W9-BLN-068

JAPAN

Titles in ABC-CLIO's *Asia in Focus* Series

China Robert André LaFleur, Editor

Japan Lucien Ellington

The Koreas Mary E. Connor, Editor

JAPAN

Lucien Ellington

ABC CLIO

Santa Barbara, California • Denver, Colorado • Oxford, England

Library of Congress Cataloging-in-Publication Data

Ellington, Lucien.

Japan / Lucien Ellington.

p. cm. — (Asia in focus)

Includes bibliographical references and index.

ISBN 978-1-59884-162-6 (hardcopy : alk. paper) —
ISBN 978-1-59884-163-3 (eBook) 1. Japan—Civilization. I. Title.

DS821.E5127 2009

952—dc22 2009014904

13 12 11 10 9 1 2 3 4 5

This book is also available on the World Wide Web as an eBook.
Visit www.abc-clio.com for details.

ABC-CLIO, LLC
130 Cremona Drive, P.O. Box 1911
Santa Barbara, California 93116–1911

This book is printed on acid-free paper ∞

Manufactured in the United States of America

Contents

About the Author

Lucien Ellington is Codirector of the Asia Program and UC Foundation Professor of Education at the University of Tennessee at Chattanooga. Ellington, who is founding editor of the Association for Asian Studies teaching journal Education About Asia, has authored three previous books and numerous articles and reviews on Japan.

Preface

It is my hope that *Asia in Focus: Japan* will be an informative and useful introduction for American readers to one of the world's most important countries. Currently, the rise of two other important Asian countries, the People's Republic of China and India, seem to have diverted many Americans' attentions from Japan. Although I would be the last to argue that Americans shouldn't better understand both of these nations, knowledge of Japan remains crucial for American global literacy for at least three reasons.

Japan remains the world's second-largest economy in terms of GDP, and Japan and the United States are heavily invested in each other's well-being. Millions of Americans and Japanese earn their livelihoods from one of the world's most extensive economic relationships.

Japan is also crucial to the United States because it has been a staunch ally since the end of World War II. In recent years, Japan has supported the United States in several ways in the global struggle against radical Islamic terrorism. Japan's geographical location in Northeast Asia near some of the world's most critical hot spots makes the bilateral political relationship vital for the continued peaceful existence of not only Americans and Japanese but many other peoples as well.

In a world made increasingly smaller through technology, it is also important that Americans become more knowledgeable of the significant accomplishments of such non-Western cultures as Japan. Anyone who presumes to have a basic education in the 21st century should be familiar with *The Tale of Genji*, haiku, Japanese gardens, Zen, and other important elements of Japan's traditional culture. For at least a decade and a half, Japanese popular culture has been a particular favorite with young people throughout the world. Anime, manga, Hello Kitty, karaoke, and sushi are enjoyed by people everywhere.

No one work can provide in-depth understanding of another culture, but hopefully this book will be of assistance to those readers who want to begin to understand Japan. *Asia in Focus: Japan* is written for the widest possible audience including businesspeople, educators, high school and university students, school teachers, tourists, and virtually anyone who wants to know more about Japan. Every attempt has been made to provide readers with accurate and fair information.

The book includes chapters on Japan's geography, history, economy, society, culture, and contemporary issues and problems. There is a resources section that contains a variety of information about Japan including lists of organizations based on the topics of earlier chapters. This compilation of Japan-related organizations features Web sites and addresses on a wide range of subjects for readers with particular interests. The resources section also includes an annotated bibliography for readers who have a special interest in topics that appear in earlier chapters. Since I believe that many of the people who read this book will either travel to Japan or interact with Japanese in the United States, I've tried to include practical information in the resources section.

Japanese names are usually ordered with family name first and given name second but exceptions are made in a few cases where individual Japanese use Western style name placement. Diacritics are not used with Romanized Japanese terms.

I have traveled to Japan 20 times and have been interested in the country for almost 30 years. Every day, I still enjoy learning more about a culture that has meant so much to me. I hope that in addition to providing information, I have conveyed some of my enthusiasm for Japan in my prose. This book is not my creation alone although I accept responsibility for any of its weaknesses or mistakes. I thank former ABC-CLIO employee Steve Danver, who assisted with the development of the book proposal; series editor Lynn Jurgensen and submissions editor Kim Kennedy-White, who have been professional and patient in their work with me; and other dedicated ABC-CLIO employees who have assisted in this project. I have been associated with ABC-CLIO for almost a decade, and the relationship has been quite positive. I also thank Colleen Simeral of Cadmus Communications for her work.

Thanks go to Katie Goss, Lauren Crump, and Peggy Pollock for their hard work in assisting me in the development of this manuscript. Last, but certainly not least, I thank my wife, Charlotte Ellington, for her patience with me while I was working on this project and for her help as well in assisting me in the development of portions of the book.

Maps

Japan superimposed on the United States.

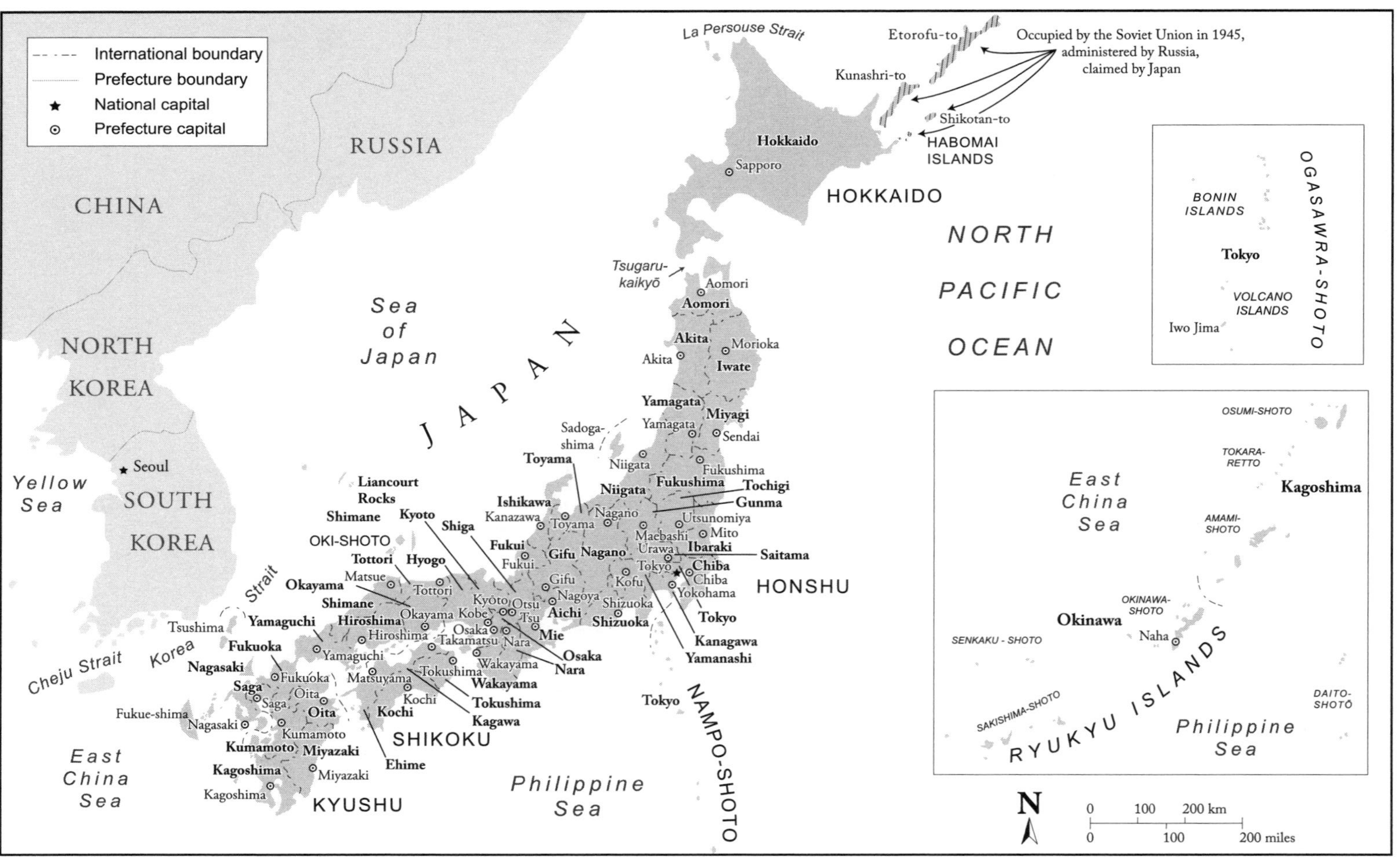

Map of Japan showing prefecture boundaries and capitals.

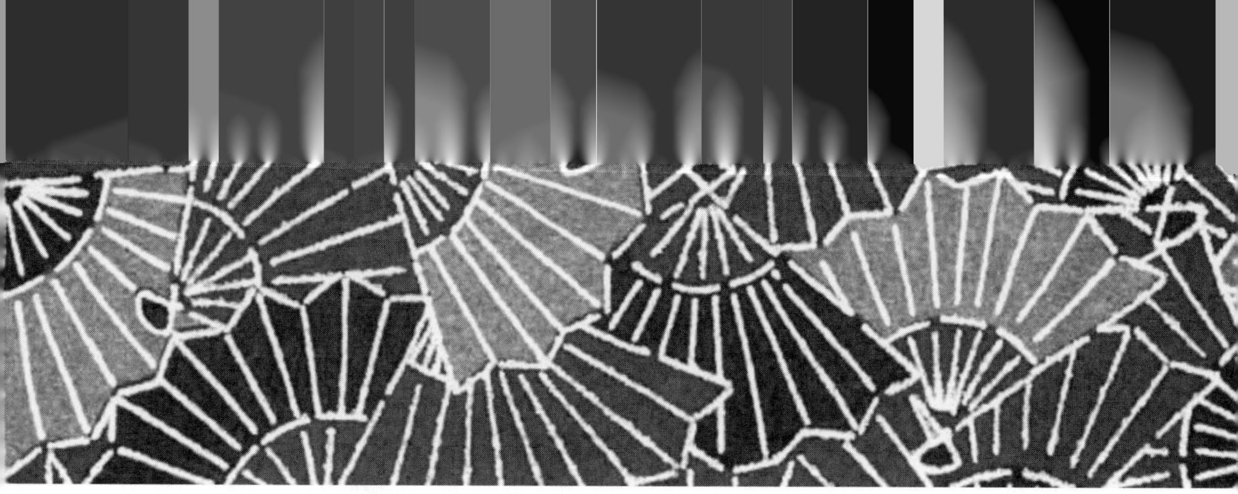

Geography

As is the case with any people, geography influences contemporary Japanese, and Japan's physical geography has helped shape culture, the economy, politics, and religions. Geography, while offering some impressive advantages for Japan's inhabitants, has also often been an obstacle rather than an asset in the Japanese quest for economic development, safety, and security. Beginning with prehistoric times, some Japanese always had varying levels of contact with other Asian peoples. Intermittent contact even occurred with South, Southeast, and Southwest Asians, and by the middle of the 16th century, Europeans reached Japan. Still, the historical remoteness of the Japanese islands from the rest of the world and even from the Asian mainland helped shape Japanese culture in ways that are still influential today.

THE PHYSICAL AND HUMAN GEOGRAPHIES OF JAPAN

With its four major islands—Hokkaido, Honshu, Kyushu, and Shikoku—as well as thousands of smaller ones, Japan has a total land area of approximately 145,825 square miles. The distance from the northernmost tip of Hokkaido to extreme southern Kyushu is approximately the same as the distance from Bangor, Maine, to Mobile, Alabama, in the United States (please see map on page xvi).

Japan's population of more than 127 million makes it the world's 10th-most-populated nation. Japan's population is almost one-third larger than Germany's and more than twice the size of the individual populations of the United Kingdom, Italy, and France. However, since peaking at an average of four per household during the postwar "baby boom," Japan's birthrates have been steadily declining, and in 2006

ASIA, EAST ASIA, AND JAPAN

The term "Asia" has been seriously questioned for years. What is conventionally called a continent includes an enormous landmass and a much more heterogeneous collection of peoples than the world's other continents. What is believed to be Asia also includes island chains separated by large amounts of water. Eurasia, a land mass that ranges from the Atlantic to the Pacific Ocean and that includes what is known as Europe and Asia is as logical a construct, if not more so, than the notion of Asia. East Asia, by contrast, has been a coherent region since prehistoric times. There is evidence of contact between the peoples of what are now China, Japan, and the Koreas since the Neolithic period. As important, the people of East Asia all shared the first common written language, which was based on Chinese characters, in existence in the region.

Japan's population fell for the first time since the government began keeping this data in 1899. Japan's current average birthrate is 1.26 children per household, and it is likely that further population declines will occur (*Facts and Figures of Japan* 2007, 28). While the number of children as a proportion of the Japanese population continues to decline, the percentage of Japanese age 65 and older grows rapidly. Currently, Japanese who are 14 years old or younger constitute approximately 14 percent of the nation's population. In the United States, people 14 years old and younger constitute 21 percent of the population. The figure for the Republic of Korea (ROK) is 19 percent. Twenty percent of Japan's population is 65 years or older compared to 12 percent in the United States and 9 percent in the ROK (Statistical Research and Training Institute 2008).

Japan is often viewed, even by many Japanese, as a small country in terms of land area. This is true if the Japanese archipelago is compared to such large countries as China or the United States. Japan is at the least a "medium-sized" nation by world standards. It is approximately 25 percent bigger than Italy or the United Kingdom, approximately 75 percent larger than the Democratic People's Republic of Korea and the ROK combined, and approximately 75 percent the size of France.

Only Bangladesh, South Korea, and the Netherlands have higher populations per square mile than Japan, but Japan is, in practical terms, much smaller than it looks on a map. Japan has the highest population density per square mile of any of the world's 10 most populous countries, but population density statistics alone do not accurately depict the Japanese space problem. Japan's total land area is a little less than 5 percent that of the United States. However, almost 75 percent of the archipelago is mountainous, and only 20 percent of the nation's land is suitable for human development (Laing 2007).

Most of the arable land is in quite scarce flatlands. Although Japan's average population density per square mile is comparable to such small countries as

Japanese policy makers hope that oil deposits off the coast of Sakhalin Island will be a greater future energy source for Japan. (Dreamstime.com)

Belgium and the Netherlands, these countries are flat with far more arable land. Unlike the latter countries, which have the luxury of more usable space, in much of Japan, including parts of urban areas, large amounts of people are crowded between farm plots. Population density per unit of area cultivated is the largest in the world.

Japan's location relative to other nations has been significant in shaping Japanese culture and attitudes. To Japan's north, the nearest foreign soil is the Russian-controlled island of Sakhalin. Although China and Korea have always been important neighbors to Japan, the distances between them and Japan are relatively great. One must travel 500 miles across the East China Sea to reach mainland China or travel 120 miles through the Korea Strait to land on Korean soil. Many writers, when considering the United Kingdom, emphasize how important the geographic isolation of the British from the rest of Western Europe was in shaping many of the distinctive features of life on the British Isles. Yet Japan is 5 times further away from the Korean Peninsula and 20 times further away from China than the 20-mile distance from the white cliffs of Dover to France.

Today, technology makes physical distances between Japan and other countries seem slight. Yet the culture of any nation remains influenced by the past, and until the last half of the 19th century, Japan was relatively isolated compared to many other countries. The archipelago's remote location helped the Japanese avoid being successfully invaded from ancient times until the American occupation in 1945. Historically, the government carefully controlled foreign influences and for long periods of time chose to have little contact with foreign countries. Modern Japanese culture contains foods, words, tools, and practices from other countries that were allowed into Japan in earlier times and also many uniquely Japanese objects and ways of doing things that developed during isolationist periods.

Japan's early geographic isolation and later government policies also influenced the ethnic makeup of Japan's population. The Japanese are, like their nearest neighbors on the Asian continent, a Mongoloid people. Archeological evidence indicates the earliest human settlements in what is now Japan were approximately

HISTORICAL GEOGRAPHY: "JAPAN"

In Japan's earliest history, the Japanese referred to the archipelago as Yamato, but in the early 7th century they began to employ the term "Nippon" (or "Nihon"), which was written using the Chinese characters for "sun" and "source." One theory is that the leaders of the emerging Japanese state felt that since the sun rose more quickly in Japan, which is situated to China's east, this would give them equal or perhaps more prestige than the Chinese. Marco Polo allegedly transmitted the Chinese pronunciation for Nihon, "Jiphen," to Europe when he returned to the West in the 13th century.

30,000 years ago or more. The fall in sea levels due to successive ice ages created temporary land bridges between Japan and the Asian continent. People probably came to Japan by bridges located in what is now Manchuria in the north, the Korean Peninsula in the west, and the Ryukyu island chain toward central and south China. The Ainu, a people who share some characteristics of Caucasians, also settled in early times on the present-day island of Hokkaido and on part of what is now Honshu.

Once humans arrived, geographical remoteness and a temperate climate meant that they usually remained. Although scholars disagree, the best evidence indicates that since the early part of the sixth century CE, there has been no major infusion of immigrants into the Japanese isles. The end product of an absence of immigration or migration, along with no successful foreign invasion, is a relatively high level of racial homogeneity, and the Japanese are one of the more ethnically homogeneous peoples in the world. Although it is difficult to precisely calculate because of illegal immigrants, somewhere between 1.5 and 2.5 percent of Japan's population are ethnic minorities. Until the end of 2007 Koreans were Japan's largest ethnic group but the Chinese have taken their place. Chinese residents are from both the People's Republic of China and Taiwan and have moved to Japan for educational opportunities or industrial or services employment. However, Brazilians of Japanese ancestry (most of whom speak no Japanese), Southeast Asians, and people from South and Southwest Asia as well as several Middle Eastern nations have all come to Japan through guest worker programs or illegally in the last two decades seeking economic opportunities. Japan is clearly becoming less a homogeneous nation than was the case a few decades ago.

In the past, racial homogeneity has in part spawned a deep-seated notion among some Japanese that they are so unique that foreigners cannot ever really understand their language or culture. Despite recent changes in these attitudes, Japan still does not have a particularly positive reputation among the nations of the world as being an especially welcoming place for medium-term or permanent foreign residents. Koreans

AINU

The Ainu are a people indigenous to Japan who are ethnically and culturally similar to Eskimos. Historically, they inhabited northern Honshu and Hokkaido as well as southern Sakhalin and the Kurile Islands. They hunted deer and seal and fished for salmon. The Japanese launched successful military campaigns against the Ainu that were similar to U.S. government efforts against Native Americans. Most full-blooded or mixed-blood Ainu live in Hokkaido and a small but undetermined number of Ainu live in other parts of the country. However, estimates of how many Japanese have some Ainu blood vary wildly and range from 30,000 to 300,000. There are probably 50,000 people whose ethnicity is over half Ainu. Many Ainu have been assimilated into mainstream Japanese culture, but there is preservation of Ainu customs, festivals, and crafts in Hokkaido, which draws Japanese tourists much like Native American tourist attractions do in the United States.

whose families moved to Japan in the 19th century and before World War II historically faced discrimination and were denied easy access to citizenship. Although this situation has dramatically improved between the 1980s and the present, in many instances Koreans still encounter social discrimination, as does the new wave of foreigners in Japan. How Japanese interact with foreign residents is becoming ever more important and will be addressed in more depth elsewhere in this book.

Japan's climatic and physical features have also contributed to molding culture. Mountains are the most common topographical feature of Japan, with 75 percent of the land area classified as mountainous. Japanese mountains, while not particularly high by world standards, tend to be extremely wooded and quite beautiful. Most mountains are only a few thousand feet high, although in central Honshu in the Japanese Alps there are ranges that soar as high as 10,000 feet.

Japan's mountains, although beautiful, have been more of a hindrance than an asset to people; because of the high percentage of mountainous terrain in Japan, there are few level areas. The 120-square-mile Kanto Plain on Honshu, which includes Tokyo, is the most extensive plain in Japan. Historically, the mountains were barriers to communication, trade, and political unification within Japan. Today, they still constitute largely wasted space from an economic utilization perspective. Most Japanese are reluctant to live in the mountains for fear of volcanic activity and landslides, expense, and inconvenience. Throughout Japan one observes homes, factories, businesses, and farms jammed next to each other on the scarce level land.

Japan is fortunate to have, by and large, a quite temperate climate. Although there are substantial climatic variations within Japan, particularly in sparsely populated and cold Hokkaido and in warm southern Kyushu, in general, Japanese weather is similar to that of the U.S. East Coast. However, Japan experiences more

MOUNT FUJI

Located in central Honshu on the border between Shizuoka and Yamanashi prefectures, this 12,385-foot dormant volcano is a universal symbol of Japan. The climbing of Fujisan—Fuji is so highly regarded that it is given the honorific *san*—began as a religious practice. One religious sect with both Buddhist and Shinto elements, Fujiko, considers the mountain sacred. The Shinto shrine Fujisan Hongu Sengen Jinja, located south of the mountain in Fujinomiya City, maintains a smaller shrine on the summit. Many Japanese and foreigners alike with no religious connections climb Fuji annually for pleasure. Thousands of climbers scale Fuji during the climbing season, July 1–August 26. There are 10 stations along the way. Fuji will always be special to the Japanese people. Local mountains that resemble Fujisan are often admired simply for that reason.

annual rainfall, and most of Japan is warmer, both in the winter and in the summer, than the northeastern section of the East Coast.

Most of Japan's great cities on the main island of Honshu enjoy weather remarkably similar to that of the American states of North Carolina and Virginia. For example, the average January and August Tokyo temperatures of 41.9°F and 78.8°F and the humidity levels are similar to what might be found in Norfolk, Virginia.

Because of the temperate climate, there are long growing seasons in all of Japan except for Hokkaido. Historically, scarce agricultural land could be used very productively to support large numbers of people. Vegetables and rice constitute Japan's largest crops. Nonirrigated fields are devoted to fruits and vegetables, and most rice is grown in irrigated fields. Since farms are quite small, averaging only a little more than four acres, considerably less than 5 percent of total cultivable land in Japan is used as pastureland for beef or other animals. Japan's large population and the small space available for farming have meant that since around 1900 Japan has been forced to depend on foreign countries for a portion of its food. Currently, imported food accounts for approximately 60 percent of all the calories Japanese annually consume. Japanese purchase large amounts of beans, cereals, fruit, meat, and even fish from abroad. Even though Japan has one of the world's largest economies, all students are taught in school that the nation is incapable of feeding itself, and the public is aware of the necessity of maintaining a steady supply of agricultural imports.

Beginning in the 20th century, the lives of Japanese farm families began to dramatically change, and this process has accelerated even more in the 21st century. In the early 1990s, farmers made up 60 percent of Japanese workers. By 1950, about 50 percent of the nation's workforce were in agriculture. By 2002, less than 3 percent of all Japanese were employed in agriculture (Tanaka 2007, 98).

Although rice consumption has steadily declined since World War II, rice paddies are very much in evidence throughout much of Japan. Here, workers are planting rice. (Corel)

Although Japanese agricultural production has increased in recent years, farm mechanization and the enormous expansion of industry have transformed Japan into one of the world's most urban countries. This means the end of traditional rural living and working patterns for most people. Many farmers, as in other developed countries, don't derive all their income from the land. Estimates are that today less than a quarter of Japanese farmers earn all of their income from agriculture. In several developed countries, commercial agriculture is increasingly an occupation performed by the elderly. This is true in Japan, where estimates are that more than half of all farmers are 65 years or older.

Cities have been part of Japan's geography since the early 8th century CE. By 1700, Edo (present-day Tokyo) had an estimated population of more than 1 million people, making it possibly the world's largest city. Still, until well into the 20th century most Japanese lived in rural areas. Today more than 75 percent of Japanese live in cities, and an even higher percentage of the population works in urban environments.

The highest concentration of people is in the Kanto Plain in central Honshu, which includes the two largest cities: Tokyo and Yokohama. Tokyo's population is more than 8 million people, but it is only 1 of 12 Japanese cities whose population exceeds a million. The 300-mile distance along the eastern Honshu coast from Tokyo south to Osaka, the third-largest Japanese city, is almost completely urbanized. Approximately 50 percent of the Japanese population live in three great clusters: Greater Tokyo (including Kawasaki, Yokohama, and Chiba), Greater Nagoya (including Aichi and Mie prefectures), and Greater Osaka (including Hyogo and

Because most Japanese live in densely populated urban areas congested streets are common. (Corel)

Kyoto prefectures). All of these megalopoli are located on Honshu, making it Japan's most populous island by far. Although massive urbanization has been beneficial to Japan's economy, it has also complicated Japan's living space problem and caused major air and water pollution.

Developed nations in particular must have access to both a great variety and amount of natural resources. The Japanese are not self-sufficient, with the exception of limestone, in such vitally important commodities as iron ore, petroleum, lead, zinc, and copper. Japan has an ideal climate for tree growth and enjoys substantially more timber than mineral resources. Forests comprise at least 65 percent of Japan's land area. However, Japan's total land area is relatively small, deforestation has occurred at various times in the past, and the range of commercial timber is primarily limited to cedar, cypress, and larch. Wood has a special place in traditional and contemporary Japanese culture. Temples, shrines, chopsticks, and, still today, contemporary home construction all rely on wood, ensuring great domestic demand. However, the domestic timber industry cannot meet Japanese demand for wood, and its prices are higher than foreign competition. Japan continues to be a major world timber importer.

Japan has high energy demand and scarce natural energy resources. Oil, the most critical energy resource, accounts for about half of energy consumption, and Japan relies almost entirely on imports. There are oil deposits off Japan's shores in the East China Sea, but competing territorial claims with China have seriously impeded their development.

A forest in Hokkaido. Although forestry is still a viable Japanese industry, wood is also imported to meet the nation's massive needs. (Corel)

Japan trails only the United States and the People's Republic of China in annual oil consumption and each year imports the world's third-largest amount of oil. Historically, the Middle East has supplied Japan with more than 80 percent of its oil, and the Japanese are more vulnerable than any major nation to the negative effects of wars or economic and political crises in that volatile region. Any lengthy disruption of oil supply would negatively affect Japan's manufacturing output and unemployment rates. Japanese companies are actively engaged in joint crude oil production ventures in more stable areas of the Middle East while also seeking production and import opportunities in Latin America, the Caspian Sea region, and the Russian Far East. The Japanese have high hopes that oil-rich Sakhalin in eastern Russia and quite close to Japan will be a major new source of oil. Japan also for the most part lacks and must import natural gas, which accounts for about 13 percent of Japanese energy needs. Most of the natural gas that the Japanese use is imported as liquid natural gas from Indonesia, Malaysia, Brunei, Australia, and elsewhere (Karan 2005).

Despite being the only country upon which nuclear weapons have been employed, the Japanese government and private companies have built a substantial nuclear energy program. Japan now is 14th in the world in electricity generation through nuclear power while the United States ranks 18th. Japan obtains over 25 percent of its electricity from nuclear power. Although the latter percentage is expected to rise, several well-publicized accidents at plants, including one in 1999 in Tokaimura, north of Tokyo, that left two workers dead, have caused considerable public anxiety about nuclear power (Australian Uranium Association 2007).

Japan presently accounts for about five percent of its total energy needs from hydroelectric, geothermal, and other alternative energy sources such as wind power.

Since Japan has considerable thermal activity because of the large numbers of volcanoes and hot springs, geothermal energy could be a major future domestic source of power for electricity and other energy needs.

The resource picture is not completely dark for the Japanese, however, since there are two great resources with which Japan has been blessed. One is the sea. No part of Japan is more than 70 miles from the sea, and Japan has a total of 16,800 miles of coastline as well as a large inland sea. In Japanese history, the ocean was a great boon for transportation, and the sea has always been a wonderful source of food. Herring, cod, halibut, salmon, crab, sardines, tuna, skipjack, sea breams, mackerel, yellowtail, octopus, eel, seaweed, and squid are just some of the sea life that ends up on Japanese tables. In traditional Japanese cuisine, it is most unusual to eat a meal that does not include some kind of food from the sea. However, in the last few years, overfishing, stricter international regulations, and rising world prices for such specialty fish as tuna, which are used in sushi bars throughout the world, have adversely affected domestic supply and introduced new competition for the Japanese fishing industry.

Japan has long been criticized by many nations and international organizations because it continues the practice of whaling. In 1986, in response to an international moratorium, the Japanese ended commercial whaling but still engage in scientific whaling. Many young people have never eaten whale, and its availability has declined, but some whale meat is still consumed. The Japanese who support whaling argue that the current excess population of whales reduces the supply of a number of other edible fish.

The second-greatest resource within Japan is undoubtedly its people. Throughout history, the Japanese have proven to be hardworking, intelligent, accepting, and resourceful. These traits are especially important in a crowded country with almost no resources.

THE SPACE PROBLEM

Because much of Japan's land does not lend itself to development, with the exception of Hokkaido, lack of space is a permanent problem. The space squeeze is most serious in cities and particularly acute in such huge metropolitan centers as Nagoya, Osaka, and Tokyo and numerous other urban areas. When one negotiates Japanese cities, example after example of space affecting human activities is in evidence. Multistoried large apartment complexes with much smaller individual units than those Americans are accustomed to are common in urban areas. Foreigners visiting Japanese cities also almost always notice the multilevel golf driving ranges with nets that take up a relatively small amount of space. They also take note of the voluminous number of multistoried buildings with one or more restaurants or nightclubs on each floor.

Because of the space problem in urban areas, the Japanese have, more than people of any other nation, developed extensive urban underground streets for retail shopping and dining out. Typically, underground commercial areas are near or under subway and train stations. One of the largest in Japan is in Nagoya under the central train station where the train and subway systems converge. This shopping complex features one of Japan's largest malls as well as several lesser malls, all connected by more than 5 miles of hallways. Strolling through this area as well as similar underground commercial districts in Japan, one finds entire streets of restaurants, coffee houses, and food stores, with other streets featuring outlets representing large Tokyo-based chain stores that sell clothing, books, and other consumer goods.

The daily task of getting from one place to another is more problematic for the average Japanese than for the average American or European. Even though Japan has only a little more than half the number of cars as in the United States, many Japanese city streets average several times as many cars daily as U.S. streets. A major reason that Japanese streets are so crowded for vehicles and pedestrians is that there is little room to build adequate expressways in urban areas. This intense congestion makes it impossible for Japanese to depend on the car to the extent that it is used in the United States.

Fortunately, the Japanese enjoy one of the best train and subway systems in the world. Japanese trains link the entire nation, and all major cities and some medium-sized cities have subway systems as well. The Japan Railways Group, or JR, consists of eight for-profit companies that took over the assets of the old government-owned Japan National Railways when the national government privatized that organization in 1987. JR owns and operates about 70 percent of Japan's rail networks, with dozens of private companies also providing rail service, particularly in and around major metropolitan areas. In a recent year, almost 10 times as many Japanese annually used Japan's public rail systems as Americans used the same kind of transport.

Although there are a variety of types of Japanese trains, the Shinkansen, or bullet train, is the most famous. The Tokaido Shinkansen, the first bullet train and the first high-speed train in the world, was launched in 1964 and connected Tokyo, Nagoya, Osaka, and Kyoto. Originally, Shinkansen traveled up to 200 kilometers per hour but now exceed 300 kilometers per hour. Shinkansen service now reaches parts of Japan's four major islands. Shinkansen manage to travel at these impressive speeds quietly and smoothly and almost always on time. Wind and earthquake detectors as well as rain gauges are installed throughout the entire Shinkansen rail lines to monitor possible natural disasters. If an earthquake occurs, the electrical current helping to power the trains automatically ceases, and trains in the danger area stop. In high winds and heavy rains, train speed is automatically reduced, or the train stops. Many Japanese, because of auto highway congestion getting to and from airports, find it easier to take the Shinkansen to domestic destinations than to fly (Karan 2005, The Japan Railways Group).

Still, in Tokyo and other large Japanese cities, using subways and trains during rush hours can be uncomfortable at best and, because of the enormous number of users, dangerous at times. During rush hour, Tokyo subway cars often are jammed to over twice their capacity, and passengers are warned not to board subways with their arms in awkward positions because of potential broken bones. In rare cases, babies have suffocated on crowded Japanese subways. Windows sometimes shatter because of the crowds, and dozens of riders lose shoes daily. Station attendants often must shove the last few people on commuting trains or subways on board in order to close the doors. In winter, heavy clothing increases the average rider's bulk and forces officials to employ more shovers.

The Shinkansen not only provides high-speed service, but is famous for strictly adhering to railway time schedules. (Corel)

Lack of adequate living space makes housing and land prices atypically high by world standards. However, the daily quality of life of typical Japanese is an even more important factor than simply the high cost of housing. The average Japanese home or apartment by American standards is often small and somewhat noisy. Individual privacy is usually difficult or impossible to fully attain. The amount of space in typical Japanese homes compared to residential space in the United States makes privacy a precious commodity. In a recent year, new Japanese homes averaged just 1,435 square feet, compared to 2,204 square feet for new American homes. Japanese homes, however, seem less cramped when Japan is compared to several Western European countries rather than the United States.

Japan's postwar economic affluence changed the utilization of space within homes. Traditionally, Japanese used the limited space available in their homes in very flexible ways. Rooms contained little furniture. Instead of a sofa and chairs, there would be only a low table in the middle of the room. Family members would sit on the floor on straw tatami mats, and at night the table would be pushed aside and futons, the traditional Japanese sleeping rolls, taken from the closet and spread out. One room could easily be used for eating, recreation, and sleeping. In the past, traditional Japanese homes were also pleasing in appearance because of the lack of big, heavy furniture.

Japanese homes are now in some ways more difficult places in which to spend large amounts of time than in years past. The rise in living standards and changes

OKINAWA

Okinawa is the only one of Japan's 47 prefectures that is totally located in a subtropical climate. Okinawa, known historically as the Ryukyu Islands, has a culture that is markedly different than the Japanese main islands in many ways. Although often dominated by Japan and subject to Chinese influences, the Ryukyu Islands were a separate kingdom until they were formally annexed by Japan in 1879. The United States gained control of Okinawa at the end of World War II, and the island chain was returned to Japan in 1972. Okinawa has its own language, although younger people use Japanese, and distinctive traditional architecture. Its population of approximately 1.31 million people is situated on 48 different islands, with a large majority of the population living on Okinawa, the main island. Okinawa is famous for its beautiful beaches and coral reefs. Its relations with Japan are complex and often trouble-ridden.

in cultural preferences mean that even though the average family size is smaller and the available living space is larger now, the interiors of houses tend to appear somewhat cluttered. In most Japanese homes, much of the wall space is now taken up with wardrobes, bureaus, and furniture. Typically, rooms include a large variety of such decorative objects as stuffed animals and Japanese or French dolls, and other ornaments are likely to be found on top of furniture and pianos. Although many Japanese still retain a traditional room with tatami mats, Western-style interior furnishings, particularly in urban areas, are the norm.

Lack of adequate home space forces Japanese to pursue a number of activities outside the house that people in the United States and many other developed countries engage in at home. For example, almost no homes in urban areas have lawn space or outside play equipment for children. Because of the lack of space and sometimes high noise level at home, many students do their homework in study areas provided by their schools or in public libraries. Friends are often entertained at restaurants or other public places.

Insufficient space is so widespread in Japan that primary school students are assigned the exercise of finding the best way to get from one to another section of their town or city. Japanese children learn early how to read detailed train and subway maps because it is unlikely some youngsters will be driven to school or other activities on the country's crowded roads. Lack of adequate habitable space affects how Japanese people live, travel, spend leisure time, and work.

THE HAZARDS OF BEING JAPANESE

Although virtually all cultures have some level of appreciation for nature, it is particularly pronounced in Japanese culture. The constant attention to the changing seasons in Japanese literature and culture, the classical Japanese garden that is deliberately constructed to celebrate nature, the mass cherry blossom viewing parties of Tokyo office workers, and the deep appreciation of autumnal and other natural colors are all evidence of the Japanese people's appreciation for the world of nature. It is ironic that this appreciation developed in a country that has always been more prone to a variety of natural disasters than is the case in much of the rest of the world.

An author who has studied Japan's most publicized hazard partially titled his work *Earthquake Nation* (Clancey 2006). Since antiquity, the Japanese have been well aware of this hazard. Earthquakes are the topic of one of the earliest-surviving written poems (about 500 CE) by Emperor Buretsu (Bates 2007, 13). Japan is one of the most vulnerable nations in the world to earthquakes and ranks second only to Indonesia, a much larger country, in total annual number of recorded earthquakes. The Japanese archipelago is situated where three tectonic plates, the Eurasian Plate, the Pacific Plate, and the Philippines Plate, intersect. Approximately 11 percent of the world's seismic energy is released each year under the Japanese islands. About 20 percent of the world's earthquakes that reach 6.0 magnitude and higher annually take place in Japan. Throughout Japan, an average of 7,500 earthquakes is recorded annually, and approximately 1,500 can be felt by people. Because of the frequency of earthquakes, tremors strong enough to gently shake a sleeper in bed often receive relatively minor coverage in the Japanese media.

The sudden movement of the earth occasioned by a quake can also cause giant tidal waves, or tsunami, which literally means "harbor wave." Some of Japan's worst and most complicated seismic faults are located offshore of the heavily industrialized and populated Tokai region situated southwest of Tokyo. Some scientists estimate that the secondary effect of a major earthquake could very well be a tsunami as high as 27 feet that could reach Tokyo's waterfront within three or four minutes.

Earthquakes can occur in many parts of Japan, as evidenced by the 1995 Kobe earthquake in which 6,400 people died and the 2004 Niigata earthquake that killed 7 and injured more than 830 people. Unfortunately, however, the Kanto Plain, where Tokyo and Yokohama are located, is the most earthquake-prone area in the archipelago.

The worst natural disaster in Japan's recorded history, the Great Kanto Earthquake, struck Tokyo at 11:58 A.M. on September 1, 1923. Today, the nation commemorates this event by observing Natural Disaster Prevention Day on the anniversary of the earthquake. Although the epicenter of the 7.9-magnitude earthquake was more than 40 miles south to southwest from Tokyo, the earthquake released energy equivalent to the detonation of almost 400 atomic bombs of the size dropped on Hiroshima. The first jolt, lasting a little more than 14 seconds, caused the collapse of most of the Kanto region's brick and unreinforced concrete buildings. Fires proved even more destructive for buildings and deadly for humans than the earthquake itself. In Tokyo, 130 fires began within an hour of the earthquake in many of the most populated areas of the city. As the temperature and winds increased, five cyclone-like firestorms engulfed sections of the city. At the Honjo Military Clothing Depot near the banks of the Sumida River, where large numbers

The great Kanto earthquake in 1923 killed over 110,000 people and destroyed most of Tokyo and Yokohama. (The Illustrated London News Picture Library)

of displaced people had gathered, nearly 40,000 people suffocated and burned to death in one of the firestorms. Eyewitness survivors virtually all referred to the area as a hell on earth.

Four days later, more than 20 square miles of Tokyo had burned to the ground. Before a week had elapsed, the earthquake and ensuing fires destroyed most of Tokyo and almost all of Yokohama. The disaster was responsible for the deaths of more than 110,000 people, left 1.5 million people homeless, and required major relief efforts. The earthquake's total amount of damages of 6.5 billion yen was approximately four times larger than the Japanese national government's budget for the preceding year (Schencking 2007).

In addition to the great Kanto disaster, much of Tokyo was also destroyed in 1657 and 1703 by earthquakes and accompanying fires. The Japanese people and their government are well aware of virtually the entire archipelago's vulnerability to earthquakes. Although earthquake prediction is difficult, Japan's program, which began in 1963, is one of the country's largest and oldest scientific research endeavors. Earthquake preparation strategies are widespread and include earthquake drills in schools, extensive regulations for the construction of "earthquake-proof" structures, sophisticated warning systems, and careful evacuation route planning.

The Japanese must also annually deal with an average of three to four tropical cyclones—better known as typhoons. Typhoons, most of which originate in the Philippine Sea in the late summer and early fall, can be devastating to both humans

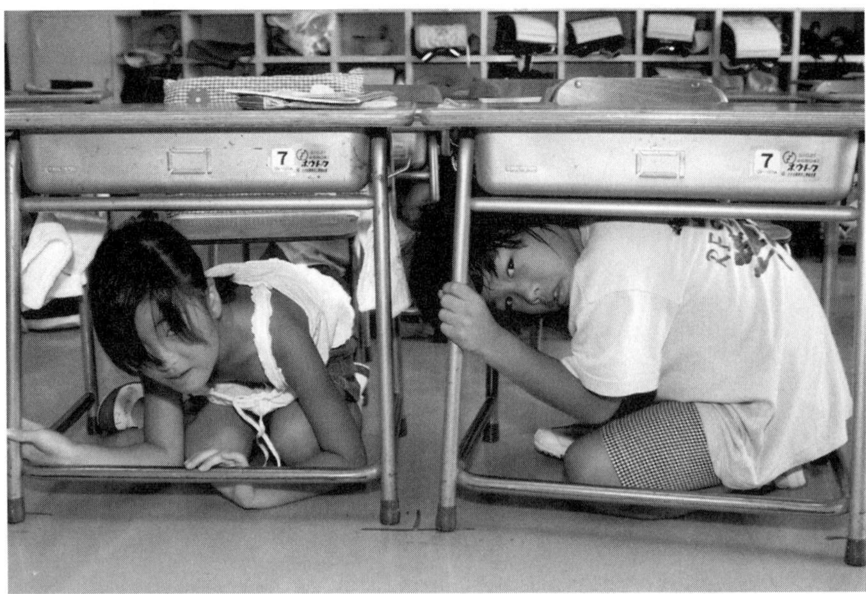

Earthquake safety drills are an integral part of Japan's school curriculum. Here, elementary students crouch under desks during a drill. (AP/World Wide Photos)

and property. In 2004, a year that brought an abnormally high 10 typhoons, one of the tropical megastorms left 63 people dead and injured more than 340 Japanese. In October 1959, a massive typhoon crashed through Nagoya, Japan's fourth-largest city, killing 5,000 people and leaving 400,000 homeless. Seven days after the storm, more than 25,000 people were still stranded on their roofs because of the water. Although typhoons killed thousands of people from the 1930s through the 1950s, the numbers of deaths they cause have plummeted in recent decades due to technological advances, including the positioning of breakwaters and sophisticated warning systems. Today, typhoons' effects are primarily limited to often extensive property damage as a result of flooding and landslides (*Life* 1959, 38–39).

As if earthquakes, tsunami, and typhoons were not bad enough, Japan has two volcanic zones with approximately 50 active volcanoes that encompass much of Japan, with the exception of Shikoku, the Kansai region in the southern-central part of Honshu, part of western Honshu, and the Kanto Plain. Although it has not erupted since the early 18th century, even Japan's greatest icon, Mount Fuji, is volcanic. Volcanoes have erupted throughout Japanese history, and evidence exists documenting a large eruption approximately 7,000 years ago off Kyushu's southern coast that did massive damage to southern Kyushu and spewed ash as far north as Hokkaido. The layer of volcanic debris from this eruption still seriously impedes agriculture in southern Kyushu.

Mount Unzen, a large volcano consisting of several overlapping and proximate lava domes in the Shimabara Peninsula in Kyushu, erupted in 1792 and caused an avalanche and tsunami that killed an estimated 15,000 people. Between 1990 and

Japanese not only consider Mount Fuji special, but the mountain has become a global symbol of Japan. (Corel)

1994, Mount Unzen again became active, and 43 scientists and journalists were killed in a 1993 eruption. Thousands of people were evacuated at different times during the volcano's latest cycle activity, and more than 2,000 buildings were destroyed by debris flows in the summer of 1993. In 2000, volcanic eruptions in southwest Hokkaido and in the Izu Islands about 90 miles from Tokyo seriously disrupted local economies and also caused thousands of evacuations ("Mount Unzen," Wikipedia).

Little usable land, almost no natural resources, incredible urban congestion, earthquakes, typhoons, volcanoes—the list of seemingly ill-fated aspects of Japanese life caused by the physical and human geography of the archipelago is long. Still, recent life expectancy averages indicate that Japanese women on average live to be older than 86, making them number one among the world's countries, while the average Japanese male lives to be 79 and is slightly surpassed only by men who live in Iceland and San Marino. This statistic is at least partial evidence that despite the seemingly cruel hand nature dealt Japan, its people are amazingly flexible and resilient.

REFERENCES

Australian Uranium Association. *Nuclear Power in the World Today: Briefing Paper 7.* August 2007. http://www.uic.com.au/nip07.htm (accessed September 2007).

Bates, Alex. "Catfish, Super Frog, and the End of the World: Earthquakes (and Natural Disaster) in the Japanese Cultural Imagination." *Education About Asia* 12, No. 2 (Fall 2007): 13–19.

Callick, Rowan. "Make Way for Japan." *The American* (July–August 2007): 60–69.

Clancey, Gregory. *Earthquake Nation: The Cultural Politics of Japanese Seismicity, 1868–1930*. Berkeley: University of California Press, 2006.

"East Asia in Geographic Perspective: China, Japan, Korea, and Vietnam," *Asia for Educators*. Columbia University. 2008. http://afe.easia.columbia.edu/geography.

Energy Information Administration. "Japan: Oil." December 2006. http://www.eia.doe.gov/emeu/cabs/Japan/Oil.html (accessed September 19, 2007).

Facts and Figures of Japan 2007. Tokyo: Foreign Press Center, 2007.

Hidenori, Sakanaka. "The Future of Japan's Immigration Policy: A Battle Diary." *Japan Focus Online*, September 22, 2007. http://www.japanfocus.org/products/details/2396 (accessed September 22, 2007).

"International House Sizes." *Demographia*. 2005. http://www.demographia.com/db-intlhouse.htm (accessed September 2007).

Japan Railways Group. http://www.japanrail.com (accessed September 2007).

Karan, Pradyumna P. *Japan in the 21st Century: Environment, Economy, and Society*. Lexington: University Press of Kentucky, 2005.

Laing, Craig R. "Japanese Cultural Landscapes." *Japan In-service/Pre-service Teacher Module*. University of Tennessee at Chattanooga. http://www.utc.edu/asia/teaching (accessed October 8, 2007).

Masaki, Hisane. "Oil-Hungry Japan Looks to Other Sources." *Asia Times Online*, February 21, 2007. http://www.atimes.com/atimes/Japan/IB21Dh01.html (accessed September 2007).

Ministry of Foreign Affairs: Okinawa. http://www.mofa.go.jp/policy/economy/summit/2000/outline/eng/fukuoka/fko0102.html (accessed July 2008).

Mount Unzen, Wikipedia. http://en.wikipedia.org/wiki/Mount_Unzen (accessed September 2007).

Schencking, J. Charles. "The Great Kanto Earthquake of 1923 and the Japanese Nation: Responding to an Urban Calamity of an Unprecedented Nature." *Education About Asia* 12, No. 2 (Fall 2007): 20–25.

"Shinkansen." The Japan Railways Group. http://www.japanrail.com/JR_shinkansen.html (accessed September 2007).

Statistical Research and Training Institute, MIC, ed. *Statistical Handbook of Japan 2008*. Tokyo: Statistics Bureau, Japan. September 2008. http://www.stat.go.jp/english/data/handbook/index/htm (accessed October 2008).

Tanaka, Hideaki, ed. *Japan 2007: An International Comparison*. Tokyo: Keizai Koho Center, 2007.

Tym, Alice L. "Centripetal Forces in Japan." *Japan Teaching Module*. University of Tennessee at Chattanooga. http://www.utc.edu/asia/teaching (accessed October 8, 2007).

"Typhoon!" *Life*, October 12, 1959, 38–39.

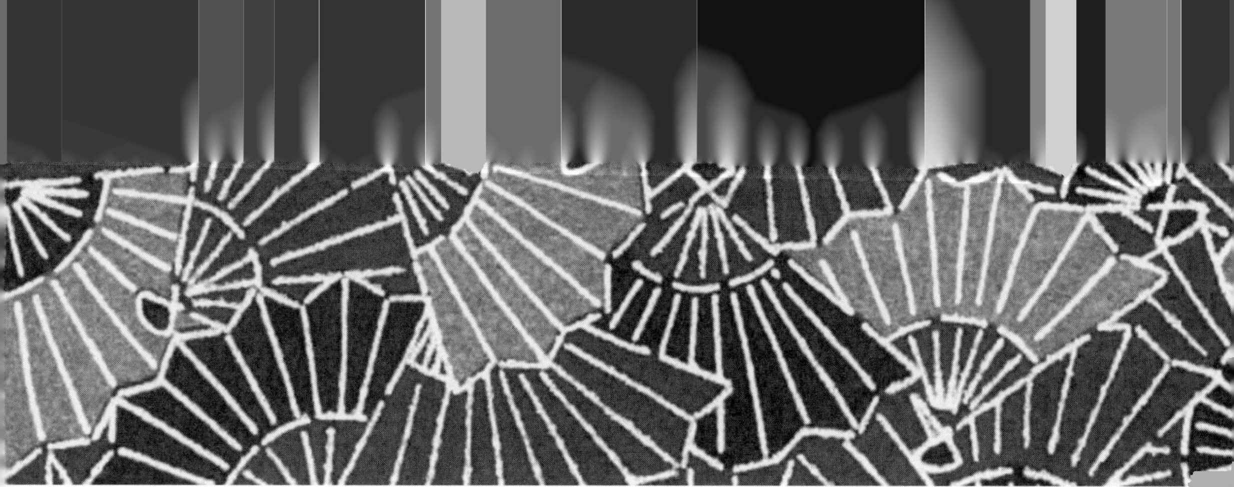

History

KEY EVENTS IN JAPANESE HISTORY

11,000–300 BCE	Jomon culture
300 BCE–250 CE	Yayoi culture
250–552 CE	Tomb period (Kofun)
552–710	Late Yamato period
552	Buddhism is transported from Korea to Japan
604	Japan's 17-point "constitution" is ascribed to Prince Shotoku
645	So-called Taika Reforms are enacted
710	Japan's first permanent capital is established at Nara
710–794	Nara period
794–1156	Heian period
794	Capital is moved to Heian (Kyoto)
ca. 1010	Murasaki Shikibu authors *The Tale of Genji*
1156–1185	Taira clan controls the government
1180–1185	Gempei War between Taira and Minamoto
1185–1333	Kamakura period
1192	The emperor appoints Minamoto Yoritomo as Japan's first shogun
1274, 1281	Two Mongol attempts to conquer Japan fail
1333–1336	Kemmu Restoration attempt to increase imperial power fails
1336–1573	Ashikaga period
1338	Ashikaga Takauji is formally appointed shogun and rules from Kyoto

1467–1477	Onin War marks the beginning of Japanese disunification and civil strife
1543	Portuguese are the first Europeans to reach Japan
1573–1600	Unification period
1600	Tokugawa Ieyasu defeats rivals for political power at the battle of Sekigahara
1600–1868	Tokugawa period
1603	Tokugawa Ieyasu assumes the title of shogun, ruling from Edo (modern-day Tokyo)
1615	The unification of Japan is completed with the defeat of Tokugawa's opponents at Osaka Castle
1630	Japan is closed to almost all foreigners
1630–1853	Tokugawa period is marked by peace and prosperity
1853	Commodore Matthew C. Perry "opens" Japan to foreign countries
1868–1912	Meiji period
1868	A group of disaffected samurai overthrows the Tokugawas and establishes an oligarchy ruling in the emperor's name
1889	Japan becomes the first Asian country to adopt a Western-style Constitution
1904–1905	Japan defeats Russia and gains control of Korea
1910	Korea is formally annexed
1912–1926	Taisho period
1919	Japan, having fought with the Allies in World War I, fails to get a racial equality clause in the Versailles Treaty
1926–1989	Showa period
1931	Japan seizes Manchuria
1937	Start of the Chinese-Japanese War
1941	The Japanese bomb Pearl Harbor, starting World War II in the Pacific
1945	Atomic bombings of Hiroshima (August 6) and Nagasaki (August 9); Japan surrenders
1952	End of the U.S. occupation of Japan
1980	Japanese automobile production exceeds that of the United States for the first time
1989–present	Heisei period
1990	Japanese economic bubble bursts, bringing more than a decade of economic stagnation
2001–2006	Prime Minister Koizumi provides strong and visionary leadership to Japan during a troubled time
2003	Japan's economy begins to recover from the long downturn
2008	Democratic Party of Japan becomes the first single party ever to gain control of the Upper House of the Diet from the Liberal Democratic Party

INTRODUCTION: JAPAN, EAST ASIA, AND THE WORLD

Many have the stereotype that until relatively recently, the archipelago's culture developed largely in isolation from the rest of the world. Although there are critical elements of truth in this assumption, it is incorrect in many respects. Throughout history, some Japanese have interacted in a variety of ways with other East Asians and, at times, with South and Southeast Asians. Japanese and Europeans made important connections in the 16th century. By the latter part of the 19th century, Japan was inextricably involved in world events.

Although a primitive indigenous culture developed on the archipelago that is briefly discussed later, understanding Chinese civilization and its influences on East Asia, including Japan, is as critical a key to historical literacy as comprehending the profound influence of the ancient Greeks on Western cultures. Parts of what we now know as China already possessed an advanced civilization for at least 1,200 years before Japan began this process. The Chinese, just as was the case with the Greeks throughout the Mediterranean and elsewhere, transmitted advanced ways of doing things—and of thinking—first to the northern area of what is today northern Vietnam, then to the Korean Peninsula, and later to Japan.

The Chinese, even more than their Greek counterparts, gave the gift of the first writing systems to the rest of the region. Early China scholar Charles Holcombe describes China as "an empire of writing" (2001, 75). Although Japanese and other early East Asians already possessed spoken languages, educated Chinese introduced writing to peoples who previously could only speak. The critical importance of this action is demonstrated by the fact that the literal meaning for the word "culture" in Korean, Vietnamese, and Japanese is identical: "the transformation caused by writing." The Japanese word for Chinese written characters, kanji, literally means "the writing of the Han"—Han being the name of the Chinese dynasty in power when the Japanese imported a writing system. Even the conventional so-called native term for Japan, Nihon, was chosen in the seventh century for the meaning of the Chinese characters ("origin of the sun").

Even more than Greece in the West, to educated East Asians, China was an admired civilization rather than a place. Most Hellenes, with the notable exception of Alexander the Great, dismissed all non-Greeks as "barbarians." In contrast with the Greek attitude, educated Chinese accepted other peoples who could read written characters and considered only those who could not read Chinese characters and understand China's belief systems, literature, and history to be barbarians. Educated elites throughout East Asia would share many classical Chinese core beliefs until well into the 19th century. Despite the occasional use of military force, the Chinese state did not, for the most part, force its culture on the region. Thus, the infusion of Chinese culture freely intermingled with existing local cultural practices. Chinese influence was more indirect in Japan than in the rest of the region. Not only were the Japanese islands more remote from China than was the case with northern Vietnam and Korea, but also in crucial early centuries of contact, the Koreans were transmitting *their* version of Chinese ideas to the Japanese.

JAPAN'S PREHISTORY AND EARLY MAINLAND ASIA INFLUENCES

The first people in the archipelago probably walked there via temporary land bridges from the Asian mainland more than 30,000 years ago. There is some archeological evidence that people from Southeast Asia also reached Japan by water in prehistoric times.

Archaeologists have used the art of Japan's earliest known culture to name the first period of Japanese prehistory. A *jomon* was a rope pressed into a clay vessel to form a design; the clay pot was then fired to imprint the design. It is now the name given to a people who from approximately 11,000 to 300 BCE lived a simple nomadic lifestyle of hunting, fishing, and gathering edibles. Evidence of Jomon culture has been found from Okinawa to Hokkaido. The only surviving evidence of early Jomon culture are remains of their pottery used as containers, but more sophisticated implements from the late Jomon period (2000 BCE), such as the remains of serving bowls, have been unearthed.

By approximately 300 BCE, in parts of the present-day islands of Kyushu and Honshu, individuals were engaged in a much more sophisticated lifestyle than in the Jomon era. More important, the people of the Yayoi culture, named after an excavation site in the Tokyo area, were assured a steady food supply because they adopted wet field or irrigated rice cultivation. Agriculture enabled these early Japanese to build permanent communities and devote time to activities other than hunting for food. Even during these times, the more advanced Chinese and Korean

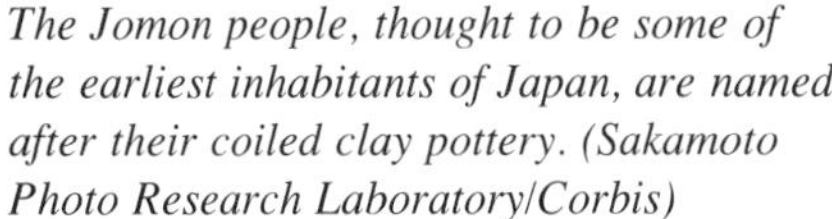

The Jomon people, thought to be some of the earliest inhabitants of Japan, are named after their coiled clay pottery. (Sakamoto Photo Research Laboratory/Corbis)

During the latter part of Japan's Yayoi period, evidence of contact with continental Asia is found in designs of artifacts such as this pot. (Sakamoto Photo Research Laboratory/Corbis)

civilizations were important in Japanese development since wet field rice cultivation almost certainly came to Japan from the Asian mainland.

Although there is still some controversy, wet rice agriculture almost certainly reached Kyushu from Korea around 400 BCE and had gradually spread north by the beginnings of the Common Era. People during the Yayoi period produced a variety of implements, including large jars and urns; used two other East Asian imports, bronze and iron, for making weapons; and established some sea trade with the Korean Peninsula and China. Surviving Chinese records reveal that representatives of that nation's government visited Japan as early as 57 CE.

Although the Chinese had visited the archipelago probably beginning sometime between the third and fourth centuries CE, a wave of Korean immigrants militarily and technologically dominated the more primitive Yayoi culture. These Korean intruders also engaged in some of the same practices in their new land as on the Korean mainland. These immigrants have come to be known as Kofun, or "Tomb People," because they buried their leaders in huge keyhole-shaped tombs. By 250 CE, Japanese culture resembled that of Korea more than it did earlier Yayoi culture. Such tomb artifacts as textiles, pottery, coins, and mirrors indicate that regular contact was maintained with the Asian mainland. Also, the arrival of military technology from the Asian mainland, particularly the skill of riding horses, enabled some powerful families to gain power through coalitions.

One such coalition, who lived on the Yamato plain near present-day Osaka and Kyoto, extended their political power to the point that they controlled all of Japan

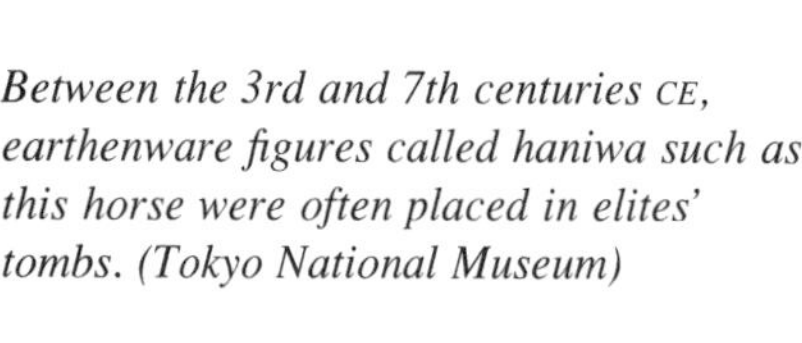

Between the 3rd and 7th centuries CE, *earthenware figures called haniwa such as this horse were often placed in elites' tombs. (Tokyo National Museum)*

except northern Honshu and Hokkaido. The Yamato rulers were in contact with the Chinese and built alliances with Korean sovereigns. Also, Yamato leaders, who were both male and female, established the principle of hereditary succession to the throne. The first Yamato rulers were probably both religious and political leaders as well as prosperous rice farmers. Wet rice cultivation formed the base for the emerging Yamato state, and for much of Yamato clan power. The first Japanese emperors emerged from the Yamato rulers. Rice is much more than a food in Japanese culture, and even today, Japanese imperial rituals are mostly about planting and harvesting rice.

By the time of the Yamato rulers, elements of indigenous religious practices that are now organized as Shinto, or "way of the gods," were already present in the archipelago. Shinto, which will be discussed in detail in a later chapter, is based on nature worship and is intimately connected to such venerable Japanese cultural icons as rice, sake, sumo, and even Mount Fuji.

An event as historically significant as the beginnings of Shinto occurred in 552 CE when Buddhism was introduced to Japan from the Asian mainland. Buddhism, which originated in India and spread to China, eventually reached Korea and then Japan. According to legend, the king of the Korean state of Paekche, in the process of requesting Japanese military assistance, sent gifts to the Yamato rulers that included Buddhist sutras, a statue of Buddha, and a letter of praise for the religion.

The advent of Buddhism in Japan, whose influence would be limited to aristocrats for hundreds of years, caused extreme controversy in Yamato ruling circles. Although two powerful clans, the Nakatomi and the Mononobe, opposed the strange new spiritual import, a third influential clan, the Sogas, who had ties to the Yamato ruler, were leading proponents of Buddhism. Buddhism had initial setbacks. After the Soga clan adopted a Buddhist image as their house kami, an epidemic occurred that the Nakatomis, who were Shinto ritualists, blamed on the new

Prince Shotoku is considered the earliest influential Japanese political leader ruling as regent from 593–622 CE. *Shotoku was a leading advocate of Buddhism and Confucianism. (Instructional Resources Corporation)*

religion. Eventually, though, the Soga clan defeated the Mononobe clan in war in 587 CE, thereby insuring Buddhism's survival in Japan. Buddhism is still an important religion in contemporary Japan, and it is extensively discussed later in this book.

Koreans probably played an important role as an organized Japanese state emerged in the sixth and seventh centuries. The first head of organized Buddhism in Japan was a Korean Paekche priest, several of the compilers of the first Japanese law codes were Korean, and at least one member of the imperial family was Korean. However, early Korean influences on Japan waned with the fall of the Paekche kingdom; the assimilation of the original Korean immigrants, many of whom were granted land and Japanese surnames; and increased Japanese direct contact with imperial China.

The desire of educated Japanese to learn more about Buddhism not only had profound eventual religious implications but also helped to increase the level of general knowledge in Japan. Japanese Buddhist priests traveled to China for religious instruction and then returned to Japan with technology and ideas ranging from better tools and weapons to governmental innovations and philosophy.

Although several important Chinese imports, including wet rice cultivation, iron, and a writing system, had come to Japan through Korea or directly from China, a Chinese-based knowledge explosion occurred between the late sixth century and 838 CE. The Japanese government, eager to learn from what was perhaps the world's most advanced civilization at the time, sent at least 19 separate missions to China between 600 and 838 CE. Missions, usually numbering more than 500 individuals, included official envoys, students, Buddhist monks, and translators. Many

Japanese who braved these often dangerous trips stayed in China for as long as 20 to 30 years.

Confucianism, another Chinese belief system that would eventually be just as influential on Japanese thinking as Buddhism, also gained the attention of those Japanese elites who were eagerly absorbing new knowledge from China. Early Japanese political leaders valued the teaching of Confucius for its practical utility—its stress on the need for good government along with ethics, social hierarchy, harmony, duty, and respect for authority. Confucianism's teachings are still an important part of the belief systems of contemporary Japanese, and they are addressed later in this book.

Buddhism and Confucianism as well as other Chinese-derived ideas received a powerful boost from Prince Shotoku, who served as imperial Yamato regent from 593 until his death in 622 CE. Shotoku was a strong advocate of Buddhism and gave it official government approval. Although there was some opposition to Buddhism from Shinto priests and powerful families, Buddhism took root in Japan without the substantial bloodshed that historically accompanied the introduction of a new belief in many other countries. While it would be centuries before Buddhism became a popular religion with the common people, it was highly favored among the nobility, at least partially because Buddhism was known to be the religion of an advanced Chinese civilization.

As Japan moved from a land ruled by a clan to a country with an organized government, Shotoku also promoted Chinese ideas in his so-called 17-point constitution in 604, which affirmed the power of the emperor, Buddhism, and the Confucian

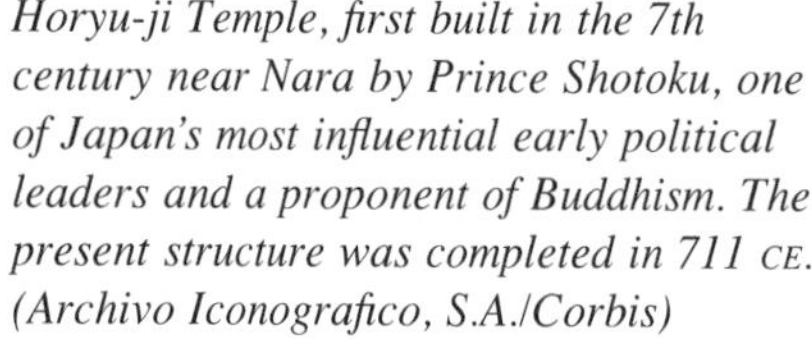

Horyu-ji Temple, first built in the 7th century near Nara by Prince Shotoku, one of Japan's most influential early political leaders and a proponent of Buddhism. The present structure was completed in 711 CE. (Archivo Iconografico, S.A./Corbis)

SHOTOKU TAISHI (574–622)

Possibly of Korean lineage, Prince Shotoku was appointed regent as a young man by Empress Suiko and is considered Japan's first great leader. Shotoku was educated in Chinese and was a proponent of learning from China's more advanced empire. He introduced Chinese technology, science, and governmental procedures to Japanese political elites although he encountered stiff opposition from conservative quarters. He is most remembered for the promulgation of Japan's so-called 17-point constitution in 604. The short document was actually not a plan of government but mostly a set of moral injunctions based on Confucianism and Buddhism. The first point in the document is a Confucian call for harmony.

notion of harmony. Following Shotoku's death in 622, there were blood feuds between factions for power, but in 645 a pro-China faction led by the founder of the Fujiwara family and an imperial prince engineered a coup d'état. The next year, the new government initiated the Taika, or "Great Reforms."

The intent of these reforms, most of which were modeled after the Chinese Tang dynasty and based on Confucian ideas, was to transfer power from clan and family leaders to the throne and its representatives. The separate domains ruled by clans became provinces, and Chinese taxation systems and law codes were adopted. All agricultural land supposedly belonged to the Yamato emperor, and bureaucrats of different ranks, who theoretically earned their positions by merit, were to run the national government.

Even as many Chinese-based reforms took root in Japan, its leaders altered or ignored Chinese political models that did not fit their culture. In Japan, powerful families not only had extensive property and armed retainers but also monopolized leading government positions. In China, by contrast, important positions in the imperial bureaucracy were increasingly awarded to candidates who had successfully passed examinations and weren't necessarily from powerful aristocratic families. This situation provided the Chinese emperor with a means to disempower the aristocracy. The Japanese emperor had no such political weapon. While China had powerful emperors, Japanese emperors gradually became politically weak leaders, and individuals acting in the emperor's name made important decisions.

Although Japanese culture would later become quite sophisticated, in the sixth through the ninth centuries, the upper classes in Japan viewed Chinese civilization as much the superior source of knowledge. The few literate Japanese were extremely familiar with Chinese literature. Japanese also adopted many Chinese techniques in weaving, lacquerware, metallurgy, orchestral music, dance, architecture, sculpture, and painting. Still, as in government and politics, the Japanese either changed certain Chinese practices to fit their culture or rejected them entirely.

Chinese food and eating habits were not accepted during this time in Japan. Even the emperor might have a Chinese-style palace but live in private quarters that would retain the Japanese tradition of cedar-bark roofs and pillars of plain, undecorated wood. Until 694, after the death of an emperor the capital would be moved, but on that date, Emperor Temmu's widow, who succeeded Temmu, moved the capital to a new site that was named Fujiwara a few miles in the southern part of the Nara plain. The new capital was modeled after the then Chinese capital Loyang, but political infighting and natural disasters influenced the court in 710 to move the capital a few miles north to a site that has historically come to be known as Nara. The new capital, which became Japan's first permanent seat of government, was laid out in direct imitation of the Chinese Tang dynasty capital, Chang'an.

Shortly after the capital's founding, the earliest two surviving Japanese books, the *Kojiki*, or *Record of Ancient Matters*, and the *Nihon Shoki*, or *Chronicles of Japan*, were completed in 712 and 720, respectively. These books contain both mythology and historical information. The *Kojiki* attempted to use written Chinese to represent the Japanese language phonetically, but the *Nihon Shoki* was written in conventional Chinese script. The modest number of books that circulated in Japan at this time were written with Chinese characters. It would not be until the 800s that Japanese people would devise their own writing systems to accompany the already centuries-old spoken language.

However, Japanese technology was already significantly advancing. While Nara was the Japanese capital, one of the world's greatest architectural projects, the construction of the enormous Todaiji Temple containing the more than 52-foot-high Great Buddha, was completed under the leadership of Emperor Shomu, perhaps the most devoutly Buddhist sovereign in Japanese history. An estimated 10 percent of the Japanese population contributed to the project, and 50,000 carpenters and more than 370,000 sheet metal workers were involved in construction. Approximately 10,000 Buddhist priests were in attendance as well as many other visitors from foreign countries during the dedication ceremony in 752 (Stanley-Baker 1984, 46–47; Varley 1973, 24–25).

Emperor Shomu's project probably did imperial power more harm than good as the costs of Todaiji placed enormous strains on government finances. Also, after Todaiji was built, the Buddhist temples that surrounded Nara housed many priests who attempted to intervene in politics. Partially because of a fear of the growing influence of the great Nara temples, in 784 Emperor Kammu first moved the capital 30 miles to Nagaoka. However, feuding families, the assassination of the emperor's brother, and a series of natural disasters caused the emperor in 794 to move the capital to a village 10 miles north of Nagaoka. The new capital was named Heian ("peace and tranquility"). The new city that was laid out on the checkerboard pattern of Chinese cities would later come to be known as Kyoto. Kyoto remained Japan's imperial capital until 1868.

CLASSICAL JAPAN

The Heian period (794–1185) is a critical period of Japanese history. Although the cultural heritage imparted by China and the early Korean states remains a part of

Todaiji Temple in Nara houses one of Japan's two great Buddhas. The dedication for the temple occurred in 752. (Dreamstime.com)

Japan, distinct and sophisticated Japanese cultural forms emerged during this period. The new capital city was situated in a nation with an estimated population of 5 million people. Heian, by the millennium, had a population of around 100,000, making it larger than any European city of the time but significantly smaller than the Chinese capital of Chang'an or classical Rome. Through most of the period, the powerful Fujiwara family successfully exercised "marriage politics." Rather than make the mistake of actually trying to assume the imperial title, the family would marry their daughters to child emperors, and a Fujiwara male aristocrat would be the de facto head of government. As Buddhism continued to be important among the upper classes, emperors would abdicate relatively young—the average age was 31—ostensibly to focus on religious practices. During the Heian period, the imperial family and a few hundred high-ranking aristocrats played a major part in creating aspects of Japanese culture that are still present in contemporary Japan.

Heian aristocrats operated within a complex social system with 10 rankings. Those members of the top ranks had enormous economic, social, and political advantages over everyone else. One's social rank determined everything from the permissible size of a gatepost at a private home to the number of folds in a fan an individual might be allowed. This preoccupation with rank and status was in contrast with China, where important government positions that brought high status were increasingly awarded to men who exhibited "virtue" through passing Confucian-based examinations. Aristocratic marriages were arranged, and what today would be considered illicit love affairs were commonly conducted, usually under cover of night. While they lived lives largely confined indoors except for festivals and religious holidays, aristocratic women in some ways had more status in Heian Japan than

Kyoto's Heian Shrine, built in 1895 to commemorate the 1,100th anniversary of the city, is an impressive Shinto shrine that also features a beautiful garden. (PhotoDisc/Getty Images)

in several of the subsequent historical periods. High-ranking women were important because of marriage politics and could inherit property.

Because of imperial records and surviving memoirs, written mostly by women, there is considerable existing knowledge about aristocratic lifestyles. However, all that is known about the daily lives of ordinary people are revealed through the documents and writings of the educated upper classes. Also, there were no large urban centers outside of Heian, so knowledge of daily life in the archipelago is scarce. A complicated manorial system existed, with individuals holding rights on fiefs in the provinces and accumulating private military forces for estate protection. Aristocrat absentee landlords resided in the capital, and the worst possible social misfortune that could happen to an aristocrat was to be sent to the provinces. While the political system perpetuated Fujiwara power, it further weakened the throne and central government authority and finances. Still, this unusual governance system brought domestic peace, and the separation of the island nation from the mainland was a barrier to foreign invasion. These factors allowed many of the capital's aristocrats to concentrate on varieties of leisure and aesthetic pursuits.

In 894 the Japanese government ceased sending missions to China, and over the next two centuries Japan had little official contact with the continent. The defeat of Paekche more than a century earlier lessened Japanese interactions with Korea. Although core imported Chinese belief systems such as Confucianism remained influential, the literature and nonfiction that formed the curriculum of the state university were culled from the earlier Tang dynasty, and little or nothing new came to Japan from the contemporary Chinese Song court. Heian aristocrats began to pay less attention to China and increasingly focus their aesthetic and literary interests on their daily lives.

Heian-era aristocrats considered one's visual appearance and whether it was pleasing to others as a mark of one's sensitivity. Women were expected to pluck their eyebrows and blacken their teeth because both were considered marks of beauty. The following description of the dress of a Heian nobleman attending a court ceremony illustrates the importance placed on appearance: "Michitaka wore a summer tunic with a violet mantle, laced violet trousers, underwear of deep red, and a stiff unlined brilliantly white overgarment. All gentlemen carried fans with them whose ribs were lacquered in various colors with paper of brilliant red" (Sansom 1964, 192–193). This original aristocratic emphasis on form as equal with function remains a widespread cultural proclivity in contemporary Japan.

However, deeper spiritual and religious values particular to Heian aristocrats lay beneath the emphasis on visual appearances. While Buddhism had not become a religion of the common people during this period of Japanese history, it profoundly influenced the aristocracy. The impermanence of all things, a fundamental tenet of Buddhism, found expression in Japan in the concept of *mono no aware*, or a recognition of the pathos of life. The cherry blossom became a particular symbol of beauty because its bloom exists only for a short time. Mono no aware also found expression in an appreciation of the beauty of a young girl in the early stages of adolescence because in a short time her appearance would substantially change. Long-time Shinto reverence of nature and simplicity found expression in the spare style of Japanese architecture compared to more ornate Chinese homes.

Although Japanese aristocratic males continued to write in classical Chinese, dramatic earlier changes in Japanese writing were beginning to exert profound cultural effects. For centuries the Japanese had no written language, and educated people wrote in Chinese. Because spoken Chinese and Japanese sounds are completely different, it is extremely difficult to write down spoken Japanese in Chinese. In the 9th and 10th centuries, the Japanese took certain Chinese characters, greatly abbreviated them, and created a phonetic system and written syllabary, called kana, which, combined with Chinese characters, provided the basis for a unique written language. By the latter part of the 10th century, members of the nobility were using kana to write books and poems. Women in particular used kana because written Japanese was still considered to be less appropriate for educated men than written Chinese.

Heian aristocrats focused most of their attention on the pursuit of pleasurable activities that included unwritten courtship rituals for both sexes and various recreational activities that focused on aesthetic pursuits. Males played a ball game, *kemuri*, that was similar to hacky sack in that the object was to keep the ball in the air as long as possible. However, judges evaluated one's skill on how graceful the player appeared while engaging in the sport. Heian aristocrats also played musical instruments such as the lute and the zither, and both the sound of the music and the appearance of the player were important.

Poetry and letter writing abilities could make or break an aristocrat's reputation. Poems were used for a variety of functions including even that of one government official using the medium to criticize another official for not reporting to his post. The ideas alone that were represented in a poem or letter were not enough. Calligraphy or writing ability was also important in determining reputation since the visual quality of one's writing was considered a mirror to the soul. Letter writing was an art form that combined a number of aesthetic elements including the excellence of the poem or prose, the appearance of written characters, the quality of the paper, and even its perfumed scent or the blossom or sprig that was enclosed with the letter.

As described earlier, Japanese women aristocrats freely employed the new Japanese script in writing, and much of what we know about the Heian era is because of the surviving works of such authors as Sei Shonagon and Murasaki Shikibu. Murasaki wrote the *Tale of Genji* during the first two decades of the millennium. The book, now considered to be a masterpiece of world literature and the world's first psychological novel, reveals much of the life and values of Heian aristocrats. The hero, Prince Genji ("shining prince"), epitomizes what Heian nobility considered to be superb personal qualities. He is handsome, a thoughtful lover, a graceful athlete, and a musician, and he also possesses impeccable taste. Genji's love affairs constitute much of the story. However, poetry permeates the work, and the vivid human interactions have made the book timeless. Also, women don't just constitute a backdrop for Genji but have their own unique voices. In contemporary Japan, *The Tale of Genji* both occupies a similar high position in Japan as Shakespeare's works enjoy in the West and is a perpetual subject in such popular media as animation and cartoons.

This scene from "The Tale of Genji" is illustrative of the little time that aristocrats of different genders actually saw each other during the Heian period. (Library of Congress)

MURASAKI SHIKIBU (973?–1014)

Murasaki is the most famous Japanese novelist and a world literary figure. It is questionable whether Murasaki's birth date and date of death are actually known, but these are accurate approximations. Her father was a Chinese literature scholar who also served in the Imperial Bureau of Rites. Murasaki was educated in both Japanese prose and the Chinese classics, the latter being unusual for a Heian woman. She became a lady-in-waiting for the Empress Shoshi in 1006 or 1007. It is likely that Murasaki received the post in recognition of the masterpiece that she was then writing and distributing serially. Murasaki, who probably finished her masterpiece while in imperial service, is also famous for her diary. *The Tale of Genji* occupies a place in the Japanese literary canon equivalent to the status in the English-speaking world of Shakespeare's entire works. Murasaki describes, in a novel that focuses on a quintessential Japanese aristocrat, elite values and aesthetics during Japan's classical period that through the centuries became larger Japanese cultural propensities.

Cultural achievements notwithstanding, the inattention of Heian elites to the practical business of governing a nation resulted in an increasingly dysfunctional government. Crime and other forms of disorder increased in the capital and elsewhere. Provincial families with their private warrior-retainers became increasingly

The Gempei War, which was a fierce battle between two powerful clans for control of Japan in the latter part of the 12th century, also spawned the later creation of the Tale of the Heike, a classic of Japanese literature. (Instructional Resources Corporation)

powerful. As the central government asked for more and more taxes, many peasants in the provinces began to band together behind these rural lords. While the Fujiwara regents and other aristocrats in the capital concerned themselves with the arts, powerful landowners were gaining experience managing large estates, amassing wealth, and becoming quite proficient at fighting on horseback. Political change was imminent.

MEDIEVAL JAPAN

As the influence of the Fujiwara clan and the central government declined, two powerful provincial families, the Taira and Minamoto, warred against each other in what historians refer to as the Gempei War. In 1185, Yoritomo, the leader of the Minamoto family, defeated the Taira and Fujiwara clans and obtained military control of Japan. In 1192 the emperor "appointed" Yoritomo shogun, or "barbarian suppressing general," making him the most powerful political and military leader in Japan.

Yoritomo chose not to live in Kyoto, the imperial capital, but remained in his headquarters in the seaside town of Kamakura, located near the modern city of Tokyo. Yoritomo's headquarters in Kamakura, which came to be known as the *bakafu*, or "tent government," was Japan's major but not exclusive center of political power and its unofficial capital. At the same time, the imperial court and emperor continued to reside in Kyoto, the official capital.

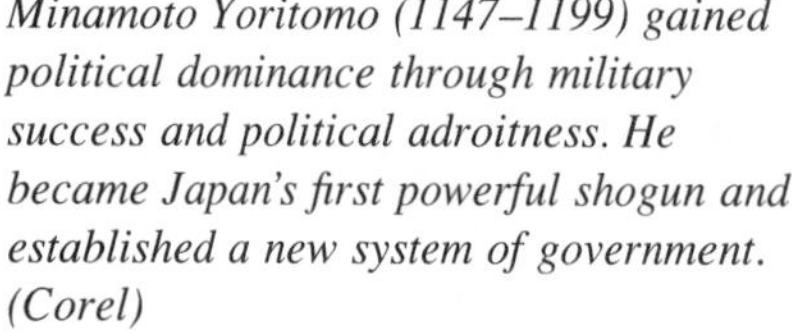

Minamoto Yoritomo (1147–1199) gained political dominance through military success and political adroitness. He became Japan's first powerful shogun and established a new system of government. (Corel)

The emperor and imperial court were much more culturally than politically influential. This pattern of rule from behind the scenes became even more pronounced in the power struggle following Yoritomo's death in 1199. The family of Yoritomo's widow, the Hojo, emerged victorious. By placing Hojo family members in key positions, the family exercised actual political power. The shogunate, first occupied by a Minamoto, then by Fujiwaras, and later by princes of royal blood, became a figurehead.

Political power was quite decentralized. Yoritomo established a system throughout Japan where his vassals, or *gokenin*, and their warrior-retainers, known as samurai, fulfilled many of the old imperial government functions. Even though there were differences in the two systems, medieval Japanese, as did their European counterparts, developed a feudal system where landowners were responsible to overlords, who, in turn, were often loyal to higher authorities. Japanese feudalism came later than in Europe but remained in place until the last half of the 19th century.

The warrior class was the backbone of Japanese feudalism. By the late 1100s, a general code of ethics for the samurai was already being observed, though it was not written down until much later. As in Europe, it was of vital importance that samurai learn such techniques of war as swordsmanship. As in Europe, heroism, honor, and loyalty were highly valued. The samurai, however, were particularly enamored with the last two characteristics. Honor of family name was something a samurai would die for, but loyalty to superiors was perhaps the most treasured of ideals.

Ideally, warriors did not question a superior's commands, and a warrior's obedience to a superior was expected regardless of family, all private interests, and even life itself. One samurai, who had a reputation for being especially brave, was in danger from a robber and evaded the assailant in what seemed to be a cowardly manner. This samurai could not risk his life to protect his own property because he needed to preserve himself to serve his lord. Yoritomo was once presented with the head of an opponent by a samurai who had sworn loyalty to the dead opponent. The founder of the Kamakura government eventually had the samurai executed for disloyalty.

Samurai also were taught not to fear death and, as mental training, to become comfortable with the notion that death is preferable to dishonor or failure. This attitude is illustrated by words from the very first page of *Hagakure*, or *The Book of the Samurai*. Although the author, Yamamoto Tsunetomo, wrote this classic much later than Japan's Kamakura period, samurai were already practicing the following injunction:

> The way of the samurai is found in death. When it comes to either/or, there is only the quick choice of death. It is not particularly difficult. Be determined and advance. To say that dying without reaching one's aim is a dog's death is the frivolous way of sophisticates. When pressed with the choice of life or death it is not necessary to gain one's aim.
>
> We all want to live. And in large part we make our logic according to what we like. But not having attained our aim and continuing to live is cowardice. (Yamamoto 1983, 17)

The ability of many samurai to focus the mind to exhibit self-discipline, as well as their appreciation for beauty, was in part stimulated by the popularity of Zen Buddhism among the warrior class. Though Zen was a sect that largely appealed to elites, Buddhism in general during the Kamakura years grew from a religion practiced by a few to a widespread belief system. Popular variants of Buddhism flourished, including the Pure Land sects, whose adherents worshipped Amida Buddha. Buddhism is discussed in more detail later in this book.

Self-discipline and bravery were qualities very much in demand during Japan's medieval period, which were marked by strife. One of the major crises in Japanese history occurred in the late 1200s as outside invaders threatened the archipelago. Mongol nomads from the steppe lands north of China conquered Central Asia, southern Russia, parts of the Middle East and Eastern Europe, Korea, and China. The Mongols tried twice to subdue Japan, sending a large seaborne force of almost 30,000 men in 1274 and a much larger contingent of 140,000 troops in 1281. In both cases, the Japanese fought fiercely with the Mongols but received enormous help from nature when typhoons, which the Japanese called kamikaze, or "divine winds," destroyed the foreign fleets.

The Kamakura system lasted a little more than 50 years after the repulsion of the Mongol invaders. The Hojo family was overthrown in 1333 by Emperor Go-Daigo, who attempted to revive imperial rule in the Kemmu Restoration. In turn, Ashikaga Takauji, the leader of a powerful family who was an early imperial ally, later broke with Go-Daigo, seized Kyoto, and installed a rival puppet emperor. Shortly afterward, Go-Daigo escaped from Kyoto and established a second imperial court in Kyushu. From 1336 until 1392, when the Kyushu-based emperor was forced to return to Kyoto, Japan had two sets of emperors. However, Takauji became the major political power in Japan and in 1338 had his handpicked emperor appoint him shogun. Takauji and his Ashikaga successors ruled from Kyoto.

The political system became more hierarchical during the Ashikaga period (1333–1573), as warrior-retainers were responsible to more powerful provincial lords, or daimyo, who in turn were theoretically responsible to the shogun. The actual situation during most of the Ashikaga years, however, was that power was even more decentralized than in the Kamakura era. Ashikaga shoguns were relatively weak, and powerful families fought each other and the shogun for control of Japan.

The Ashikaga period was marked by constant strife, including the bloody Onin War, which lasted from 1467 until 1477 and was fought all over Japan. During these confused years while the Ashikaga shogunate was virtually powerless, emperors continued to reign but were often reduced to near poverty because they had no access to stable income. It is not surprising that the Ashikaga years are considered one of the darkest political times in Japan's history.

Political problems notwithstanding, in other human endeavors the Ashikaga period was one of excitement and growth. The Ashikaga shoguns were quite interested in Zen Buddhism and the arts. They built in Kyoto the Golden and Silver

Shogun Ashikaga Yoshimitsu built what is now known as the Golden Temple as a retirement residence in 1397. After his death it became a Zen temple. Although a disturbed monk burned the original down in 1950, the temple was rebuilt and is today a Kyoto world tourist attraction. (Corel)

Pavilions, two of the most beautiful temples in all Japan. Many world-famous aspects of Japanese culture, such as the tea ceremony and flower arranging, were fully developed during this period. Japanese art today often emphasizes the value of the natural over the artificial, irregularly shaped pottery over the symmetrical, the small over the large, and the simple over the complex. These values were a lasting result of the refined artistic taste of the Ashikaga shoguns.

Two classical forms of Japanese drama, *noh* and *kyogen*, also developed during the Ashikaga period. Although noh's roots go back even earlier, a Shinto priest named Kan'ami (1333–1384) and his son Zeami (1363–1443) fully developed noh theater during the Ashikaga years. Noh, a musical dance drama where the characters wear masks, is still performed in contemporary Japan. Buddhist themes permeate noh plays. Noh drama usually features a meeting of a troubled spirit who is still attached to an earthly incident and either a priest or other mortal. Noh is danced more than acted, accompanied by a chorus as well as flute and drum music. The noh actor's dance is controlled, slow, and intense. The unearthly voices (due in part to the effects of the masks), intensity of the dance, spare music, and grave themes create an air of great seriousness and mystery.

Shorter *kyogen* plays were performed between different noh dramas as changes of pace. Kyogen translates to "mad and wild words" and is completely opposite from noh. These comic plays featured provincial bumpkins in the capital, servants

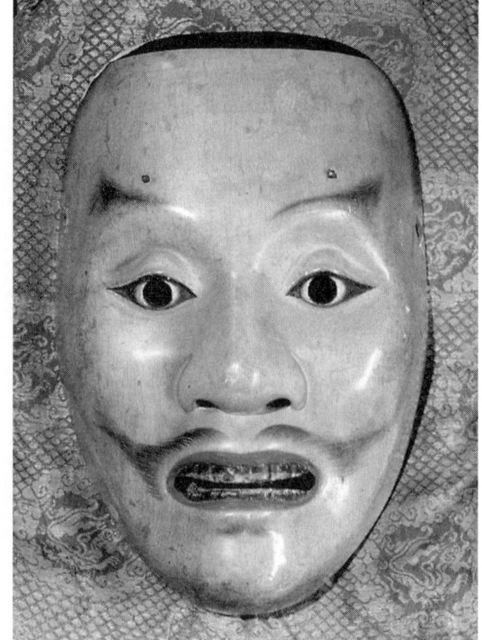

Buddhist-inspired noh drama developed in the 14th and 15th centuries. Noh actors wear masks such as this one. (Werner Forman/Art Resource)

who were smarter than their masters, and other such light-hearted themes. Kyogen plays are also still part of modern Japanese theater.

As noted, most Ashikaga shoguns were not effective political leaders. Ashikaga Yoshimasa (1443–1473), who was by all accounts a totally inept shogun, has gone down in Japanese history as one of the strongest patrons of virtually every traditional Japanese cultural form that was flowering during this period. Yoshimasa's name is associated with the Silver Pavilion (Ginkakuji), which he had constructed in the then outskirts of Kyoto as a retirement villa. It was converted into a Buddhist temple after his death and today is a cultural landmark and tourist attraction. However, Yoshimasa's cultural legacy runs much deeper in Japanese society. Japan scholar Donald Keene credits Yoshimasa in playing a seminal role in helping to create what is considered today to be much of traditional Japanese culture.

Yoshimasa practiced Pure Land Buddhism but was heavily influenced by Zen aesthetics, where the focus is on subtle, simple, and understated art forms. He favored the *rikkya* ("standing") style of carefully arranging a few flowers in the floral displays in his palace. Yoshimasa played a major part in elevating flower arranging to the same status as other art forms such as calligraphy or painting. The development of Zen-influenced gardens that often made maximum use of carefully arranged rocks accelerated during the 15th century. Many of the builders of gardens actually responsible for moving and placing rocks were *kawaramono*, or "people of the riverbed," who were the lowest class in Japanese society. Yoshimasa took the quite unconventional step of placing many *kawaramono*, including Zen'ami, who would become one of the most famous garden designers in Japanese history, under

Ashikaga Yoshimasa who built a retirement villa beginning in 1482 at the foot of the eastern mountains of Kyoto, never completed the structure what went on to become the world famous Silver Pavilion. (Corel)

his personal protection. Yoshimasa also patronized and participated in the *chanoyu*, or tea ceremonies, that often took place in modest tea houses that were part of larger Zen rock gardens and temple complexes.

Of all the art forms he promoted, Yoshimasa may have been most devoted to the noh theater, and he was involved as a spectator, as well as promoter and patron of noh, his entire life. Although at least one other shogun of this period had been a strong patron of noh, when Yoshimasa was shogun he issued a proclamation identifying noh to be "the music of the state." According to Confucian tradition, rites and music were essential to the well-ordered and harmonious state. Yoshimasa believed that noh both fulfilled a societal need for the ordered continuity that rites and music create and that a person's participation as a spectator in a noh performance helped evoke an individual sense of the existence of a world beyond the visible one.

Ashikaga Yoshimasa's reliance on Confucian beliefs to bolster noh, a Japanese creation, is an example of how Japanese valued elements of a mother culture yet extensively immersed themselves in their own practices. Zen Buddhism originated in China but took new Japanese forms and was more influential in Japan than its country of origin. Zen monks of the Ashikaga period, especially those who resided in five great protected Kyoto temples, were the intellectual elite of the time. They were skilled in classical Chinese and worldly in that many had visited the mainland. These monks, who were protected by the state during these often turbulent times, managed to preserve classical Chinese learning in a similar way to what occurred with Christian monastic preservation of Greco-Roman heritage in medieval Europe. The monks even developed a genre of prose and poetry written in classical Chinese that included works of distinction.

Technological and economic progress also occurred during medieval Japan in part because other Japanese met and learned from foreigners. Although after 894 there had been no official government contact between Japan and China, during the mid-1100s the Japanese government began sending "tribute" to China's Song dynasty and receiving gifts in return from the Chinese court. By the Kamakura years, Japan and China engaged in an officially condoned and quite lively trade. Japanese society was enriched by Chinese imports, including silk, perfumes, sandalwood, porcelain, and copper coins, and Japanese swords, fans, and lacquerware were highly prized in China.

When Portuguese traders landed off southern Kyushu in 1543, Japan was exposed to both technology and ideas significantly different from anything ever introduced from Asia. Japanese immediately became interested in European guns and in less than 25 years were manufacturing enough guns that in one battle between rival families, the winning side had several thousand riflemen. Also, the Portuguese and other Europeans who followed included Catholic priests and protestant clergy who viewed the Japanese as excellent candidates for Christian conversion. The Europeans proceeded immediately to win converts.

TOKUGAWA JAPAN: AN ERA OF PEACE

European influence, particularly new technology, served as a partial catalyst for political change in Japan. Only a few years after Europeans introduced guns to Japan, three powerful leaders—Oda Nobunaga, Toyotomi Hideyoshi, and Tokugawa Ieyasu—used advanced firepower to achieve brilliant military successes that resulted in the political unification of Japan.

In 1568, at the invitation of the emperor and Ashikaga Yoshiaki, an unsuccessful candidate for shogun, Oda Nobunaga and his forces occupied Kyoto and took control of much of central Japan. Nobunaga allowed Yoshiaki to hold the title of shogun until 1573 and then removed him from office, ending forever the Ashikaga family claim to the shogunate. Nobunaga was in control, although he installed a member of another family as puppet shogun. Nobunaga was extremely ruthless in attempting to unify Japan. He killed every man, woman, and child in one major Buddhist stronghold that opposed him.

After taking control of all of central Japan, Nobunaga was betrayed by one of his own generals, who surrounded the warlord and forced Nobunaga to commit suicide in 1582. With Japan again threatened by civil war, a second powerful leader emerged. Toyotomi Hideyoshi was a man of peasant origins who rose to become Nobunaga's chief general. Hideyoshi first successfully defeated rival daimyo and, after subduing Kyushu and Honshu, in 1590 gained control of Japan. He reorganized the government, made it illegal for peasants to own weapons, and dispatched

Tokugawa Yoshinobu (1837–1913), although initially highly regarded, was destined to be Japan's last shogun. (Alinari Archives/ Corbis)

an army to attempt the conquest of Korea in a bloody war on the peninsula. Because of his lower-class background, Hideyoshi did not claim the title of shogun but instead had himself declared regent to the emperor.

When Hideyoshi died in 1598, he left a young son as an heir and a group of five powerful daimyo as collective regents. The daimyo soon divided among themselves, and the most powerful of the five, Tokugawa Ieyasu, after winning the battle of Sekigahara near Kyoto in 1600, attained virtual mastery of Japan. Tokugawa, whose original power base was a huge fief that included Edo (modern Tokyo), by 1615 defeated his last opponents at Osaka Castle. A competent military man and a prudent and painstaking administrator and politician, Ieyasu assumed the title of hereditary shogun in 1603 by claiming descent from Minamoto Yoritomo. Not only did Tokugawa reunify Japan, but also his heirs occupied the shogunate for more than 250 years. Beginning in the early 17th century, the Japanese enjoyed more than 250 years of peace.

Ruling from Edo, the Tokugawa shoguns controlled a system that included a relatively authoritarian, but certainly not totalitarian, central government and three descending ranks of daimyo, feudal lords who controlled domains and lived throughout Japan. Elite hereditary daimyo also served on several councils that with the shogunate shared governance of Japan. Daimyo were required to reside in Edo in alternate years so that the shogun could control them. Meanwhile, the emperor remained in Kyoto. Although Japanese emperors still had no appreciable political power, they continued to be living symbols of the nation.

TOKUGAWA IEYASU (1542–1616)

Tokugawa Ieyasu completed the unification of Japan after almost a century of widespread civil and military discord. He used alliances with Oda Nobunaga and then Toyotomi Hideyoshi, two military leaders who began the unification process, to build his own power base in eastern Japan and three years after his victory at Sekigahara was appointed shogun in 1603. The Tokugawa family would retain this title for more than 250 years, with Tokugawa shoguns either actually or nominally ruling Japan during this time. Ieyasu made an obscure fishing village, Edo (now Tokyo), his political base. He and his successors ruled Japan until the 1868 Meiji Restoration.

Tokugawa Japan was characterized by rather rigid divisions between social groups based on Neo-Confucian teachings. At the top were the samurai, who constituted about 5 to 6 percent of the total population. The Tokugawas continued Hideyoshi's policy that only samurai could bear weapons. Samurai could also not marry into the lower classes. Samurai were freed from earning a living because of guaranteed government stipends. They were expected to be not only warriors but also models of virtue as well as government bureaucrats. Samurai were also expected to be familiar with the Confucian canon and such Japanese arts as calligraphy, the tea

Tokugawa Ieyasu unified Japan in 1600 and began an era of over 250 years of political stability. (Ric Ergenbright/Corbis)

ZHU XI AND NEO-CONFUCIANISM (1130–1200)

Although he was Chinese and never visited Japan, this great Neo-Confucian philosopher had a tremendous impact on Tokugawa-era government and social class structure since the shogunate adopted Neo-Confucianism as state orthodoxy. Neo-Confucianism was a reaction to Buddhism and had a metaphysical aspect, but what appealed to the shogunate was the hierarchical class structure that placed samurai elites imbued with a sense of moral responsibility and duty at the top. Government officials also appreciated Neo-Confucianism's stress on active pursuit of learning and activity in this world as opposed to Buddhism's rejection of daily life as an illusion. Neo-Confucianism, although it sometimes placed too much emphasis on overconformity, also played a positive role in the peace and prosperity of the Tokugawa years.

ceremony, and noh. However, higher- and lower-ranked samurai had tremendous gaps in their respective levels of wealth and status. Lower-level samurai were often on the brink of poverty or, in the latter Tokugawa years, poor.

Peasants, who constituted 85 percent of Tokugawa Japan's population, were considered the second-most-important class because they produced the food. The artisans, because they made useful products, ranked just below the peasants. Since the merchants were considered nonproducing parasites, they had the lowest status. However, as time passed and the merchant class accumulated great wealth, it was impossible to restrain their influence. Even though in theory artisans were above merchants, the economy depended on the business class. By the latter part of the Tokugawa period, rich merchants could use their wealth to acquire samurai status. In addition, there were groups of people such as scholars, priests, and physicians who did not fit into the four major classes and groups such as beggars and Burakumin who were shunned because they engaged in such "unclean" trades as garbage collection, butchery, and slaughterhouse work.

Through much of the Tokugawa era, Japan distanced itself from most of the rest of the world. Fear of European Christianity and possible economic and political domination were the reasons behind the official Tokugawa policy of seclusion, which took effect during the 1630s. For a time before then, Christianity and trade with Europeans flourished. By the 1500s, several daimyo encouraged their subjects to adopt Christianity because they either believed in the new religion or desired more trade with Europeans. In 1580 there were an estimated 150,000 Japanese Christian converts, and some accounts indicate that by 1600 there were twice this number.

However, such leaders as Hideyoshi and Tokugawa Ieyasu felt that Christians, particularly Catholics, could not be completely trusted as loyal Japanese because their true allegiance would be to the pope. Also, the Japanese leadership was aware that the Spanish had conquered the Philippines under the guise of Christianity. The Buddhist religious establishment supported anti-Christian sentiments because it viewed the new religion as competition. From 1597 until the late 1630s, the government persecuted and executed thousands of Christians. By 1640, except for some underground Kyushu Christians, the government had managed to abolish the religion in Japan. Also, the Tokugawa seclusion policies largely limited contact with foreigners in the archipelago to a few Chinese, Korean, and Dutch traders and officials. Tokugawa Ieyasu had negotiated a peace treaty in 1605 with the Korean throne, thus reestablishing relations. The Japanese government would directly trade with only one European power, the Netherlands, because they viewed the Dutch as much more interested in commercial activity than spreading Christianity. However, Dutch merchants were limited to residing on a small island in Nagasaki Bay and were closely supervised when required to travel to Edo for an audience with the shogun. No Japanese were allowed to travel abroad, and any Japanese persons living overseas were forbidden to return.

Although the government substantially reduced foreign contacts, contrary to what many believe, Japan was not closed off from the outside world, particularly throughout the 17th century when Japan's silver exports intended primarily for China constituted 30 percent of world silver circulation and Japanese copper exports to the Dutch were a major factor in the Netherlands' economic rise. By the beginning of the 18th century, Japan's domestic economic growth and a drying up of the silver supply caused foreign trade to decline relative to the early Tokugawa period. However, Japan, in addition to trading with the Chinese and Koreans, also did business with the Dutch, therefore maintaining a window to the West throughout the Tokugawa years.

Within Japan the arts, economic development, and learning in areas other than science were in some ways equal or superior to that of the United States or Western Europe during the same period. The city became the focal point for many advances, concurrent with Edo's growth to more than 1 million people by the 1700s. In addition to the great urban areas of Osaka and Kyoto, approximately 250 smaller cities, with populations ranging from 3,000 to 20,000, gained residents during the Tokugawa years.

Tokugawa art forms are still treasured throughout Japan and the world. Woodblock prints, or *ukiyo-e*, which featured beautiful women, actors, and scenes of travelers and natural geographic beauty, became popular. The Japanese had been interested in poetry for centuries, and its culmination came with the 17-syllable haiku, which in a few words often suggests entire worlds.

It was in the Tokugawa era that two forms of popular Japanese theater, *kabuki* and *bunraku*, flourished. The Chinese characters for kabuki (*ka-bu-ki*) mean "song," "dance," and "skill," and the actors in these dramas certainly exhibited these attributes. Kabuki plays today feature action, romance, and elaborate sets. A reoccurring kabuki theme that made Tokugawa officials particularly nervous was the conflict between feudal duty and human concerns and feelings. Often to avoid censorship, playwrights would portray actual contemporary events as occurring in the distant past. Because early Tokugawa kabuki plays were often accompanied by

Kabuki theater is now considered a classic Japanese art form. During the Tokugawa period, kabuki was popular theater. (Library of Congress)

disruption in the audience, authorities first banned women from acting in kabuki and then a few years later banned young men as well. Today men play both gender roles in kabuki.

While kabuki was popular in Edo, bunraku theater, also still alive today, was the rage in Tokugawa-era Osaka. In bunraku, three male puppeteers control large wooden puppets that act while chanters tell the story, accompanied by stringed instruments called samisen. Although originally kabuki and bunraku were theater for commoners, they are considered today, along with noh and *kyogen*, to be classic Japanese theater.

The peaceful Tokugawa years allowed the Japanese economy to expand. Because the country was unified, domestic trade flourished and some merchants acquired enormous fortunes in wholesaling, retailing, and banking. The use of money, always an indicator of societal economic sophistication, was widespread.

Cultural and economic developments were in part due to the spread of formal learning throughout Japan. The daimyo maintained schools for the offspring of samurai, and common children attended schools operated by Buddhist temples, merchants, wealthy farmers, and local teachers. Estimates are that by the mid-19th century, 40 percent of all Japanese men and 10 to 15 percent of all Japanese women could read and write, making Japan one of the world's most literate societies at the time.

Despite advances, Japan's lack of frequent contact with the rest of the world led to some stagnation, particularly in science and technology. Also, other nations took a dim view of Japan's seclusion policies, and eventually the restrictions contributed to the Tokugawa government's collapse. Although the shogunate endured for 15 more years, the real death knell for Tokugawa Japan sounded when Commodore Matthew Perry and the U.S. Navy steamed into what is now Tokyo Bay in July 1853.

JAPAN AND THE WORLD: 1853–1945

Few events in Japan's history have proven as significant as Commodore Perry and his "black ships," as the Japanese called them. In the years since Perry first arrived, Japan would become the first Asian nation to modernize, attain world power status, lose a disastrous war, and recover to develop a democratic government and the second-largest economy in the world.

The United States was interested in opening Japan for several reasons. The U.S. government wanted to expand Pacific trade, and Japan was considered both an excellent fueling station for China-bound ships and a lucrative potential market. The American government also claimed to be concerned about the fate of sailors who were cast ashore in Japan. During his first visit, Perry presented U.S. demands, including better treatment for shipwrecked sailors and the opening of ports where foreign ships could procure supplies and trade. The commodore then left Japanese waters after promising to return the following spring with a larger and more formidable fleet.

Perry's ultimatum caused turmoil within the Japanese government, and a debate raged in the months that followed over what the response should be to the Americans. Although some individuals within the Tokugawa government wanted war, most were painfully aware of the military technology gap. When Perry returned in the spring of 1854, the Japanese offered no resistance and reluctantly gave in to almost all of the American demands. The Americans and Japanese signed the Treaty of Kanagawa on March 31, 1854, granting the United States access to the ports of Hakodate and Shimoda to provision their ships and providing for the appointment of an American consul at Shimoda. The treaty did not grant the Americans trading rights, however.

Although numerous gifts were exchanged to celebrate the treaty, Japan's leaders were in no real mood to celebrate, and debates raged over future policy toward the United States and other Western countries. The Americans were not completely happy with the Kanagawa Treaty either, since the right to trade with Japan was not included, and began almost immediately to demand trading concessions. Antiforeign elements, including Emperor Komei and a group of young samurai, urged the government not to grant trading rights to the United States. Nevertheless, in 1858 the Tokugawa government signed a trade treaty despite these strong objections.

The Harris Treaty, named after the American diplomat who negotiated it, did far more than simply open Japan for trade. It placed Japan, for the first time in history, under the partial control of foreign powers as Americans, and later the Dutch, Russians, British, Germans, and French, obtained both trading rights and the power to determine the tariff amounts for all imports without consulting the Japanese. Also, the United States and European powers were granted the right of

Japanese artist's impression of one of Commodore Perry's "black ships" probably completed in 1854. Fortunately, both American and Japanese artists provide an ample visual record of the Perry visit to Japan. (Library of Congress)

extraterritoriality, which meant that foreign residents were subject to their own rather than Japanese law. The shogunate's decision to acquiesce to violations of national sovereignty, although practical considering Japan's military weakness, proved to be a major reason for the overthrow of the Tokugawa government a few years later.

By the mid-1800s, the Tokugawa government was in trouble over domestic as well as foreign problems. Although public expenditures exceeded revenues, the government seemed incapable of developing adequate measures to derive more income from business and manufacturing. This chronic revenue shortage forced the government to cut back as much as 50 percent the monies paid to samurai. By the latter Tokugawa period, some samurai were living in such austere circumstances that they were reduced to pawning family armor and even putting babies to death to avoid economic destitution.

Also, increasing numbers of people became unhappy with the class system. Many merchants and manufacturers felt discriminated against because even though rich, they were still considered socially inferior to samurai. Lower-ranking samurai, in turn, were discontented with the system because high-ranking samurai, regardless of their qualifications, were awarded upper-level government positions.

By the 1860s a group of younger samurai and commoners, adopting the slogan *sonno-joi*, "revere the emperor and repel the barbarians," were plotting to use the throne as a symbol in an attempt to overthrow the Tokugawa government. Early in

1868, antigovernment forces took over the shogun's Kyoto palace, and the 15-year-old emperor issued a decree establishing a new government. Despite Tokugawa resistance, there was little support for the old regime, and in 1868 the revolutionaries forced the government army to surrender, ending two and one-half centuries of Tokugawa rule relatively bloodlessly. The new emperor, who from the beginning was a symbol rather than an actual leader, took the reign name Meiji, or "Enlightened Rule." Meiji has also become the name for the period of Japanese history from 1868 to 1912.

The small group of men who would modernize Japan was unusual in several respects. They were mainly younger, lower-ranking samurai, and many were in their thirties. Despite earlier rhetoric about driving out foreigners, Meiji leaders were mostly pragmatic and understood that knowledge of Western science, technology, and institutions was vital in the development of a strong economy and military. Then Japan could rid itself of the unequal treaties and assume its own destiny.

The Meiji leaders first established their authority throughout Japan, which meant drastic governmental reform. By 1871, the Meiji government had transformed the old domains into new administrative units called prefectures. During the Tokugawa years, farmers were allowed to pay taxes in rice rather than money, and rates were based on annual harvests instead of land values, making it impossible for the government to plan expenditures in advance. In 1873, the government began requiring that all taxes be paid in money and basing annual collections on land values rather than harvests. Payments to samurai, a tremendous burden to the Tokugawa government, were first reduced and eventually terminated in 1876, when the government

The Meiji Emperor. The emperor's name was Mutsuhito, but he is best known for the reign name, Meiji, which means "enlightened rule". During the Meiji period Japan became a world power. (Ridpath, John Clark, Ridpath's History of the World, 1901)

converted them to interest-bearing nonrenewable bonds. The Tokugawa class system was also ended the same year by abolishing samurai privileges.

Economic advancement was also vital for Japan to become equal with the West. Western expert Kanda Kohei wrote early in the Meiji years: "The nations that depend upon business are always rich while those that depend on agriculture are always poor. Therefore the Eastern countries are always poor and the Western ones always rich" (Duus 1976, 83). As they began to shape new economic and political institutions, Meiji leaders systematically studied various elements of American and European economic and political systems. The Meiji government sent representatives abroad to examine institutions and practices ranging from banking to education. The Japanese government also paid foreigners handsome salaries to serve as technical advisers and teachers.

After attempting socialist policies that failed, Meiji leaders sold factories, mines, and shipyards to private businessmen. Meiji leaders systematically studied various economic models and made the decision to adopt a Prussian-style state-directed capitalism, where the government plays a significant role in determining what is produced and allocates capital through control of the financial system. The Japanese rejected the Anglo-American laissez-faire model in which the market largely determines what products are produced and banks and the stock market allocate capital.

Remaining internal trade barriers and most export restrictions were abolished as Japanese businesses were encouraged to sell rice, copper, and raw silk abroad. The government developed a supportive infrastructure through a widespread railroad- and telegraph-building program. Japan's first railroad line, connecting Tokyo and Yokohama, was completed in 1872, and by 1900, 5,000 miles of railroad track had been laid. By 1880, telegraphs linked all major Japanese cities.

By the late 1880s and early 1890s, Japan's strategy of government-aided business development was beginning to pay off. Tea and silk export profits were providing capital for industrial growth, and textile factories were supplying Japanese needs and earning profits in international markets as well. Even though as late as 1902 only 14 percent of the Japanese workforce was employed in industry, the foundation for a modern economy was firmly in place.

The new government also viewed education as a major priority and recognized several advantages in the creation of a national educational system. More educated people were needed for the new factories and government, and a national school system could promote loyalty and patriotism. In 1872 a national educational system was created and elementary education made compulsory. At first Japanese children were allowed to leave school after 16 months, but by 1886 the required time in school was raised to four years. The highly centralized French system was used as an administrative model, but American curricula, textbooks, and teacher training methods were also influential in the creation of Japanese elementary schools.

The 1870s witnessed a Western craze of sorts, particularly in the cities, as numbers of people wore Western clothes and bought diamonds and gold watches. Some believed that if foreigners could be convinced that the Japanese were becoming "civilized and enlightened," the Western powers could be cajoled into modifying the unequal treaties. Others even came to believe that the West was a superior

FUKUZAWA YUKICHI (1835–1901)

As a young man, Fukuzawa learned first Dutch and later English to better understand the West. He was part of the first Japanese mission to the United States in 1860 and two years later visited several European countries as part of a similar mission. In 1866, 1868, and 1870, he published one each of a three-volume series titled *Conditions in the West*. In this, his most famous work, Fukuzawa provided readers with clear accounts of specific Western institutions as well as customs. Fukuzawa viewed his major role throughout much of the Meiji period as that of helping the Japanese people better understand two very positive aspects of Western civilization, science and an independent spirit. Although he was critical of much about traditional Japan, Fukuzawa saw Western learning as a way to make Japan strong and independent of foreign domination. Fukuzawa never entered government service but championed a number of political causes, including women's rights. He also controlled a newspaper and founded Keio University, which remains today one of Japan's most prestigious private institutions of higher learning.

civilization compared with Asia, and some pro-Western writers were condescending toward traditional Confucian values and enamored with Western individualism.

The spread of Western ideas had important ramifications for Japanese government and politics. By the 1870s and 1880s, intellectuals had read Western political tracts, and support mounted for the initiation of such foreign institutions as popularly elected legislatures and a written constitution. Although the majority of Meiji leaders viewed such democratic sentiments as a threat to their power, the idea of a constitution was attractive. Those government leaders who favored it thought the creation and adoption of a constitution would give Japan greater status with the West since it would be the first Asian country to develop one. Other Meiji leaders saw a written constitution as promoting national unification and increasing governmental authority.

Japan's leaders were particularly interested in recently unified Germany's Constitution. Ito Hirobumi traveled to Germany to study and, after returning to Japan, wrote a constitution that was implemented by imperial decree in 1889, impressing Western nations as predicted. Although the Constitution gave some power to factions other than the Meiji oligarchs, it did not create a democratic Japan. The Constitution provided for a bicameral legislative assembly, or Diet, with power to enact legislation and debate and approve the annual budget. The House of Peers consisted of appointed members whereas the House of Representatives was elected. However, only one percent of the 1890 population, male taxpayers above a set income level, could vote in legislative elections. The cabinet, consisting of several original architects of the Meiji revolution, was quite powerful and for many years determined who would be prime minister. The Constitution, the national school system, and the creation of a merit-based bureaucracy all contributed greatly to a growing government power and nationalism.

During the 1880s and 1890s, opposition to foreign influences was also increasing. Cultural conservatives worried that Japan was becoming too much like the West. Government leaders used both Shinto and schools to promote Japanese values and patriotism. Promotion of loyalty to the emperor and state became increasingly important. The emperor was described in the 1890 Imperial Rescript on Education as "being coeval with heaven and earth," and his photograph was placed in every Japanese school. The indoctrination appeared to be working because, as Japan began imperialistic adventures, the government enjoyed enthusiastic support and strong loyalty from the majority of its citizens.

The Japanese government then followed the lead of Western powers and used force to gain territories and foreign markets. Japan engaged in imperialism for several reasons, including a desire for equality with the West, which in 1894 was partially achieved when Western powers agreed to sign treaties ending extraterritoriality. The Japanese government also wanted more East Asian natural resources and markets and feared that if no action was taken, Western powers would gain control of the tottering Chinese and Korean governments and threaten Japan.

Korea, a country that had been loosely controlled by the Chinese empire, was the major cause of the Meiji government's first foreign war. Because of fear that Korea might be taken over by a stronger Western power, in 1894 Japan went to war in Korea with Korean and then Chinese forces and won a quick victory. In the ensuing 1895 treaty with China, Japan forced China to renounce all claims to Korea, pay a substantial indemnity, relinquish Taiwan, and turn over the Liaotung Peninsula in southern Manchuria. Acting quickly, Russia, along with France and Germany, forced Japan to return the Liaotung Peninsula to China. The Japanese resented the Western action and were even more humiliated when the Russians attained a lease of Liaotung in 1898.

The Japanese viewed Russia, which desired Manchuria and Korea, as a major threat. In 1904, after negotiations over Korea broke down, Japan engaged Russia in war by a surprise attack on the Russian fleet at Port Arthur. Most military observers incorrectly thought Russia would easily win. In a hard-fought struggle, the Japanese army won several land victories, and in May 1905 the fleet under Admiral Togo attracted world attention by defeating the Russians in the Tsushima Strait. Japan and Russia agreed to allow the United States to act as mediator at peace talks in Portsmouth, New Hampshire, and the resulting 1905 treaty secured a number of Russian concessions to Japan, including a lease on Liaotung, the southern half of Sakhalin Island, Russian holdings in Manchuria, and freedom of action in Korea. Japan quickly made Korea a protectorate in 1905 and colony in 1910. The Japanese ruled Korea, which had been a sovereign unified kingdom since 1392, until 1945. Although their colonial policies varied, in general, the Japanese were harsh rulers as they attempted to subdue a fiercely independent people with a mixture of force, cooption, and modernization.

During these heady days of empire building, influential leaders and the public began to develop two beliefs that later led to trouble: the feeling that Japan had a

Japan's victory in the 1904–05 Russo-Japanese war gave the world evidence that the nation was a new world power. Above is a Japanese war map of the attack on Port Arthur. (Ridpath, John Clark, Ridpath's History of the World, 1901)

mission to protect and civilize "backward" Asian nations and the belief that the Japanese military was invincible.

As the Meiji years reached their conclusion and the new century began, Japan had become a truly important actor on the world stage for the first time in the country's history. With the exception of the Koreans, most Asians celebrated a nonwhite nation's victory over a European country. The Europeans and Americans were impressed with Japan's economic, military, and political accomplishments. Such world leaders as U.S. President Theodore Roosevelt deeply respected the Japanese for their accomplishments but worried that they could become a Pacific rival. Western democratic leaders also had to contend with backlashes against Japanese immigrants in their own countries. In the West, the Japanese were both admired and thought of as the "yellow peril."

In the summer of 1912, the Meiji period ended with the emperor's death, and Yoshihito, the new emperor, gave the name Taisho, or "Great Righteousness," to his reign. The Taisho emperor ruled from 1912 to 1926. The emperor was an ineffectual ruler who was physically weak and frequently ill, but Japan economically expanded, experimented with representative government, and was a growing presence in world politics. Yet Japan had problems in the Taisho years. Economic development worked to the advantage of some urban residents while many rural people struggled. Because European powers were preoccupied with World War I, Japan, with a smaller role in the war, began to sell products in Asian countries that had been European markets. However, European partial recapture of those markets after World War I in part contributed to a major Japanese postwar recession. Also, by the 1920s, expansion of heavy industry exhausted Japan's scarce domestic

RUSSO-JAPANESE WAR (1904–1905)

This struggle between imperial Russia and an emergent imperial Japan over control of Korea not only identified Japan as a major player in geopolitics but also is significant in world history because it was similar in a number of ways to what the ensuing world wars would be like. Both sides engaged in mass mobilizations of troops, but belligerents received economic support from international financiers, and several of the battles were not only large scale but featured unprecedented deadly technology. The Japanese used the largest artillery attack in history at the time to sink the Russian fleet in Port Arthur. In the battle of Mukden, a quarter of a million Japanese fought 320,000 Russians. Japan, the victor in the war, gained control over the Korean peninsula and formally made Korea a Japanese colony in 1910. The war also had long-range effects on relations between the Western powers and Japan.

supplies of such raw materials as coal, increasing the necessity for access to cheap raw materials.

Still, the Taisho and the Showa years that followed were prosperous times for many Japanese, and the standard of living of average families more than doubled. *Zaibatsu*, or "money cliques," were in large part responsible for economic growth. A few powerful families used government financial assistance and keen business acumen to build economic empires controlling a variety of enterprises including banking, manufacturing, mining, and foreign trade concerns. Although the zaibatsu served the government's needs by fueling economic growth, particularly in heavy industries vital for defense, elements of the public became concerned about the great political influence of the zaibatsu and the tremendous concentration of wealth in the hands of a few influential families.

Life for many employees in large industrial concerns became increasingly good, and some male managers and industrial workers even received the security of lifetime employment. However, women factory workers in large companies and workers in small businesses and industries were subject to low pay in good times and layoffs during bad times. Japanese farmers faced hard times during much of the 1920s and early 1930s. Although a few years were good, from the end of World War I until the 1930s there was a long-term drop in crop prices.

Many rural people and urban working-class people felt bewildered and angry about the rapid social change that seemed to be occurring in Japanese cities. Young people were shedding traditional Japanese habits and values in favor of Western fads and ideas. Many were reading adventure and love story magazines, listening to radios, flocking to Western and Japanese movies, attending baseball games, listening to jazz music, and wearing Western clothes. The pendulum seemed to have swung back again in favor of Western over Japanese culture.

Western ideas influenced politics as well during the Taisho years. Even before the 20th century, political parties developed in Japan, and they continued to grow in influence. From 1918 until 1932, mostly civilian politicians controlled the Japanese Diet, or legislature, with heads of major parties becoming premier and forming governments. Political parties tended to be corrupt, however, and they constantly made deals with local officials and big business. Some Japanese became increasingly dissatisfied with political corruption and in the 1920s began to work for more democratic government. In 1925 Japan appeared to be moving toward democracy when the Diet gave all men the right to vote, regardless of whether they owned property.

Still, there were ominous political trends. Elements from the military and other nationalist groups checked the democratization movement, and the Diet passed the Peace Preservation Law, making it a crime to argue that the present government should be abolished or that private property ownership should be challenged, the same year it approved universal male suffrage. The law enabled police to imprison or harass people who opposed the political status quo.

During the Taisho period, there was considerable internal debate among political leaders over what policy was best regarding imperial expansion and Japan's relations with the West. Japan fought World War I on the side of the Allied powers and, as a result, acquired German Pacific territories including the Marianna, Caroline, and Marshall Islands and economic privileges in Manchuria and China. Still, factions in the military, particularly young army officers, wanted more. Even though many politicians opposed the army, politicians, discontented rural people, and struggling city dwellers helped to strengthen the power of the militaristic expansionists. Although Japan suffered less than many nations in the 1930s world depression, the event further fueled antigovernment and promilitary sentiments.

Many Japanese disliked advocates of Western-style political institutions for other reasons. The Americans and Europeans appeared hypocritical when they talked of democracy and equality but practiced racism. At the 1919 Paris Peace Conference, the Japanese tried to convince the other major powers to include a racial equality clause in the treaty. However, the Japanese demand for this clause failed primarily because of the opposition of Australia, the United Kingdom, and the United States. Leaders from these democracies were against approving the clause because they feared the domestic political repercussions of declaring an Asian race equal to their largely Caucasian populations. In 1924 the U.S. Congress passed an Exclusion Act that made it virtually impossible for Japanese to immigrate to the United States. Almost all Japanese considered the American law a national insult.

In 1926, the Taisho emperor died, and his son and successor, Hirohito, selected Showa, or "Enlightened Peace," as the name for his reign. Subsequent events, however, made the reign name choice ironic. By the late 1920s, the Japanese army was taking direct action in defiance of civilian government. Powerful army elements coveted Chinese-controlled Manchuria for its food and natural resources and because it was a buffer zone against the Soviet Union.

In 1928, young Japanese officers of the Kwantung Army stationed in Manchuria bombed a train carrying a local warlord, and the army did little to bring the perpetrators to justice. In 1931, army factions precipitated an even more serious international incident. Army officers blew up part of a railway owned by Japan and, claiming local sabotage, took over Manchuria, and the civilian Tokyo government was helpless in the face of popular support for the action. In January 1932, the army separated Manchuria from China and created the puppet state of Manchukuo, causing world outrage. In early 1933, the League of Nations condemned this aggression, and Japan responded by withdrawing from the league.

The Manchurian takeover and further incidents involving Japanese army units in China strengthened the will of the Chinese government to resist Japanese expansion. Fighting began on the night of July 7, 1937, with a minor skirmish between Japanese and Chinese troops at the Marco Polo Bridge, and quickly expanded into an undeclared but full-scale war between China and Japan.

The Japanese enjoyed several early victories and in December 1937 captured the Chinese capital of Nanjing. In what was to become one of the worst atrocities of the 20th century, Japanese troops murdered, robbed, and raped thousands of civilians in the city. Soon the Japanese army encountered stiff Chinese resistance, and although Japan continued to win victories, it could not score the knockout blow to end the war. Japan had become involved in a quagmire in China.

The United States by this time was increasingly using economic weapons in an attempt to get Japan out of China. In the summer of 1938, the United States placed an embargo on shipments of war material to Japan. In the fall of 1940, after Japan moved into French Indochina to gain vital rubber and oil supplies, the United States stopped exporting scrap iron and steel to Japan. In the summer of 1941, the U.S. government, in response to further Japanese advances into Indochina, froze all Japanese assets in the United States. Also, the U.S., British, and Dutch governments ended oil exports to Japan. Although Japan attempted negotiations, the oil embargo, which cut off 90 percent of Japan's oil supply, pushed Japan toward a decision to fight the Western powers.

In the late fall of 1941, high officials of the Japanese government, in a last attempt to avoid war, proposed to Washington that Japan withdraw from Indochina if the United States ended the oil embargo and assisted in peace negotiations with China. The U.S. government responded that it would agree to nothing less than Japanese withdrawal from China, Manchuria, and Indochina. The Japanese government found the American demand unacceptable and secretly decided on war.

On Sunday, December 7, 1941, Japanese aircraft carrier–based planes carried out a successful surprise attack on the U.S. Pacific fleet moored in Pearl Harbor, Hawaii. The attack, which sunk or severely damaged 19 naval vessels and killed more than 2,000 U.S. sailors and soldiers, resulted in the United States' declaration of war against Japan on December 8. Many Japanese realized the decision to attack was a bold gamble since Japan possessed much less wealth than the United States. Japan hoped for a quick war and that victories in the Pacific and the conquest of Europe by Japan's ally, Germany, would cause the Americans to negotiate an end to the war with the ensuing peace settlement, leaving Japan dominant in Asia.

The Japanese people accepted this strategy in part because of a popular belief that Japan was a moral alternative to the materialistic West for all of Asia. The Japanese government early in the war formulated the Greater East Asia Co-prosperity

Japanese Imperial Army soldiers prepare to behead a Chinese man in Nanjing in 1937 during the Japanese occuption of the city. One of the worst atrocities committed by the Japanese during the Sino-Japanese War of 1937–1945, the occupation of Nanjing resulted in the murder and rape of thousands of Chinese civilians. (AFP/Getty Images)

Sphere. According to this plan, victory was only the first objective in attaining the goal of building a strong and unified Asia and Pacific community under Japanese leadership. At first, Japan achieved impressive victories and by the spring of 1942 had conquered Singapore, the Dutch East Indies, and the Philippines. The Japanese also established island bases throughout the southwestern and central Pacific in such places as Guam, Wake Island, and the Solomon Islands. The Japanese seriously underestimated American determination and economic might, however, and by May 1942 the tides of war were already beginning to turn. In June 1942, a Japanese attempt to finish the U.S. Pacific fleet for good backfired when Japan lost four valuable aircraft carriers at the battle of Midway. In 1943 and 1944, the Americans defeated Japanese imperial forces in several Pacific island campaigns.

The war between the United States and its allies against the Japanese was bloody, bitter, and tinged with racism on both sides. Japanese were taught to view the Americans and British as "foreign devils" with no morals. Most Japanese soldiers considered fighting to the death preferable to the indignity of surrender. Twenty-seven percent of Allied troops who surrendered to the imperial Japanese military died in captivity compared to only 4 percent of Allied prisoners who surrendered to the Germans. In the United States, racism was one reason why few Americans objected to the government's forced internment under armed guard of more than 110,000 Japanese Americans for portions of or the entire war years. The United States was at war with Germany and Italy, but the government didn't intern German or Italian Americans.

YAMAMOTO ISOROKU (1884–1943)

It is ironic that an admirer of the United States planned the Pearl Harbor attack. Born outside Nagaoka, the Japanese Naval Academy graduate distinguished himself a year later in Russo-Japanese War combat. Brilliant and energetic, his rise in the navy was rapid. In the 1920s, Yamamoto was attached to the Japanese Embassy in Washington, studied at Harvard, and admired the United States. In Japan, his innovations won Yamamoto command of the navy's first aircraft carrier, but many disliked his moderate views. Still, superiors recognized talent and appointed Yamamoto Japanese naval operational head in 1939. Familiar with American power, Yamamoto thought war with the United States was foolish, but when war plans were formulated, he argued that Japan's only hope was a quick knockout blow. He strongly advocated and masterminded the Pearl Harbor attack. The attack was a tactical success but a strategic failure since U.S. aircraft carriers survived. In April 1943, Yamamoto was killed when a plane in which he was traveling was shot down over the Pacific by an American fighter.

USS Arizona, Tennessee, and West Virgina in flames during the Japanese December 7, 1941 Pearl Harbor attack. (Library of Congress)

By the summer of 1944, U.S. forces captured the island of Saipan, allowing American planes to conduct regular bombing raids on the Japanese home islands. In October 1944, U.S. forces under General Douglas MacArthur began retaking the Philippines by landing at Leyte Gulf. Japan's situation was desperate, but the Japanese military fought on and civilians persevered even as American bombing raids on the home islands intensified. In one night alone in March 1945, the firebombing of Tokyo left 78,000 people dead and 43,480 wounded. By 1945 young Japanese kamikaze, or "divine wind," pilots were engaging in suicide missions while civilians were training with sharpened spears to resist to the death the expected U.S. invasion of Japan.

At the July 1945 Potsdam Conference, the United States, the United Kingdom, and the Soviet Union, which was then not yet at war with Japan, reaffirmed their previous demand of unconditional surrender and threatened complete destruction if Japan refused. Just a few days later, on August 6, 1945, the United States dropped an atomic bomb on the Japanese city of Hiroshima, killing an estimated 100,000 people. Three days later, a second U.S. bomb killed an estimated 75,000 people in the city of Nagasaki. By then the Soviet Union had also declared war on Japan and sent troops into Manchuria. The Japanese government, undecided whether to surrender, was finally persuaded to do so by the emperor. On August 15, 1945, Hirohito addressed the nation by radio for the first time ever with the news that the war was lost. Japan's drive for empire in China and the Pacific resulted in nearly 3 million Japanese deaths.

JAPAN'S PATH TO PROSPERITY: 1945 TO THE PRESENT

The years following World War II resulted in more change in Japan than any time since the beginning of the Meiji period. The U.S. occupation under the leadership of General Douglas MacArthur initiated this peaceful reconstitution of much of Japanese society. The general almost immediately won the respect and admiration of the Japanese people through his dedication to duty and his regal bearing. Partially because of the influence of MacArthur, and a widespread belief among the Japanese that the militarist course had been a disastrous one, the Japanese people were cooperative with their American conquerors, and the occupation was peaceful and orderly. MacArthur and his staff sought nothing less than a democratic and peaceful Japan and initiated sweeping reforms to achieve this goal. The wartime leadership was quickly purged from government. Despite the fact that many Americans wanted the imperial line abolished, MacArthur decided to allow the Japanese to retain their national symbol in hopes of ensuring stability.

A major event of the occupation was the largely U.S.-written constitution, which went into effect in May 1947 and established a framework for democratic government. The emperor was retained but only as a symbol of state. A democratic parliamentary system and an independent judiciary were established. Universal suffrage for both sexes was guaranteed for the first time in Japanese history. The Japanese Constitution also theoretically guaranteed equal rights for both sexes and for the right of labor unions to exist. Article 9 contained a renunciation of war and included the clause "land, sea, and air forces, as well as other war potential, will

TOJO HIDEKI (1884–1948)

Tojo was born in Tokyo and graduated from a military academy and the Army Staff College with excellent records. He was an efficient officer and cultivated bureaucratic skills as well. In the 1930s serving in Manchuria, Tojo advocated war with China. In May 1938, he returned to Tokyo and served as army vice minister and chief of the Manchuria bureau in Prime Minister Konoe's cabinet. Tojo also strongly supported the Tripartite Pact with Germany and Italy and the invasion of French Indochina. After serving as army minister and opposing reconciliation with the United States, Tojo became prime minister in October 1941 and allowed U.S. negotiations to continue while authorizing plans for the Pearl Harbor attack. After the war began, Tojo temporarily managed to suppress most opposition to it, but as Japan's fortunes waned, he was ousted from his position in July 1944 by a group led by former prime minister Konoe and top navy officers. After the conclusion of World War II, Tojo was indicted and convicted as a war criminal by the International Military Tribunal. He was hanged on December 23, 1948.

never be maintained." Later, because Japan became a Cold War ally, American policy makers had second thoughts about this prohibition, and Japan developed land, sea, and air Self-Defense Forces (SDF) that are to be used only in defense of the home islands. In the decades that followed, the SDF have been deployed in other countries as part of United Nations peacekeeping forces. In 2004, the Japanese government deployed the SDF to Iraq in a noncombatant support role for coalition forces fighting insurgents.

In addition to bringing about the massive restructuring of the Japanese political system, the U.S. occupation produced major economic reforms. The zaibatsu were broken up, and the Americans made good their guarantee of labor unions by actively promoting them in the occupation's early years. The occupation land reform policy brought about even more widespread economic change. Absentee landlordism was prohibited, and farmers could own no more than seven and one-half acres (an exception was allowed in Hokkaido). The land reform policy ended long-standing rural inequities and stimulated agricultural productivity, as that sector was the first to recover.

Not content with just economic and political reform, MacArthur wanted to change Japanese thinking so as to create the appropriate climate for democracy. In 1947 occupation authorities forced the Japanese to radically change education. Japan's schools were modeled after the American six-year elementary school, three-year junior high, and three-year senior high school system. The new curriculum included social studies courses designed to foster democratic thinking. American reformers also attempted to decentralize the Japanese public school system by including locally elected school boards in the education laws.

HIROSHIMA ATOMIC BOMBING

On August 6, 1945, the United States dropped an atomic bomb on Hiroshima in southwestern Honshu, making it the first target for such a weapon in history. More than 80 percent of Hiroshima's buildings were destroyed, and although casualty estimates greatly vary, somewhere close to 200,000 people were killed or injured by the blast. On August 9, a second atomic bomb was dropped on Nagasaki in Kyushu, and it did considerable damage but less than at Hiroshima, where the bomb struck close to the center of the city. Japan surrendered nine days after the Hiroshima bombing. Today, although both Hiroshima and Nagasaki maintain peace parks, the former facilities receive far more visitors because of Hiroshima's place in history as the first city where nuclear weapons were employed.

By the late 1940s, however, the United States was becoming less idealistic about changing Japan. Initially, occupation authorities gave higher priority to democratization than to rebuilding Japan's economy. Once the Cold War began, U.S. policy makers feared that an economically weakened Japan could fall to the communists.

Hiroshima's Industrial Promotion Hall, one of the few buildings left standing after the dropping of the atomic bomb on August 6, 1945. Today the building is part of the Hiroshima Peace Memorial, designated a UNESCO World Heritage Site in 1996. (Library of Congress)

THE JAPANESE EMPEROR

Tenno, the Japanese term for emperor, is literally translated as "heavenly sovereign." The Japanese imperial system is now the world's oldest hereditary monarchy. There is no consensus on who was the first Japanese emperor and when this occurred, but probably emperors existed by the fourth century CE. Through most of Japanese history, the emperor has functioned as a symbol of either the state or Shinto, but others have actually held political power. The only lengthy period of time when emperors actually ruled the country was from the latter part of the seventh century through the early years of the ninth century. Before 1945, emperors could have political influence, but the contrast between Japanese emperors' limited executive authority and the power of the emperor in the Chinese imperial system is striking. The current Constitution clearly gives no power to the emperor. The current emperor, Akihito, was born on December 23, 1933, and became emperor on January 7, 1989, upon the death of his father, Hirohito.

By 1948 Americans ceased to encourage labor unions and backed off attempts to break up large business concerns. The new U.S. thinking was shared by a number of Japanese political leaders, including Yoshida Shigeru, prime minister during most of the occupation years. Shifts in U.S. policy, the good fortune of the Japanese to be convenient suppliers of American forces during the 1950–1953 Korean War, and the hard work of the Japanese people succeeded. By the early 1950s, the Japanese economy was on the way to recovery.

The U.S. occupation officially ended in September 1952, following the signing of a peace treaty in San Francisco the previous year. Although the Japanese later abolished some American reforms, such as the attempt to decentralize public schools, Japan today, as a democratic and free society, continues to benefit from the sweeping outside-initiated changes of the occupation years. It should be noted, though, that some of MacArthur's decisions are controversial today. There is substantial evidence that Emperor Hirohito may have had more to do with promoting Japanese aggression in Asia than was earlier believed. Some scholars make the case that by allowing Hirohito to retain the throne and not to be tried as a war criminal, the United States enabled Japan to escape responsibility for causing the Pacific War.

Also, although most diplomatic historians consider the U.S. occupation a success, it should be emphasized that the process that eventually resulted in the democratization of Japan was a *joint* endeavor. It almost certainly would have failed had not the Japanese been already a relatively highly educated people who worked hard and cooperated with the Americans. Japan also had a critical mass of private citizens and bureaucrats with industrial and economic development expertise as well as substantial experience with parliamentary government. U.S. policies worked because, in addition to good leadership and organization,

Emperor Hirohito's 63-year reign encompassed World War II and the Japanese postwar economic "miracle". The question of whether Hirohito shares some responsibility for the war remains controversial. (Library of Congress)

the Americans believed in the benefits of liberal democracy, had confidence in their Japanese partners, were working with a relatively homogenous culture, and were highly motivated to check the advances of both Chinese and Soviet communism.

On February 24, 1989, on a cold, rainy day in Tokyo, thousands of mourners, including political leaders from 163 nations, attended the funeral service of Emperor Hirohito, marking the end of his 63-year reign and the accession of his son Akihito, who named his reign Heisei, or "May There Be Peace." Hirohito's death was symbolically significant because it marked the end of a period of Japanese history that included World War II and the "economic miracle."

Since the democratization of Japan, the economic miracle has been the most important development in Japanese history. From 1954 until the 1970s, Japan led all nations in annual economic growth rates. Although economic growth slowed in the 1970s, Japan continued to have impressive annual growth rates until the early 1990s. Today Japan has one of the world's largest economies, and the lifestyle of the typical Japanese is an affluent one by the standards of any country. Japan's postwar economic boom years carried costs, however. Until the 1970s, the government and private business concentrated so much on first rebuilding the nation and later fueling the economic miracle that such social concerns as adequate housing, protection against pollution, and attention to health and old age–related issues were ignored. By 2009, Japan's economy, as was the case with many counties, felt significant effects from what appeared to be a global recession.

By the early 1990s, the economic situation also began to darken, and for the rest of the century Japan endured some serious economic problems, including low economic growth, postwar record unemployment rates, and high government deficits. There was general consensus among economists that Japan has structural economic problems, including an overregulated economy, a capital allocation system in need of overhaul, and an archaic lifetime employment system that helped to raise product costs to unacceptable levels. Japanese government and corporate decision makers struggled with these problems for more than a decade, but beginning in 2005, the economy, though not as impressive as the miracle years, has been performing relatively well.

The 1990s and the early years of the 21st century were a time of political as well as economic turbulence. In 1993 the Liberal Democratic Party (LDP) lost control over the Japanese government for the first time since its inception in 1955. Although the LDP soon returned to power in various coalition governments, Japanese domestic politics were extremely volatile throughout the 1990s. Parliamentary government after government fell, reflecting a general voter dissatisfaction with the economic and political status quo. The election of Koizumi Junichiro, who served as prime minister from 2001 to 2006, restored political stability, and the public largely appreciated this charismatic leader's policies. The end of the Cold War, the North Korean threat, the rise of China, and the war on terrorism have caused significant changes in Japanese foreign policy as the nation's leaders now give much more priority to regional and international security questions than was the case in previous decades.

The 1995 Tokyo subway poison gas attack by members of the Aum Shinriyko religious cult, which killed 12 people, was an extreme example of what many Japanese view as mounting social problems in a society that had been stable for almost half a century. Less dramatic but still troubling trends surfaced in the Japan of the 1990s and in the first decade of the 21st century, including rising divorce rates and some increases in certain types of crime. Still, both divorce and crime rates are lower in Japan than in other developed countries.

Despite these problems, postwar Japan rose from defeat in World War II to develop an economy that is still strong, societal support for democratic politics, and a relatively trouble-free society when compared with those of most other nations. Since the war, Japan has also achieved world leadership peacefully, which is a tremendous compliment to the hard work and resourcefulness of millions of ordinary Japanese.

REFERENCES

Arntzen, Sonja. "The Heart of History: *The Tale of Genji*." *Education About Asia* 10, No. 3 (Winter 2005): 25–30.

Beasley, W. G. *The Japanese Experience: A Short History of Japan*. Berkeley: University of California Press, 2000.

Buckley, Roger. *Japan Today*. 3rd ed. Cambridge, UK: Cambridge University Press, 1998.

Chubb, Merrel. "My Pacific War Revisited" in *America's Wars in Asia: A Cultural Approach to History and Memory*, edited by Philip West, Steven I. Levine, and Jackie Hiltz, 145–160. Armonk, NY: East Gate Press, 1998.

Duus, Peter. *Modern Japan*. Boston: Houghton Mifflin, 1976.

Farris, William Wayne. *Sacred Texts and Buried Treasures: Issues in the Historical Archaeology of Ancient Japan*. Honolulu: University of Hawaii Press, 1998.

Henning, Joseph M. "Breaking Company: Meiji Japan and East Asia." *Education About Asia* 5, No. 3 (Winter 2000): 40–43.

Holcombe, Charles. *The Genesis of East Asia, 221 B.C.–A.D. 907: Asian Interactions and Comparisons*. Honolulu: University of Hawaii Press, 2001.

Jansen, Marius. 2002. *The Making of Modern Japan*. Cambridge, MA: Belknap Press, 2002.

Keene, Donald. *Yoshimasa and the Silver Pavilion: The Creation of the Soul of Japan*. New York: Columbia University Press, 2003.

Morris, Ivan. *The World of the Shining Prince: Court Life in Ancient Japan*. New York: Kodansha Globe, 1997.

Ohnuki-Tierney, Emiko. "Rice as Self: Japanese Identities through Time." *Education About Asia* 9, No. 3 (Winter 2004): 4–9.

Packard, George. "Another Look at the Occupation of Japan: Through the Minefields of Japanese History." *Education About Asia* 8, No. 2 (Fall 2003): 34–38.

Perez, Louis G. *The History of Japan*. Westport, CT: Greenwood Press, 1998.

Pyle, Kenneth. *The Making of Modern Japan*. 2nd ed. Lexington, MA: D. C. Heath, 1996.

Reischauer, Edwin O. *Japan: The Story of a Nation*. New York: Alfred A. Knopf, Inc., 1981.

Sansom, George. *A History of Japan to 1334*. Stanford, CA: Stanford University Press, 1964.

Schirokauer, Conrad, Miranda Brown, David Lurie, and Suzanne Gay. *A Brief History of Chinese and Japanese Civilizations*. 3rd ed. Boston: Houghton Mifflin, 2005.

Stanley-Baker, Joan. *Japanese Art*. New York: Thames & Hudson, 1984.

Steinberg, John W. "The Russo-Japanese War and World History." *Education About Asia* 13, No. 2 (Fall 2008): 19–24.

Totman, Conrad. *Japan before Perry*. Berkeley: University of California Press, 1982.

Varley, Paul. *Japanese Culture: A Short History*. New York: Praeger, Inc., 1977.

Weston, Mark. *Giants of Japan*. New York: Kodansha International, 1999.

Yamamoto, Tsunetomo. *Hagakure: The Book of the Samurai*. Translated by William Scott Wilson. New York: Kodansha, 1982.

Young, Arthur Morgan. *Japan in Recent Times: 1912–1926*. New York: W. Morrow Co., 1929.

CHAPTER 3

Government and Politics

INTRODUCTION: THE ROOTS OF JAPAN'S CONTEMPORARY GOVERNMENT AND POLITICS

Most readers of this book are Americans, and they have studied U.S. government. Imagine attempting to learn about how the American government works without some knowledge of the influence of Great Britain, the motives of the founders of the United States, the Declaration of Independence, the Articles of Confederation, and the formulation of the present U.S. Constitution. Without some understanding of these seminal American political developments, even rudimentary understanding of the present system would be difficult at best. Yet primarily because the Japanese suffered a catastrophic defeat in World War II and then experienced widespread change, many foreigners inaccurately assume that Japan's contemporary government and attendant political processes are entirely new creations that are considerably less than 100 years old. Despite sweeping postwar changes, to understand modern Japanese politics and government, the best beginning point is 1600 and not 1945. Those readers who want an even more complete understanding of Japan's government and politics should also consult the previous history chapter. The historical content in this chapter is limited to helping readers understand those parts of the political system and political goals that are still important in contemporary Japan.

Although a few institutions such as the imperial system go back much further in time, since 1600, stable and successful government in Japan has been dependent on particular leadership behaviors. Leaders must not only exert power over but also communicate and negotiate with the public and in particular the middle classes. Also since the early 1600s, the existence of a strong bureaucracy concerned with both social order and generating tax revenues through wide latitude for private economic productivity, as well as the formulation of successful state international relations policies, has been important in Japan. These vital political behaviors characteristic of Japan's political history for more than 400 years constituted strategic tools for the achievement of larger societal short- and long-term objectives. The short-term objectives included public order, known routines, and harmony while national adaptability and flexibility in the face of changing events were long-term objectives.

With the exceptions of the periods between 1853–1868 and 1931–1945, Japan's political system has succeeded much more than it has failed. As Japan undergoes rapid contemporary changes, even though new key factors for political success have emerged, the critical political tools mentioned above remain important. Even though the maintenance of democratic freedom is an objective that does date back only to 1945, since Japan is now a densely populated nation without self-sufficient food or energy supplies, the earlier political objectives described above are more important than ever.

GOVERNMENT AND POLITICS IN THE TOKUGAWA PERIOD: 1600–1868

As depicted in the prior chapter, in 1600 Tokugawa Ieyasu, through force of arms and diplomacy, managed to unify a Japan that had been torn by civil war for most of the previous century and intermittent internal strife for much of the 14th century as well. Tokugawa and his descendents who ruled Japan as shoguns established an authoritarian but not totalitarian regime. The distinction here is important. The Tokugawa family directly controlled one-quarter of all lands in Japan but needed to maintain the allegiance of leaders of other powerful families who controlled land, the samurai, and a larger public that included, in the first part of the period, agricultural villages. As time progressed, an expanding urban middle class of merchants and artisans also became important interest groups.

The Tokugawas were successful, and Japan enjoyed unprecedented peace throughout virtually the entire period. Occasional force or the threat of force worked to maintain the loyalty of the powerful daimyo and created a law-abiding citizenry. However, public administration, infrastructure development, and economic growth were substantially developed by a competent bureaucracy; communications and negotiations by political leaders and bureaucrats with key individuals and groups as well as central government incentives and disincentives were also essential. The samurai were an important part of this success. As societal elites, this class had a monopoly on the privilege of carrying arms and, through most of the period, constituted the majority of citizenry who possessed, in the context of the times, an advanced (Confucian) education. Samurai were expected to serve the state as warrior-bureaucrats. However, long-term peace greatly magnified their latter role. Inculcated with deep beliefs in the virtue of allegiance and duty to superiors, samurai served as regional and local bureaucrats responsible for managing important projects ranging from road maintenance and provision of public water supplies to tax collection. In achieving these objectives, samurai interacted and negotiated with village headmen who in turn communicated with subordinates and commoners. Cooperation and negotiation between authorities at different levels were important.

The central government imposed varying tax quotas at the local levels, and this provided an incentive for samurai bureaucrats to see that their local charges were economically productive since the samurai were responsible for tax collection. Tokugawa bureaucrats were involved in both maintaining public order and working for economic development. They achieved the latter objective by allowing private market forces substantial latitude. The result was both agricultural and commercial productivity. Still today, the Japanese bureaucracy, more so than its counterparts in the United States or the United Kingdom, focuses more extensively on public order, harmony, and economic development.

As described in the history chapter, although the Tokugawa government strictly controlled the populace's interactions with foreigners as well as foreign ideas, Tokugawa shoguns closely monitored many international developments through select interactions with the Dutch and the establishment of a branch of scholarship devoted to "Dutch learning." The shogunate also monitored international events through contacts with China, the Korean Peninsula, and the Ryukyu Islands (present-day Okinawa). Through most of the period, fear of losing national sovereignty was a motivating factor in the political leadership's policies. Japanese leaders, partially because China was the focal point of Westerners' attention and partially because of better negotiations on the part of the Japanese government, were able to avoid much of the misery that 19th-century China experienced at the hands of imperialistic powers. Despite the societal trauma caused by the American and European forced "opening" of Japan in the 1850s, the Tokugawa leaders were aware that Siam was having better luck dealing with Westerners through negotiations than China was through confrontation and were partially successful in delaying and modifying American and European demands.

JAPAN'S IMPERIAL PERIOD: 1868–1945

Although parts of the domestic political system such as the class structure and tax collection had also become dysfunctional, the crisis caused by the unwanted incursion of American and European powers eventually was the primary reason the Tokugawa government fell. In 1868 a group of young samurai from two domains that had always grudgingly accepted the regime led a successful revolution. The new leaders immediately returned to a political tactic employed in medieval Japan. They communicated to the country that they were restoring imperial authority and moved a very cooperative young emperor from Kyoto to Edo. The years encompassed in his reign name Meiji, or "Enlightened Rule," 1868 to 1912, mark the time that Japan became an international power. The Meiji emperor, although he did not wield direct political power, agreed with the leadership's desire to modernize

The Meiji Emperor served as a convincing symbol of a rising Japan. Apparently he loved martial uniforms but, ironically, was deeply devoted to peace. (Library of Congress)

the country and quite competently fulfilled his function as a symbol of state authority. Although far from an all-powerful, absolute ruler, the emperor exerted significant political influence through interactions with top political leaders.

Japan's new political leaders managed to make revolutionary changes yet retain key elements of the political system that emerged during the Tokugawa era. The samurai bureaucracy was gradually changed to a systematic national bureaucracy in which positions were filled based on meritocratic educational performance. The bureaucratic functions of promoting public order and stability continued as well as the task of economic development within the framework of state supervision and freedom for private companies and entrepreneurs to operate. The Tokugawa political system had been authoritarian with an individual, the shogun, having disproportionate but certainly not exclusive power. Japanese governments during the imperial period were oligarchies in which a small group of powerful leaders made decisions. However, by the latter part of the 19th century, the adoption of the 1889 Constitution and the rise of party politics meant that even more consultation and negotiations between key political actors and representatives of special public and private interests occurred. The short- and long-term political objectives of the Tokugawa years were modified but certainly did not disappear.

Meiji political leaders were confronted with both foreign demands and the physical presence of Americans and Europeans. The biggest threat to the Japanese was complete loss of their national sovereignty since Japan's military capability was

OKUBO TOSHIMICHI (1830–1878)

Okubo Toshimichi was one of the most effective leaders in creating Japan's Meiji government and epitomizes the efficient, capable, honest, and intelligent bureaucrat. Of samurai origins, Okubo and his father were in trouble with the Tokugawa government before the younger Okubo was 21 for trying to create a strong defense against what they perceived as the threat of European colonialism. Active in the Meiji Restoration that overthrew the Tokugawas, Okubo served in a variety of posts in the new government including minister of finance and home minister. As minister of finance, Okubo created the yen and initiated a money-based rather than a crop-based tax system. He was assassinated by reactionary samurai for playing a major role in stopping the last major armed challenge to Japan's new government.

much weaker than the more technologically advanced foreigners. Even before the Meiji years, Japan had suffered national humiliations at the hands of foreigners. In the 1850s, Japan was forced to open ports for trade and lost the right to try European or American nationals accused of crimes while in Japan. In 1866 tariff negotiations, foreigners imposed a forced uniform tariff ceiling of 5 percent of the declared value of imported foreign products on Japan. The Japanese even lost the right to charge foreign ships for entering and leaving Japanese ports.

The Meiji leaders realized that the only ways to prevent foreign control in an age of imperialism was to build a strong economy and a strong military. As discussed in more detail in the history chapter, the new government in the 1860s and 1870s sent missions to scour the developed world for practical information that could speed economic, military, and political modernization. Between 1868 and 1902, more than 11,000 passports were issued for foreign study. The 1871–1873 Iwakura mission visited 12 countries and met with high officials. Japan was opened to foreign teachers, ideas, and visiting leaders. In the summer of 1879, former U.S. President Grant visited Japan for several weeks and provided extensive advice to the attentive political leadership. Japan's ruling oligarchs, armed with the latest technology but focusing on dominant political values of the past, used a combination of political leadership and the power of market incentives to make rapid progress toward a manufacturing economy. They also relied heavily on British and German knowledge to build an increasingly strong navy and army.

In order to achieve economic and military modernization, Meiji leaders instigated a wide variety of administrative, economic, and social changes as soon as possible. The domains were abolished, and prefectures, which are roughly similar to American states or British counties, were established with efficient taxation systems. Japan's Neo-Confucian class system was abolished although former samurai, because of their educations, continued to dominate bureaucratic and political leadership positions for several decades.

MORI ARINORI (1847–1889)

Mori was one of the most brilliant of Japan's architects of the government that would make the country a world power, but he also struggled with modernization and traditional Japanese values. A highly promising student who received traditional and Western educations, Mori was sent in 1865 to the United Kingdom to study mathematics and physics. Mori was, in effect, appointed as Japan's first ambassador to the United States in 1871. He also served as ambassador to China and the UK. Mori pushed hard for Western learning and was responsible as education minister for creating compulsory elementary and advocated combining the inculcation of Confucian values and Japanese nationalism in lower schools with more Western education in secondary school. He was assassinated by ultranationalists for not showing enough respect to traditional Japanese values.

Before the Meiji years, common Japanese had no particular sense of patriotism and nationalism. The Japanese political leadership realized the importance of inculcating these beliefs in the general population and used religion and education to promote these values. The government organized the nation's Shinto shrines, accentuated the beliefs of one particular cult that linked the emperor to legendary Japanese gods, and gave Shintoism special favor relative to Buddhism. A national public school system with elite and common tracks was created and compulsory elementary education made mandatory. The government used the schools to promote nationalistic ideology. Education Minister Mori Arinori, who believed in physical as well as mental training, also linked the army to Japanese schools by involving noncommissioned officers in physical training. By 1890, political leaders had forged an ideology that combined Western modernization with Japanese nationalism. The 1890 Imperial Rescript on Education, Japan's seminal educational document until 1945, promoted the pursuit of learning and loyalty to parents, both Confucian traditions, while associating these behaviors with Japanese beliefs. The same document also specifically encouraged absolute loyalty to the emperor.

In the closing decades of the 19th century, Meiji leaders exhibited impressive political pragmatism in the face of a broad influx of foreign ideas. Nascent political parties emerged whose proponents advocated Western-style rights and political representation for various constituencies. Ito Hirobumi and others who were responsible for Asia's first Western-style constitution managed to partially co-opt several of these movements yet maintain oligarchic control by creating a plan of government. The 1889 Constitution, while allowing limited suffrage in the case of the lower house of the bicameral imperial legislature, or Diet, affirmed the notion of the monarchy as the apex of the political system. Ito and other Meiji oligarchs were essentially conservatives and monarchists, but they were also pragmatic. The Constitution they designed allowed affluent male taxpayers to vote for the lower

Ito Hirobumi rose from modest means to be deeply involved in the building of Japan's Meiji Government including the creation of the 1889 Constitution. He was assassinated by a Korean nationalist in 1909. (Library of Congress)

House of Representatives. This provision was included in part to placate a growing people's rights movement in Japan.

When Japan's leaders were studying constitutions, the American and British versions were rejected as too liberal and prone to promoting societal disorder. The German Constitution instead was used as a model. Ito had studied in Germany and was influenced by that country's recent unification and by the role of the German emperor in relationship to the national government. Although, as discussed in the history chapter, the Diet had powers, the Meiji oligarchs constituted the cabinet, and they were responsible to the emperor and not the legislature. Eventually, during the imperial period, party governments became the norm as the Meiji leaders died, but cabinets were still theoretically responsible to the throne and not to the Diet. The 1889 Constitution was advantageous to the political leadership in three ways: It was partially the result of negotiation and compromise, it achieved the oligarchs' goal of order, and it increased Japan's reputation among European and Western nations.

Meiji leaders gained even more international respect in a time of social Darwinism and colonialism through the accomplishments of their military forces, first by establishing Japan as the dominant East Asian power through victory over China in the 1894–1895 Sino-Japanese War and then astounding the world by defeating imperial Russia in 1905. By the emperor's death in 1912 and the end of the Meiji period, Japan was an imperial power with Taiwan and Korea as colonies, had

Two Diet members who both would serve as Prime Minister, Miyazawa Kiichi and Mori Yoshiro, bow during a June 2, 2000 Japanese Diet meeting. (AP/Wide World Photos)

achieved success at economic modernization, successfully reestablished national sovereignty by peacefully negotiating an end to Western-imposed treaties, and created a more intellectually diverse society than existed during the Tokugawa years. In less than 50 years, Japan's political leadership had shown remarkable adaptability and flexibility in the face of a changing world.

However, new problems emerged and, coupled with intended and unintended consequences of the 1889 Constitution, they eventually caused the political system to break down. These constitutionally unresolved questions included who was responsible for executive decision making, the role of the emperor in actual governance, and the ambiguity about the separation of military and civil authority.

Also, by the beginning of the 20th century Japanese leaders had a resources problem that is still a major political and economic issue today; the nation is not self-sufficient in either food or energy. Although Western countries respected the Japanese, they were wary of the emergence of a new Asian power.

The Taisho emperor's reign was short (1912–1926), and he had, unlike his predecessor, no influence on government. Japan economically benefited from World War I, and the 1920s were a time of urban economic growth and an apparently diverse political and intellectual environment characterized by rival political parties, socialists, Marxists, a women's movement, and an ultimately successful drive for universal male suffrage. However, Japanese political leaders were sharply divided into internationalist pro-Western and more conservative and traditional factions.

Rural areas experienced hard times, and flaws in the political system that was crafted between the late 1860s and 1890 made the situation worse.

As described in the previous chapter, internationalists lost the important political battles to traditionalists partially because of European and American discrimination toward Japan and Japanese. Elements of the public—particularly hard-pressed rural residents, whose income declined on average by more than half between the mid-1920s and mid-1930s, and an increasingly aggressive military—were scornful of corrupt politicians. The 1889 Constitution had not effectively separated military from civilian leadership since the former could serve in the cabinet. Theoretically, the emperor was the final source of authority, but in practice this was rarely the case. Also, partially because of Japan's group-oriented culture and partially due to the 1889 Constitution, executive responsibility was not clearly assigned. Between 1885 and 1934, there were 43 different cabinets headed by 30 different prime ministers, of whom more than half were military figures (Prime Minister of Japan and His Cabinet n.d.). The 1920s witnessed several high-profile assassinations of civilian politicians, and the military increasingly gained support from the Japanese people by tightening domestic controls on dissidents. The new Showa emperor, who ascended the throne in 1926, probably had almost as little power over political leaders as his predecessor, although his level of influence is a subject of some scholarly dispute. Most historians believe that the emperor was, for the most part, a figurehead. However, 2001 Pulitzer Prize winner Herbert P. Bix made a strong case that while the emperor did not rule, his support of or opposition to certain factions could influence public policy decisions.

In 1931, military leaders who desired increased energy and food resources as well as a buffer zone against communist Russia took over Manchuria and established a puppet government while civilian politicians and the emperor stood by helplessly.

In 1937, the Japanese army provoked a war with China. By this time, European powers and the United States, already concerned about Japanese aggression, condemned Japan for the China war and for its 1940 Axis power treaty formulated with Nazi Germany and Italy. In 1941, the Japanese military entered Indochina to secure needed vital resources, and the United States, the United Kingdom, and the Netherlands ceased exporting oil to Japan. The Japanese retaliated by bombing Pearl Harbor, made the China war part of a world war, and suffered in 1945 a calamitous defeat at the hands of the Allies that devastated the country.

Despite unprecedented government repression of dissidents relative to earlier times in the Imperial period, and even during World War II and immediately afterward, some elements of the political system that began in the Tokugawa period remained or were strengthened. Japan never had a totalitarian government such as was the case in Nazi Germany or the Soviet Union. Political parties were dissolved in 1940, and then Prime Minister Konoe created a new organization for national unity, the Imperial Rule Assistance Association (IRAA). However, in the 1942 Diet elections, IRAA candidates could manage to win only two-thirds of the seats. As had been the case since the Tokugawa years, some latitude was allowed for negotiations and differing opinions. Also, due to wartime mobilization, bureaucrats gained even more power to manage important portions of the economy during World War II than they exercised during earlier periods. Much of this power would be retained for many years after the war's end, and economic bureaucrats, although weakened relative to the 20th century, still remain an important part of Japanese politics today. The imperial system also survived the war and the democratic transformation of Japan.

POSTWAR GOVERNMENT AND POLITICS: THE CREATION OF JAPANESE DEMOCRACY AND ITS STRUCTURE

Japan became a democratic country with the adoption of the 1947 Constitution, which has never been amended and remains in effect today. However, since roughly 1985, domestic and international factors have resulted in new challenges and changes for Japan's political leadership. Before contemporary government and politics can be understood, a discussion of the creation of Japanese democracy and the structure of postwar government is appropriate. To fully understand how Japan's democracy was created and has evolved, as well as the challenges it now faces and its responses, it is also important to read other relevant sections of this book including the chapters on history, the economy, and contemporary issues.

As recent world events confirm, building democracies when prior significantly different forms of government have existed is no easy task. In retrospect, Japan rapidly changed course after World War II, but a closer examination indicates that several features of Japanese pre–World War II society provided solid foundations for later democratic government. Japan had been a politically unified country since 1600. Also, the Japanese possessed an important ingredient for building a successful democratic society; thanks to a compulsory educational system that had been in place for much more than 50 years by 1945, the Japanese had high literacy rates by world standards. Despite short periods of turmoil in the beginning of the Tokugawa and Meiji eras and during World War II, Japanese political history has been also largely evolutionary and nonviolent since the early 1600s. This climate of stability proved to be a fertile one for the growth of mass democracy in Japan. Certain political institutions vital to the growth of democracy also evolved in the 19th and early 20th centuries. As noted earlier, Japanese in 1945 had experiences with a prior Constitution that was more than 50 years old, which provided for some legislative representation. They also had experience with a political system that had adopted universal male suffrage and allowed for, despite periods of repression, contrasting ideologies, social movements, and political parties.

After experiencing displeasure with initial efforts on the part of the Japanese government, American occupational authorities wrote the present 1947 Constitution and successfully managed its adoption. The Constitution includes a bicameral Diet with both houses elected, a judicial branch that includes a 15-member Supreme Court appointed by the executive, and an executive branch composed of the prime minister and cabinet. The Constitution provides for universal suffrage for both sexes as well as other such individual rights as freedom of speech and the press. Much to the consternation of some conservatives to this day, the Constitution limits the emperor's governmental powers and states that he is solely "a symbol of the state and of the unity of the people" (Reischauer 1981, 229). Article 9, whereby the Japanese people forever renounce war as a sovereign right of the nation, also remains controversial, even though Japan now has substantial air, land, and sea self-defense forces.

The 1947 Constitution did not change the prefectural governmental structure that has existed since the Meiji period. Today, Japan has 47 prefectures, each with its own elected governor and legislature who serve four-year terms. The governor is responsible for prefectural administration. There are 43 regular prefectures, 3 urban prefectures (Tokyo, Osaka, and Kyoto), and one special prefecture, Hokkaido. Hokkaido is classified as "special" because the entire island is one self-contained prefecture. Although prefectures are roughly analogous to U.S. states, there is a significant difference: While prefectures have some control over such policy matters as public law and order and hiring teachers, they do not have the degree of autonomy from the national government as is the case with American states. More than 40 percent of monies for Japan's local government expenses—such as public hygiene, education, police, and similar areas of local responsibility—come from the national government. Prefectural and local governments regularly negotiate with national government bureaucrats regarding many policy matters because numerous national guidelines and directives accompany these central government revenues.

A major innovation of the 1947 Constitution was to make the Diet, in theory, the highest organ of state power with sole law-making authority. The more powerful of the two houses is the 480-member lower house, the House of Representatives, whose members are all elected at the same time for four-year terms. The 242 members of the upper House of Councilors replaced the pre–World War II nonelective House of Peers. Members are elected for six-year terms with one-half of members elected every third year. The House of Councilors is considered the upper house since there are no parliamentary rules that can result in its dissolution. The House of Representatives is considered the lower house, or the house that is most sensitive to public opinion, since it can be dissolved either by the prime minister or by a successful legislative "no confidence" vote.

Although both houses have power, the House of Councilors' power is more limited than that of the House of Representatives. If the lower house passes a bill and the upper house votes it down, it can still become law if a two-thirds majority of the lower house votes for the bill a second time. The annual national government budget is presented to the lower house first. If the lower house passes the budget, the upper house formulates a different version, and no compromise can be reached by a bicameral conference committee, then the lower house's version becomes law. Also, if the two houses fail to agree on who should become prime minister, the lower house has the prerogative of choosing the executive.

Once elections to the lower house are concluded, the leader of the party that either has a majority in the lower house or assembles a majority coalition of parties normally becomes prime minister. In 1994, an exception occurred when Liberal Democratic Party (LDP) leaders built a coalition government by awarding Socialist Party chair Murayama Tomiichi the prime ministership. Upon election, the prime minister names a cabinet of 14 to 17 ministers consisting of heads of government ministries and various other agencies. Prime ministers and governments change relatively frequently in Japan because of cabinet reshuffles, votes of no confidence, and elections. As of the publication of this book, since 1996 there have been seven different prime ministers and 12 different cabinets. Cabinet ministers, who are politically appointed, serve as titular heads of major departments within the bureaucracy, such as the Ministry of Finance (MOF), the Ministry of Health, Labor, and Welfare, and the Ministry of Economy, Trade, and Industry, and all have significant policy and administrative responsibilities.

National Diet elections in Japan are held for both houses, and citizens 20 years or older are eligible to vote. Although there have been several changes in election laws over the past few decades, currently, 300 of the 480 members of the House of Representatives are elected from single-seat constituencies, and the remaining 180 representatives are elected by proportional representation. Japan is divided into 11 electoral blocs, with each bloc electing between 6 and 40 members according to its size. Voters cast two ballots in elections. One is for the individual candidate in the single-district constituency. The second ballot is for a political party in the proportional representation election. Dual candidacies are legal, so a party may run a candidate for both a single-member district seat and for election by proportional representation. Candidates must be at least 25 years of age to run for the House of Representatives.

Ninety-six of the 242 members of the House of Councilors are elected by proportional representation from a single national electoral district, and the remaining 146 are elected in the 47 prefectures, with each prefecture electing a varying number of members depending on its size. As is the case in the House of Representatives elections, voters cast two ballots, one in the proportional vote and one for the individual candidate in a constituency. Candidates for the House of Councilors must be at least 30 years of age.

These electoral law changes were initiated in 1994. Until then, the House of Representatives consisted of 512 members elected from 130 districts, with each electoral district having anywhere from 2 to 6 Diet seats. Voters would vote for only one candidate, but the winners in any given district would be the 2 to 6 candidates who received the most votes among perhaps 10 to 12 candidates running. This proportional system was the subject of much criticism in Japan due to perceptions that it promoted legislator overaccentuation on constituency services, factionalism, and personality. Because one political party, the LDP, dominated the Diet, candidates for seats often would be elected based on how much money and favors could be doled out to supporters rather than based on their stances on political issues.

Electoral campaigns in Japan are much shorter than the United States, being limited by law to only 40 days. Despite this, many Japanese politicians, like their counterparts elsewhere, are always unofficially campaigning. Door-to-door campaigning is prohibited during the official campaign period, and there are stricter rules on Internet campaign use than in the United States, but citizens in urban areas are constantly subjected to candidates' supporters blaring out platitudes on loudspeakers. National elections, which were until a few years ago always held on Sundays, drew a much higher percentage of voters than in the United States until recently. As of late, cynicism about politicians has resulted in a substantial drop in voter participation rates.

Since the advent of democracy in Japan, multiple political parties have existed but, as noted, the LDP has been dominant since its creation in 1955. However, as will be discussed at some length, this dominance is in dire jeopardy. Other current active political parties include the Democratic Party of Japan (DPJ), the New Komeito Party, the Social Democratic Party, and the Japanese Communist Party. There are numerous smaller parties as well.

THE REAL WORLD OF JAPANESE POLITICS: 1945–1985

As discussed both here and in the history chapter, democracy grew relatively rapidly in Japan, and the Japanese now have a more than 60-year democratic history. However, Japan's political history, culture, geography, economy, and changing position in the world, just as is the case with any nation, makes the nature of Japanese democracy unique in many ways. Before further discussion of how democracy has worked in practice in Japan and the changes and challenges the system faces, it is important to review those objectives that have been part of the political culture and motivated Japanese political leaders in power before 1945 that remain unchanged: communications and negotiations, particularly with the middle classes; reliance on a strong bureaucracy; generation of ample tax revenues and private prosperity through allowing private enterprise freedom; ensuring food and energy supplies; and successfully coping with foreign policy problems.

During the American occupation which began in 1945 women would be granted the right to vote. (Library of Congress)

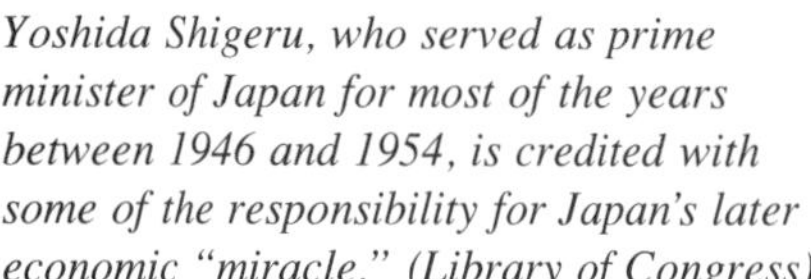

Yoshida Shigeru, who served as prime minister of Japan for most of the years between 1946 and 1954, is credited with some of the responsibility for Japan's later economic "miracle." (Library of Congress)

Although the Japanese people embraced democracy during the years of the American occupation, pragmatic leaders were elected who did not deviate from objectives they saw as vital to national and individual prosperity and survival. Often, because Japan is a group-oriented culture that focuses more on collective than individual leadership, who is actually exercising political power and decision making is still not always easy to determine. However, historians agree that Yoshida Shigeru (1878–1967) was the Japanese political leader most responsible for shaping the contours of the early postwar political system. Yoshida was a well-educated, conservative former Ministry of Foreign Affairs bureaucrat and diplomat who served in Italy, China, and the United Kingdom before the outbreak of World War II. Although a conservative and supporter of the emperor, Yoshida was also an Anglophile who had disdain for the chauvinism of Japan's wartime military leaders. Near the end of World War II, he was briefly jailed by the Japanese police for assisting former Prime Minister Konoe in attempting to communicate a message to the emperor urging surrender to save Japan. As a 68-year-old, with MacArthur's approval as well as the approval of Japanese voters for his party, Yoshida became prime minister of Japan as head of the Liberal Party. He would go on to be prime minister four more times between 1946 and 1954.

Yoshida personally thought the American-imposed Constitution was too liberal but pragmatically realized that accepting the new Constitution, and making such changes as the land reform that made many landless poor tenants into independent farmers, was essential to make Japan stable, keep the archipelago from a possible communist revolution, and retain imperial institutions, all goals he and his political associates strongly favored.

YOSHIDA SHIGERU (1878–1967)

Yoshida was by far Japan's most successful 20th-century political leader through his instrumental role in creating the nation's postwar prosperity. Given up by his politician father to a childless couple when he was a newborn, Yoshida's wealthy adoptive father had studied in the United Kingdom and worked for a British firm. Yoshida had a lifelong affinity for the United Kingdom. Yoshida graduated in law from Tokyo Imperial University in 1906, married the daughter of the second son of Okubo Toshimichi, and served as a diplomat in China, the United Kingdom, and Italy. Yoshida's great understanding of economic development, which he gained in the foreign ministry assisting Japanese companies in China, his knowledge of the West, his respect for the emperor as a symbol of the nation, and his contempt for ultranationalists all served him well as he helped to lead Japan out of the disaster of World War II.

Yoshida went on to formulate what has come to be known as the "Yoshida Doctrine." Although there was nothing in writing, the Japanese government followed this important prime minister's foreign and domestic strategies for decades. Domestically, Japan should focus its national energies on economic reconstruction and growth using a combination of economic management by bureaucracy and considerable support for big business. In foreign policy, the Japanese should maintain an extremely low profile and defer to the United States in its Cold War positions. Furthermore, the Japanese government should adhere to Article 9 of the Constitution, which prevents the creation of a military, and allow American forces to protect Japan through the maintenance of military bases long after the end of the occupation.

The question of how to craft Japan's foreign policy immediately after a crushing defeat in World War II was, at one level, simple but, from another perspective, complex. Yoshida had to solve the difficult problem of how to both build a domestic coalition that would support a particular foreign policy and secure U.S. approval of Japan's course of action. The easy part, at least for the short term, was following the American lead. Based on militarist government wartime propaganda, many of the Japanese people expected draconian treatment at the hands of the Americans. When the Americans treated the conquered people in much more positive ways than feared, there was a groundswell of public gratitude. This attitude on the part of average Japanese, despite the tough economic situation of the first few years of the occupation, worked to Yoshida's advantage. So did a prewar affinity for American popular culture on the part of many and the moral triumph of pro-Western and democratic elements within Japanese society when they were liberated from military rule and encouraged by the occupiers to develop democratic institutions. The enthusiasm for creating a democratic government for the first time spread to the man and woman on the street in the early part of the occupation. To be democratic at that time was to be pro-American.

The hard part for Yoshida was developing a foreign policy that would insure Japan's survival and placate the more ideological elements of Japanese society. Japan specialist and advisor to two American presidents, Michael Green identified the foreign policy dilemma Japan faced at this time as a classic one for weaker states that was noted by Thucydides during the Peloponnesian Wars between Athens and Sparta and has resurfaced many times in history. How does the less-powerful state strike a balance between being so tied to the powerful ally that it is trapped into wars it would rather not fight yet not be so distanced from the ally that it would be abandoned in a crisis?

Many of Yoshida's fellow conservatives wanted to rebuild Japan's military through significant weapons expenditures and by promoting Japan as a bulwark against communism. The Japanese Left, which suffered the most by far during World War II at the hands of its own government, eagerly embraced Article 9 of the Constitution, making Japan the first "pacifist nation." Although Yoshida shared none of the Left's idealistic beliefs that Japan could renounce possession of military forces into perpetuity, he saw Article 9 as a highly useful short- to medium-term tool to set Japan on a course of reconstruction, satisfy the Left and Right, and both embrace the Americans and fend them off from putting too much pressure on the Japanese to rapidly build a military if U.S. interests were threatened by communism in Asia.

The conservatives, who were anticommunist, had to live with, at least for a short time, Japan having no military but benefiting from U.S. protection against communism and support for a more conservative government. The Japanese Left was mollified by having a nation, first with no military and then later, when Article 9 was reinterpreted, with no offensive military and no foreign bases.

One of the attributes of any great political leader, as opposed to a politician, is that he or she has a long-term vision and, even if compromises are in order at times, never loses sight of end goals. Yoshida was farsighted and a good student of history. He was well aware that throughout the history of East Asia, China had been a dominant power. By the time Yoshida was formulating his plans, China was both a poor developing nation and firmly on the side of the USSR in the Cold War. Yoshida went on record as predicting that one day China would break with the USSR and rise again in the region as a major power with which Japan would need to contend. Yoshida kept a solid foot in the Western camp through his policies but was certain that there would come a time when his country would need to formulate its own China policy as a sovereign nation. Given Japan's wartime actions in China and the bitterness that those actions caused, another benefit from Article 9 is that the lack of a major Japanese military buildup a relatively short period after World War II paved the way later for Japan to develop mutually advantageous economic relations with the People's Republic of China in the 1970s after Mao's demise.

Yoshida successfully convinced the Americans of Japan's support for military bases and helped to broker both a peace treaty and the Japan-U.S. Security Treaty,

THE 1960 SECURITY TREATY REVISION

This massive political battle in the Diet accompanied by major demonstrations in Tokyo caused President Eisenhower to cancel a scheduled trip to Japan. It is important in understanding Japanese politics because it marked a new phase in Japan-U.S. relations and revealed the deep fissures between the pacifists and proponents of increased Japanese military power. These divisions still exist today. Prime Minister Kishi was an advocate of revising the original U.S.-Japan Treaty and of the continuation of American military bases in Japan. However, Japan's SDF would assume responsibility for defending Japan until U.S. forces arrived. This proposed enhancement of Japanese force utilization, which Kishi pushed through the Diet at the cost of his position, assigned Japan's armed forces a primary military function for the first time since World War II.

which he signed in San Francisco in 1951, with the occupation formally ending a year later. Neither the Japanese Right nor Left was satisfied with the treaties. Japanese conservatives, given the nation's military heritage, disliked the country's dependence on the American military, while Leftists and many moderates were troubled that adherence to U.S. foreign policy might drag Japan into another unwanted war. However, Yoshida helped to sow the seeds for Japan's prosperity and the stabilization of a democratic government through his policies. As a believer in an elite bureaucracy, Yoshida's policies also continued Japan's reliance on well-educated bureaucrats as an essential component of government.

Although the blunt Yoshida was eventually permanently driven from the prime minister's office by his enemies and some of his former allies, his conceptualization of Japan's political course of action was soon solidified and enhanced. Facing what appeared to be serious political instability and fearing the rise of socialism, powerful business groups proposed and helped to implement a plan that in 1955 resulted in the merger of two conservative parties, the Liberals and the Democrats. The new party became the Liberal Democratic Party (LDP). The LDP quickly dominated Japanese politics and remained in power for 38 years, until it was defeated by a seven-party coalition in 1993. LDP dominance, the style of Japanese democracy that ensued based on one-party legislative rule, and the implementation of Yoshida's policies lasted for so long that many political analysts use the expression "1955 system," the date of the LDP's birth, to categorize the era from that date until the mid-1980s.

The LDP, in conjunction with the Japanese bureaucracy, large and small businesses, and an increasingly prosperous public, developed the Yoshida Doctrine into a system that managed to make Japan rich, peaceful, and democratic for decades despite encountering sporadic and sometimes serious problems. Domestically, the LDP, although conservative, was a big-tent party. In close association with elite bureaucrats, the Japanese government managed to focus the nation's attention on

TANAKA KAKUEI (1918–1993)

Tanaka, from impoverished Niigata Prefecture and with only a junior high education, used connections with the construction industry and later telecommunications to vastly expand LDP "money politics" in postwar Japan. He became the nation's most powerful politician in 1972 until massive strokes ended his career in 1985. Even though Tanaka served as prime minister for only two years, resigned, and was later convicted of bribery, his power was so great that he played a major role in determining who would become prime minister even while he appealed a jail sentence. Public unhappiness with the corruption of the Tanaka machine helped to bring about needed political reforms.

economic development. Large corporations that went on to become powerful multinational economic actors were allowed the freedom to innovate and be productive. National government ministries involved in the economy also provided assistance for these companies through research, advice, subsidies, and, at times, restriction of foreign competition. Government bureaucrats managed to develop budgets that the Diet passed that kept corporate and personal income taxes low for economic growth. Employees of national ministries were so powerful that often Japan was referred to as a government by bureaucracy, but this was an oversimplification. The bureaucrats' expectation of LDP Diet members was that they would cultivate popular support from other groups besides multinational corporations, most notably the nation's large number of (mostly) rice farmers, small self-employed business people, and such industries as construction and food processing that employed many people but were not particularly productive. LDP politicians specialized in procuring government monies and subsidies for these groups and in doing local constituents a wide variety of favors including showing up at weddings and distributing money.

As Japan's economy and standard of living grew impressively from the 1950s through most of the 1980s, the LDP was able to claim credit for this achievement with Japan's large, increasingly affluent urban middle class. The opposition parties, most notably the Japanese Socialist Party and the Communist Party, were able to successfully negotiate with the LDP for economic benefits for their core constituencies but gained no experience in actually governing the country. Even though these parties won seats in the Diet, they were not able to convince voters, given Japan's prosperity.

As mentioned, important elements of the Japanese public, although for different reasons, were troubled about the national government's postwar foreign policy. Yoshida and subsequent Japanese prime ministers faced the problem of how to rehabilitate Japan's Asian and world reputation, how closely to be allied to the United States in the Cold War, and how to eventually gain an acceptable degree of national sovereignty over foreign policy. As the Cold War became more serious, the Americans in 1954 authorized Japan to develop what would eventually become air, naval, and ground Self-Defense Forces (SDF). However, political leaders were also able to use Article 9 to resist spending even one percent of the gross domestic product on the SDF since Japan was constitutionally a pacifist state.

The U.S.-Security Treaty was renewed by the LDP-dominated Diet in 1960 in the midst of substantial opposition from the socialist party and demonstrations by Leftists on the grounds that Japan was in danger of letting American dominance potentially drag the nation into a nuclear war. However, this opposition died down because Japan's government diverted public attention away from security issues through successful economic development. The 1970s thawing of U.S.-USSR tensions through détente also helped to ease fears in Japan about nuclear war. Meanwhile, after Mao's death, Japan was able to initiate a successful economic bilateral relationship with the new, more market-oriented Chinese communist leadership.

When the USSR invaded Afghanistan and superpower confrontation by proxy heated up in Africa and Latin America in the 1980s, the Reagan administration successfully negotiated with Japan that its SDF forces would be poised to defend the home islands in case of home attack. Japan's political leadership was able to spend more on the SDF in the 1980s than earlier by telling the public the increase was for defense of the home islands. However, because of geographical proximity to the USSR, not only was Japan helping to defend itself in this new era, but also its military forces were now a key part of U.S. East Asian Cold War strategy. Thus, until 1989 and the end of the Cold War, Japan followed the American lead on security issues, had the benefit of the American nuclear umbrella, and the countries' leaders largely did not need to make national defense a major concern.

Domestically, entrenched bureaucrats and LDP Diet members, throughout the 1960s, 1970s, and much of the 1980s, became increasingly close in their social and working relationships as the country continued to grow wealthy. Theoretically, Japanese prime ministers had relatively strong executive powers along British lines, but Japanese political culture in the postwar years resulted in, with the exception of Prime Ministers Tanaka Kakuei in the 1970s and Nakasone Yasuhiro in the 1980s, relatively weak prime ministers. LDP faction leaders anointed party leaders in smoke-filled back rooms, and then LDP Diet members usually approved the choice by vote. The proportional election system, dominated by a large number of LDP candidates who often ran against each other, meant that elections were determined by personalities, personal loyalties, and promises of pet projects, rather than policy debates. District candidates with the most powerful *koenkai*, or support groups, who could raise cash, won elections.

Candidates and their *koenkai* were often part of four or five powerful factions within the LDP, and when a new government was formed, the factions would negotiate for seats in the cabinet based on their respective power bases. The LDP and bureaucrats assuaged opposition parties such as the socialists by supporting wage increases for their core constituents or other legislative concessions such as environmental legislation.

The LDP developed a well-oiled machine throughout Japan where businesses contributed in return for influence with the bureaucracy while LDP politicians also

Nakasone Yasuhiro, prime minister from 1982–1987, was an advocate of a stronger Japanese national security stance than was the case with many of his post World War II predecessors. (Reuters/Corbis)

worked in the Diet and through the national ministries to bring pork-barrel government spending projects home to their constituents, regardless of need. As the decades progressed, and particularly by the 1980s, pork-barrel projects involving the construction industry, a pet beneficiary of government funds, meant that much of Japan's beautiful environment was despoiled with wasteful public works programs, such as Shinkansen routes in relatively rural areas or technological colleges in prefectures with few young people.

But as briefly mentioned earlier, the LDP carefully cultivated a number of special interest groups that included many voters. Small farmers were one important group. Because of legislative apportionment, rural areas containing farmers, whom the LDP heavily subsidized and who had a disproportionately high amount of electoral clout compared to urban dwellers, consistently voted LDP. Urban residents had to both pay for government subsidies to farmers and pay higher prices for food because of government-protected agricultural interests.

Another favorite constituency of the LDP and of some in the national bureaucracy were small mom-and-pop businesses. LDP elected officials and sympathetic bureaucrats prevented large stores with lower prices from opening through excessive regulation of large stores. Small business people voted LDP to show their gratitude, and the public paid much higher retail prices for many such goods and services as clothing, hardware, and food than citizens paid in other developed countries.

It had been a longtime government policy that low taxes should be the norm to increase the incentive for Japanese to work hard, but coupled with this policy were policies from which employees in noncompetitive industries received government favors, including protectionism from foreign competition and subsidies, so that they could make a successful living. This resulted in such high prices that Japanese, particularly those who traveled abroad and shopped, began to call themselves poor people living in a rich country.

Although the Diet had more power than a number of the prime ministers, during the years of the Yoshida Doctrine, many analysts contended that Japan had as much a government by bureaucracy as a government by Diet and prime minister. Most important legislation, including the national government budget, emanated from or was heavily influenced by elite bureaucrats. Even though Diet members occupying cabinet positions were the nominal policy makers, often they reflected the views of the civil servants in the ministries who had the real expertise on the issues.

Japan's national bureaucracy, as discussed, had long been powerful throughout history, but the elite civil servants who constituted career bureaucrats in the most powerful national ministries became even more influential in the 20th century both before and after the war. Top officials in government ministries graduate from the most prestigious Japanese universities. The University of Tokyo Law Faculty (law is an undergraduate degree in Japan similar to political science in the United States) has traditionally been the most important source for top bureaucrats.

Those university graduates who aspire to a top-tier position in a government ministry take a rigorous "class 1 examination," and only about 3 to 4 percent annually, or less than 1,000 people, of all those who take this examination are hired for elite bureaucratic fast-track positions. There is a class 2 examination to fill temporary, more menial jobs. Although some young women are now hired, the typical top-tier civil servant is still a male who has spent his student life with the single-minded goal of career preparation.

Among the national government ministries, the MOF has been seen as particularly important. During the 20th century, the MOF exercised, among other powers, unchallenged de facto control of the budget, responsibility for design of the national tax system, and regulatory authority over the banking and securities sectors. The elected politician serving as the official minister of finance has a very tough job, to say the least, in actually shaping the direction of this vast ministry. By contrast, in the United States, although career high-level civil service employees with permanent positions also wield considerable influence, a change in the White House also means political appointees in major departments who often have the power to change policy directions. While a few strong politicians like Tanaka, who served as prime minister during the years of the 1955 system, managed to get Diet members more involved in developing expertise in policy matters to challenge senior civil servants, this was the rule rather than the exception.

LDP dominance in electoral politics increased bureaucratic influence. Senior-level bureaucrats, most of whom encountered mandatory retirement in their fifties, engaged in the practice of *amakudari*, or "descent from heaven." The former bureaucrats subsequently accepted positions as executives in nonprofit government corporations or with private firms that they previously regulated. This often created special advantages for the private firms that hired these retired bureaucrats since the latter were able to effectively lobby their former public-sector associates on behalf of their private employers. Similar practices occur to some extent in the United States and other democracies but were, and still are to an extent, more widespread in Japan. The result is often collusion between representatives of different organizations who should be independent of each other.

As the LDP continued to win elections, increasingly bureaucrats retired and then successfully ran as LDP candidates for the Diet. Approximately 25 to 30 percent of LDP Diet members were ex-bureaucrats. Diet members, often in return for contributions from businesses, acted as go-betweens to the bureaucracy on behalf of their private-sector contributors. The result of such cozy interactions often meant special favors for both big business and bureaucrats, with the typical Japanese consumer paying higher prices due to government-arranged cartels or monopolies.

Years of LDP dominance and cementing of the bureaucratic relations also resulted in abuses of power. The combination of political dominance by one party and great bureaucratic influence coupled with the political and bureaucratic incentives to protect clients led to a great deal of corruption that beginning in the 1980s was regularly reported in the media. One LDP vice president was discovered to have about $50 million in cash and gold bullion in his office, most of which was thought to be construction industry kickbacks. One prime minister and several other top LDP members were implicated as recipients of insider trading information from a firm in return for political favors.

Throughout the same time period, the media reported instance after instance of situations in which bureaucrats were bribed or given special gifts by both elected officials and private-sector interests in return for favors. By the 1980s and early 1990s, the level of overt public criticism of national bureaucrats in Japan reached higher levels, due to several widely reported scandals, than at any time in Japanese political history. One exposé by a former Ministry of Health bureaucrat even became a best-selling book in Japan and elsewhere. It should be emphasized that elected politicians in Japan are no more prone to corruption than Western democratic leaders. Japanese top-tier national bureaucrats are some of the most intelligent and hard-working professionals in the world, but the 1955 system eventually encouraged corruption. Also, by the latter years of the 20th century, the 1980s combination of LDP/bureaucratic rule was proving dysfunctional, given the great changes in the domestic and international economy and in Japan's international relations.

THE REAL WORLD OF JAPANESE POLITICS: 1985 TO THE PRESENT

The 1985 Plaza Accords, discussed extensively in the following chapter of this book, where Japan signed an agreement with other major developed nations to raise the value of its artificially undervalued yen, is now looked on as having subsequent major political as well as economic ramifications for Japan. After that agreement, Japan was forced to become more fully integrated into the global economy. The

NAKASONE YASUHIRO (1917–)

Educated at Tokyo Imperial University and a World War II naval officer, Nakasone became the first Japanese prime minister in postwar politics to be an overt major player on the world stage. His forceful public style and demeanor captured international media attention as did Nakasone's friendship with U.S. President Ronald Reagan. Domestically, Nakasone advocated educational reforms and economic privatization. He began the process that led to the privatization of the national railway system. Interested in international affairs and winning the Cold War, he publicly proclaimed in his first official visit to the United States in 1982 that the United States and Japan were bound together by common values. Nakasone, who was part of the Tanaka faction, and served as prime minister from 1982 to 1987, eventually resigned as prime minister in the wide-ranging recruit scandal.

government could no longer keep export prices low and import prices high. Thus, the MOF bureaucrats, in an effort to make up for a projected fall in export sales, created a domestic boom by drastically lowering interest rates. The Japanese government's reaction to the Plaza Accords triggered the economic malaise of the 1990s. These events are discussed in the next chapter, but the important point here is that the government-induced economic boom and bust had significant political ramifications.

Also, other domestic and international issues that had begun before 1985 and continue today would, along with economic problems, cause Japanese democracy to enter a new phase. These political changes are causing several elements of the Yoshida Doctrine and the LDP-created 1955 system to either largely no longer apply to Japan's government and politics or to be seriously weakened. Domestically, political leaders and the public in the 1980s began to realize that people were living longer than ever before, and if the trend continued (as it has), Japan would have a larger percentage of old people than any other nation. By the beginning of the 1990s, the public and political leaders recognized that the related trend of low birthrates, which has also continued, was not only a demographic but also a political issue. Such social programs as pensions and health care were designed during a time when the majority of people were young, had much higher costs by the 1980s, and needed reform. More and more women were better educated, but Japan lagged behind Western Europe and the United States in providing professional opportunities for educated women.

As mentioned, the heating up of the Cold War in the 1980s had already caused a change in Japan's national security policies as Prime Minister Nakasone Yasuhiro, who served as chief executive between 2002 and 2007, expanded the SDF's role in occupying a maritime frontline position against the USSR. Nakasone and other political leaders also realized that with the death of Mao a new China as well as a rising threat from the Democratic People's Republic of Korea meant Japan had to

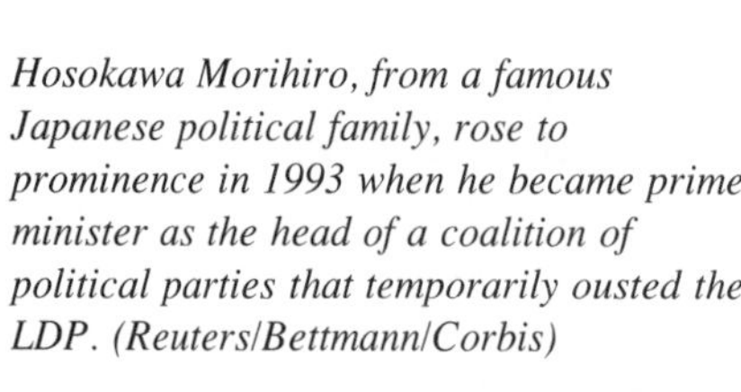

Hosokawa Morihiro, from a famous Japanese political family, rose to prominence in 1993 when he became prime minister as the head of a coalition of political parties that temporarily ousted the LDP. (Reuters/Bettmann/Corbis)

take a more active role in its own national defense. Although Nakasone was unsuccessful in many of his efforts to strengthen Japan's military forces, his lack of reticence in improving defense capability was a change from the low national security profile of typical Japanese prime ministers. Nakasone also spoke out on the need for economic deregulation. The prime minister's willingness to articulately voice opinions and his charismatic personal style made him popular with large numbers of the public who were proud to have a prime minister who was a strong chief executive and an international figure. This success would serve to lay the groundwork for later strengthening of chief executive powers in Japan.

Other international events, in particular the end of the Cold War and accelerated globalization, put additional pressure for change on a political system and government that seemed not able to cope. During the decades-long struggle with the USSR, the United States had been content to overlook many of the Japanese government's policies that prevented American imports, but the end of the Cold War brought changes. With the USSR no longer a threat, the United States exerted more pressure on Japan's government to open its economy to foreign goods, services, and investments. Global dissemination of technology and liberalization of markets in many countries around the world created efficient multinational corporations that were in a better position to compete than a number of Japanese firms that were either subsidized by the government into comfort levels that hindered their productivity or unable to act in a flexible way because of excessive bureaucratic

Murayama Tomiichi who was prime minister from 1994–1996 was a socialist who was supported by the pro-business LDP. (Reuters/Eric Miller/Archive Photos)

regulation. A growing number of urban consumers were also increasingly tired of high prices caused by LDP subsidies for farmers and other inefficient industries.

All of these events unleashed an unprecedented level of public dissatisfaction with the old Yoshida/1955 system. In 1993 the LDP, for the first time in its 38-year history, lost a national election. A multiparty coalition of all sizable opposition parties except the communists led by Hosokawa Morihiro, scion of an aristocratic family and former LDP member and journalist, captured a majority in the House of Representatives. Although Hosokawa's coalition government and his party lasted less than a year before being replaced when he had to resign in 1994 because of allegations of past misuse of funds, in retrospect the election was important. Japan ever since has been experiencing what appears to be, in the words of political and economic analyst Richard Katz, "a long, tumultuous transition toward a political system that is more suited to the needs of the present day economy and security situation, a government in which parties (or coalitions) alternate in power. This process has its own ebbs and flows" (Katz 2008, 1).

The LDP regained power but temporarily conceded the prime minister's office by coalescing in 1994 with its major longtime political party opponent, the socialists (Social Democratic Party of Japan). Socialist leader Murayama Tomiichi served as prime minister for two years. Even though the LDP entered the 1994 coalition with the socialists in order to regain power, it was the socialists who repudiated their platform through joining the LDP, and they permanently appear to have lost credibility with much of the public. Since the late 1990s, the socialists have declined and the Democratic Party of Japan (DPJ), a centrist/liberal party, has become the LDP's major opponent. Many political analysts consider the DPJ, created in 1998 and which quickly gained popularity, to constitute a major step toward a Japanese two-party system. The party bills itself as reform-minded and representative of a variety of professionals including attorneys, bankers, and journalists as well as workers.

The LDP managed to regain the prime minister's office in 1996 but since then has primarily retained control of the House of Representatives through forming coalition governments with other parties, most notably the New Komeito Party, now the third-largest political party in Japan and associated with the Japanese Buddhist Soka Gakkai organization. New Komeito, a moderate party dedicated to clean government and abolishment of nuclear weapons, brings the LDP a reliable, disproportionately high working-class vote. However, the party is not controlled by the LDP, so withdrawal of coalition support is an ever-present possibility.

As of the publication of this book, the LDP retains a greatly reduced power over the Diet, relative to the past, and the prime minister's office through a pragmatic combination of political reform and continuing voter disenchantment—support for the DPJ notwithstanding—with the other party alternatives. Also, the LDP, which

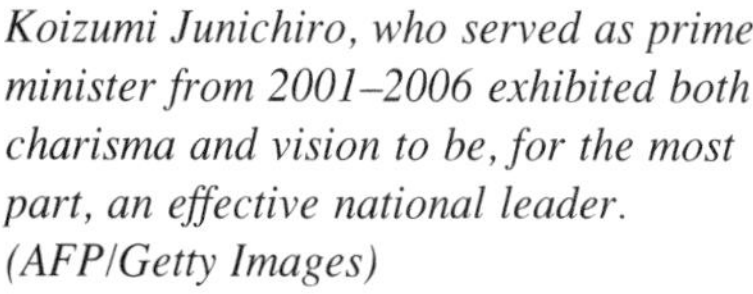

Koizumi Junichiro, who served as prime minister from 2001–2006 exhibited both charisma and vision to be, for the most part, an effective national leader. (AFP/Getty Images)

KOIZUMI JUNICHIRO (1942–)

Typical Japanese politicians have avoided the limelight and, perhaps because of traditional Japanese cultural notions about appropriate behavior, have been anything but flamboyant. Koizumi Junichiro managed to be successfully reelected while becoming somewhat of a cult figure at times. He recorded a karaoke album of Elvis Presley songs after being elected, a chewing gum named after him appeared, and Koizumi dolls featuring his famous permed hair were a hot commodity for a time. Although substantive, Koizumi was also a master politician, and he effectively used media to cultivate an antiestablishment persona. Koizumi had other advantages; his father and grandfather were successfully elected and reelected to the Diet, and he was the first candidate elected to the LDP presidency chosen (automatically becoming prime minister) after the party had changed its rules in response to public complaints about excessive LDP secrecy and cronyism.

supports a stronger military, has mostly benefited from public recognition that post–Cold War security issues pose new challenges for Japan and simple reliance on the United States or general pacifist sentiments do not constitute viable policies. The LDP also survived most of the first decade of the 21st century because of the public popularity of Koizumi Junichiro, who served as prime minister from 2001 to 2006.

Until 1994, the multiple-member, exclusive, proportional lower-house electoral system favored LDP candidates because the party was the only one with ample enough funds to run several candidates in a single district. Since in most districts a large number of candidates running against each other were from the LDP, policy issues usually didn't matter, which diminished real choices for many voters. In 1994, before his own coalition government that had ousted the LDP fell, Prime Minister Hosokawa managed to get the Diet to approve the current House of Representatives election system whereby a majority of representatives are elected from single-seat constituencies rather than proportionately. This has created more of a policy focus on the part of many LDP candidates since they aren't running against each other. Also, a number of LDP candidates are now getting elected on their positions on policy.

More independent LDP Diet members who were elected on their own, sometimes because of their policy stances, have weakened but not eliminated the power of LDP factions that in earlier times could control more Diet seats through money and favors. In 2000, the LDP changed its party leader selection process (party leaders are Diet members who become prime minister according to LDP rules if a government can be formed) and made it more transparent. Each of the LDP's 47 prefectural chapters now have three votes for party leader while each LDP Diet member gets one vote in the selection. In the spring of 2001, after the new LDP party leader selection process was employed, Japan had its 11th prime minister in almost 12 years. The new LDP party selection process made a difference as the prefectural LDP chapter representatives bucked the old-guard party leadership and voted heavily for a reform candidate, Koizumi Junichiro, who subsequently became Japan's first strong prime minister in almost 14 years.

Koizumi, who served as prime minister from 2001 to 2006, both was a strong executive and employed a new style of politics. He was photogenic, made an effective communicator, sported a popular hair style, let the public know about his interests including a deep affection for the American pop icon Elvis Presley, and gained a reputation as a maverick who was going to make needed changes in Japanese politics and government. Although from a longtime LDP family, Koizumi's educational background was different than many of the Japanese political elite. Instead of attending such "old boy" former imperial institutions as Tokyo University, Koizumi graduated from Keio University, a highly regarded private school, where he studied economics. Koizumi studied abroad in London as well.

Perhaps most important, Koizumi entered office with an understanding of how globalization was changing Japan and with a vision of what he intended to do to reform the political system. Although Koizumi failed as much as he succeeded, his mixture of successful reform, adroit politics, and personal courage even when taking unpopular stances won the respect of elements of the media and the public. Koizumi, who gained nicknames like "Lion Heart" for his boldness in publicly challenging political enemies, managed to remain in office and make changes in government that appear to be long-lasting.

The prime minister and his inner circle recognized that economic globalization was irreversible. If Japan wished to recover from the more than decadelong economic malaise, old political and financial structures that gave the Japanese government too much control over economic management and overrelied on a political system that allocated enormous amounts of public monies to unproductive activities had to be greatly reduced. This meant fixing Japan's serious financial and banking problems, deregulating of much of the economy, and ending a substantial portion of pork-barrel spending. In order to achieve policy success, Koizumi had to battle not only the bureaucracy but also entrenched elements within the LDP, his own party, who bitterly opposed economic liberalization and government spending reductions.

Koizumi initiated several major economic reforms, which are described in more detail in the next chapter, that were designed to strengthen Japan's corporate sector domestically and internationally through deregulation, solve the financial crisis that had lasted more than a decade, privatize inefficient government corporations, and make the LDP more responsive to large numbers of Japan's urban residents and less beholden to rural interests. He also attempted to make higher education more responsive to government and corporate needs through wide-ranging reforms including creating incentives for national universities to compete for government research funds.

Whenever possible, Koizumi seized power from the bureaucracy. For example, MOF bureaucrats had been ineffectual in solving the bank bad loans crisis, but Koizumi was able to do it through making maximum use of minimal executive appointments and through Diet action. Koizumi governments also managed to slow down the national government spending that had been occurring through local grants, subsidies to special interests, and public works spending for local governments. Koizumi both cut national spending and required significant local matching funds, usually half the total projected expenditures or more, before central government fund allocations would be distributed for public works projects.

The prime minister also tried to address the question of how to deal with the economic needs of the elderly, Japan's fastest growing population. In an effort to keep an increasingly expensive national pension system under control, the LDP-dominated Diet during the Koizumi years passed a law that restructured the system by increasing payment premiums from working adults but promised to collect enough tax revenues that the total of an individual basic pension would not fall below 50 percent of the average income of a working person.

Koizumi attempted to continue a process intended to transfer power from the central governments to prefectural and local ones that had begun shortly before he became prime minister. In January 2001, a major Diet-approved governmental reorganization went into effect. The reorganization package had several objectives. Two important ones were to give prefectural and local governments more flexibility in meeting the needs of their citizens and to increase local officials' power while decreasing the authority of central government bureaucrats. Objectives of the reorganization package included making the units of government closer to the people more responsive. The number of national ministries and agencies was cut from 22 to 12 in an attempt to promote more efficient policy making and implementation by eliminating ministry and agency turf wars. This was affected by merging several ministries and agencies and creating two gigantic cabinet ministries, the National Land and Transportation Ministry and the General Affairs Ministry. The idea was that the reduction in the number of separate bureaucratic agencies and ministries would make elected officials' jobs easier in interacting with government bureaucracy. Another objective of the reorganization was to strengthen elected officials' power by increasing the executive authority of the prime minister. Koizumi met resistance from central government bureaucrats in his efforts to decrease the ministry's power over the economy and in his attempts to implement government decentralization. He was much more successful with the former objective than the latter.

Perhaps Koizumi's major victory over both bureaucrats and strong opposition from his own party was his successful privatization of Japan's huge postal savings program. For decades the postal savings program, the largest source for individual savings deposits in Japan, provided interest rates to savers that were slightly higher than commercial banks. Ministry of Posts bureaucrats then funneled the monies to various government agencies for a host of projects. Koizumi, who had campaigned on the promise to privatize the postal banking system, dissolved the lower house in 2005 when the Diet refused to pass a bill achieving his objective and called for an election depicting it as a national referendum on his proposal. Koizumi as party leader also refused to support LDP Diet members who opposed the measure. A large number of voters viewed these moves as daring and felt that voting to retain an LDP government with Koizumi as head constituted a vote for needed reform.

The fall 2005 election was the biggest LDP victory of the new century, and the privatization legislation passed during the 2006 Diet session.

In foreign policy, Koizumi saw increased national security as essential for the new circumstances Japan faced. He increased the size of the SDF and continually made public comments to the effect that Japan needed a "normal" military like other sovereign nations. Koizumi also, despite public division on the issue, assertively supported the U.S.-led war on terrorism. Shortly after the September 11, 2001, attack, Koizumi was one of the first world leaders to contact then President Bush and assure him that he agreed with him in fighting a global war on terrorism. Koizumi wrote the president, "You must win and Japan will help" (Green 2007, 28). Koizumi and the Diet then passed legislation deploying maritime SDF forces to refuel coalition forces operating against the Taliban in Afghanistan.

In January 2004, he became the first prime minister in postwar history to send Japanese troops who were not a part of United Nations (UN) peacekeeping forces to Iraq, a combat zone. In order to constitutionally do this, even though the troops were in a noncombatant role, Koizumi managed to enact controversial legislation in the Diet. The Japanese government also contributed $5 billion to the war against terrorism. Koizumi also introduced legislation in 2006, enacted after he left office, that elevated the former Japan Defense Agency to Japan Ministry of Defense. The law took effect in 2007 and makes the civilian head of SDF part of the cabinet.

Although Koizumi pushed the constitutionality of SDF utilization to new boundaries, there was established legal precedent for international deployment of the SDF. As of 2005, Japan's SDF had been sent to 14 countries, mostly for humanitarian purposes or as part of UN peacekeeping forces, since its first international mission in Cambodia in 1992. In the most recent year for which statistics are available, Japan's SDF forces now have the fifth-biggest budget of all militaries in the world, trailing only the United States, the United Kingdom, France, and China.

As mentioned, Koizumi did not succeed in a number of items on his ambitious agenda, and some policy changes that he enacted remain controversial with elements of the Japanese public and with other Japanese politicians, including LDP members whose self-interests were tied to maintaining the 1955 system. Bureaucrats were able to join forces with LDP Diet members and defeat his plans to privatize the Japan Highway Public Corporation and the National Mail Services. Koizumi, although able to wrest much power away from the national ministries, was unable to secure control of the central government budget formulation process. Since the postal bank privatization law is incrementally enacted, even the eventual success of this much-touted measure is unsure at this time. Pension reforms proved to be insufficient since Japanese families continue to have low birthrates, and the question of how to fund retirement income is a serious political issue again. In his foreign policy, Koizumi was viewed by the Japanese Left, and at times other East Asian nations, as being too much of a hawk. His several visits to Yasukuni, the Shinto shrine that honors imperial Japan's war dead, provoked riots in China in which Japanese property was destroyed and formal protests from the Republic of Korea.

Still, by having a clear political vision, skillfully articulating it to the Japanese people, taking decisive action that at times produced clear results, and engaging in, for Japan, what were considered daring political tactics, Koizumi's political and policy legacy resonate in the archipelago's politics and government. One of the reasons the Democratic Party of Japan (DPJ) has become apparently a viable second party in Japan is through appearing more realistic to voters in its policy proposals than such earlier parties as the socialists and communists. However, by engaging in imaginative political campaigns, DPJ politicians lifted at least some tactics and strategy from the Koizumi playbook.

The DPJ first became popular because the party leaders offered practical policy alternatives to the LDP. The DPJ issued very specific positions including a proposal that elected politicians gain more control over government by expanding the central government's authority to appoint more high-level bureaucrats. In 2003 the DPJ made inroads against the LDP in Diet elections through its policy proposals and by tying many LDP politicians to the bureaucracy despite the fact that Koizumi was an opponent of the bureaucrats. These 2003 gains were particularly impressive considering that the party was experiencing growing pains and organizational problems because of a recent merger with a smaller left-of-center party shortly before the election.

The DPJ also had political leaders who were effective in personal-style campaigning that captured the attention and imagination of voters. In 2006 the DPJ won a special election to fill a vacant lower house seat in Chiba Prefecture that Koizumi wanted for the LDP. Party leader Ozawa Ichiro secured the support of enough groups in the Chiba district through imaginative campaigning that included bicycling around for high-profile meetings with voters. Then, in July 2007, after Koizumi had left the prime minister's office a year earlier having reached the constitutional term limit for service in the office, the DPJ dealt his successor, then LDP Prime Minister Abe Shintaro, a humiliating defeat by winning a majority in the upper house elections. This was the first time that the LDP had ever lost control of the House of Councilors in the history of the party. Ozawa skillfully took advantage of a period of time marked by higher taxes and increasing gaps between the rich and the poor. He organized campaigns in hundreds of smaller locales and particularly appealed to those Japanese who were not benefiting from recent reforms enacted by the Japanese government in response to economic globalization. Furthermore, Ozawa effectively captured media attention by promising beforehand to resign if the DPJ lost the upper house election and challenged Abe to do the same. Abe refused to resign after the humiliating defeat but went on to leave the prime minister's office in September 2007, citing ill health. He was replaced by Fukuda Yasuo, a caretaker prime minister who subsequently resigned in September 2008 and was replaced by longtime LDP politician Aso Taro, the grandson of Yoshida Shigeru. As this book is published, the LDP clings to a majority in the lower house in coalition with the New Komeito Party, with the DPJ in solid control of the upper house.

Events, particularly in the Diet and in the prime minister's office, are indicative of the nonlinear course of change from the death of the old 1955 system to a new phase of Japanese politics. The Japanese Diet has been in virtual gridlock on a host of issues since the unprecedented DPJ upper house victory. Important prime ministerial appointments, including the presidency of the Bank of Japan, have been blocked by two-thirds upper house majorities. Similar bottlenecks have occurred

OZAWA ICHIRO (1942–)

Analysts have predicted for years that Japan is on the verge of a political transition from LDP party dominance amid a host of smaller parties to a two-party competitive system. In July 2007, Ozawa Ichiro led the DPJ to defeat the LDP in upper house elections for the first time ever. Ozawa, born in Iwate Prefecture and the son of a self-made man who was elected to the Diet, has been a force in Japanese politics since the 1990s. Originally an LDP member, he broke with the party, cofounded the Renewal Party, and then worked with another small party leader, Hosokawa Morihiro, in causing the LDP to lose Japan's lower house in 1993 for the first time. After forming yet another new political party, eventually Ozawa joined forces with the DPJ. Ozawa, who graduated from Keio University and is recognized to have policy as well as political expertise, is difficult to categorize ideologically. He is a controversial figure but has played a major role in the birth of a party that is a serious contender for power.

with legislation including, in a period marked by rising gasoline prices, a controversial gas tax bill. This situation was not lost on Japanese who were also experiencing a 2008 economic downturn. Throughout the latter part of 2007 and much of 2008, opposing parties in the Diet spent time blocking legislation and wrangling over rules, and there was virtually no sign of compromise. As a result, national polls indicated that public support, already low for the LDP as evidenced by the 2007 elections, had now plummeted, and politicians of both parties were proving to be, at least temporarily, more unpopular than bureaucrats.

According to both political scientists and such seasoned politicians as former Prime Minister Nakasone Yasuhiro, these recent events point to a structural problem in Japan's government that will need to be addressed given the transitions that are occurring. When Japan is compared to other democracies with bicameral legislatures, the Japanese House of Councilors is considerably stronger than other nations' upper houses. Constitutionally, only the Japanese lower house can nominate the prime minister, ratify treaties, and approve the budget. In all other matters, the two houses are equal except that the lower house can override an upper house veto by a two-thirds majority, difficult at best with the current party divisions. Upper houses in the United Kingdom and Germany have nothing like this kind of power. Although the Italian upper house is roughly as powerful as its Japanese equivalent, it can be dissolved, as is the case with Italy's lower house. In Japan, only the lower house can be dissolved. In the United States, the Senate's and the House of Representatives' powers are roughly equivalent but, unlike the Japanese prime minister who must control events in the Diet to have virtually any power, the American president has an independent source of power because of direct election by the voters. The president can take much more policy action, even when the chief executive's party is in a minority.

This structural imbalance can be traced to Japan's 1947 Constitution, which was developed by Americans who were then supported by like-minded Japanese. Occupation authorities held the concept of checks and balances and two powerful legislative chambers in high esteem but were unfamiliar with how parliaments best operated. Japanese involved in developing the 1947 Constitution were operating from the traditions of the 1889 Constitution, which envisioned less of a role for the legislative body than would be the case in a viable democracy. Thus, the issue of a deeply divided Diet was probably not concretely conceptualized.

If Japan is to continue to develop a form of democratic legislative politics in which parties contest for voters on policy issues and more than one party is strong, the situation just described must be rectified. There are two possibilities. One is revision of the 1947 Constitution to alter the current legislative status quo. In 2008, DPJ secretary-general Hatoyama Yukio anticipated the current problem and wrote a recommended constitutional revision that was publicly disseminated. His proposal called for abolishing the upper house and creating a unicameral legislature. Former Prime Minister Nakasone Yasuhiro has also developed his own suggested constitutional revision that he thinks will solve the problem. Nakasone proposes that in the event of an upper/lower house division, the lower house can override the upper house with a simple majority.

The problem with constitutional revision, which has been discussed on several issues including, most notably, Article 9 is that there is a sense of general apprehension on the part of many Japanese about the unintended ramifications of beginning a process of constitutional revision. Postwar Japan has risen from the ashes of defeat and authoritarian rule and transformed itself into a prosperous and free democracy. This has occurred with the current Constitution, which has never been amended, as the overarching framework of government.

Many Japanese consider the Constitution in almost reverential terms. Those who remember World War II as well as large numbers of people born afterward, who have been taught that Japan is the first "pacifist" country, see the Constitution as a major reason why Japan has not been directly involved as a combatant in war since 1945. Although other Japanese feel quite differently, in a society where harmony is still highly valued relative to many cultures, proposed constitutional reform of any kind is a sensitive issue.

Another more immediately practical way to solve the problem of party deadlock is for Diet members to create bipartisan or multipartisan parliamentary precedents. Foreign examples could be useful. The British have a rule called the Salisbury Doctrine that was designed to avoid legislative deadlock. The House of Lords may modify but cannot oppose legislation passed by a House of Commons majority if the legislation had been included as part of the ruling government's campaign manifesto and received, because its sponsors won an election and could form a government, the electorate's implicit approval. Although the U.S. government does not have a parliamentary system, it is common procedure in the U.S. Congress that joint committees are established with members from both houses to resolve disagreements about a particular bill. There have been calls for the creation of a special bicameral Diet committee to study foreign procedures used in bicameral legislatures to solve the kind of problems that have recently occurred in Japan.

In the spring of 2008, a few Diet members publicly proposed changes in some historic Diet procedural rules that appear to be contributing to gridlock in light of the unique situation in postwar Japan of two parties with virtually equal legislative power. For example, there is a Diet rule dating back to the 19th century that bills must be passed in the same session in which they are introduced and cannot be carried over from one session to the next. This means that in a divided legislature where one party has enough power to seriously challenge another, incentives exist for members of any powerful opposition party to focus on scheduling maneuvers and on attacking administration scandals rather than debating issues. Opponents of a government-sponsored bill can simply waste enough time, and the legislation will automatically die at the end of the Diet session.

Japan has been a successful country for virtually all of its existence in comparison to many of the world's nations because it benefited from pragmatic, intelligent, and farsighted leaders who solved such problems as the one just described. If the Diet log jam continues to hinder the passage of needed legislation, leaders who put the nation's welfare above partisan politics will emerge because of strong electoral support.

CONCLUSION: POLITICAL CHALLENGES AND EVOLVING GOVERNMENT STRUCTURES

Much change has occurred in Japan's political system since roughly the mid-1980s. However, further progress needs to be made. Like any large nation in an increasingly interconnected and fast-changing world, Japan's problems are complex. The economy is always a paramount issue, and Japan has made substantial progress in rebounding from the serious malaise that lasted more than a decade. However, as readers of the next chapter will discover, additional legal and policy reforms are needed to make portions of the Japanese economy more competitive and productive and thus the larger population more prosperous.

As is the case with many affluent countries, education and training are now even more critically important in Japan than in the past. Japan has enjoyed a rising tide since the 1950s that lifted up most people, but changing international and domestic circumstances have caused income gaps between the skilled and the relatively unskilled to noticeably grow. This is reflected in a growth in the percentage of Japanese children who now attend private high schools and the situation in which many adults without skills find themselves in the new economy.

At present, more than 30 percent of high school students attend private schools. Twenty percent of high school students attended private schools 15 years ago. Until the first years of the 21st century, approximately 98 percent of all Japanese elementary and junior high students attended public schools. Although less than 10 percent of younger students attend private schools, the percentages that do so have steadily climbed in the past five years. The primary reason for the defections from public schools is that increasingly, students admitted to the better Japanese universities first attended private schools. For most of the postwar period, Japan's public schools were

WHAT DO JAPANESE CONSTITUENTS WANT?

All democratic societies confront pork-barrel spending, in which elected legislators gain support in their own districts through procuring public funds for unnecessary and wasteful projects. However, longtime one-party rule and Prime Minister Tanaka's expansion of money politics created a particularly intensive pork-barrel problem in Japan that added to the 1990s' economic problems. The Japanese system has also been characterized by politicians overtly doing favors for individual constituents. There are signs that Japanese voters are helping to diminish pork-barrel spending by supporting reformists in the LDP and the DPJ. Also, data from one often-cited public opinion poll in Ibaraki Prefecture indicated that in 1986 almost 20 percent of respondents claimed to have benefited from subsidies or individual favors provided by politicians. Just a little more than one percent of respondents in Ibaraki Prefecture indicated this was the case in 2003.

vehicles whereby children of modest circumstances could succeed and then become successful adults. For a group-oriented society, a public education system that does not help poor families advance constitutes a serious national political problem.

Also, Japanese politicians must continue to facilitate economic changes that prevent another "lost decade" like the 1990s with high unemployment and several recessions. However, low-skill workers who lose jobs in industries that no longer receive government subsidies must be retrained and not forgotten. Recently, Japanese political leaders are paying close attention to such Scandinavian countries as Norway and Sweden, that managed to both make their economies more flexible and retrain displaced workers.

As discussed elsewhere, the quality of life for Japan's elderly and the problem of younger Japanese not having enough children to sustain population increases are interrelated problems that have major political and social implications for the future, as does the influx of people such as Japanese Brazilians who aren't culturally Japanese and Southeast Asians who aren't ethnically Japanese. How Japan addresses diversity, including the accommodation of well-educated women, is an important domestic political issue.

Foreign policy challenges, discussed at some length in the Contemporary Issues chapter, also loom importantly for the future. Japan has always been part of the greater Northeast Asia region, but China's rise means new problems and opportunities for Japan's leaders as they determine in what ways to accommodate the largest country in the world while retaining their own existing alliances, commitments, and sovereignty. U.S. relations and the American military presence on Japanese soil and what form it should take is another political issue with far-reaching implications, as are relations with a volatile Democratic People's Republic of Korea and an ally, the Republic of Korea, that still have a collective memory of colonization by Japan.

Changes in Japan's political structures have occurred but are still needed. In addition to procedural changes in the Diet that have become apparent with the growth of a second strong political party, there is somewhat of a DPJ/LDP bipartisan perspective about the continuing need to decrease national bureaucratic power. Although a strong national bureaucracy has been largely a political asset for Japan for hundreds of years, the country is becoming a mature democracy. This means the elected representatives of the people should have general authority over the officials who are hired to implement government policy.

In the 1990s and into this century, consistent problems in the bureaucracy occurred. They ranged from ineptness in response to the 1995 Kobe earthquake, to cover ups of AIDS-tainted blood supplies, to the recent sensational 2008 news of the misplacement of more than 50 million pension premium payments. The DPJ built its policy reputation in large part on increasing democratically elected officials' power over bureaucrats. Since Koizumi left office, a Diet power vacuum has occurred and national ministries, often in collusion with such traditional LDP Diet members as the "road tribe" representatives who want to build often unnecessary roads through their districts, are attempting to reassert power. These LDP members are opposed by a reform wing within their own party. Furthermore, public opinion polls consistently indicate that majorities of Japanese citizens support the reduction of bureaucracies' power. How this will occur and what party (or parties) will accomplish these changes remain to be seen.

The whole issue of constitutional revision and its consequences is a political challenge that has been discussed in various quarters since 1947, is deeply controversial, has both domestic and international ramifications, and is the most unpredictable. The LDP has long supported constitutional revision, although not very intensely, for much of Japan's postwar history. While the July 2007 loss of the upper house elections was a major blow to LDP revision hopes, events a few months before that loss placed the possibility of constitutional reform on a national agenda.

In order to amend Japan's current Constitution, two-thirds of both houses of the Diet must approve formal constitutional revision, and then a majority of Japanese voters must also vote affirmatively in a national referendum. For decades the possibility of getting the required two-thirds majorities in both houses was so remote that procedures for conducting a national referendum were not in existence. However, Abe Shintaro, the LDP prime minister who succeeded Koizumi, was an enthusiastic proponent of constitutional reform and immediately worked with his own party as well as the coalition New Komeito to get necessary approval through both houses of the Diet. The legislation was introduced just before Constitution Day and passed the House of Representatives on April 12, 2007, and the House of Councilors on May 14 of that year. Abe and his revision proponents did provide a concession for opponents of the legislation that any further revision would be delayed for three years, which meant that both houses of the Diet would have conducted scheduled elections before a national referendum will be conducted.

Why was Abe, an unpopular prime minister, able to find the Diet votes to advance the possibility of constitutional revision the furthest in Japan's postwar history? Although there are groups and individuals who are interested in other issues related to constitutional revision, Article 9 dwarfs all other topics. This is *the* constitutional revision issue that will resurface as 2010 approaches. Postwar polls have always shown general support on the part of large numbers of Japanese for constitutional revision, but not for abolishment of Article 9.

However, recent national surveys of Japanese citizens, including a 2004 poll, indicated more than 90 percent of Japanese considered the world a more dangerous place than 25 years ago. Such East Asian countries as China and North and South Korea all pay close attention to SDF commitments, and discussion of constitutional revision receives international attention. U.S. policy, which is always subject to change through electoral politics, has for decades been largely in favor of a Japanese ally freed from the constitutional constraints of Article 9. Although the Cabinet Legislative Bureau has consistently given the majority party and prime minister freedom to reinterpret Article 9, two substantial constraints of the Constitution are limitations on offensive military force capability and limitations on collective self-defense activities with militaries of other countries. Most constitutional experts believe these constraints will always exist without constitutional reform. The vision to negotiate the unprecedented event of constitutional reform will tax the skills of the most capable political leaders.

This much is certain about Japanese politics. The days of the old 1955 political system are gone. Ten years ago, noted Columbia political scientist Gerald Curtis observed, "Old verities—a prestigious and competent bureaucracy, a public consensus on national goals, one party dominance, an opposition that opposes for opposition's sake and does not offer a creditable alternative to the party in power—are gone" (Curtis 1999, 241–242). As depicted in this chapter, in the subsequent decade that has passed, new political structures are now visible and operative but are not a new system as they are currently still evolving while emerging leaders deal with vestiges of the old order.

Still, in Japan, as reiterated in different ways throughout this chapter, political leadership has been sound for most of the years that have passed since 1600. In the years after 1945, Japan has become richer and freer and enjoys a stable democracy. This history, along with one of the hardest-working and better-educated populations on the planet, constitutes a good track record for meeting present and future political challenges.

REFERENCES

Anderson, Gregory E. "Lionheart or Paper Tiger? A First-Term Koizumi Retrospective." *Asian Perspective* 28 (March 2004): 149–182.

Appleton, Andrew, and Wilhelm Vosse. *An International Study of Attitudes and Global Engagement, 2004*. Pullman: Washington State University and International Christian University, 2005.

Auslin, Michael R. *Negotiating with Imperialism: The Unequal Treaties and the Culture of Japanese Diplomacy*. Cambridge, MA: Harvard University Press, 2004.

Bix, Herbert P. *Hirohito and the Making of Modern Japan*. New York: Harper Perennial, 2001.

Curtis, Gerald. *The Logic of Japanese Politics: Leaders, Institutions, and the Limits of Change*. New York: Columbia University Press, 1999.

Dolan, Ronald E., and Robert L. Worden. *Japan: A Country Study*. Washington, DC: GPO for the Library of Congress, 1994. http://countrystudies.us/japan/ (accessed June 2008).

Duke, Benjamin C. ed. *Ten Great Educators of Modern Japan: A Japanese Perspective*. Japan: University of Tokyo Press, 1989.

Green, Michael J. "The US-Japan Alliance: A Brief Strategic History." *Education About Asia* 12, No. 3 (Winter 2007): 25–30.

Hidehiko, Hamada, ed. *Japan: Eyes on the Country, Views of the 47 Prefectures*. Tokyo: Foreign Press Center, 1997.

Inoguchi, Takashi. "Can the LDP Survive Globalization?" *Education About Asia* 12, No. 3 (Winter 2007): 45–49.

———. *Japanese Politics: An Introduction*. Melbourne, Australia: Trans Pacific Press, 2005.

Iinuma, Yoshisuke. "LDP Divided: Curb the Bureaucrats?" *Oriental Economist Report* 76, No. 3 (March 2008): 9–10

———. "Legacy of One-Party State: Fiddling in the Divided Diet." *Oriental Economist Report* 76, No. 4 (April 2008): 7–8.

———. "Pension Politics: How to Pay for Aging." *Oriental Economist Report* 76, No. 2 (February 2008): 7–8.

Jansen, Marius B. *The Making of Modern Japan*. Cambridge, MA: Belknap Press of Harvard University Press, 2002.

Japan Considered. http://www.japanconsidered.com/ (accessed June 2008).

Karan, Pradyumna P. *Japan in the 21st Century: Environment, Economy, and Society*. Lexington: University Press of Kentucky, 2005.

Katz, Richard. "Countdown on Fukuda." *Oriental Economist Report* 76, No. 4 (April 2008a): 1–2.

———. "'Flexicurity' & Reform: A Nordic Mirror for Japan, Part 1." *Oriental Economist Report* 76, No. 2 (February 2008b): 5–6.

———. "'Japanizing' the Nordic Model: A Nordic Mirror for Japan, Part 2." *Oriental Economist Report* 76, No. 3 (March 2008c): 7–8.

Katz, Richard, and Peter Ennis. "Drift Continues: Who's Willing to Take the Helm?" *Oriental Economist Report* 76, No. 2 (February 2008d): 1–2.

Kawashima, Yutaka. *Japanese Foreign Policy at The Crossroads*. Washington, DC: Brookings Institution Press, 2003.

"Koizumi, Junichiro." Wikipedia. http://en.wikipedia.org/wiki/Junichiro_Koizumi (accessed June 2008).

Lincoln, Edward J. "The Japanese Government and the Economy: Twenty-first Century Challenges." *Education About Asia* 12, No. 3 (Winter 2007): 31–38.

Masuzoe, Yoichi, ed. *Years of Trial: Japan in the 1990s*. Tokyo: Japan Echo, Inc., 2000.

Métraux, Daniel A. "The Mikado, Guranto Shōgun, and the Rhapsody of US-Japan Relations in Early Meiji." *Education About Asia* 11, No. 3 (Winter 2006): 39–44.

Miyamoto, Masao. *Straitjacket Society: An Insider's Irreverent View of Bureaucratic Japan.* Translated by Juliet Winters Carpenter. Tokyo: Kodansha International, 1994.

Online Dictionary of Politics and Media in Japan. "Nakasone Yasuhiro." http://www.docoja.com:8080/jisho/mainword?dbname=polg&mainword=Nakasone_Yasuhiro (accessed March 2009).

Oros, Andrew L. "The Domestic and International Politics of Constitutional Change in Japan." *Education About Asia* 12, No. 3 (Winter 2007): 39–44.

Pempel, T. J., et al. "Roundtable Discussion of Richard J. Samuels's *Machiavelli's Children: Leaders and Their Legacies in Italy and Japan.*" *Journal of East Asian Studies* 6 (2006): 1–29.

Prime Minister of Japan and His Cabinet. "Archives." n.d. http://www.kantei.go.jp/foreign/index-e.html (accessed June 2008).

Reid, T. R. *Confucius Lives Next Door: What Living in the East Teaches Us About Living in the West.* New York: Vintage, 1999.

Reischauer, Edwin O. *Japan: The Story of a Nation.* 3rd ed. New York: Alfred Knopf, 1981.

Tanaka, Hideaki, ed. *Japan 2007: An International Comparison.* Tokyo: Keizai Koho Center, 2007.

Weston, Mark. *Giants of Japan: The Lives of Japan's Most Influential Men and Women.* New York: Kodansha International, 1999.

Yamamoto, Tadashi, ed. *Deciding the Public Good: Governance and Civil Society in Japan.* New York: Japan Center for International Exchange, 1999.

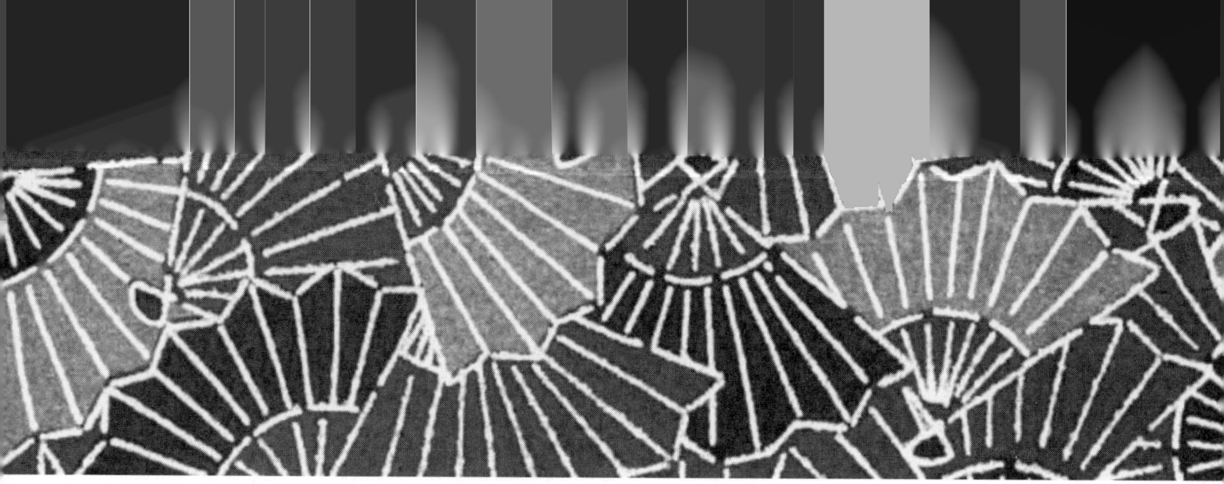

Economy

The rise of the Japanese economy from the ashes of World War II is one of the most important world events since that conflict. Today, Japan ranks with the U.S. and China as one of the world's largest economies. The United States, the United Kingdom, and Japan respectively have the world's three-largest stock markets, and Japan ranks among world leaders in manufacturing and international trade. After more than two decades of high-speed growth and another decade of slower but still impressive economic advancement, in 1990 Japan began a period of economic malaise that would last until 2005. Although serious problems remain from the recent period of stagnation, Japan appears to be back on course. However, like the rest of the world, Japan suffered from the 2008 global financial crisis.

Even when Japan and other nations recover from recent economic difficulties, the archipelago faces its own unique economic challenges. These include the aging of its population, a shrinking workforce, too many inefficient small manufacturers and service providers, and business restructuring that threatens traditional cultural practices. In subsequent sections of this chapter, readers will gain a basic understanding of both Japan's economy and potential barriers to economic prosperity that the Japanese must successfully overcome.

ECONOMIC SYSTEMS: THE ROOTS OF SUCCESS (1600–1868)

Even though Japan's spectacular economic rise did not occur until the three decades after World War II, the foundations for the so-called economic miracle were laid

Trading floor of the Tokyo Stock Exchange. New York, London, and Tokyo have the world's biggest stock exchanges. (Obremski/Corbis)

during the Tokugawa era (1600–1868). Although technologically behind parts of Western Europe and the United States that were industrializing and had more advanced technology, the Tokugawa economy was certainly not primitive by world standards. Tokugawa Japan, despite occasional, localized severe food shortages, was in general a prosperous society. A substantial number of small and large businesses, particularly in urban areas, existed, and the use of money was widespread. By the 1850s, larger percentages of Japanese were literate than was the case in most of the world's countries. The Japan that Perry "opened" contained an economic base for future commercial and industrial expansion and a segment of the population well educated enough to make good use of new Western technology.

Several economic conditions important for this stable and relatively healthy economy existed in Tokugawa Japan. The entire Tokugawa period was, with the exception of some isolated peasants' revolts, a time of domestic peace accompanied by no unwanted foreign presence in the archipelago. The samurai, the institutionalized upper class, were theoretically warriors and bureaucrats, but the absence of a need for the military meant these educated elites devoted their time to efficiently supervising and maintaining the infrastructure of Japan's domains so irrigation, water supplies, tax collection, and a transportation system were, for the most part, effectively administered. A daimyo, or great lord, controlled each domain. In order to prevent daimyo opposition, the Tokugawa shoguns required daimyo to spend alternating years residing in Edo. A system of five national highways, originally

Green tea is an integral part of the Japanese agricultural economy. Uji, near Kyoto, is a famous area for its production. (Library of Congress)

constructed so that daimyo and their entourages could travel to and from Edo, had the positive unintended consequence of facilitating the exchange of goods and services through making most of Japan a national market.

The great highways, an efficient agricultural sector, the use of money throughout most of Japan by the mid Tokugawa years, and population growth in cities and market towns created national demand for agricultural and nonagricultural goods. A large number of peasants, especially in central Honshu, produced food surpluses. In rural areas, this overproduction of food led to two subsequent developments that further stimulated economic prosperity: the commercialization of agriculture and what economic historians identify as protoindustries, or small manufacturing enterprises. Commercialization of agriculture was a change in the scope of how agricultural goods were consumed as regions producing more food sold surpluses to consumers in towns and cities and in less fertile areas. Much of Japanese agriculture was transformed into a "for-profit" enterprise.

The development of rural protoindustries was also significant for the Tokugawa economy and for later economic growth because protoindustrialization brought infusions of investor capital, raw materials, and hired labor in efforts to produce products for regional or national consumption. Daimyo, samurai, and especially merchants from towns and cities in the latter Tokugawa years were using rural people to brew sake and soy sauce, produce silk, make paper, engage in small-scale iron- and metalworking, and process indigo and fertilizer. These goods were then sold throughout Japan. Protoindustrialization in the Tokugawa years meant that

Japanese women provided a cheap source of labor for the silk industry. This photograph of women working in a silk factory was taken sometime between 1935 and 1938. (Library of Congress)

throughout Japan, because they earned extra income through nonagricultural labor, many peasants achieved increased prosperity. Peasants also learned such work habits as time management that facilitated production, and families became accustomed to work not exclusively dependent on seasonal agricultural cycles. This better positioned many Japanese for work in the industrializing economy of the later Meiji years (1868–1912).

As readers of the history chapter are aware, Tokugawa Japan had a vibrant urban culture. This meant city- and town-based retail and wholesale sectors that interacted with peasants who supplied food and goods while also serving the needs of the urban consumers of a wide range of goods and services. Japan had a highly successful preindustrial economy by the late Tokugawa years. Per capita incomes had been rising for a century before the 1868 Meiji Restoration.

INDUSTRIALIZATION AND STATE-GUIDED CAPITALISM: 1868–1945

In the early 1870s, shortly after the Meiji Restoration, Japan's new political leadership faced the problem of Western imperialism. Japan's oligarchs quickly decided to build both a strong economy and a strong military in order to negotiate with Western Europe and the United States on an equal footing. Meiji leaders systematically studied various economic models and decided to adopt a system of government-directed capitalism based on recently unified Germany rather than the Anglo-American capitalist system.

SHIBUSAWA EIICHI (1840–1931)

Shibusawa is one of the most famous businessmen and philanthropists in Japanese history. Born of a family of small farmers in what is today Saitama Prefecture, Shibusawa's father had, through dealing in indigo, become the richest man in their village and was able to provide his son with a solid Confucian-based education. Leaving home, Shibusawa was made a samurai in a branch Tokugawa family and had a chance to visit the Paris Exposition shortly before the 1868 Meiji Restoration. When Shibusawa returned home, despite the Tokugawa connections, and because of Shibusawa's knowledge of the West, the government helped him start a trading company. Shibusawa was involved in organizing or founding 59 different businesses and manufacturing concerns ranging from textiles to chemical fertilizer to railways. He demonstrated exemplary ethics through all of this and practiced both Confucian and Christian principles through serving the nation by creating wealth and founding and donating to schools and homes for the elderly. Shibusawa regarded himself as a friend of the United States and was active in promoting positive Japan-U.S. relations.

Although private markets function in both systems, in government-directed capitalism, particularly in the case of heavy industry and exports, the state plays a larger role in determining what is produced and then allocates capital to private business through state control of the financial system. In government-directed capitalism, free trade is considered harmful much of the time, and politicians and bureaucrats exert more efforts than in the Adam Smith–influenced Anglo-American laissez-faire model to protect domestic industries from foreign competition. Most important, in the Japanese version of state-assisted capitalism, the economy was primarily viewed as existing to serve the interests of the nation and not the individual.

To aid industry, the Meiji government quickly established a national currency and banking system, which in turn greatly facilitated the flow of savings to the private sector. Meiji leaders were highly successful in establishing a modern national communications and transportation infrastructure by building telegraph and railroad lines. The government began such large-scale economic enterprises as coal mining and shipbuilding and later sold them to private interests. Meiji leaders also engaged in activities including educational improvements, export promotion, importation of foreign technology, and encouragement of private business.

Meiji Japan's successes in exporting and industrialization were particularly important because these actions helped to cause even greater economic success in the early 20th century. The Japanese were also fortunate in the early Meiji years in that raw silk, a large peasant industry that had roots in the Tokugawa years, enjoyed high worldwide demand. This demand, partially due to a disastrous European silk blight, subsequently enabled Japan to export massive amounts of silk and thereby

Japan was making great strides in heavy industry by 1925 as evidenced by this photograph of the interior of the Mitsubishi plant in Kobe. (Library of Congress)

raise the money to import equipment and raw materials for heavy industrialization. By the Meiji emperor's death in 1912, Japan was well on its way to developing heavy industry. Japan's economy grew despite a few setbacks and steadily improved during the Taisho period (1912–1926) and during the first years of the Showa period (1926–1989).

In the early part of the 20th century, World War I was a tremendous boon for the Japanese economy. Exports quadrupled and such important heavy industries as shipbuilding, iron, and steel, although still minor compared with textiles and agriculture, showed steady growth. Despite hard agricultural times and a world depression, the 1920s and 1930s brought continued long-term growth in Japanese manufacturing. In 1935, industrial production became, for the first time, more financially valuable to the economy than agriculture. Although textiles remained a leading export, such other industries as steel, rayon, and shipbuilding made major gains. By 1937, Japan possessed the world's largest merchant marine fleet. In the same year, largely because of the military buildup, total heavy industrial production for the first time surpassed light industry in value.

As the Japanese empire expanded into Manchuria and then China in the 1930s, government bureaucrats and private company employees gained experience, as had been the case earlier in the colonies of Taiwan and Korea, in joint economic planning and even in successful foreign investment. Although Japan incurred a tremendous human and economic cost because of World War II, it is important to understand that this catastrophe could not erase the human know-how in industrial production, management-labor relations, and government and business economic development that had been growing in Japan for decades. This knowledge would prove vitally important as Japan struggled to rebound from the worst disaster in the nation's history.

JAPAN BECOMES A WORLD ECONOMIC POWER: 1945–1973

Despite the experience and knowledge of its people, Japan was a devastated nation at the end of World War II. Millions of Japanese were without the basic necessities of life. Approximately one-fourth of all Japanese homes, as well as a high proportion of factories and shops, had been destroyed by the war. Japan was also stripped of its entire empire, which had been a vital source of low-cost raw materials, and of its investments in China and Manchuria.

Yet Japan, beginning just a few years later in the early 1950s, would grow its economy at an annual rate of approximately 10 percent for almost 20 years. By 1957, Japan's recovery from World War II was complete. Foreigners who came to Japan for the 1964 Tokyo Olympics returned to their respective countries with stories of the economic vitality of the Japanese. By the 1970s, these long-term Japanese economic growth rates were commonly being referred to as "an economic miracle." Even though in the early 1970s the Arab oil shocks and other factors ended Japan's whirlwind growth, the Japanese would still lead advanced nations in economic growth until the 1990s.

Perhaps the best way to understand the significance of the miracle for millions of ordinary Japanese is to examine the fortunes of one person and his family in the years before and during the high-growth era. Tanaka Sanosuke was a real-life Japanese blue-collar worker whom the late David Halberstam depicted in his award-winning book *The Reckoning*. Tanaka was born into a peasant family on a tiny farm near Tokyo in 1915. The Tanaka family lived a hard life. Both parents and children 11 years of age or older worked long hours in the rice paddies, but the family had to render four-fifths of their annual crops to the landowner. The Tanakas lived in a tiny one-room, thatch-roofed hut and usually ate only rice mixed with millet. During the occasional good times, the family could replace the hard millet with vegetables. On rare occasions, the Tanakas ate fish, but they could never afford meat.

The village of 500 where the Tanakas lived was almost entirely cut off from the outside world. As was true with most Japanese in the early and mid-20th century, the villagers owned no radios to keep up with the news or cars to visit other parts of Japan. In fact, young Tanaka was 8 years old before he saw his first gas-driven vehicle, a bus.

Although Tanaka dreamed of an education, poverty made this impossible. After completing the eighth grade and delivering coal for a small business in a neighboring village, in 1937 he moved to Yokohama and was hired as an assembly worker by Nissan (then Datsun), a new company that was part of a small Japanese automotive industry. Although Mr. Tanaka's pay was modest, he earned almost as much in a month with Nissan than he made in a whole year working in an earlier job. The young worker was the first member of his family to afford the purchase of a suit.

Eleven years later, after returning to Japan from military service during World War II and going back to work at Nissan, Tanaka's life seemed worse than before the war. For several years, this now father of two children could not even buy enough food to feed his family and was reduced to foraging the countryside for edibles. On Sundays during the first months after the war, Tanaka spent his day off hanging around American occupation troops, hoping to get work as a day laborer or at least scrounge food scraps the rich Americans threw away. Then the miracle years began.

By 1954, Nissan profits and salaries had grown, and Mr. Tanaka could purchase a small three-room house. It was a proud day for all five members of the family when they moved from their one-room house into these larger quarters. By the mid-1950s, Nissan and many other Japanese companies were already rebounding from the effects of World War II and exceeding prewar production levels.

As the years passed, the Tanaka family's standard of living steadily improved. In 1957, they acquired a television, and in 1963, the family joined the middle class through purchasing the ultimate status symbol: a first car.

The gains in wealth that the Tanakas and many other Japanese enjoyed in the 1950s and 1960s did not come easily. Japanese worked long and hard to rebuild their country and then take the economy to undreamed heights. In Mr. Tanaka's company, Nissan, for example, each year it seemed workers toiled harder than ever to meet increasing consumer demand.

Annual automobile production increases staggered the imagination. In 1957 Tanaka and his coworkers celebrated when the company attained the monthly production goal of 5,000 cars and trucks. At the time, virtually no company employee dreamed that three years later the monthly number would double to 10,000. Nissan was only one of many companies where people worked incredibly long hours and, by the early 1960s, were somewhat awestruck at the fruits of their labor. Japan had arrived as an economic power.

What were the reasons why Tanaka Sanosuke and millions of others like him experienced dramatic improvements in their material well-being during the two decades of the economic miracle? Economists concur that Japan's postwar economic rise can be attributed to a number of factors.

After World War II, the Japanese government continued to practice state-directed capitalism, but with the repudiation of militarism, economic development was *the* top national priority. Ministry of International Trade and Industry bureaucrats attempted to identify potential blue-chip industries and subsidize them while discouraging foreign and even domestic competition. Although scholars debate the effectiveness of these policies, during the miracle years several industries, such as steel and electronics, seemed to have benefited from initial government assistance and then gone on to be highly successful domestically and globally.

The U.S. occupation of Japan was beneficial to eventual economic growth. Although there was no Marshall Plan in Japan that directly funded rebuilding economic infrastructure, the Americans encouraged the Japanese government to initiate anti-inflation and prosavings policies that stabilized the yen and helped build capital for business expansion. The famous Article 9 of the U.S.-imposed Constitution forbidding the establishment of armed forces resulted in long-term economic benefits. Even today, Japan still spends a low percentage of national wealth on defense compared to other nations, thereby freeing resources for the civilian economy. The United States, as recounted in an earlier chapter, also unintentionally helped the Japanese economy through the American military's high demand for goods and services while fighting the Korean War. During the early postwar years, the United States and the United Kingdom played leading roles in creating a world climate much more conducive to free trade than in the past. This helped to create a favorable situation for Japanese exports in the United States and a number of other countries.

The miracle received a boost from Japan's shift from more resource-dependent to less-dependent industries. Before the 1950s, a number of leading Japanese industries, epitomized by textiles, were heavily dependent on expensive raw materials. By the latter part of the same decade, the Japanese were producing goods, such as cars, that required fewer imports. This made Japanese exports less expensive. Even though Japan's miracle was not export led and the country did not begin substantial exporting until the 1960s, when the export boom did occur in Japan, it made a strong economy even stronger.

Enhancements in both human capital (worker skill levels) and financial capital available for investment powered the economy. As late as 1950, 50 percent of Japan's population lived on farms. Japan's excellent schools and a high birthrate placed employers from the 1950s until the late 1960s in the enviable situation of having a large supply of young, well-educated, rural high school or junior high school graduates who were no longer needed on farms and who desired industrial employment. Japan's booming industries were also aided by the population's high personal saving rates. Government policies both provided savings incentives for Japanese and, for the most part, limited their saving and investing options to banks, which then made large amounts of funds available to companies for industrial expansion at low interest rates.

Cultural and structural aspects of Japan's postwar workplace environments also contributed to the nation's impressive economic growth. Japan has industrial rather than craft labor unions, which means management negotiates with one labor union rather than several. This form of union system encourages efficient use of human resources through facilitating communication between management and labor.

The so-called lifetime employment system has been cited as another cause of the miracle. In Japan, beginning with a few experiments before World War II but becoming widespread in the 1950s, many firms institutionalized the practice of giving permanent positions to both white-collar employees as well as many blue-collar workers. The rationale behind this practice, which still continues, has been that permanent employees will be more loyal to the company and also more productive because their job security is guaranteed. Despite the misconceptions of some foreigners that everyone in Japan is guaranteed employment, formal permanent employment has traditionally been largely a male privilege and is primarily limited to large companies in the private sector. Government employees in Japan as well as most other developed countries usually have stable long-term employment prospects.

Whether or not lifetime employment is extended to workers, societal beliefs that firms should take care of employees and government policies supporting employee retention have caused employees in businesses of all sizes to be more reluctant to lay off Japanese workers than is true in the United States. This Japanese cultural propensity was a positive force in the high-economic-growth years, as was a corporate "welfare" system in which the larger companies provided subsidized rental housing for single workers, annual employee bonuses, and special financial benefits from affiliated banks. Harmony within Japanese firms was also promoted by a seniority system that provided virtually automatic pay raises that were usually based on age and/or the number of years an individual worked for the company.

Also, Japanese manufacturing companies pioneered "quality control circles," a worker-participatory decision-making system that dramatically improved the quality of manufactured products and captured the attention of businesses worldwide. Quality control circles are groups of 6 to 12 workers in the same assembly section who meet regularly to identify, discuss, and pass on to management possible innovations for improvement of efficiency and product quality. In the late 1940s and early 1950s, W. E. Deming, an American statistician and college professor, after unsuccessfully attempting to convince American corporate managers to involve assembly workers in production decisions, traveled to Japan for a series of lectures. A number of large Japanese companies during the miracle years, beginning with Toyota Motor Corporation, adopted Deming's idea of quality control circles.

Today the Japanese have made the late W. E. Deming and quality control circles famous all over the world. Many large Japanese companies consistently produce fine manufactured goods because millions of ordinary workers in quality control circles formulate useful suggestions on how to improve work processes or product quality, and these are adopted by management. It is not unusual for such multinational companies such as Toyota and Hitachi to receive more than a million suggestions each year and to adopt the majority of these.

Japan's climb to world economic leadership was also greatly abetted by the domestic and foreign postwar political situation. Since its inception in 1955, with two exceptions, the probusiness Liberal Democratic Party elected all of Japan's prime ministers. Thus, the Japanese enjoyed a stable domestic political situation with a party in leadership that unquestionably ranked economic development as the major national goal. U.S. involvement in the Cold War also indirectly benefited the Japanese economy. U.S. government officials considered Japan, with its close proximity to China, the Korean Peninsula, and the then Soviet Union, to be so strategically important that it largely ignored questionable Japanese trade policies in return for loyalty in the long superpower confrontation. Therefore, Japan was able to exclude many foreign products while selling its own products in other countries without garnering extensive foreign, and especially American, criticism.

Despite Japan's good fortune and beneficial government policy, the economic miracle would not have occurred without the incredible hard work of Japanese of

HONDA SOICHIRO (1906–1991)

Honda was unusual in postwar Japan in that he built Honda Motor Corporation into a world famous corporation despite his humble background that included only an elementary education and no establishment connections. He was also independent, a nonconformist, and not reticent about speaking his mind. Born in Shizuoka Prefecture and the son of a blacksmith, after finishing school Honda left his small town and moved to Tokyo to become an apprentice mechanic. In 1928, he returned to Hamamatsu in his home prefecture and organized a company that manufactured piston rings. He also raced cars and developed a deep interest in motorcycles. In the mid-1940s, Honda designed and manufactured a small engine that was attachable to a bicycle. In 1948, he established Honda Motor Company, which manufactured motorcycles, and within a decade it was the world's leading motorcycle manufacturer. Honda then turned his attention to automobiles but had to fight the Japanese government for permission to compete with such major established firms as Toyota and Datsun (now Nissan). Although Honda automobile sales were small in the 1960s, by the late 1970s the company was competitive in the United States and today ranks in the top five companies in the world in automobile production. Honda Soichiro consistently attracted press attention because he was talkative and generally did not behave in ways that were typical for Japanese businessmen. He dressed casually, was considered flamboyant, and most interestingly, promoted executives based on their ability and not seniority, making him ahead of his time in corporate Japan.

all walks of life and the fierce competitiveness and innovative entrepreneurship of businesspeople. During most of the miracle years, Japanese workers led the world in annual number of hours worked. Successful Japanese corporate leaders were intensely competitive at home and abroad, pursuing economic success with extremely high levels of dedication. Honda Motor Company founder, the late Honda Soichiro, made this statement at the time he established his company: "If my company becomes bankrupt because of the rate at which I expand my plant, the plant itself will remain to be used for the development of Japanese industry. So I will take the risk" (Allen 1981, 234). This devotion to both economic growth and Japan's welfare encompassed in Honda's words symbolized a national spirit during the miracle years that served to help make Japan's economy a world leader today.

RESPONSE TO GLOBALIZATION: 1973 TO THE PRESENT

The Japanese economic miracle ended in 1973 when some Arab nations embargoed oil due to their opposition to American and allied Middle Eastern policies and energy prices subsequently rose throughout the developed world. Still, Japan enjoyed the highest average annual growth rates for a developed country all through the 1970s and 1980s. By the 1980s, Japan then occupied second place only to the United Kingdom as a foreign investor in the United States and trailed only Canada as a U.S. trading partner. The United States was (and still is) the leading foreign investor in Japan, making the U.S.-Japan economic relationship one of the most important bilateral business and financial relationships in the world. Americans were buying enormous amounts of such high-profile Japanese-produced goods as automobiles and stereos.

Because the major developed economies were incurring merchandise trade deficits with Japan in the 1980s, they pressured the Japanese not only to open their markets but also to raise the value of the yen, which had been artificially low for some time. The Americans and Europeans hoped that a higher yen would help their trade deficits by making exports to Japan cheaper and Japanese imports more expensive. In the 1985 Plaza Accord, five major industrialized nations—the United Kingdom, the United States, West Germany, France, and Japan—increased the value of the yen, thereby threatening Japan's export-sector growth.

The Japanese government responded a short time later by lowering interest rates and substantially increasing the money supply in order to prevent the value of the yen from rising so high as to inhibit exports and reduce domestic economic activity. This action led to an increase in bank loans and an economic bubble that caused rapid and astronomical rises in the prices of stocks and especially real estate. After the Ministry of Finance, fearing inflation, raised interest rates in 1990, the bubble burst and Japan's real estate prices, which had risen in value to four times the value

The yen is the basic Japanese currency. This 1000 yen note series, printed before 2004, features the famous author, Natsume Soseki. (Corel)

of U.S. real estate, collapsed and the stock market quickly lost about half its former value. Japanese real estate also plummeted in value. Japan's banks were left with an unspecified but staggering amount of bad loans.

Although what occurred in 1990 was immediately triggered by mistaken government monetary policies, the bursting of the assets bubble was prolonged because of more deep-rooted structural defects in Japan's economy. Japan, although far from economically collapsing, experienced more than a decade of relatively hard times compared to the rest of the postwar period. The 1990s and the first few years of the 21st century were marked by several recessions despite very low interest rates, record post-occupation unemployment rates, low and, at times, negative annual economic growth rates, and a major crisis of confidence on the part of both businesses and consumers.

The 1990s economic malaise affected all sectors of the economy, but perhaps what was most striking was the blow suffered by Japan's manufacturers. At the end of 1997, industrial production barely exceeded 1990 levels. The Japanese economy lost 1 million manufacturing jobs between 1992 and 1996 and continued to lose manufacturing jobs for the rest of the decade. Such Japanese blue-chip industries as Toshiba, Hitachi, and Nippon Electronic Corporation (NEC) as well as many other manufacturing firms suffered (Katz 1998, 10).

The economy began to recover from this long-term downturn only in 2003. By that time, the Japanese government was making significant progress in stabilizing the financial system and banks. Also, businesses throughout Japan were cutting costs in an effort to avoid bankruptcy or to become profitable again. Since then, for the most part, annual growth rates have returned to what would be considered normal for a developed country, Japanese enterprises reporting favorable business conditions have outnumbered those reporting unfavorable situations for several recent years, unemployment has declined to acceptable levels, and exports have increased. However, the Japanese economy is in the process of a broad structural transformation from what existed during the miracle years. This transformation is probably most vital for Japan's continued prosperity but also promises to change the larger culture in substantial ways.

Most economists believe that Japan's previously highly successful economy faltered in the 1990s because global and domestic economic circumstances had drastically changed. Increased globalization meant more intense competition between multinational corporations. Firms that could quickly lower a wide range of costs to meet the competition had advantages in the new economy. A wide range of economists and policy makers agreed that because of too much government direction, subsidies, and overregulation, Japan's economy was not well-positioned to meet these challenges.

During the miracle years and beyond, Japan faced relatively little economic competition from Europe and most of Asia. The U.S. government considered Japan so valuable an ally in the Cold War that it gave, with some exceptions such as the "voluntary" automobile export limitations of the early 1980s, relatively low priority to Japan's significant inroads into a few American markets. When the Japanese economy was experiencing its most dramatic growth, the global information technology revolution had not yet occurred. Business decision-making time horizons

By the 1970s and 1980s, Japan's successes in the American auto market created consternation among both US automobile management and the United Auto Workers. (Library of Congress)

were slower, which meant that government and business could be deliberate in strategy consultations without overly worrying about foreign competition.

Then globalization brought dramatic change. By the end of the 1980s, Japan was contending with new European competition as well as competition from such Asian countries as South Korea, Taiwan, and Singapore. The Cold War's end meant that the United States, apparently freed from that profound national security concern, began to pay even more attention to economic competitiveness and to issues such as trade deficits with Japan.

In the 1990s, American businesses and companies began to exhibit dramatic growths in productivity and flexibility because the private sector was free to initiate an information technology revolution. In the early part of the 1990s, such newly industrialized Asian countries as South Korea were now also competing with the Japanese in manufacturing computer chips, stereos, and automobiles. Often hindered by government regulation, Japanese companies lost ground to the United States and other countries. Japanese top-down capitalism, with its myriad regulations and cartels for specific sectors of the economy, made flexible responses to foreign competition and entrepreneurship difficult.

In order to regain economic momentum, Japan needed widespread structural economic reform in a number of areas including banking, financial and capital markets, public works, employment practices, technology, regulation, state-run enterprises, higher education, productivity, and international trade and investment. Many of these reforms would have the effect of moving parts of the economic system away from the old government-directed capitalism and more in the direction of a system

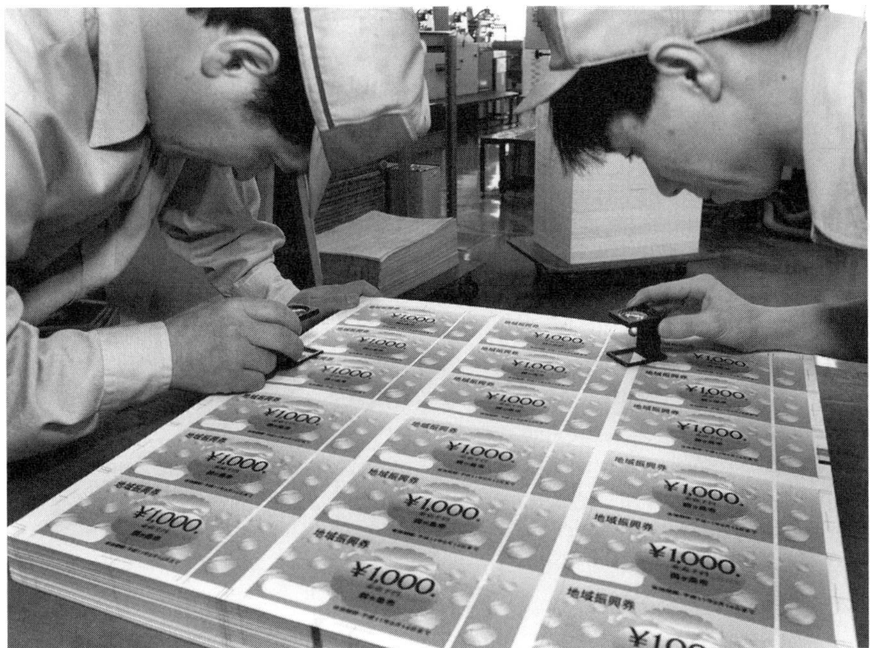

The government tried many strategies to end Japan's 1990s economic malaise. Here printing company workers check government-distributed shopping vouchers that would be distributed. (AP/Wide World Photos)

similar in many ways to what was formerly known as the Anglo-American model but now, in an era of globalization, has come to be known as neoliberalism. Neoliberal economies are characterized by more private-sector freedom and less government regulation. Reform efforts gathered steam during Japan's economic stagnation years, and enough substantial progress has been made that Japan's economy has recovered from the doldrums of the 1990s and the ensuing few years.

The problem of bad, nonperforming bank loans to questionable commercial borrowers that became evident after the real estate collapse was in large part caused by government monetary policies and by bankers who were encouraged by the Ministry of Finance to make loans. Bank officials also often based loans to private borrowers on such noneconomic reasons as common friendship ties or previous university or other long-term relationships. The solution to the bank loan problem was slow going until 1998, took until 2004 to largely solve, and included a variety of measures such as bank mergers, some bank closings, regulatory changes and tougher investigation, accounting practices, and monitoring. Prime Minister Koizumi, who provided much-needed stability and national leadership from 2001 until 2006, took on one of the biggest drags on the Japanese economy, the government-run Postal Savings Bank.

The government-run Postal Savings Bank—which possessed approximately $3 trillion worth of U.S. assets, about 30 percent of all Japan's household assets, 35,000 offices, and 260,000 employees—performed the dual role of Japan's largest savings bank and largest life insurer (Lincoln 2007, 34). This financial institution is one of the most affluent in the world. The Postal Savings Bank deposits, excluding insurance assets, are three times as valuable as deposits in the largest U.S. bank (Progressive Policy Institute 2006). The money that Japanese savers and life insurance customers put into the bank was funneled through the Ministry of Finance to a variety of government programs, which often resulted in unnecessary public works projects that benefited the construction industry but generally hurt the economy by diverting capital from more productive uses and subsidizing an already noncompetitive and inefficient industry. As discussed in a previous chapter, Koizumi successfully challenged a wide array of public and private special interest groups and began the process to transform this massive government agency into a public corporation that would make loan and investment decisions based on market forces and not politics.

As Japan continues the process of economic liberalization, some of the most profound transformations that have already begun and will continue involve the reconfigurations and more efficient use of a variety of resources, and it is to this topic that we now turn.

NATURAL RESOURCES OVERVIEW

Although readers of the earlier section of this chapter as well as chapter 2 are familiar with the term "economic miracle," which describes Japan's high-growth years (mid-1950s–early 1970s), in some ways the real miracle is that the Japanese were able to become the second-richest major nation on earth despite the fact that they have almost no natural resources when compared with most of the rest of the world. In Asia, only Singapore could lay claim to having fewer natural resources than Japan. Japan's natural resources predicament and its economic effects will become clearer in what follows. Those who are particularly interested in this subject should also read chapter 1.

Primary Resources: Agriculture, Timber, Mining, and Fishing

Food supply is the most critical resource for any economy, and 2004 Japanese government statistics indicate that only 12.7 percent of land in the archipelago can be used for agriculture. The rest of the Japanese islands are either too densely populated, too mountainous, or in the case of a substantial part of Hokkaido, too cold for productive agriculture. The agricultural land that is utilized is intensively cultivated, and Japanese farmers are highly productive. Because of agricultural efficiency, Ministry of Agriculture, Forestry, and Fisheries (MAFF) data indicate that as recently as 1980, Japan's farmers could provide 53 percent of national food supplies. By 2005, Japanese farmers could produce only an estimated 40 percent of the food Japanese consumed. In 2005, Japan's Ministry of Economics, Trade, and Industry data illustrated that Japanese must now depend on 10 nations (the United States and China being leading providers) and a number of other countries to make up the food supply gap. Rice, whose production is heavily subsidized by the government, constitutes one of the few widely consumed agricultural products where the Japanese are self-sufficient.

Japan is even less self-sufficient in its need for timber products than for food. Until the first years of the 1960s, Japan's forestry industry was able to meet consumer demand, but with increasing economic growth, the situation changed dramatically as demand increased for a wide variety of timber products ranging from wood for construction to paper. According to MAFF, by 1980 Japan could produce only about 32 percent of the timber it needed, and by 2005 the nation's forestry industry managed to supply 20 percent of the nation's demand for timber. Japan does have a mining industry, but its output was responsible for a miniscule 0.16 percent of the gross domestic product (GDP) at the end of the 20th century.

Japan is still a major fishing nation, but the industry has declined because of diminishing ocean fish supplies, difficult environmental conditions, effective competition from foreign fisheries, and changes in international regulations. In 1960, Japan was the world's leading fishing nation, and according to Japan's Foreign Press Center, 1.5 percent of the workforce was employed in the industry. By 2006, only 0.3 percent of the workforce was still employed in fishing enterprises. United Nations statistics indicate that by 2004, Japan had dropped to fifth among the world's fishing nations, with world-leading China catching more than four times as much fish that year as Japan. Because seafood is exceptionally important in the Japanese diet, Japan now is the world's leading importer of fish.

Natural Resources: Energy

Ample energy supplies are critical to the survival of any economy and especially one as developed as Japan's. Japan is highly dependent on foreign sources for its energy supply. International Energy Agency statistics indicate that in 2004 imports constituted about 82 percent of the national energy supply, and approximately 99 percent of oil consumed in Japan was imported. In the same year, Japan obtained approximately 90 percent of its oil from the Middle East, leaving the Japanese vulnerable to geopolitical events that might disrupt supply in that region of the world. The government began stockpiling oil after the first world oil crisis in 1973. Japanese Agency for Natural Resources and Energy statistics indicate that as of January 2007, the government had enough oil stockpiled for 177 days if supplies were disrupted. Serious efforts have been underway for some time to reduce oil as an energy source. According to government and international statistics published by Japan's Foreign Press Center in 2007, while Japan's reliance on oil as a share of all energy sources remains higher at 50 percent than those of the United States or Western European countries, in 1973, 78 percent of all the nation's energy was produced through oil.

In 2006, Japan's government announced a new energy strategy based on both economic and security considerations. By 2030, targets have been set that include reducing oil to 40 percent or less as a source for all energy needs, reducing Japan's transportation sector's reliance on oil as a source of energy from 100 percent to 80 percent, reducing the costs for solar energy development, and developing nuclear power plants so that energy source will account for 40 percent of the nation's power generation. In addition to the political volatility of the region of the world that supplies Japan with most of its oil, international economic developments, most notably increasing demand for oil by China and to a lesser extent India, also motivated the Japanese government to refocus on reducing oil supplies. In 2008, China passed Japan as the second-largest importer of oil in the world. Increasing need for oil by these growing economies will likely drive oil prices even higher for the Japanese. As of the fall of 2008, a liter of gasoline (slightly less than a quarter of a gallon) was selling for 126 yen, or about $1.20, at Japanese gasoline stations.

Eighty two percent of Japan's electrical power output, according to the Agency for Natural Resources and Energy, is produced by nuclear, coal, and natural gas–powered plants, so even though Japan must import large amounts of natural gas and coal, oil dependence has been reduced. However, when international comparisons are considered regarding energy dependence in general and oil dependence specifically, it is apparent that Japan, because of a lack of energy resources, will be dependent to some extent on other nations for imported energy for the foreseeable future. Statistics published by Japan's Foreign Press Center that are compilations of private-sector, government, and international agency sources indicate that as of 2004, Japan was the most dependent country on imported energy of seven major industrialized nations, including the United States, Germany, and China. When oil in particular is considered, only the Republic of Korea (ROK; 99.6 percent) exceeded Japan's dependence (99.1 percent) on foreign sources.

Labor Resources: A Workforce Overview

Japan's almost 67 million workers are highly educated by world standards, and the distribution of their employment conforms in general to what would be expected in a developed country. As mentioned earlier, less than 5 percent of all Japanese are employed in primary (mining, fishing, forestry, agriculture) industries. As of the beginning of 2007, according to economist Richard Katz, approximately 17 percent of all Japanese workers are employed in manufacturing enterprises, with the majority of workers (69 percent) in services industries (Katz 2008, 8). Even though the majority of Japanese workers, as is true in other highly developed economies, are employed in services, a substantially higher percentage of Japanese are in manufacturing than in the United States, where only 10.2 percent of workers are employed in the secondary sector (AFL-CIO 2007). Comparative statistics from Japan's Institute of Labor indicate that in 2005, 18.2 percent of workers belonged to labor unions. This was a higher percentage than in the ROK or the United States, where unionization rates ranged from 12 to 12.5 percent of unionized workers. However, the percentage of Japanese workers in unions was much lower than in Western European countries like the United Kingdom and Germany, where 29 and 26 percent, respectively, of the workforce was unionized.

In most of the postwar years, Japan has enjoyed, even during the tough 1990s, low unemployment rates compared to other developed countries, particularly those in Western Europe. In 1990, the Japanese unemployment rate was 2.1 percent, according to the MHLW. Japan's unemployment rate rose steadily during the economic problems of the 1990s, and by 2002, 5.4 percent of the Japanese workforce was unemployed. As Japan's economy recovered, it dropped to 4.1 percent by 2006. MHLW comparative data for the same time frame is 4.6 percent for the United States and approximately 10 percent each for France and Germany. As of the publication of this book, Japan's unemployment rate, as is true of most other nations, is rising again due to the 2008 world economic situation.

Japan is comparable to other developed countries in the percentages of women who work outside the home. Between 1980 and 2006, MHLW data indicated that the number of employed female women grew by 9.2 million or 68.2 percent. In 2006 women made up well over 41 percent of the nation's workers. Explanatory factors for this change include women's desire to work and improved opportunities as a result of equal employment laws, enhanced family leave laws, and more educated women than in earlier times. Japan now has about the same percentages of women working outside the home as most Western European countries and the ROK but still trails the US.

With a shrinking workforce because of population decline and the need to more effectively use human resources, the question of the role of women in Japan's economy is more important for the nation than in the past. Approximately 48 percent of all adult women are employed outside the home, and for women ages 25–34, workplace participation has grown from 49 percent in 1980 to 68 percent at present. Although significantly fewer numbers of women earn university degrees in Japan in such technical fields as engineering, the number of women who complete higher education is roughly comparable to the number of men. However on average, Japanese wives in two earner households' wages are so modest, they account for substantially lower percentages of family incomes when compared to two-earner households in other developed countries. One reason that Japanese women earn so little income from work is that higher percentages of Japanese women work part time compared to Western European or American women. Another reason for the low earnings of women is that despite a more than 20-year-old equal employment law, the Japanese workplace, partially because of traditional attitudes and also because of company employment tracks that favor permanent employees, is still not effectively utilizing women.

One traditional term, *kanai*, that Japanese men use when referring to their wives literally means "inside the house," and usually, even until the 1970s, only poor women and those of questionable reputations worked outside the home. During that decade, women were still supposed to married by age 25 and have two or perhaps three children. During the 1980s, Japanese attitudes had changed to the point that it was socially acceptable if middle-class women worked part-time, and many, because fertility rates had dropped, were in a position to seek outside employment. By the 1990s, massive numbers of women were entering the Japanese workplace. Even so, a large number of married women still stop working when they have young children and return when their children are in school. The overall female workforce participation rate slightly dropped from 50 percent in 1980 to 48 percent now because Japan's overall population, including women, is aging (Katz 2007, 7).

Although estimates vary greatly because it is difficult to collect precise data on part-time employees, women, especially part-timers without tertiary educations, often do the same work in Japan as their male counterparts but earn substantially less money. MHLW 2006 statistics indicate that in workplaces employing more than 30 people, on average, women's earnings are about 60 percent those of men. This Japanese pattern is in contrast to much smaller salary gaps between women and men doing the same work in the United States and other developed countries. Despite recent improvements and such long-standing exceptions as in the education and fashion industries, it is still difficult for female graduates of universities to obtain salaries commensurate with their educational levels. The majority of large Japanese companies do not make permanent managerial positions available to women university graduates because of a belief that after becoming mothers, women will devote more time to child rearing than work if they continue employment at all. There does seem to be some progress, however, in the earning power of women under 30 relative to men, as recent statistics indicate women in this age cohort now earn 86 percent of the hourly wages of their male peers. This progress may be primarily due to the fact that fewer women in this age group are married than has been the case in the past, and divorce rates have risen. One-third of all 30-year-old women are now single.

Japan's effort to escape the economic doldrums of the 1990s also affected women in the workplace. Approximately 60 percent of all "freeters" (mostly younger people during the 1990s who began a pattern of intentionally seeking a series of temporary jobs) are women (Miyamoto 2006, 23–26). Also, a substantial portion of women who work full-time with one company are contract rather than permanent employees. As is the case with anyone regardless of gender, people in these job categories usually have lower salaries than permanent employees, and health and pension benefits are low to nonexistent. Women freeters who are unmarried are particularly vulnerable. They often don't have a second breadwinner on whom to rely, and because they are women, it will be even more difficult for them to move into permanent employment than for their male counterparts.

As noted, *the* major problem with the Japanese workplace and women is that many business leaders in major and medium-sized firms still do not even consider women for regular-employment management-level positions. Also, unlike in the United States and several other developed nations, Japanese management has been reluctant to experiment with flexible work schedules and job configurations that allow ambitious and talented women to have both children and a career.

Many working females are typically young, unmarried women, for whom the Japanese have a nickname that may be translated as "office ladies." These young women do menial work for a corporation for five to six years after they graduate from high school, junior college, or even a university and upon marrying are expected to leave the company. Traditionally, male Japanese view these work years for a woman as a time she can learn about the world before settling down. Office ladies are usually not given meaningful work but instead are expected to create a pleasant environment for the permanent, mostly male employees by making and serving tea and running errands. Many executives in Japanese companies feel obligated to help their young male employees find wives. Management often views the pool of office ladies as a good source of brides for these young men. Women are an underused resource in Japan's economy.

Despite substantial remaining economic barriers for women, there are signs of progress. When starting salaries are compared, Japanese women with graduate degrees receive approximately equal pay as their male counterparts while university graduates who are women are receiving about 10 percent less than their male counterparts. Males with high school educations received about a 9 percent higher starting salary than their female counterparts (*Facts and Figures* 2007). Although statistics are unavailable, the salary differential in favor of men in the private sector probably becomes even higher later in working careers since a larger percentage of women than men take extended time off from working when they have small children and because of a glass ceiling that still exists at management levels in Japanese companies. Although change is occurring, it takes place in the face of cultural traditions that date back to the introduction of Confucianism.

Two segments of the Japanese workforce, older workers and the young, also face some particular problems that are more pronounced in Japan than in other developed countries. Senior citizens who are over 65 constituted almost 20 percent of the population in 2005. This number is expected to rise to 28 percent of the population in 2020 and approximately 30 percent of the population in 2030. At the same time, percentages of young people annually entering the Japanese workforce are steadily dropping. Children constitute less of a share of Japan's population year after year. Currently, children who are 14 years old or younger are a smaller percentage of the population than people over 65 (Lincoln 2007, 36–37).

This decline in young workers and increase in retirees presents significant problems for such social programs as pensions and health insurance since unless significant increases in immigrants or birthrates occur, fewer numbers of workers will be funding larger numbers of senior citizens each year.

In the postwar years, Japan's mandatory retirement has always been lower than a number of other developed countries; MHLW statistics indicate that as late as 1960 the mandatory retirement age for approximately 77 percent of Japanese workers was between 50 and 59. Since 1990, the mandatory retirement age for most Japanese workers has been 60, and this was still true for 90.5 percent of workers as of 2006. The combination of inadequate government and private-sector pension funds and increasingly long life spans has meant that larger percentages of Japanese workers, particularly males, remain in the part-time workforce at 65 or older than is the case in the United States or Western Europe. Comparative MHLW 2006 data indicate that almost 29 percent of Japanese males 65 or older still had at least part-time jobs compared to 19 percent of their American, 9 percent of their UK, 5 percent of their German, and less than 2 percent of their French counterparts. The problem is now compounded by the aging of Japanese baby boomers, 6.8 million of whom began to retire in 2007. In response, the government has enacted laws mandating that employers either raise the retirement age to 65, abolish mandatory retirement, or rehire in part-time positions formerly full-time employees who have retired. More than 90 percent of employers are responding to the new laws by hiring their retired employees as part-timers. Previously, retirees had to find jobs elsewhere than the firm where they had worked, so the new option usually provides more attractive part-time options for the average senior employee. The 1990s transition of Japan's employment structure from a situation where many workers had either permanent employment or full-time positions to a more market-based system that depends on more part-time employees than was the case in the past poses even more widespread challenges for young people than for their older counterparts. This is discussed in detail in the next section.

The Transformation of Employment

Around April 1 of each year all over Japan, induction ceremonies for employees entering new firms are conducted with much fanfare. This account of an induction ceremony at NEC is typical of what occurs in large and medium-sized firms: The "entering the company" ceremony, or *Nyu Sha Shiki*, for 1,400 recently hired young people is about to begin. Many Japanese consider such a ceremony as this one to be a profound moment for the individuals honored, the company, and society. There is the attendant feeling that if group harmony and teamwork are to be promoted, young employees must be celebrated by this ritual.

All the new inductees are required to be present at 8:25 A.M., before the ceremony, and roll is taken. The ceremony begins promptly at 9:00 A.M. with new inductees and assembled corporate dignitaries singing the company song accompanied by the corporate band. After speeches by corporate officials, including the president, each new member reaches under his or her seat and opens a packet that contains business cards, a corporate lapel badge, and a 520-page textbook containing all kinds of information about the company, company expectations, and suggestions for employees. Then a young, new female inductee, chosen to represent the entering class, comes forward and recites the new company member pledge, which is a promise to improve the daily lives of people with electronics and communication. Finally, the president of the company leads the entire assembly in the company oath (Reid 1999, 153–155).

The entrance ceremony epitomizes the Japanese notion of company as family. Japan is famous for being a society that places high importance on the group, and this notion has historically been as true in the world of work as in other aspects of Japanese life. In Tokugawa times and even before, artisans took in apprentices, or *deshi*, and if they proved worthy gave them status similar to family members in the Japanese household, or *Ie*. A few industrial concerns were experimenting with permanent employment for skilled blue-collar workers around the time of World War I. Companies that tried this tactic during this time did it for pragmatic reasons; rapid industrialization meant rapidly rising wage rates for machinists, mechanics, and others with technical skills. The promise of a lifetime job could keep a worker in high demand from leaving. However, the practice had cultural resonance in a group society.

During Japan's postwar high-growth years, permanent employment and the related seniority pay system became regular and much-touted parts of corporate Japan. Although permanent employment linked to seniority-based pay systems and entrance ceremonies are still part of Japanese life, the proportion of employees who can access "lifetime" and regular employment tied to guaranteed salary increases based on tenure with the firm has been in decline for more than a decade and a half. Throughout the high-growth years, these practices promoted teamwork within the company, discouraged office politics based on ambition for higher salaries, and contributed to the production of excellent goods and services.

In the early 1990s, many of the Japanese companies that suffered through years with low profits or even losses were operating in an economy characterized by low growth and faced increasingly intense domestic and foreign competition. Hiring large numbers of lifetime or regular employees each year threatened to bankrupt many firms.

At one point in the early 1990s, estimates of even some of Japan's most successful companies indicated that top management reported the number of surplus workers ranged from 5 percent to almost 20 percent. Foreign companies could downsize in bad years, but this was difficult for Japanese firms, so they initiated changes. Because the public and their elected representatives strongly endorsed the company-as-family concept, there were only a few well-publicized cases of actual situations where longtime employees of large firms lost their jobs. As discussed earlier, even before World War II a few companies were offering lifetime positions to new recruits. Even today, those Japanese who are hired by firms as so-called permanent employees will lose their jobs only if companies go bankrupt.

However, by the mid-1990s, the survival strategy that Japanese firms adopted was to hire many fewer regular employees and drastically increase the recruitment of part-time workers. These part-timers were paid much lower salaries and benefits than regular employees and could be laid off when particular businesses and industries faced hard times. Ministry of Internal Affairs and Communications statistics over a 15-year period indicate the number of regular employees in Japanese business declined from about 35 million to 34 million during a time when the number of potential job seekers was slowly growing, while the number of nonregular and part-time employees almost doubled, from almost 9 million to more than 16 million workers. As a result, many Japanese firms have managed to survive and even make high profits while average pay in private-sector companies failed to increase for 8 consecutive years during the time for which statistics were compiled.

This change in the use of human resources in the workplace that began in the 1990s resulted in a new word as well as work pattern, "freeter," a term that is a combination of the English word "free" and the German word for worker, *Arbeiter*. A recent government estimate indicates there are more than 2 million young people, most of whom are in their twenties and many of whom have university educations, who are freeters. Freeters earn a living by changing from one part-time or temporary job to another, and the jobs pay less and offer fewer opportunities than regular employment. Many of the freeters are now approaching or in their thirties, and even though companies are hiring more full-time workers again, freeters lack job skills that are often gained through regular employment. Also, the fact that they are older than other applicants coming out of school and seeking employment means freeters are less attractive to employers because the seniority system, which can be based on age as well as time, means management would theoretically be obligated to pay the older freeter looking for permanent employment a higher salary than the younger recruit. The national government is concerned about the freeter problem and has established a special council to provide assistance in job training for them. As noted earlier, it is estimated that 60 percent of all freeters are women, who have historically experienced institutional gender discrimination in most Japanese workplaces (Miyamoto 2006, 23).

Japanese firms that cut back on hiring full-time employees in order to survive the "lost decade," as many in Japan label the 1990s and the early part of this century, are not the only example of the reconfiguration of human resources in Japan in the face of a changed economy. Japanese human resources experts report and statistics confirm that by the year 2000, substantially more employees with such desirable university degrees as engineering were more narrowly focused on their own careers and much more willing than in the past to leave one firm for more lucrative employment in another firm. One study indicates that the job turnover rate among employees in their first three years with a firm was about 20 percent in 1992 but had risen to 35 percent by 2006, with no sign that the trend was reversing. This pattern has both positive and potentially negative effects for Japan's economic health (Jo 2006, 18–22).

More employees who are willing to change jobs to advance themselves could very well boost productivity and also give firms a chance to hire skilled people in a much more flexible manner than in the past. This new trend, as does the strategy of hiring part-time rather than full-time employees, helps Japanese companies compete on a more level playing field with foreign competition. However, the substantial number of freeters who move from job to job as well as the rise in career-focused rather than organizationally loyal workers puts the traditional Japanese company-as-family model, and the societal stability that it created, considerably at risk. How significant will company entrance ceremonies remain given the changing environment?

There are already indications as well that the freeter problem is increasing income inequalities in Japan since permanent employees are considerably more affluent on average than part-timers. Having too many part-time workers also reduces national government revenues for maintaining the expected level of social services that are sorely needed in a country with a rapidly aging population since the government collects less tax revenues from part-time than full-time workers. Also, the aging of the Japanese population along with the substantial present and projected future numbers of nonworking to working Japanese threatens to increase a recently growing gap between rich and poor. In order for Japan to increase or improve existing affluence levels, barring massive immigration or dramatic increases in birthrates, almost all economists concur that increasing worker productivity is the only strategy open to a nation with fewer and fewer workers and a growing elderly population.

Improving Productivity

Often when one hears the word "resources," such natural resources as oil, copper, or perhaps agricultural land come to mind. Although an extensive discussion of these kinds of resources is included in chapter 1, Japan is by world standards a poor nation in nonhuman resources. Japan's greatest resource is its workforce, which is, by world standards, highly skilled.

Labor productivity, or the amount of goods or services a worker can produce in a given amount of time, is a vital ingredient in any economy. Productivity or the lack of it is a key determinant of standards of living in any country. Japan is one of the world's richest countries because, like the United States and Western Europe, the workforce is well educated, possesses high skill levels, and works with large amounts of excellent equipment and machinery. Although Japanese workers, like their American and European counterparts, enjoy high salaries by world standards because they are productive, Japan is substantially less productive than the United States and several Western European countries in such important sectors of the economy as construction and services.

As noted, the "graying" of Japan and a shrinking overall population makes improving productivity a critical imperative for the nation. Studies indicate that in the next 20 years Japan's working-age population will shrink by about 16 percent compared to an overall population decline of 9 percent. Specifically, until 2025 the percentage of Japanese workers is expected to annually drop almost one percent faster than the general population (Lincoln 2007, 36–37). If increasingly fewer workers are creating goods and services in this environment, employees must produce higher quantities of output relative to the past to maintain or improve prosperity levels. If all kinds of taxes and not just income tax are considered, Japan already has relatively high tax rates. Its aging population will need more social security and health care in the future than ever before. If productivity doesn't improve at some point in time, future economic growth could be further jeopardized by the imposition of even higher levels of taxation.

Fundamental changes in Japan's economy mean that some traditional ways in which the Japanese bolstered productivity probably won't be options in strategies for future improvement. Throughout the 1980s, Japanese led developed nations in the annual number of hours worked, and Japan is still, along with South Korea and the United States, a world leader in this category. However, annual working hours in Japan are about 5 percent lower than was the case in 1990 because the increased number of part-time workers hired earlier is cumulatively putting in fewer total hours than was the case with Japanese employees when a higher percentage of the workforce was full-time. Also, education and training are critical in improving employee productivity. In the past, when the lifetime employment system was more pervasive than now, large companies had a strong incentive to constantly improve employee skills through in-house training. Now Japanese business is more dependent than in the past on educational institutions for what economists call the improvement of their employees' human capital.

Even though the Japanese face some daunting challenges, significant future improvements in labor and overall productivity are certainly possible. During the high-growth years and beyond, the Japanese were either the world leaders or near the top in average annual manufacturing productivity growth rates. Today, Japanese automobile and semiconductor companies, along with a number of other firms involved in international business, are some of the most productive companies in the world.

Still, when Japanese productivity rates are compared to other industrialized, developed countries over the last 10 to 15 years, a clear pattern emerges. Japan's manufacturing workers are 30 percent less productive on average than their American counterparts, who are world leaders. However, Japanese employee annual manufacturing productivity growth rates and already high manufacturing productivity levels place Japan somewhere among the top five nations in the world each year in manufacturing productivity. But Japan, because of low productivity among workers in services and distribution industries, tends to rank average at best and often below average in overall productivity when compared with other affluent nations.

The major root of Japan's productivity problem is the continued existence of the dual, or two-tiered, economy, a situation that has existed in Japan since the early part of the 20th century in one form or another. During the economic miracle years, Japan was making such massive improvements in manufacturing technology that a "rising tide," assisted by government redistribution of monies from productive to nonproductive sectors of the economy, "lifted all boats." The situation is different now.

The major drag on Japan's economy is unusual among the world's developed nations in that there is such a wide discrepancy between the high productivity levels of large industries that export and are thus exposed to intense foreign competition and the low productivity of manufacturing firms and entire sectors of the economy that sell only to the domestic market. Examples of industries and sectors of the economy that are clearly in the lower tier include those segments of Japanese manufacturing not exposed to the global market: food processing, construction, and much of retail and wholesale distribution. These industries in general suffer from low productivity levels, and most actually experienced productivity drops while the Japanese economy was improving after the lost decade.

Viable strategies for improving productivity in the lower tier of Japan's economy are also important because, as is the case in other highly developed economies, recently in Japan manufacturing jobs have been declining and service sector jobs increasing. Factory jobs have fallen since 1997 to 17 percent of all jobs while during the same period service jobs have risen from 26 to 34 percent of all employment (Katz 2007, 8). When the total output of workers in services, construction, distribution, and low-productivity manufacturing sectors is considered, the typical worker in the lower tier produces less than half the output of the average worker in the highly productive segment of the Japanese manufacturing sector. Employees in the lower tier of Japan's economy constitute 60 percent of the nation's workforce.

Human Capital Development

Although education is addressed more extensively in a future chapter, in an information economy the quality of education and training is crucial. Just as financial capital is needed to buy machines that make for more efficient production of goods or services, high levels of what economists call human capital, or the knowledge and skills workers possess, are crucial to productivity growth and national affluence. Japan has a tradition dating back to Tokugawa times and before of deep respect for education. One of the keys to the development of the Japanese economy during the Meiji years was the successful implementation of universal elementary education. During the American occupation, access to secondary and higher education was dramatically expanded. Today, Japanese literacy rates are more than 95 percent, and about the same number of the high school cohort graduates, compared to 89 percent of American students. Japanese mathematics education, especially important as a foundation for later technical training, ranks among the world's best. One leading scholar of Japanese education asserts that the typical Japanese graduates from high school with the same level of content knowledge as the average American who completes two years of college. Comparable percentages of Japanese and Americans go on to some form of postsecondary education. An extensive network of mostly private postsecondary vocational schools and public technical colleges provide advanced technical training, and the Japanese have, behind the United States, the second-largest university system in the developed world.

Still, throughout the 1990s and beyond, large numbers of the public as well as many business and political leaders increasingly felt, whether correctly or not, that the educational system was failing to meet the needs of the workplace. At the elementary and secondary levels, Japanese mathematics scores in international testing, while still quite high, fell behind such countries as Singapore and the ROK. According to Organization for Economic Co-operation and Development 2006 international test data, first-year Japanese high school students scored 14th out of 15 developed nations in reading comprehension. First-year students also indicated a lack of interest in their studies and typically did not read any books for pleasure. Also, increasing numbers of Japanese felt that the education system was too fact- and examination-orientated and did not promote the kind of critical thinking and creativity needed by future workers in an intensely globalized economy. During the 1990s, there were also much-publicized cases of student violence that led many to believe that young people were not receiving the kind of moral education that facilitates the development of a disciplined and principled workforce.

In response to these concerns in 2002, the Ministry of Education began to implement widespread educational reforms that officials labeled the most significant since World War II. In an attempt to develop better independent and critical thinkers, one-third of the national curriculum was eliminated, and Japanese students in grades 3–9 were required to take a course titled "Integrated Studies," in which they and their teachers jointly planned projects, field trips, and other hands-on activities. The long-term results of these reforms, which have been controversial since their inception, are impossible to determine at this time but indicate a deep societal concern about the adequacy of a heretofore impressive educational system for the new economic environment. The Japanese government has also recently initiated policy discussions focusing on ending public schoolteachers' iron-clad tenure protection, liberalizing teacher certification to attract talented and creative "outsiders" to education, and facilitating the hiring of school principals who have experience in the private sector and fields other than education. All of these proposed policy changes are primarily intended to more adequately address the larger question of how to develop a more effective future workforce.

Virtually all educational policy analysts, Japanese and foreign, agree that the one educational institution most in need of reform is the Japanese university, particularly in regard to shaping it to better meet the needs of the economy. Although about the same percentage of Japanese students as their American counterparts attend university, there is substantial evidence that the structure of the typical university causes most undergraduates to learn less than their counterparts in other countries. In Japan, the majority of students attend private universities because the national government has historically limited the supply of public universities relative to demand so that the more elite students qualify for low-cost, tax payer–subsidized education. Although some private institutions are top flight, most are inferior to public Japanese universities, and funding for professors, laboratories, and other facilities in private universities is modest at best compared to public universities.

Also, certain companies and government ministries tend to recruit from one or only a few public or private universities. In Japan, university entrance is primarily determined by examination, and job recruiters have traditionally not been as interested in students' majors as in what university they were able to enter. Most Japanese students tend to relax once they are admitted to a particular university and not apply themselves very diligently in their undergraduate years. Because professors are often not very demanding as a rule in many Japanese universities when compared to universities in a number of other developed countries, students can get away with not working hard—or learning much—and still graduate.

In the United States and other countries, university research and graduate programs often directly service the needs of business and industry. This has not been the case in Japan. For a variety of reasons, only a few Japanese university departments rank among world leaders in research, and Japanese industry has long complained that the private sector is not obtaining enough benefits from the nation's university system given the resources allocated to higher education. Graduate programs in Japan, particularly those for professionals instead of scholars, are still scarce compared to the United States. In fact, it is common practice in large Japanese companies to send bright young managerial employees to the United States for MBAs or graduate degrees in the sciences. The human capital levels of Japanese university graduates will improve considerably if higher education can be reformed.

On April 1, 2004, the Ministry of Education initiated a major reform intended to make the institution of higher education more beneficial to the economic needs of the nation. All 88 of Japan's public universities were turned into independent agencies. Also as a result of this policy, college faculty and staff at these universities no longer have the status of national civil servants with guaranteed jobs for life.

These sweeping reforms, specifically modeled after former British Prime Minister Margaret Thatcher's 1980s policies intended to introduce competition and flexibility in government universities, were designed to increase institutional autonomy and teaching productivity while at the same time developing financial transparency for national government assessment of institutional effectiveness. Former Prime Minister Koizumi, who aggressively pushed through the reforms, also believed in introducing market forces in higher education. A major goal of the higher educational reforms also has been to improve graduate and legal education through the initiation of a process whereby national universities competed with each other for government funds for research, the majority of which is intended to be specifically related to economic and scientific development. The Japanese reforms are creating some competition between higher educational institutions within a uniform regulatory framework, but it is still too early to tell if they will have the far-reaching effects that supporters claimed.

In a related development, the government-appointed Justice System Reform Council in 2001 moved from the undergraduate law major and called for the creation of three-year American-style law schools. This was a radical change from a legal system that changed little throughout the high-growth economy years. Because of a cultural distrust of both highly verbal people and the disharmony of an advocacy-oriented legal system, becoming an attorney has traditionally not been a highly popular profession in Japan. Perhaps even more important, until recently important sectors in the Japanese economy have been closed to foreign business, so legal expertise in contract law was not as crucial as is presently the case. Historically, the Japanese bar and Ministry of Justice kept the number of lawyers miniscule by maintaining an admission pass rate of 2 to 3 percent for the legal examinations. It was the 1960s before the number of attorneys throughout Japan surpassed 500 annually, which is fewer than Harvard Law School's annual graduating class. In 1990, 90 percent of Japan's cities and towns had only one attorney, but by 2004 the first of what are now 68 law schools were opening.

Japan, who still has only about 20,000 lawyers nationally, fewer per capita than most other developed countries, began to be hurt economically in the 1990s by this scarce human resource. As Japanese companies went bankrupt and struggled to restructure, there was an increasingly significant demand for bankruptcy attorneys and merger and acquisition specialists. Large financial institutions as well as foreign and domestic investors who needed legal assistance were frustrated by this impediment to business.

As Japan's economic system began to change from one that depended less on personal relations, whether between private companies who had historic ties or between government bureaucrats and business, and more on carefully worded contracts between strangers, the low supply of attorneys was a problem that had to be addressed. The Japanese bar is expected to increase annual admissions to the profession from the now 1,200 to 3,000 by 2010. The long-term goal is 50,000 attorneys in Japan by 2018. This particular kind of increase in human capital is for the most part a direct response to the requirements of a significantly changed economy (Stern 2006).

BUSINESS AND INDUSTRY: MANUFACTURING

Western industrialization began with the development of capitalist institutions in Europe in the 1500s, then evolved to more complex levels with the British industrial revolution beginning in the late 18th century, and culminated a century later in the industrial capitalist system of Europe and the United States. The Japanese had a much different experience in that the country quickly changed, between the years 1868 and around 1900, from a primarily agrarian-based economy to one with an already domestically important and growing industrial manufacturing sector.

During the rest of the 20th century, Japan further evolved into an economic world superpower, largely on the strength of manufacturing, and the Japanese experience constituted an economic development model for both other Asian economies and developing countries throughout the world. Because of Japan's rapid rise relative to the West and Japanese cultural propensities, Japan's manufacturing industries, while drawing from the West, are different than their European counterparts, and manufacturing is still more important to Japan's economy than is the case in the United States and some of the more advanced European economies that have moved further toward a "postindustrial" economy. In postindustrial economies, services and high-tech manufacturing are increasingly important.

It is indeed difficult to think of Japan without the notion of manufactured products coming to mind. Manufacturing still accounted for more than 26 percent of the GDP in 2005 (*Facts and Figures* 2007, 89). Japan ranked second in the world behind China in the production of crude steel, trailed only the United States in the production of four-wheeled motor vehicles, and was the world's leading producer of machine tools (Tanaka 2007, 42–43). Today, Japanese products are famous throughout the world even though the much larger American economy still produces more manufactured goods annually than Japan. Japan now leads the world in car and robot production and is among world leaders in a wide variety of manufacturing sectors including steel, semiconductors, shipbuilding, and consumer electronics. In developed countries, and especially in the United States, Japanese products have been present in large quantities throughout most or all of the lives of the majority of citizens. Honda motorcycles, Canon cameras, and Sony radios, televisions, and the Walkman were a part of life decades ago, and these companies as well as other Japanese firms continue to be responsible for originating or continuing to manufacture innovative and reliable products ranging from karaoke equipment to PlayStations. Manufacturing productivity gains have been a major reason why Japan has recovered from the economic doldrums of the 1990s.

The scope, variety, and productivity levels of Japanese manufacturing are quite diverse. There are a large number of local industries that rely on local capital and labor to make a specific product. A few examples of these products include lacquerware, bamboo ware, ceramic goods, wire, fans, handbags, and gloves. These industries are widespread throughout Japan. Such large industries as Nippon Steel, Toyota Motor Corporation, Hitachi Engineering, and Asahi Chemicals that employ thousands of workers are located in what began as company towns—Toyota is one example—and in great clusters in industrial districts in several locales primarily in

The Akihabara district in Tokyo is both an internationally famous area for electronics and also a gathering place for young people who are interested in them. (Corel)

central and southern Honshu near the Pacific coast. Many of these industrial districts are on reclaimed coastal land, and the firms that locate there have domestic and international markets. The location, particularly for multinational manufacturing industries on or near the coasts, means that major firms can cut their international shipping costs because of their location and still supply their domestic customers.

Construction and food processing are significant industries that employ large numbers of workers, serve primarily national markets, and are found throughout Japan. As noted earlier, these two industries are important not only because they employ so many people but also because they share the dubious distinction of needing substantial restructuring and much higher productivity. Japan's construction and food processing industries consistently have low productivity rates relative to their foreign counterparts.

High-technology industries are considered to be a key asset for Japan's continuing economic prosperity. Examples of these knowledge-intensive industries include microelectronic fibers, industrial robots, medical electronics, aerospace, and information technology. These industries depend on such sources for research and development as universities and other research institutes. Also, employees of these industries are highly educated and have clear preferences regarding residence locales and cultural amenities. Although these industries are located throughout Japan, they tend to be concentrated in metropolitan and urban areas like Tokyo and Osaka because of specific industry and employee requirements most in evidence in

Japan has been a world leader in robotics. These are robotic dogs produced by the Sony Corporation. (PRNewsFoto/Sony Electronics Inc. Entertainment Robot America)

high-technology firms. The northern part of Kyushu has also grown into a home for important semiconductor producers.

THE TWO-TIERED ECONOMY

One of the most distinct characteristics of the Japanese economy when it is compared to the economies of most developed nations is the high productivity of large multinational corporations and a few internationally competitive retail and wholesale distributors and the relatively mediocre to poor productivity of those manufacturers that serve primarily the domestic market as well as almost all of Japan's services and distribution industries. This lower tier of industries (as well as small shops and restaurants) is inefficient, often have too many employees, and since World War II have often been subsidized or protected from foreign and, even at times, potential domestic competition by the Japanese government.

Beginning in the late 19th century, the Japanese government gave high priority to economic development in such heavy industries as steel, railroads, and communications because they were vital to national security. By the end of World War I, a clear division was developing, especially in urban areas, between high-quality, productive heavy manufacturers that produced such products as aluminum, ships, and plastics and smaller manufacturers that produced such goods as processed food and consumer goods that were not for export. Employees in the upper-tier manufacturing sector enjoyed higher status, more attractive salaries and benefits, and secure employment in contrast to workers in small manufacturing and services.

As Japan attained world economic prominence during the high-growth years and into the 1980s, most foreigners conceptualized that all of Japanese business and industry was among the best in the world and were ignorant of this second tier of the economy. The discrepancy between the two tiers was one structural problem that contributed to Japan's recent economic problems, and improving the second tier remains, to a certain extent, a still unresolved challenge for Japan. Perhaps the best way to realize just how stark the differences are between industries in the two tiers is to contrast the Toyota Motor Corporation, and the Japanese automobile industry, with the food processing industry.

Toyota Motor Corporation is probably Japan's most famous business concern. Toyota's (originally spelled Toyoda) roots go back to the early 20th century when Toyoda Sakichi established Toyoda Spinning and Weaving. Automotive operations began in 1933 with the establishment of an automobile department within the Toyoda Automatic Loom Works, and in 1937, Toyoda Motor became an independent company. Before the war, a few large industrial concerns called "zaibatsu" controlled key sectors of the economy. After the war, such large corporations as Toyota used some of the advantages of the zaibatsu system by forming *keiretsu*, affiliated groups of suppliers that, along with the parent company, were serviced by member banks. Other foundations of Toyota's success today were laid in the years immediately after World War II. Toyota first concentrated on improving the production process by better organization and helped supply U.S. forces with trucks during the Korean War. As it slowly but surely improved the quality of its industrial plants, Toyota also continued to be a leader in human capital development. It introduced highly effective employee training programs and in the 1960s pioneered the now world-famous quality control circles, which were discussed earlier in this chapter. Toyoda Kiichiro, the motor company's founder and the son of Toyoda Sakichi, is said to have developed the "just in time" manufacturing system in which inventories of parts are kept low, thereby promoting efficiency and lowering costs in the 1930s, but this revolutionary manufacturing procedure was implemented in the 1950s.

Already a successful automobile company in Japan, Toyota along with Nissan (then named Datsun) began exporting cars to the United States in 1958. The venture was experimental, and the Japanese government did not think the venture would be successful. Many in the automotive industry shared the bureaucrats' viewpoint. For more than a decade, Japanese auto companies including Toyota were not particularly successful in the American market, but management and dealers listened closely to consumer feedback and systematically created small, fuel-efficient, mechanically reliable vehicles designed for consumers with modest economic means. Toyota and other Japanese car companies realized increasingly impressive sales results in the 1970s and early 1980s. In response to U.S. government pressure to limit exports, by the mid-1980s Toyota was moving into the mid-range and luxury American car markets and building manufacturing plants in the United States.

Japanese automobiles are famous throughout the world. Here, a new line of Toyotas is exhibited at an international automotive show in Tallinn, Estonia in 2008. (Dreamstime.com)

Today Toyota and other Japanese automotive companies such as Honda and Subaru occupy worldwide technological leadership in motor vehicle production with an array of popular vehicles. Toyota, which is in close competition with GM for worldwide leadership in motor vehicle sales, is also a pioneer in cutting-edge hybrid car design and production. Currently, Toyota and its subsidiaries produce close to 8 million motor vehicles annually, of which 6 million are produced outside of Japan. Auto sales for all companies in Japan have recently been stable and declining. Toyota, like many of Japan's leading-edge manufacturers, built plants in various parts of the world and sells so many of its products worldwide that its profits keep growing despite lower Japanese demand. Currently, Toyota and its affiliates have 22 manufacturing plants in Japan and 520 overseas manufacturing plants in 26 countries in Asia, Africa, Europe, and North America. Toyota markets vehicles in 170 different countries.

The robotics, machinery, chemicals, consumer electronics, biotechnology, and steel industries are all examples of Japanese manufacturing firms whose productivity approaches or exceeds that of the United States and leading Western European and Asian economies. They are globally successful and clearly belong to the top tier of Japan's economy.

The food processing industry, all those firms that process food after it leaves the farm, is a gigantic industry in Japan, employing more people than the automobile, steel, machine tool, and computer industries combined. Currently, it alone is responsible for employment of about 11 percent of Japan's manufacturing workers, and the industry is only approximately 40 percent as productive as the American food processing industry. The United States, with more than double Japan's population, has one-third the number of food processing firms as is the case in Japan, where many small and mostly inefficient firms exist.

Much of the domestic food processing industry, one of Japan's least successful industries by world standards, has been protected by government from foreign competition. Largely because of government protection and discouragement of imports of processed food, Japanese consumers still buy a relatively small percentage of processed food from foreign sources. Competition in the food industry is stagnant, and low foreign imports and investment in food products means little pressure on the domestic industry. Partially because of the inefficiencies in this industry and what most analysts believe to be excessive government protection and regulation, Japan's consumers pay much higher prices for food on average than is the case in the United States and Europe. This hurts not only millions of consumers but also the entire economy. However, Japanese worries about food self-sufficiency if markets are liberalized, and a tolerance for protecting jobs, make a number of consumer groups reluctant to pursue reform of this industry.

The contrast between not only Toyota but also other successful automobile companies such as Honda and Nissan and the food processing industry is a clear example of the stark difference between higher-tier and lower-tier Japanese industries. Toyota and other Japanese car manufactures constantly compete against each other in a vibrant domestic market. These companies, as has been true with other highly competitive Japanese industries such as electronics and software firms, hone their business and manufacturing skills domestically and then aggressively compete globally. These companies also gain enormous competitive advantages through their global investments in manufacturing plants as they gather constant "on the ground" information.

Japan's food processing industry is not as automated as food processing industries in other developed countries, which hurts its productivity; local food processing industries often enjoy monopolies, which tend to create disincentives for product quality; and because of government protection, Japan's food processing industry does not gain economic benefits from foreign direct investment (FDI). The industry also, unlike top-tier industries, is not export oriented. In addition to food processing, construction and textiles are two other major manufacturing industries that clearly fit into the second tier of the Japanese economy as their productivity levels range from 25 percent to 60 percent of comparable industries in the United States and several other developed countries. Their disadvantageous economic positions and low productivity are a result of virtually similar economic environments as those that influence the food processing industry.

Much of Japanese services, retail, and wholesale distribution industries are also less productive on average than Japan's first-tier manufacturers. These sectors of the economy often tend to employ more workers than are needed, and such firms as banks and small and middle-sized shops tend to be less automated than is the case in other developed economies. Collectively, 60 percent of all jobs in Japan are in

Street vendors are a highly visible part of Japan's urban economy. (Corel)

industries that average between 50 and 60 percent of Japanese manufacturers' productivity levels, and productivity in the former industries is currently stagnating.

Improving performance of the second-tier industries has become a priority for several government agencies and privately funded research institutes and think tanks. Japan has improved considerably in the last few years in the application of information technology to manufacturing. In retailing and wholesaling distribution, most business analysts and economists believe that more widespread use of microcomputers, optical scanners, and corporate reorganization, in addition to more government deregulation to promote competition and foreign investment, are all steps that can address some of the problems discussed.

A few distribution industries have, through excellent management, focused consumer-friendly goals, and superb marketing, become successful multinational firms. Japan has been famous for mom-and-pop shops since the Tokugawa era, but sole proprietorships are fast giving way to chain retail shops. Convenience stores seem to have taken Japan by storm in the last two decades, and although there are other chains, Seven-Eleven Japan is now the country's biggest retail business, with annual sales of almost 2.5 trillion yen. There are more than 11,500 Seven-Eleven Japans in the country. The chain, originally American-owned, first entered the Japanese market in Tokyo in 1974, and many erroneously predicted that U.S.-style convenience stores would fail because they were not suitable for Japanese culture. Seven-Eleven Japan is now a wholly owned subsidiary of Japan's biggest retail conglomerate, Seven & I Holdings. Seven-Eleven sells a wide range of Japanese and Western products including food, magazines, and a variety of alcoholic and nonalcoholic beverages including green tea, whiskey, fruit and yogurt drinks, and many iced coffee brands. They also offer such services as photocopying, faxes, Internet shopping, and ATMs. Customers can even pay their utility bills. Seven-Eleven's success has become international, and there are now more than 31,600 stores in 18 countries including the United States, Turkey, Thailand, and Sweden (Okada et al. 2007, 16–17).

The 100-yen shops are larger stores that have also become quite popular in Japan and internationally. These stores sell everything from office supplies to bags, books, and CDs and all for the same 100-yen price. Although there are some similarities to American dollar stores, Japanese argue that the quality of the items is better in the 100-yen stores. The 100-yen stores certainly seem to occupy a greater portion of the retail market than the American variant. Currently, 100-yen stores are the fourth-largest retail category in Japan, ranking behind only department stores, supermarkets, and convenience stores. Daiso is the biggest 100-yen shopping chain, stocks 90,000 products, and in a recent year enjoyed sales of more than 320 billion yen. Although they aren't called 100-yen shops, Daiso now has 400 outlets in 15 countries including South Korea, the United States, Thailand, and Macau (Okada et al. 2007, 16–17).

Recent changes in Japanese legal constraints for financial services investments and sales also constitute very positive developments for both Japanese consumers and the nation's economy. Over the last decade, lifts on prohibitions of sales of a variety of such financial securities as annuities, mutual funds, and other investment packages by brokerage firms and banks, 2008 global financial situations notwithstanding, have resulted in many more profitable investment opportunities for millions of Japanese whose previous savings and investment options were primarily limited to postal savings or other bank savings accounts that paid almost no interest and a stock market in which low dividend payments were the general rule. Since these changes, both domestic providers and such foreign concerns as Merrill Lynch, the Bank of New York, and Ivy Investments have either entered or dramatically expanded their Japanese operations.

Liberalization of market entry and relaxation of dense government regulation in both manufacturing and services are often a slower process in Japan than in other countries because traditionally Japanese place a high priority on maintaining societal harmony. The airlines are a good case in point. After observing U.S. air deregulation efforts in the 1970s, Ministry of Transportation (MOT) officials began to consider deregulation in 1980. However, MOT officials wanted the procedure to be fair for all companies, advocated giving the companies time to adapt, were reluctant to confront recalcitrant airlines, and worried about the effect of deregulation on employment. This meant that the deregulation process took 20 years, during which time those Japanese who flew were paying excessively high prices. Additionally during this time, Japanese airlines were losing business to their American competitors. Many economists believe the nature of international competition probably makes it important that despite the great premium placed on harmony in Japanese culture, the pace of deregulation proceed more rapidly than was the case with the airlines industry.

Cell phone use is even more popular in Japan than the US. (Rob Howard/Corbis)

Cell phones probably offer one of the best examples of how a Japanese industry improved performance dramatically because of deregulation, and millions of consumers made cell phones an integral part of their lives. In 1994 cell telephones were deregulated in Japan, and that policy change led to a 22-fold rise in ownership of cell and car telephones in the ensuing six-year period—from 2.13 million phones in the beginning of fiscal year 1994 to 47.58 million at the end of November 1999. The Japanese fascination with electronic gadgets certainly is a stimulus for mobile phones' increasing popularity, but general costs for cell phone use dropped dramatically after deregulation.

Since that time, the number of cell phones used in Japan has continued to rapidly grow and is now more than 100 million. Estimates are that about 75 percent of the Japanese population use mobile phones (Japan-Guide.com 2008). Japan's high level of technology and a seemingly cultural affinity for gadgets that is pronounced in Japan has created an environment where cell phone industry innovations appear to occur on an almost weekly basis. Japanese were using cell phones to access the Internet, interface with home computers, trade stocks, do automated grocery orders with delivery included while coming home from work on the train, and convert currency considerably earlier than Americans and Western Europeans.

As reform proceeds in Japan, a number of economists argue that in the case of large businesses in both tiers, significant corporate restructuring is an unfinished agenda item. Although widespread cost cutting has occurred and, at least in the successful companies, the problem of excess full-time employees has been addressed, some business analysts contend that a more focused approach to product prioritization and core objectives than in the past needs to occur. More Japanese than

American and Western European firms still seem to be producing a wide variety of unrelated products without really distinguishing between profitable core products and products that would be best produced elsewhere. Economist and Japan specialist Richard Katz contrasts the example of an electrical machinery firm that produced blood pressure monitors, made automotive testing equipment, and ran a catering service and insurance company with the highly successful Canon Corporation, whose goal is a global reputation for quality in a few products based on optical technology: cameras, photocopiers, and printers.

The above story has a happy ending in the case of the machinery company, whose top management has since decreed that any business divisions that were clearly not profitable be sold. In the last few years, the company, which asked not to be named, has acted on this decision and shed unprofitable divisions and product lines. Company employees in these divisions represented 15 percent of the firm's workforce. Management either gave them incentives for early retirement or transferred younger employees to other divisions in the firm. When Katz asked the machinery firm executive in charge of corporate planning why these decisions were made, he was told that globalization was the motivational factor. Foreign investors who were eager for profits owned 40 percent of the firm's shares.

Globalization is also driving some big Japanese companies that are not experiencing immediate economic pressure to divest themselves of major divisions. All Nippon Airways (ANA) sold 13 hotels it operated to Morgan Stanley. Although ANA is a successful company, the hotel division was losing money. ANA received a good price for the hotels and probably made an excellent strategic move to better position itself to take advantage of the planned conversion of Haneda Airport to an international facility.

Throughout Japan there are too many companies engaging in what Katz labels "mindless diversion," and it is uncertain whether they can make the kinds of difficult short-term decisions that most likely result in a better economic future for the companies and for Japan (Katz 2007, 2).

Since the negative experience of the 1990s, Japan's economic and business culture has experienced widespread changes that, as noted, are moving the country toward an even more competitive and freer economy than is now the case. However, it is important to bear in mind that Japan is not the United States or Western Europe. Because of a deep concern for personal relations and cultural harmony, even the "winners" in Japan often don't aggressively push for an end to protection for such industries as food processing, which employ large numbers of people. The two-tier economy model is useful in understanding Japanese industrial successes and failures, but sometimes Western economists forget that because of cultural differences, it is much more complicated in Japan to initiate long-range economic reforms than is the case in different environments.

TRADE

Economists concur that voluntary trade, whether domestic or international, promotes economic progress. The richest nations throughout history have consistently been those whose governments created legal and political environments that facilitated trade. The Japanese have engaged in domestic and foreign trade throughout their history, although there were long periods of time when past authoritarian governments severely limited international trade. Even then, some Japanese engaged in illicit trade with other Asian nations. Today, Japan enjoys the most liberal climate for domestic and international trade in its history. Compilers of the annual 2007 *Index of Economic Freedom*, a systematic comparison that includes most of the world's countries, give Japan good marks for trade freedom and economic freedom in general, ranking it 18th in the world out of 157 countries surveyed and 5th out of 30 nations in the Asia/Pacific region.

Japan is a world leader in international trade and was surpassed at the end of 2005 only by the United States, Germany, and China when the export and import values (in dollars) were added together for each country. Japan's economic recovery of the past few years has been greatly stimulated by both export and import increases, but this is particularly true in the case of exports. Since 2002 Japan's exports of goods and services have increased by approximately 65 percent, and exports account for 16 percent of Japan's GDP. Japan has been legitimately criticized, and still should be, by trading partners for first having formal barriers to trade and then later erecting informal ones. The 2008 economic crisis caused significant rises in the value of the Yen, which severely reduced Japanese export sales. In Japan, consumption of now cheaper imports continued to rise.

Even though Japan has improved import consumption, there are remaining trade-related problems that impede economic progress. Domestically, such informal trade barriers as unrealistically high consumer safety regulations keep out many foreign products. Also, Japanese consumers are denied access to many foreign goods and services because the political/legal structure in Japan still discourages foreign direct investment (FDI) even though the FDI level is now at a record high. In a recent survey of 141 countries, Japan ranked 131st in the percentage of GDP attributable to FDI. FDI accounts for only 2.4 percent of Japan's GDP compared to 23 percent in the United States and 41 percent in the United Kingdom (U.S. Department of State 2007). Fewer available foreign goods and services and the difficulties foreign firms experience buying or building facilities are major reasons why Japanese consumers pay more for most goods and services than consumers in other developed countries. The good news is that in the same survey cited here, Japan ranked 22nd out of 141 countries as a potentially attractive nation for FDI. When there is more economic freedom in Japan for FDI, there is little doubt that significant amounts will occur.

Japan should also be a larger exporter, given the size of its economy and the advanced education and skills of its workforce. Most economic analysts agree that export in services is the sector of the economy for which international trade needs to be most expanded. A wide range of service industries encompassing firms ranging from finance to entertainment are candidates for export expansion if they can be globally competitive. At present, too large a percentage of Japan's exports are manufactured goods produced by famous, internationally competitive, and well-known Japanese companies. The 2008 drop in global demand for Japanese automobiles due to the world economic slowdown illustrates the vulnerability of an export sector that depends too much on large established manufacturing companies while relying too little on services. As long as this export imbalance remains, the Japanese economy is potentially at risk if foreign demand remains low for such manufactured goods as steel, cameras, or machine tools. Most economists believe that Japan's lower-tier industries such as food processing and construction will become more proficient exporters only as a result of further economic, legal, and political reforms, which have been discussed in this chapter as well as the previous one.

Even though different sectors of the Japanese economy are in better positions than others in international trade, larger volumes of Japanese exports are being sold to new consumers throughout the world than in the past. At the end of 2004, a significant change occurred in Japanese trade patterns. For the first time since statistics were compiled in 1947, the United States lost its position as Japan's largest trading partner to China. This trend has continued. Although the United States remains an important Japanese trading partner, Japan has increased its trade not only with China but also with other parts of Asia. By 2006, Japan's overall imports and exports reached record levels. As of the publication of this book, the world economic situation has negatively affected Japan's trade balances, but with a better global economy, the situation will likely improve.

CONCLUSION: JAPAN'S ECONOMIC FUTURE

For almost 400 years, Japan has enjoyed a national economy that compared favorably with most of the world's nations. However, the post–World War II years were unprecedented as the archipelago nation became the world's second-strongest economic power. Readers of this chapter now understand that despite Japan's continuing high level of affluence, the nation faces a wide array of economic challenges. If history is a reliable guide, the odds are high that these challenges will be successfully negotiated.

REFERENCES

AFL-CIO Working for America Institute. "Manufacturing Update." April 2007. http://www.workingforamerica.org/documents/manuupdate.htm (accessed November 2008).

Allen, G. C. *A Short Economic History of Modern Japan*. New York: St. Martin's Press, 1981.

Bickers, Charles, and Ichiko Fuyuno. "Banking on the Robot Evolution." *Far Eastern Economic Review*, November 23, 2000, 38–42.

BNET Business Network. "Although Food Processing Is One of the Biggest Sectors in Japan, the Market Is Only Predicted to Increase by 2–3%." *Business Wire*, December 15, 2005. http://findarticles.com/p/articles/mi_m0EIN/is_2005_Dec_15/ai_n15946560/pg_1?tag=artBody;col1.

Callick, Rowan. "Make Way for Japan." *The American*, July–August 2007, 60–69.

"EAA Interview with Edward J. Lincoln." *Education About Asia* 5, No. 1 (Spring 2000): 22–25.

Eades, J. S., Roger Goodman, and Yumiko Hada, eds. *The "Big Bang" in Japanese Higher Education: The 2004 Reforms and the Dynamics of Change*. Melbourne, Australia: Trans Pacific Press, 2005.

———. "Learning from the Japanese Economy." *Japan Digest*, September 2004.

Energy Information Administration. October 29, 2008. http://www.eia.doe.gov (accessed November 2008).

Facts and Figures of Japan 2007. Tokyo: Foreign Press Center, 2007.

Halberstam, David. *The Reckoning*. New York: Avon Books, 1986.

Howell, David L. "Proto-Industrial Origins of Japanese Capitalism." *Journal of Asian Studies* 51, No. 2 (May 1992): 269–286.

"Japan." *Encyclopedia of the Nations*. October 28, 2008. http://www.nationsencyclopedia.com/Asia-and-Oceania/Japan.html.

Japan External Trade Organization. October 31, 2007. http://www.jetro.org (accessed November 2008).

Japan-Guide.com. "Cell Phones in Japan." http://www.japan-guide.com/e/e2223.html (accessed November 2008).

Japan Productivity Center for Socio-Economic Development. "International Comparison of Labor Productivity." 2006. http://www.jpc-sed.or.jp/eng/research/2006_03.html.

Jo, Shigeyuki. "End of the Road for the Seniority System." *Japan Echo* 33, No. 5 (October 2006): 18–22.

Kane, Tim, Kim R. Holmes, and Mary Anastasia O'Grady. "Japan" in *2007 Index of Economic Freedom*, 229–230. Washington, DC: Heritage Foundation, 2007. http://www.heritage.org/index/country.cfm?id=Japan.

Karan, Pradyumna P. *Japan in the 21st Century: Environment, Economy, and Society*. Lexington: University Press of Kentucky, 2005.

Katz, Richard. "Demographics, Growth and the Budget: Rosy Scenario." *Oriental Economist Report* 75, No. 2 (February 2007): 6–7.

———. "The Importance of Being an Exporter: The Kindness of Strangers." *Oriental Economist Report* 75, No. 6 (June 2007): 1–3.

———. *Japan, the System That Soured: The Rise and Fall of the Japanese Economic Miracle*. Armonk, NY: M. E. Sharpe, 1998.

———. "Orchestrating Productivity Revival, Part 1: Still Tuning Up." *Oriental Economist Report* 75, No. 7 (July 2007): 7–8.

———. "Promoting Productivity, Part 2: Dual Economy More Dualistic." *Oriental Economist Report* 75, No. 8 (August 2007): 8–9.

———. "Structural Dualism Worsens." *Oriental Economist Report* 68, No. 11 (November 2000): 8–11.

———. "Whither Corporate Reform? Mixed Messages." *Oriental Economist Report* 75, No. 5 (May 2007): 1–4.

Kelly, William and Merry White. "Students, Slackers, Singles, Seniors, and Strangers: Transforming a Family Nation." In Peter J. Katzenstein and Taksashi Shiraishi, eds. *Beyond Japan: The Dynamics of East Asian Regionalism*. Ithaca, NY: Cornell University Press, 2006.

Lincoln, Edward J. "The Japanese Government and the Economy: Twenty-first Century Challenges." *Education About Asia* 12, No. 3 (Winter 2007).

———. *Troubled Times: US-Japan Trade Relations in the 1990s*. Washington, DC: Brookings Institution Press, 1999.

Macpherson, W. J. *The Economic Development of Japan, 1868–1941*. New York: Cambridge University Press, 1996.

Mak, James, et al., eds. *Japan: Why It Works, Why It Doesn't*. Honolulu: University of Hawai'i Press, 1998.

Miyamoto, Michiko. "Better Work for Women." *Japan Echo* 33, No. 5 (October 2006): 23–26.

Miyauchi, Yoshihiko. "Reform Is in the National Interest." *Oriental Economist Report* 68, No. 3 (March 2000): 16.

Mulgan, Aurelia George. "Japan: A Setting Sun." *Foreign Affairs* 79, No. 4 (July–August 2000): 40–52.

Nakamura, Takafusa. *Economic Development of Modern Japan*. Singapore: Japanese Ministry of Foreign Affairs, 1985.

Okada, Shin'ichi, Tadahiro Ohkoshi, and Mayumi Nakamura. "Made in Japan: The Kanban System." *Japan+: Asia-Pacific Perspectives* 4, No. 12 (April 2007): 18–19.

———. "Made in Japan: A Retail Revolution." *Japan+: Asia-Pacific Perspectives* 4, No. 12 (April 2007): 16–17.

Olstrom, Douglas. "Prospects for a 'New Economy' in Japan." *Japan Economic Institute Report* 32 (August 18, 2000): 1–14.

Organization for Economic Co-operation and Development. "OECD Briefing Note for Japan." *Education at a Glance 2007*. 2007. http://www.oecd.org/dataoecd/22/2/39317152.pdf (accessed November 2008).

Osamu, Nariai. "A Five-Year Economic Report Card." *Japan Echo* 33, No. 5 (October 2006): 40–42.

Porter, Michael E., and Hirotaka Takeuchi. "Fixing What Really Ails Japan." *Foreign Affairs* 78, No. 3 (May–June 1999): 66–81.

Progressive Policy Institute. "The Japan Postal Service Is the World's Largest Bank." 2006. http://www.ppionline.org/ppi_ci.cfm?knlgAreaID=108&subsecID=900003&contentID=253759 (accessed November 2008).

Reid, T. R. *Confucius Lives Next Door: What Living in the East Teaches Us about Living in the West*. New York: Vintage, 1999.

Rosenberger, Nancy. *Gambling with Virtue: Japanese Women and the Search for Self in a Changing World*. Honolulu: University of Hawai'i Press, 2001.

Stern, Seth. "Engineering Lawyers: Japan Is Building Up Its Legal Profession." *Harvard Law Bulletin*, Summer 2006. http://www.law.harvard.edu/alumni/bulletin/2006/summer/feature_4.php (accessed October 2007).

Takahashi, Hiroyuki, and Jeanette Voss. "'Parasite Singles': A Uniquely Japanese Phenomenon?" *Japan Economic Institute Report* 31 (August 11, 2000): 1–12.

Tanaka, Hideaki, ed. *Japan 2007: An International Comparison*. Tokyo: Keizai Koho Center, 2007.

Toyota Corporation Web site. http://www.toyota.com.jp/en/about_toyota/index.html (accessed June 2008).

U.S. Department of State. *United States-Japan Investment Initiative: 2007 Report*. Washington, DC: June 2007. http://www.state.gov/documents/organization/86189.pdf (accessed November 2007).

Vogel, Steven. *Japan Remodeled: How Government and Industry Are Reforming Japanese Capitalism*. Ithaca, NY: Cornell University Press, 2006.

Weston, Mark. *Giants of Japan*. New York: Kodansha International, 1999.

Wright, Richard A. *A Brief History of the First 100 Years of the Automobile Industry in the United States*. Detroit: Wayne State University. http://www.theautochannel.com/mania/industry.orig/history/chap16.html.

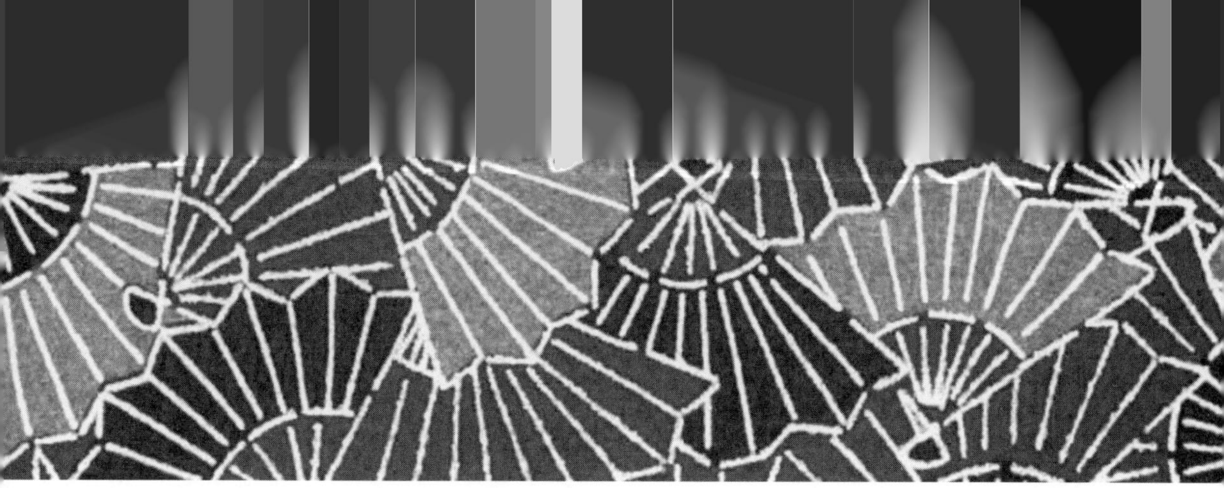

Society

Religion and Thought

INTRODUCTION

Japanese spiritual traditions are a rich blend of ancient beliefs and rites intermingled with regional and even world influences. However, culture shapes religion as much as religion shapes culture, and contemporary Japanese religious and philosophical perspectives constitute a unique mélange. Aspects of Japan's spiritual traditions have even been exported to the West. The indigenous spiritual practices known as Shinto as well as Buddhism, Confucianism, elements of Daoism, the so-called "new religions," and Christianity are all present in the archipelago. This does not necessarily mean, as will be discussed later, however, that large numbers of Japanese consider themselves "religious" in the Western meaning of the term.

The large majority of readers of this volume have spiritual traditions that emanated from the ancient Near East and that are predicated on the notions of monotheism (one god) and exclusivity—one cannot be both a Christian and a Muslim. The first step in understanding Japanese spiritual traditions is the realization that for the majority of Japanese, the aforementioned beliefs are not valid. The large majority of Japanese, as is true of most East Asians, approach religion from a syncretic perspective and have no problem with incorporating aspects of different religious creeds and practice into their lives. The assumption undergirding syncretism is that various practices and beliefs from different spiritual traditions are most useful

A typical home shrine. Buddhist, Confucian, and Shinto icons might all be present in the same shrine. (Courtesy of Lucien Ellington)

depending on the particular stage of one's life. This syncretic tradition in Japan dates back more than 1,000 years. The first historical record of the figurative transfer of a Shinto kami ("divinity") in a portable shrine was in 749 CE when a kami was taken from Kyushu to Nara to protect the construction of the Buddhist temple Todaiji, which contains one of Japan's two Great Buddhas.

Many contemporary Japanese, for example, have family shrines where Shinto and Buddhist icons are present. Large numbers of Japanese also base aspects of their daily conduct on Confucian teachings but adhere to certain Daoist beliefs about lucky and unlucky practices. Traditionally, Japanese have christened children and married in Shinto shrines and conducted funerals at Buddhist temples. Even though Christians constitute less than one percent of the Japanese population, getting married in Christian churches is now popular among Japanese young people. Recent estimates indicate that slightly over half of newlyweds have a Christian service. Sometimes, the marrying couples will have both a Christian and a Shinto wedding service. If this now more than 20-year-old Christian-style wedding trend continues, it could be evidence that the Japanese are even more eclectic than their East Asian neighbors in utilizing a variety of religious rites.

Not only have different spiritual traditions affected individual Japanese, but also the religions and belief systems present in Japan have influenced each other. Even Shinto, the "indigenous" Japanese religion, has been influenced by Buddhism, Daoism, and Confucianism.

ISE SHRINE

Located in the city of Ise in Mie Prefecture, Ise is the most important Shinto shrine in Japan. It is now less a place of worship than a historically significant tourist site, but Japanese from all walks of life are familiar with Ise today, and it receives thousands of visitors annually from Japan and foreign countries. Ise was the site of popular pilgrimages during the Tokugawa era. There are both inner and outer as well as affiliated shrines. One of the reasons Ise Shrine is so important is that it enshrines the ancestral gods of the imperial family, including Amaterasu Omikami, the mythical ancestor of the imperial family who is represented by the sacred mirror icon. The shrine is first mentioned in an eighth-century Japanese poem. The main building is elegant in its simplicity and is constructed of unpainted Japanese cypress wood. Its simple design may possibly be traced to prehistoric Japanese grain storehouses. The shrine is usually torn down and rebuilt on a regular interval of, at present, every 21 years.

Another aspect of East Asian syncretism that is a dominant feature of Japanese spiritual traditions is that practice and behavior are much more important than abstract beliefs, Western-style theological debates, and adherence to religious dogma. Nowhere is this element of East Asian syncretism truer than in the spiritual tradition that has come to be known as Shinto.

SHINTO: "THE WAY OF THE KAMI"

The bundle of spiritual rites and practices that we know today as Shinto began in Japanese antiquity and shares many characteristics of ancient early preliterate forms of Western and non-Western religions that were rooted in the earth, nature, and fertility. Like many other earth religions, Shinto has no historical founders such as Jesus, Buddha, or Mohammed, no sacred scriptures and moral injunctions, no martyrs, and no saints. The early daily and seasonal practices that came to be known as Shinto, although an integral part of life as was the case in other preliterate societies, were not rigidly compartmentalized as "religion." In fact, the term "Shinto" did not appear in written records until well after Buddhism reached Japan. In the early eighth century, the term is mentioned in the *Nihon Shoki* and the *Kojiki*, two of the earliest official chronicles of Japan, as part of a more general government-sponsored effort to both contrast and reconcile Japanese beliefs with such newly imported foreign spiritual traditions as Buddhism and Confucianism.

The definition of what Shinto precisely means is still controversial. Although Shinto is often translated as "the Way of the Gods," Shinto deities are dissimilar from Western conceptualizations of "God" in enough ways that thinking of the two terms as largely synonymous is to quite likely promote misunderstanding. Kami are any animate, mythological, or inanimate entities that promote awe, fear,

The large edifice is a Torii Gate, which always marks a Shinto Shrine. Torii Gates are a variety of sizes. (Courtesy of Lucien Ellington)

and reverence. Kami may be mountains, rocks, trees, streams, and even people. In many ways, "spirits" serve as a better equivalent Western term for kami than gods, although a precise translation is impossible.

Shinto has been described as a religion of shrines, festivals, and rituals. Large, medium, and small Shinto shrines with their torii gates are pervasive throughout Japan. Shrines, considered to be the homes of kami, are often located in such beautiful natural surroundings as the mouths of rivers or at the foot of a mountain. Many of the sites of the older shrines were considered to be sacred spaces long before the erection of any structure. Japanese consider Shinto, in contrast to the more somber Buddhism, to be an optimistic and happy religion. Children are christened at shrines and taken there during special festivals during their third, fifth, and seventh years. As noted, many couples have Shinto weddings. Shinto-related festivities take place during rice planting and harvesting cycles. Millions of Japanese observe the custom of visiting Shinto shrines on New Year's Day. Some shrines do a brisk business throughout the year selling good-luck charms for marriage, fertility, examination success, and even auto safety. A number of Shinto shrines hold annual *matsuri*, or festivals, where revelers carry large portable shrines that figuratively transport the local kami all around the immediate area of the home shrine. It is not uncommon for large companies to have small shrines honoring particular kami.

Individuals or groups who visit shrines to worship complete, often in a short period of time, three processes: purification, making an offering, and praying or making a request of the local kami. Before entering the shrine, the purification act involves the use of water to wash one's hands or wash out one's mouth. Then a

The Yaskuni Shinto Shrine was built to honor Imperial Japan's war dead. The Japanese prime ministers who have visited it since World War II have provoked intense criticism from China and South Korea. (Matsukin)

monetary offering is presented to the kami, followed by the prayer or request. Values common to most Japanese today that originated in part through early religious practices include a love of bathing and deep reverence for nature.

Shinto also bequeathed a rich mythology to the Japanese people, with stories of gods and goddesses who possessed various magical powers. The first political leaders of a Japanese state, the Yamato clan, were originally priest-chiefs. They later became the first Japanese emperors and claimed descent from Amaterasu, the sun goddess and a leading Shinto deity. The sun has gone on to play a central role in Japanese culture. The Japanese name for their country, Nippon, means "source of the sun." A number of Japanese consider many of the practices and objects associated with this indigenous set of spiritual traditions, including New Year's and agricultural rites, rice, sumo, and sake, as the traditional cultural essences of what it means to be Japanese rather than as symbols of formal religion.

During the Meiji period in the last half of the 19th century, Japan's new leaders looked for a centrifugal force that could be instrumental in promoting the high level of nationalism that was absent in the archipelago but constituted an integral feature of Western political systems. The Meiji oligarchs chose Shinto. Meiji leaders created formal hierarchical structures for Shinto shrines throughout Japan, promoted a state Shinto characterized by the inculcation in school students of the belief that the emperor was divine, and promulgated the notion that the highest calling of a citizen

An image of the historical Buddha, Siddhartha Gautama, on a Nepalese thangka scroll painting. Buddhism spread from South Asia to China, Korea, and then Japan. (Dharmapala Thangka Centre)

was to die for the emperor. With Japan's defeat in World War II and the creation of the 1947 constitution, Shinto was disestablished as the state religion, and the emperor issued a statement that he was secular and not divine. Although the Japanese government now provides official support for no religion, memories of Shinto's association with 20th-century Japanese militarism, imperialism, and the Pacific War are still present among some Japanese today. Also, since the 1970s, unofficial visits by some of Japan's prime ministers to Tokyo's Yasukuni Shrine, which honors the spirits of Japan's war dead, have resulted in domestic, Chinese, and Korean protests. Some extreme right-wing groups incorporate Shinto in general, and the Yasukuni Shrine in particular, into their ideological messages that focus on the Japanese as a special people and that exonerate Japan's role in World War II.

The syncretic nature of religious observance and, for the most part, the lack of the clergy-directed weekly services common to Western religions cause contemporary religion statistics on Japanese practitioners to be imprecise. However, Shinto shrines claim more than 106 million *ujiko*, or parishioners, making Shinto Japan's most common spiritual tradition. Shinto, with approximately 86,000 shrines, has long coexisted with Japan's various Buddhist sects that include 78,000 temples and claim more than 96 million members. Even though Japan was the last of the three major East Asian countries to adopt Buddhism, in some respects the religion is more culturally pervasive in contemporary Japan than in China or the Korean Peninsula.

BUDDHISM

Buddhism was a world religion that had existed for 1,000 years when emissaries from the king of the more advanced Korean state of Paekche introduced this complex array of beliefs to the Japanese in 552 CE. Buddha, meaning "enlightened one," was born Prince Gautama Siddhartha in the Indian Shakya nation around 563 BCE and died in 483. Siddhartha was a human and only later deified. According to the story of the founding of Buddhism, written centuries after Siddhartha's death, the young boy was brought up in luxury and protected from the evils of the world by his parents. However, Siddhartha ventured from the safe confines of the palace and encountered old age, sickness, and death. Siddhartha was extremely troubled by these ultimate realities of human existence and, abandoning his privileged life and his family, pursued the life of the wandering religious seeker.

For a number of years Siddhartha engaged in such practices as extensive fasting that almost killed him. Finally, he settled on a middle way that preserved his life but did not lead to overindulgence in the world's pleasures. After extensive

One of two Japanese Great Buddhas, the Kamakura Great Buddha was completed in 1252. (Corel)

GREAT BUDDHA OF KAMAKURA

The Great Buddha at Kamakura, while smaller than the Nara statue, has been better restored than the latter Buddha. The Kamakura Buddha is a depiction of Amida, the Buddha of Infinite Light. The Kamakura Buddha is on the grounds of Kotoku-in, a Pure Land Buddhist temple. It was completed in 1252 and was allegedly constructed through the efforts of a lady who had been in the court of the late shogun Minamoto Yoritomo, who, before he died, expressed the desire to have a great Buddha in Kamakura. A Pure Land priest, Joko, allegedly raised the money from throughout Japan for the Great Buddha. The statue, which is more than 37 feet fall, was once housed in a wooden building. The statue is partially hollow inside, and steps go to a window in Amida's back, where visitors can view surrounding scenery. However, a 1495 tidal wave destroyed the building, and today the Buddha sits in the open.

meditation under the bodhi, or "wisdom tree," Siddhartha became enlightened and spent the rest of his life bringing his teachings to a growing number of disciples. From Siddhartha's evolution to Buddha, a world religion was born.

The Four Noble Truths constitute the essence of Buddhist teachings, though they are now greatly augmented by an entire canon of theological literature. The first Truth is that life is suffering. To be human is to suffer, and such tribulations as pain and old age are impossible to avoid. Integrated with this teaching are the notions of karma, reincarnation, and nirvana. The principle of karma focuses on human action and moral results. Both good and evil deeds accrue for the individual. If an individual lives a good life, he or she will be born again, or reincarnated, in a better life. Still, all human life means suffering, so the ultimate spiritual goal is not to continue to be born or reincarnated again but rather to achieve nirvana, where one transcends the repeating life cycle and is never reborn.

The second and third Truths expand on the first Truth. In the second Truth, desire is clearly identified as the cause of human suffering. The third Truth is an injunction that if humans want to stop suffering they must extinguish desire. This goal is achieved through such religious practices as meditation and through following the fourth Truth, or the Eightfold Path, which includes right views, right intention, right speech, right action, right livelihood, right effort, right mindfulness, and right concentration.

As Buddhism matured in India, its theology became more complex, and other concepts became important to the belief system as well. One major Buddhist tenet critical to understanding the religion is that the notion that each individual possesses a "soul" is incorrect. Because to live is to change, any individual is a compilation of his or her attributes at any given point in time. Human attributes are not permanent and change as time passes. Buddhism also divided into two major schools relatively early in its history: Theravada, which is today dominant in most of Southeast Asia, and Mahayana, which spread to China, Korea, and then Japan

KIYOMIZUDERA TEMPLE

Located in Kyoto, Kiyomizudera, or Temple of Clear Water, was founded in 798 by the monk Enchin with the patronage of a general, Tamuramaro (758–811), who had fought to bring eastern Japan under central government control. The temple is part of the Hoso Buddhist sect, which was one of the more popular early esoteric variants of Buddhism in Japan. The temple's architecture is a good example of Chinese influence during the Heian period. Over the centuries, the temple has been the object of military attack as well as fires and earthquakes. The last major fire was in 1629, and the present buildings date from 1633. The main hall is built over a cliff and has a large open-air veranda that on a clear day provides viewers with one of the most impressive views of Kyoto possible.

and is still the general institutional framework for the many Buddhist denominations in existence in Northeast Asia today.

Although Mahayana and Theravada Buddhists agree on key points, there are also significant differences on some basic beliefs. While the ultimate goal of Theravada Buddhism is individual enlightenment, Mahayana Buddhists embrace the concept of Bodhisattvas, or "enlightened ones," who delay their own accession into nirvana in order to help other sentient beings realize this state. Also, Mahayana Buddhism encouraged the growth of devotion toward not only the Buddha but a pantheon of other Buddhas including Kannon, the Buddha of Mercy; Maitreya, the Buddha of the Future; and Amida, the Buddha of Infinite Light. One eventual effect of Mahayana Buddhism was to make the religion popular among common people who, lacking the education to understand complex philosophical points, could embrace specific sects that deified certain Buddhas such as Amida.

When Buddhism first reached Japan from the Korean Peninsula—along with other vestiges of traditional Chinese culture including written language, art, much of it religious in nature, and philosophical tracts—the Japanese who encountered the foreign religion considered it a form of powerful magic similar to kami. Later during the Heian period, the aristocracy began to embrace such elements of the spiritual messages of Buddhism as the intransience of life and the ideal of giving up attachments. Several sects became popular then including, most notably, Shingon, an esoteric Buddhism introduced by Kukai, who had traveled to China to study the sect. Shingon, which remains the third largest of the Japanese Buddhist sects today, includes intricate and symbolic modes of meditation, mandalas, and distinctive art forms.

By the late Heian era and particularly during the Kamakura period that followed, another Chinese import, Pure Land Buddhism, became the first sect that appealed to the masses. Today, the Pure Land and True Pure Land sects claim the largest number of adherents in Japan. In Pure Land Buddhism, salvation can be gained by

GREAT BUDDHA OF NARA

The first of two great Buddhas constructed in Japan, the Nara Great Buddha was built in 746 and is located in a city that is regarded as Japan's first permanent capital. According to historians, the Emperor Shomu commissioned the construction of the statue as protection against possible smallpox epidemics and as a symbol of imperial power. The Buddha depicted in the bronze statue is Variocana, the cosmic Buddha. The Buddha, which is more than 53 feet in length, is the largest bronze statue in the world. It is housed in Todaiji Temple, which is the largest wooden building in the world. The present building that houses the great Buddha was rebuilt in 1708, having suffered from fire at least two times. The statue has also been restored several times.

praying to Amida, the Buddha of the Western Paradise, and when salvation is gained one can be reborn in this paradise.

Although the sect had arrived earlier, it was during the Kamakura years and the Ashikaga period that followed that Japanese elites including the samurai embraced yet another Chinese import, *Ch'an*, or in Japanese, Zen Buddhism. Zen would have more profound effects on the culture of the archipelago than was the case in either China or the Korean Peninsula. Today, Zen temples and adherents rank second to

Heian Shrine in Kyoto. Shinto shrines are traditionally places where Japanese weddings have taken place. (Corel)

DOGEN (1200–1253)

Also known as Dogen Kigen, Dogen is considered to be one of Japan's greatest religious figures. Dogen is the father of the Japanese Soto school of Zen Buddhism, which places great emphasis on meditation and gradual enlightenment. Born an aristocrat and the recipient of an excellent education, Dogen, after deciding to take up the religious life as a vocation, first searched unsatisfactorily for appropriate religious instruction in Japan. Dogen then went to China to study Buddhism and, after several unfulfilling experiences, found what he was looking for in the Chinese Caodao school of Buddhism, which emphasized silent meditation with no goal in mind and gradual rather than sudden enlightenment. After returning to Japan, Dogen moved to the remote Echizen area rather than give in to Kyoto religious authorities. In addition to being regarded as a great religious thinker, Dogen also is recognized for his poetry.

the Pure Land sects in Japan, and without a doubt Zen is Japan's most famous world spiritual export. The meaning of Zen is "quietude" or "meditation," and Bodhidharma, the Indian monk who came to China and spread its teachings, perhaps best defined the sect in the following lines that are attributed to him:

> A special transmission outside the scriptures,
> Not founded upon words and letters;
> By pointing directly to [one's] mind
> It lets one see into [one's own true] nature and [thus] attain Buddhahood.
> (Dumoulin 2005, 85)

This form of Buddhism was in important ways originally a Chinese adaptation of Daoist beliefs to imported Buddhism. Japanese Zen was also influenced by Shinto's focus on nature. Although there are differences between Rinzai and Soto, Japan's two largest Zen schools, adherents of both perspectives agree on the beliefs that enlightenment is obtained not through deep reading, study, or philosophical reflection but through zazen, or meditation. Dogen (1200–1253), who was and remains the most revered Zen master in Japan's history, emphasized intense meditation and refused to compromise with the more worldly Buddhist figures of authority in Kyoto. Dogen abandoned Kyoto and moved to a more remote area of Japan.

Zen, with its emphasis on austerity, nature, the understated, and the subtle, has been responsible for influencing some of the most famous aspects of traditional Japanese culture. Zen profoundly influenced such martial arts as karate, judo, and kendo ("the way of the sword") as well as haiku, *ikebana*, calligraphy, and the construction of Japanese gardens.

Ryoanji Rock Garden, completed in the latter part of the 15th Century in Kyoto, is famous throughout the world as a symbol of Zen Buddhism. (Corel)

Thanks initially to the efforts of Suzuki Daisetsu (1870–1952), an academic, a prolific writer who was published in Japanese and English, and a master popularizer, a few accessible books about Zen were available in North America and the United States by the 1930s. Shortly after World War II and particularly in the 1950s and 1960s with the rise of the "beat" poets in the United States, such high-profile writers as Allen Ginsberg, Jack Kerouac, and Gary Snyder and the English writer Alan Watts introduced millions in the West to basic ideas of Zen. Today, Buddhism and in particular Zen (followed by Tibetan Buddhism) has adherents throughout Europe and the United States. Nishida Kitaro (1870–1945), Japan's most famous philosopher and a lifelong friend of Suzuki, integrated the Western philosophical ideas of Henri Bergson and William James with elements of Zen. Eventual translations of Nishida's work created opportunities for academics throughout the world to consider Zen-based intellectual discourse. Even though Zen Buddhism did not originate on the Japanese archipelago, its ideas have global impact because of individual Japanese who lucidly and beautifully articulated its spiritual practices and, just as important, Zen cultural aesthetics.

The post–World War II globalization of Zen ironically resulted in a rediscovery of the sect in Japan, particularly by some young people who became interested because of their awareness that it had attracted the attention of Westerners. Also, in the years since World War II, some Zen temples have formed associations with private companies who've sent recruits to be trained in hard meditation as a form of "boot camp" to inspire selflessness, concentration, and group loyalty. Both developments are partially indicative that Western popularity notwithstanding,

RYOANJI ZEN TEMPLE AND ROCK GARDEN

Ryoanji Temple was built in Kyoto in 1450 by General Hosokawa Katsumoto. The temple is part of the Rinzai Zen sect. The rock garden, which is one of Japan's most famous cultural sights, is said to be the work of the artist Soami, although this is not documented. The garden consists of a simple combination of raked white gravel and 15 rocks, which are set in three groups. The garden is bordered by the temple buildings and a wall (see photo on page 160). Some have speculated that the stones represent islands in the ocean, while others have contended that the rocks are mountains. However, the garden was designed to aid contemplation and realization through intuitive and not literal understanding. In addition to the temple and rock garden, Ryoanji also features a beautiful duck pond.

within postwar Japan the situation has not been favorable for Zen or other forms of traditional Buddhism. Although there are devout Buddhists and Zen meditation adherents, today most Japanese limit their relationship with Buddhism to using priests for funerals and visiting culturally or historically important temples. The fact that many of the younger generations were ignorant of their own Buddhist traditions until foreigners stimulated their interest is indicative of the decline of regular temple affiliation and spiritual observances on the part of most Buddhist parishioners.

During the early modern period, the Tokugawa government (1600–1868), in an effort to discover hidden Christians, forced every Japanese family to register with a Buddhist temple. Since the majority of Japanese lived in the countryside and small villages and towns until 1945, concrete relations existed between ordinary people throughout Japan and Buddhist temples and priests. However, with the great rural to urban demographic shift of the 20th century, many Japanese families lost connections with their family temples and now use whatever temple is available in the cities only for funerals or on other rare occasions. While Buddhism's influence on daily practice and individual belief systems seems to have diminished in contemporary Japan, beliefs attributed to the teachings of the Chinese sage Confucius, while challenged by the forces of modernity, apparently remain deeply rooted among many Japanese.

CONFUCIANISM: THE BRANCHES AND LEAVES OF JAPANESE CIVILIZATION?

Prince Shotoku, who as Yamato regent in 604 wrote the first guidelines for Japanese government in his "constitution," was also alleged to have written in another document that Shinto was the root, Confucianism the branches and leaves, and Buddhism the flowers and fruit of the tree of Japanese civilization. Although the prince

Stones with Confucian messages at the Temple of Confucius in Beijing. Confucian teachings are still influential in Japan today. (Instructional Resources Corporation)

didn't put this assertion in writing, Confucian ideas definitely permeate his 604 document. While Japanese learned of the doctrines that Europeans would label "Confucianism" later than Chinese and Koreans, the belief system exerted widespread influence in Japan.

Confucius justly deserves the reputation of one of the greatest teachers in world history. He lived from approximately 551 to 479 BCE and was born of a minor aristocratic family during a time in its history when China was not unified under one dynasty. A well-educated man, Confucius greatly desired to influence public policy and advise rulers. Although he held minor bureaucratic posts and consulted with several rulers, Confucius was unable to become a permanent adviser with any Chinese sovereign.

Confucius instead turned to teaching. Though he left no writings, after his death his disciples compiled his teachings in a printed work, known as *Lun Yu* in Chinese and the *Analects* in English. Later, scholars and adherents of the teachings throughout East Asia, including Japan, produced a canon of Confucian texts. Confucianism is difficult to categorize. Some scholars assert it is a philosophy while others, citing the fact that there are Confucian temples in Asia, conceptualize it as a religion. However, all concur that the impact of the belief system is profound throughout East Asia.

Although respectful of the spiritual and supernatural, Confucius was most concerned about the promotion of societal harmony at every level and of political stability in this world. He viewed the proper maintenance of important relationships as vital to the promotion of these goals. Confucius identified five basic relationships that must be nurtured: those between ruler and people, parent and child, husband and wife, older and younger siblings, and friend and friend. Confucius was an aristocrat, and his belief system was clearly hierarchical in nature but assumed reciprocity on the part of all parties. Subordinates were expected to obey and be loyal to superiors, while those at the top were obligated to be benevolent and protective of subordinates.

Confucius also stressed the importance of tradition and the cultivation of individual virtue. Rites and ceremonies were important societal centripetal forces as was veneration of ancestors. Individual virtue could be cultivated at its highest level through acquiring a true education. Like Socrates, Confucius made morality and virtue the heart of education. He stressed the cultivation of an aristocracy based on learning and virtue instead of blood. Confucius felt that the practice of virtue by heads of households, government officials, and rulers taught people proper moral behavior much more than the imposition of penalties or punishments.

Although Confucian teachings had been influential before the Tokugawa era, it was during that period of Japanese history that the government adopted so-called Neo-Confucianism as part of official state ideology. As was the case elsewhere in East Asia, the Tokugawa shogunate organized society into classes based on Confucian teachings. Samurai were at the top, followed by peasants and artisans. Merchants, who were considered money hungry and nonproductive, ranked below the other groups. Familiarity with Confucian classics was an important component of the education of samurai elites. Ideally, samurai were expected to not only be warriors but also, though never to the extent of their Chinese literati counterparts, cultivate a knowledge of classical Chinese philosophy, history, literature, and the arts as well as their own indigenous national traditions. Samurai were also obligated, as was the case in imperial China, to be virtuous government bureaucrats. As time passed and peace seemed a prominent part of Tokugawa life, the samurai became more bureaucratic and less of a warrior class.

It is important to note that as was the case with other foreign ideas and practices, the Japanese rejected elements of Confucius' teachings. Family birth status exerted much more power in Japan than in mid- and late imperial China, so the Japanese refrained from adopting a meritocratic civil service examination system as was the case in China. The Meiji government did, however, initiate a competitive educational examination system during the latter part of the 19th century.

As the Japanese rushed to Westernize during the first part of the Meiji era, Confucian ideas fell out of favor, but they were too much a part of the fabric of Japanese life to disappear. There was a resurgence of government and elite accentuation of Confucian ideas in the latter Meiji period. Today, despite changes in Japanese society because of affluence and urbanization, the influence of Confucian thought survives in Japan. The irony is that most Japanese don't even think of themselves as Confucian, but the teachings are deeply integrated into daily life. As noted, the very terms "Confucianism" and "Confucian" are Western inventions. Northeast Asians have traditionally called the belief system "the teachings of the scholars."

Despite widespread participation in Shinto and Buddhist rituals, a higher percentage of Japanese than Americans have a secular rather than a theologically based religious worldview. Confucius, while not an atheist or even agnostic, focused his teaching on appropriate virtue and conduct in this world.

The Japanese emphasis on both academic and moral education, the high school and college entrance examinations, and the rewards and high status that well-educated people accrue in Japanese society are beliefs and practices partially resulting from Confucianism. For example, most Japanese business and political elites positioned themselves for career advancement by working hard and succeeding in Japan's relatively meritocratic educational system.

Confucianism also directly affects Japanese attitudes toward work, society, gender, and the group. Confucian teachings strongly stress the virtues of hard work, obligation, and reciprocity. In all Northeast Asian countries, a widely accepted work ethic is quite apparent compared to what exists in many other nations. Countries like Japan and South Korea are annually at, or near, the top of developed countries in number of hours worked. Seemingly even more than other East Asian countries, Japan is a status-conscious society. Many Japanese have a propensity to find few things equal and to assign differing levels of status to both individuals and institutions. Within public and private institutions, superiors and subordinates traditionally owed each other protection, loyalty, and good team play. These propensities manifested themselves in such Japanese business practices as superiors helping to find potential spouses for subordinates and employees voluntarily not taking their full annual vacation time so as to put in more hours in their offices. Economic globalization and recent deregulation in light of a more intense competitive environment seem to be causing at least some changes in these practices. For example, although Confucian notions of hierarchy survive in the Japanese corporate world, many employees now don't have a particularly deep-seated loyalty to their supervisors for various reasons. Japanese companies are hiring fewer permanent employees, and an increasing number of employees have specific skills that enable them to more easily change jobs than in the past.

The Confucian notion that the family is the all-important unit in society is deeply embedded in Japanese culture. The most obvious sign is Japan's still-low divorce rate compared to other developed countries, but it is important to point out that Japan's rate has been steadily rising on an annual basis in recent years. Traditional East Asian family structures have been more hierarchical and status driven than in the West. Although elderly people are now more and more living apart from their children, there still seems to be somewhat higher levels of respect for old people compared to other developed countries, and many Japanese continue to honor dead family members. Despite equal opportunity employment laws, Japanese women often still have a much more difficult time obtaining employment that is commensurate with their qualifications than is the case in the United States or Western Europe. This situation is at least partially a legacy of the influence of Confucian beliefs that resulted in lower status for women than was the case in the West.

Confucius was very concerned about public as well as family life. Rule by virtuous leaders was a constant subject that the sage addressed in his teaching. Confucius felt that rulers should lead by example and that developing a sense of shame in people was a much better tool to make them behave than specified and detailed legal codes. The traditional Japanese propensity to first ascertain the trustworthiness of a potential business partner rather than heavily relying on contracts, the somewhat general nature of Japan's statutory laws, and the minimal role of litigation as a problem-solving method each partially reflect Confucian influences. Recent economic reforms designed to make the Japanese economy more competitive in a new era of globalization are creating a demand for more statutory commercial law and for the services of attorneys that constitute challenges to two of these Confucian-inspired traditions.

Like any belief system, Confucianism is an ideal conceptualization of human action; how people behave in the real world is often contradictory to cultural belief systems. Japan's political leaders have certainly engaged in corrupt practices. Still, despite recent increases, Japanese rates of violent crime, theft, drug abuse, and divorce are lower than many developed countries. For example, Japan has approximately 33 percent as many police per capita as the United States, about 20 percent as many judges per capita, and approximately five percent as many jail cells per capita (Reid 1999, 16).

It is also quite common throughout Japan to see government-financed signs and billboards exhorting people to do the right thing. Upon entering an urban Tokyo park, for instance, a visitor encounters a host of messages requesting park patrons to keep things clean for others, preserve the grass, jog on designated paths and not cut corners, and not do anything that might bother other people who use the space. Although such good behavior admonitions are common in many countries, they are much more numerous in Japan than in the West. This practice reflects the Confucian notion that people will probably act virtuously if they are constantly reminded to do so. Although it is impossible to quantify the relationship between Confucian teachings and the relatively high level of social stability in Japan, there is little doubt that a relationship does in fact exist.

CHRISTIANITY AND THE "NEW" JAPANESE RELIGIONS

Christianity, which was present in Japan long before the end of World War II, occupies an unusual position in Japan. Only approximately one percent of Japanese are professed Christian. Yet at specific points in Japanese history, Christian institutions and individuals have exercised considerably more intellectual, social, and cultural influence than might be supposed given today's small number of believers.

To date, there are at least three distinct periods of Christian influence: the period when Christianity first came to Japan dating from the mid-16th century until the Tokugawa government banned Christianity after the first few decades of the 17th century, the period from 1873 when the Meiji government lifted the previous ban until 1945, and the postwar years.

Although Christianity has some cultural and educational influence, only about one percent of Japanese are Christians. (Michael S. Yamashita/Corbis)

In the 16th century, the Portuguese and Spanish first introduced Catholicism to Kyushu, and promulgators of European protestant sects also arrived. Some scholars have labeled this first introduction of Christianity as Japan's "Christian century" since at no subsequent time has a higher percentage of Japanese actually converted to the faith. However, the Tokugawa government, primarily fearful of foreign political domination, banned Christianity and persecuted those adherents who would not renounce their faith. Despite this treatment, some Christians secretly practiced their religion, and a small number of adherents of the tenets of underground Christianity still exist today. Because underground Christians had no access to Christian teachings or literature until the latter part of the 19th century, these few remaining practitioners of the belief system are actually much more engaged in a folk religion with many indigenous beliefs than what could be considered Christian doctrines.

During the Meiji (1868–1912) and Taisho (1912–1926) years, Christians were actively engaged in social reform, particularly in education but also in leading efforts to increase public access to health care and to develop labor union movements. Christian missionaries from primarily the United States and Canada were (and still are in more limited ways) active in Japan, and a number of young Japanese either were influenced by Christian sects in Japan or came to the United States to study at Christian educational institutions. Some of these young people gained national influence in education and other intellectual endeavors. In particular, Christians in Japan were in the vanguard in the creation of educational opportunities for women, and such Japanese Christians as Naruse Jinzo (1858–1919), the founder of Japan Woman's University, and Nitobe Inazo (1862–1933), the first president of

Tokyo Christian Women's University, were pioneers in this field. Christianity gained even wider general influence in education and the public through the activities of such prominent individuals as Uchimura Kanzo (1861–1930), Mori Arinori (1847–1889), and Nambara Shigeru (1889–1974). Uchimura, a prominent Christian and a political and social commentator, resisted rising Japanese ultranationalism. Although not a Christian, Mori, who went on to become the father of Japan's public schools, was deeply influenced by his experiences with the religion in the United States. Nambara in December 1945 became the first Christian president of Tokyo University, Japan's most prestigious institution of higher education.

Christianity's influence on a number of educational institutions in Japan continues today. The number of private Christian schools in Japan is higher than might be imagined given the low number of Christians, and such higher educational institutions as International Christian University and Doshisha University, which is not Christian but is rooted in the religion, continue to be highly respected.

After World War II, the Japanese government established freedom of religion for the first time, and a number of new religious groups rose to prominence. However, for the most part Christianity did not grow. Many Japanese have mixed or negative feelings about actually becoming Christians for a variety of reasons including associations of the faith with Western dominance and the incompatibility of much of its theology with Japan's spiritual traditions. This is much less true of the new Japanese religions.

Since roughly the 1850s, there have been at least three religion booms in Japan during which new and often quite unorthodox faiths have attracted large numbers of people. The first boom coincided with the end of Tokugawa rule, and the second occurred after World War II. Some observers assert that the third boom, which dates back to the 1970s, is still occurring. There are hundreds of the new religions, and several, of which Soka Gakkai is the largest, have millions of members. Approximately 11 million Japanese are adherents of the new religions.

Most of the new religious movements have high-profile leaders, many of whom behave in somewhat similar fashion to charismatic Christian evangelists in the United States. The new religions originally tended to promise happiness on earth and deliverance from suffering if members faithfully subscribed to the creeds. Other characteristics of the more prominent new religions include lavish headquarters and mass meetings attended by thousands. Until recently, the overwhelming majority of followers of the new religions were lower-middle-class or poor people, many of whom spent their youths in rural areas and moved to the city for economic reasons. However, there is substantial evidence dating from the 1980s and 1990s that the socioeconomic class backgrounds of people who are attracted to some of the newest religions are becoming more varied. These newest religions seem to be appealing to younger and often well-educated people who feel alienated with what they see as evil materialism and a nonsensical world.

Soka Gakkai merits special attention because of its large following, great wealth, and political activities. Soka Gakkai, or in English, "Value-Creation Society," was founded in 1930 but began to attract a large number of adherents after World War II. Soka Gakkai was originally affiliated with the more than 700-year-old Nichiren Buddhist sect, but the two religious organizations severed ties in the early 1990s. Although the statistics are highly disputed, Soka Gakkai is reputed to have somewhere between 8 and 9 million members in Japan and somewhere between 1 and 2 million members in 120 other countries including the United States. The sect's beliefs and practices are a combination of mantra chanting, positive thinking, and self-help strategies. Soka Gakkai makes generous donations to charities and claims to promote peace, culture, and education. Still, Soka Gakkai's claim that other religions are in error makes many Japanese quite ill at ease.

Large numbers of Japanese are also disturbed by the wealth and influence of Soka Gakkai. Estimates are that the sect has amassed approximately $82 billion through sale of burial plots, rental property, and publications. Soka Gakkai also has a political arm, the New Komeito (formerly Komeito), or "Clean Government" Party, which commands several million votes and has accounted in the past at times for approximately one-tenth of Japan's voting population and an estimated one-fifth of voters who turn out in most elections. Because of this political strength, the Liberal Democratic Party has in recent years included the moderate to socially conservative Komeito Party in coalition governments.

Although many Japanese continue to be uneasy about Soka Gakkai, the Japanese people were shocked by the March 20, 1995, actions of Aum Shinriyko, a doomsday new religions cult led by Shoko Asahara, a partially blind former meditation teacher. Allegedly acting to divert police attention since authorities were already investigating previous cult activities, Aum Shinrikyo members released deadly sarin nerve gas, invented by Nazi German scientists in the 1930s, inside five Tokyo subway cars during rush hour, killing 12 passengers and making more than 5,000 other passengers sick. Authorities then found weapons, poison gas, and torture chambers at the Aum Shinrikyo compound near Mount Fuji as well as clear evidence that cult members had murdered individuals who tried to leave Aum Shinrikyo. Although Aum Shinrikyo's membership (the group recently changed its name to Aleph) has now shrunk to a little more than 1,500 members, in its heyday Aum Shinrikyo claimed to have 10,000 Japanese members as well as considerable membership in Russia. The sarin gas incident caused the Japanese government, while retaining religious freedom, to tighten the legal specifications for obtaining official religious group status.

Aum Shinrikyo's actions also stimulated a discussion in Japan that went far beyond the specific crimes that the cult perpetrated. Many of the cult's leaders were young, well-educated Japanese with university degrees. A number of social commentators as well as some young people feel that too many young Japanese are now experiencing a spiritual malaise. Those concerned about what is perceived as a spiritual vacuum believe that since the end of World War II the most highly valued goals of most Japanese have been economic development and materialism. There does appear to be evidence that a number of young people want something more from life than simply affluence.

PHILOSOPHY: JAPAN, ASIA, AND THE WEST

Readers of the chapter are obviously aware that the interplay between foreign and indigenous ideas and practices is a major theme in Japanese spiritual traditions, and the same is true regarding philosophical thought. Foreign ideas and concepts that

Shoko Asahara, the leader of the Japanese new religion, Aum Shinrikyo who utilized sarin gas to kill 12 people in the Tokyo subway in 1995. (Getty Images)

seem to work are retained and modified so as to fit into the culture while what does not fit the Japanese situation is rejected. Since Japanese began to interact with the West in the mid-19th century, one reoccurring dilemma that some of Japan's greatest thinkers have pondered is how to learn from Europe and the United States yet retain traditional Japanese and East Asian spiritual and philosophical values.

In some cases, there has been a good fit. Neo-Confucianism, which was influential during parts of the Tokugawa period and afterward, stressed the investigation of a variety of phenomena, which was a good fit with the Western emphasis on science. The 19th-century samurai, artist, and proponent of Western science and medicine Watanabe Kazan epitomized this combination of East and West in his life's work, yet Tokugawa government persecution led him eventually to suicide. The religious leader and educator Uchimura Kanzo, who described himself as Japanese, the son of a samurai, and an independent Christian, also successfully synthesized Eastern and Western ideas, as did the philosopher Nishida Kitaro, who was influenced by both William James and Zen. Other Western and Asian ideas—the Chinese notion that the emperor has a mandate of heaven that can be revoked or the reliance of South Asians, Muslims, and Christians on a sacred text—have largely been rejected.

Since the latter part of the 19th century, public intellectuals, university philosophers, social critics, and the increasingly well-educated public have been steeped in Western ideas ranging from Marxism to classic liberalism. Just as was the case with earlier continental Asian influences, many Japanese have borrowed some elements of Western ideologies and belief systems that met their needs while rejecting other components of various doctrines. So what are some modes of thought that can be identified as ones that many Japanese hold? One is a tendency in spiritual traditions to emphasize the immanent, or the notion that divinity is in all things including humans, rather than the idea of a transcendent god. Another Japanese approach to life is a kind of situational pragmatism, or the use of a mode of thinking for concrete real-life situations, rather than a reliance on a set of overarching absolute principles. Most Japanese at some level also seem to manage to critique Western notions of the overarching importance of the rational while still employing this mode of thinking in their everyday lives. These modes of thought that have just been described must be taken with many grains of salt. Japan is a free society and a dynamic one. Still, these propensities exist and have been commented on extensively by both Japanese and foreigners.

ARE THE JAPANESE RELIGIOUS?

When sociological surveys are conducted of contemporary Japanese, only about 26 percent of the public and 12 percent of university students indicate they are religious. Less than a third of Japanese typically indicate they belong to a religious group. When asked to name Japanese religions, few respondents even mention Shinto. Twenty percent of Japanese in one survey described themselves as atheists. Sixty-nine percent of respondents trusted the police, and 63 percent had faith in the legal system, but only 12 percent of Japanese trusted religious institutions, with 40 percent of respondents indicating religious groups were just out to make money. Yet one-half of respondents believed in God or Buddhas and almost two-thirds believed in an unseen higher power. Almost 20 percent of atheists indicated they believed in God (Swanson 2006, 1–12; Bodiford 2006)!

What does all this information tell us? The term "religion" is a Western one in the minds of most Japanese and in many ways does not apply to the rites and practices, especially those associated with Shinto, in which many Japanese engage. Traditional Western notions of what constitutes a religion also often do not fit with widely held beliefs associated with Buddhism. Dominant Japanese religions lack the highly specific prescriptive codes of conduct found in such faiths as Christianity, Judaism, and Islam. Thus, Japan is characterized by more religious toleration than many societies and by a lack of clearly defined religious-based moral laws. Many Japanese are frightened of the new religions, especially in light of the Aum Shinriyko incident. First and foremost, in the words of the scholar of Japanese religions William Bodiford (2006), in Japan, "no religion does not mean non-religion."

REFERENCES

"Aum Followers Down by 10." *Japan Times Online*, August 16, 2000. http://www.japantimes.com (July 2001).

Bodiford, William. "Religion and No Religion in Asian Religions." Paper presented at the Asia in the Curriculum: 5th Annual Symposium, Los Angeles, CA, 2006.

Dawkins, William. "New Religions Have Been a Feature of Japan's Modern History." *Financial Times* (London), April 3, 1995. http://www.lexis-nexis.com (accessed January 2008).

Dawson, Chester. "In God's Country." *Far Eastern Economic Review*, June 22, 2000, 26–27.

DharmaNet International. 2007. http://www.dharmanet.org (accessed January 2008).

Duke, Benjamin C. ed. *Ten Great Educators of Modern Japan: A Japanese Perspective*. Japan: University of Tokyo Press, 1989.

Dumoulin, Heinrich. *Zen Buddhism: A History, India and China*. Bloomington, IN: World Wisdom, 2005.

French, Howard W. "A Sect's Political Rise Creates Uneasiness in Japan." *New York Times*, November 14, 1999. http://www.nytimes.com (accessed January 2008).

Kasulis, Thomas P. (1998). "Japanese Philosophy." In E. Craig (ed.), *Routledge Encyclopedia of Philosophy*. London: Routledge. (January 2008). http://www.rep.routledge.com/article/G100.

Marshall, Andrew. "It Gassed the Tokyo Subway, Microwaved Its Enemies, and Tortured Its Members. So Why Is the Aum Cult Thriving?" *The Guardian* (London), July 15, 1999. http://www.guardian.co.uk (accessed June 2001).

Minoru, Sonoda. *The World of Shinto: Reflections of a Shinto Priest*. Tokyo: International Society for Educational Information, 2002.

Moore, Joe, ed. *The Other Japan: Conflict, Compromise, and Resistance since 1945*. New ed. Armonk: NY: M. E. Sharpe, 1997.

"New Religions Rivaling Old Traditions in Japan." *Los Angeles Times*, May 13, 1995. http://www.latimes.com (accessed January 2008).

Parry, Richard Lloyd. "Japan Braced for the Party of Mantra and Machiavelli." *The Independent* (London), June 25, 2000. http://www.independent.co.uk (accessed June 2001).

"Popularity of Cults Reflects Japan's Gaping Spiritual Void." *Japan Times*, December 22, 1999. http://www.lexis-nexis.com (accessed June 2001).

Radin, Charles A. "Young Adults in Japan Find Spirituality in New Forms." *Boston Globe*, May 21, 1995. http://www.lexis-nexis.com (accessed June 2001).

Reader, Ian. *Religious Violence in Contemporary Japan: The Case of Aum Shinrikyo*. Honolulu: University of Hawai'i Press, 2000.

Reid, T. R. *Confucius Lives Next Door: What Living in the East Teaches Us about Living in the West*. New York: Vintage, 1999.

Sadao, Asami. "New Religions Tend to Thrive Amid Social Malaise." *Daily Yomiuri*, May 24, 1995. http://www.lexis-nexis.com (accessed June 2001).

Suzuki, Daisetz T. *Zen and Japanese Culture*. Rutland, VT: Charles E. Tuttle Company, 1959.

Swanson, Paul, and Clark Chilson, eds. *Nanzan Guide to Japanese Religions*. Honolulu: University of Hawaii Press, 2006.

Watt, Paul. "Buddhism in Japan." *Asia for Educators*. 5 January 2008. http://afe.easia.columbia.edu/japan/japanworkbook/religion/jbuddhis.html.

———. "Shinto." *Asia for Educators*. 5 January 2008. http://afe/easia.columbia.edu/japan/japanworkbook/religion/shinto.htm.

Webster, Fiona. "The Wellspring of Pacifism in Japan." Review of *Prophets of Peace: Pacifism and Cultural Identity in Japan's New Religions*, by Robert Kisala. *Japan Times Online*, April 12, 2000. http://www.japantimes.co.jp (accessed June 2001).

Social Classes and Ethnicity

INTRODUCTION: SOCIAL CLASSES AND ETHNICITY IN A NON-WESTERN SOCIETY

Both many Japanese and Westerners consider Japan to be unique among nations in its ethnic homogeneity and high levels of egalitarianism and social harmony. Most social scientists who study Japanese society strongly disagree with these stereotypes. Japan is homogenous compared to such nations as India, the United States, and Singapore, but such Northern European countries as Sweden and Norway are comparable to Japan. Furthermore, as indicated in the geography chapter, Japan is steadily becoming more ethnically heterogeneous.

Although Japan is not a starkly inequitable society by world standards, identifiable socioeconomic classes have always existed in Japan. Most sociologists agree that contemporary social stratification patterns in Japan are generally quite similar to what exists in other developed capitalist democracies. Both Japan's growing ethnic minorities and the historic and contemporary presence of social classes mean that people have always existed in Japan who have scarce economic resources or who deviate from widely held social expectations, despite the deserved reputation of Japanese for achieving societal stability through much of their history.

In addition to understanding that Japanese social relations are in many ways similar to what exists in many other nations, it is also important to realize that Japan is not a Western society. Just as was the case with religion, a narrow social class and ethnicity-based analysis of Japan is Eurocentric and ignores fundamental differences between Japanese and Western interpersonal relations that have existed for thousands of years.

First and foremost, historically as well as presently, Japan is one of the most group-oriented societies on earth. In the words of the late Harvard professor and famous Japanologist Edwin Reischauer, "Certainly no difference is more significant between Japanese and Americans, or Westerners in general, than the greater Japanese tendency to emphasize the group, somewhat at the expense of the individual" (Reischauer 1977, 127).

Also, Japan, despite its democratic political system, is markedly more hierarchical in social relations than is the case in Europe or the United States. Confucianism, as well as other historical and cultural factors, helped to shape a society where situations in which individuals or institutions that are considered equal in status are much rarer than is the case with the West. The concepts of egalitarianism and democracy as known in Western Europe and the United States, although there have been competing ideologies, were born in ancient Athens and grew significantly in

A group of Japanese secondary school students most probably on a school excursion. (Corel)

the 18th century in the United States and France. Therefore, there is more of a tradition in the West of social and political equality and individualism than is the case in Japan.

The concepts of group culture and Japan as a vertical society where equal status is the exception rather than the rule so fundamentally affect social class and minority/ethnicity issues in the archipelago that they are the starting point for any understanding of these topics.

THE GROUP AND THE VERTICAL SOCIETY

Despite increasing signs of individualism among the young, more often than not the expected behavior for Japanese in a wide range of social relations is to subordinate individual desires to group interests. Group loyalty, which is still taught early and reinforced in almost every aspect of Japanese life, has a long history in Japan. Confucianism, with its major objective of the achievement of societal harmony through, among other factors, an individual's understanding of his or her status and role in the group, greatly influenced Japanese thinking about the importance of the group over individual interest. A fundamental tenet of Buddhism is that all animate and even inanimate beings are one. This basic tenet serves to de-emphasize focus on individual wants and needs. In contrast to these East Asian belief systems that accentuate the hierarchy and the group, Christianity, the most influential Western belief system, teaches that every person has a soul separate from the rest of the universe. Even Westerners who are not Christians have been influenced by thousands of years of greater emphasis on the individual than is the case elsewhere.

Other forces have influenced the growth of the power of the group. As readers of the history chapter are aware, the importation of wet paddy rice cultivation constituted one of the earliest and most vital economic developments in early Japan. As is the case in the rest of East Asia, this agricultural process depends on effective group cooperation. The Tokugawa shoguns created a long-lived (1600–1868) stable government characterized by a clearly defined Neo-Confucian class system, peace, and, for most people, a lack of contact with the outside world. A major difference in Neo-Confucianism and earlier versions of Confucianism was that the former placed great emphasis on class hierarchy. During the Tokugawa period of Japanese history, most people were socialized to know their status and subsequently expected roles within groups that in turn related to each other within the context of a predetermined class hierarchy. Samurai were the elites, followed in status by farmers, artisans, and merchants. Certain groups such as priests enjoyed relatively high status but did not fit into a class, while other groups such as Burakumin were considered low status because they engaged in work such as butchery or tanning that Buddhists considered unclean.

Japan's historic high levels of homogeneity also made it much easier for group cooperation to be nurtured than in many other countries, including even its neighbor, imperial China. Geographically, Japan has always been a hazardous place compared to most countries—and frequent earthquakes, typhoons, and fires often forced people to work together to survive disasters.

The family has been the fundamental microcosm of Japan's group culture. Until the mid-20th century, the majority of Japanese lived in rural areas and extended families were the norm. Husbands and wives as well as older relatives, children, and siblings usually worked together as farmers or proprietors of small enterprises. As Japan experienced the post–World War II "economic miracle," in which the nation averaged annual economic growth rates of 10 percent for approximately 20 years, family structure became much more like the United States and Western Europe. A larger percentage of retired adults in Japan than in the United States still live with or near their children, but the nuclear family is now the norm. Readers of the next section of this chapter will learn that family structure has also become more diverse in Japan as is true in the West. However, despite significant recent changes, most Japanese still expect adults to inculcate young children in appropriate behavior, and subordinating one's desires to a larger group remains important in the socialization process.

As noted, Japan is also a hierarchal or "vertical" society in which traditionally people both within an organization and from different organizations are rarely equal in status. Not only are Japanese loyal to particular groups to which they belong, but also within a particular group a clear hierarchy exists, with different members having different amounts of status. Also, at times, many Japanese tend to use more formal language and behave in a cool and distant manner to people who are not members of their specific group. Interpersonal relations can become complex. Within a government agency, for example, members of a particular department will be much more informal with each other than with members of another department but have a different interpersonal style entirely when dealing with people who are not part of their particular government agency. The Japanese are more acutely aware not only of organizational status but also of an individual's place in the hierarchy than are people in many cultures. Sociologists commonly use the terms "in-groups" and "out-groups" when describing the varying interpersonal relations styles Japanese might employ depending on circumstances.

It is difficult to overestimate the vertical society's influence on Japanese interpersonal relations. Back in the 1970s and 1980s, Sekigun, or the Japanese Red Army, was a notorious group of Marxist terrorists who engaged in much-publicized bank robberies and murders as they fought against capitalism, unequal social relations, and other forms of oppression that prevented the achievement of an egalitarian society. A disproportionate number of Sekigun members, as is the case with most terrorist groups, had attended a university or were graduates. However, in the process of stopping an attack on the prime minister's residence, the police obtained a Sekigun organizational chart. What they learned is typical of most Japanese organizations with respect to issues of hierarchy and status. The Sekigun membership was organized into separate attack squads, with graduates of the most prestigious universities responsible for the more critical and dangerous tasks. Even in a Japanese organization devoted to abolishing hierarchy, hierarchy mattered (Steinhoff 1989, 224–40).

Typically, two businesspeople, government bureaucrats, or academics who have never met will, when introduced, exchange and carefully study each other's business cards. Vigilant observers might notice that each of the two people will appear to be carefully studying the other's business card. This is because each party is trying to quickly gain a sense of the status of both the other person as well as, if not known, his or her organization. Often (but not necessarily always), the status of the organization with which the individual is affiliated determines individual status. As the Sekigun example should indicate, these vertical and in-group/out-group relations are true not just of workplace groups and organizations but also virtually the entire range of Japanese organizations from literary clubs to the yakuza, or Japanese mafia.

Historically, even certain family members would lose in-group status in one family through marriage but gain it in another. When a younger son or a daughter in one family married, often he or she moved away, joined another family, and was no longer considered a member of the original family. Similarly, in a family with only daughters, when the oldest married, her husband would often become part of her family and sometimes would even adopt his wife's family name. Although this kind of change has become less the norm today, it has not disappeared.

GROUP SOCIALIZATION: THE SCHOOL

Most Japanese learn appropriate social behavior toward in- and out-groups first as children at home and then in school; many continue these patterns of interactions at work. Understanding how groupism and hierarchy play out at school and work is essential to understanding social class and ethnicity in Japan.

Although Japanese parents, as is briefly addressed in the next section, begin inculcating culturally appropriate behaviors in infants and young children, the

Junior high school students lining up for exercises. (Corel)

socialization of the young is considered more of a priority in Japanese schools than is the case in the West. The process begins in Japanese kindergartens, where getting along with others is considered more important than academics. American preschool teachers are invariably surprised when they visit Japanese kindergartens and find less emphasis on academics than in the United States. Although academics become more important in first grade, there is still more time placed on the affective than the academic during this school year in Japan compared to the United States. Japanese students usually remain together as a class with the same teachers through the first and second grades. Classes, or *kumi*, as the Japanese call them, constantly learn, play, and even eat together for two years, and children often develop a strong attachment to the kumi. Japanese teachers work hard to foster this attachment by focusing their attention on the kumi as a whole at the expense of individualized instruction. Whole-class instruction is more prevalent in Japan than in the United States throughout the school years, and one of the reasons for this is Japan's focus on the group rather than the individual.

Most Japanese elementary schools do not have cafeterias, and kumi eat together in the classroom along with the teacher. Within each kumi, smaller groups of students, called *han*, are responsible on a rotating basis for bringing the food to and from the school kitchen to the classroom. The hans also take turns cleaning the classroom.

Each kumi and han in elementary school also incorporates student leaders, often in the case of han on a rotational basis, who assist the larger classroom group and the smaller groups within in operating effectively. Teachers sometimes give classroom assignments to the han, and group loyalty is fostered as children work together to complete tasks. Almost all Japanese sixth and ninth graders take field trips lasting several days to famous cultural and historical sites. Children are often assigned bus or train seats on the basis of their particular kumi and han, and teachers check attendance by consulting the kumi and han leaders.

Extracurricular clubs are important in junior and senior high school. Although there are exceptions, when a Japanese student joins a club—a tennis, flower arranging, or dramatics group—he or she is expected to exhibit total group commitment. This means the member will work hard for the club and show the appropriate amount of respect to older club members. For example, it is common in high school baseball practice for sophomores to play very little, sometimes regardless of their abilities. Instead, younger team members spend most of their time retrieving bats and balls and keeping the playing field in good shape for the juniors and seniors.

Young people who attend university and join Japanese clubs find that many expect group loyalty and respect for senior members. By the time a Japanese person reaches adulthood, much of his or her socialization has emphasized teamwork and group hierarchies and expectations. This pattern of personal interaction often continues in the workplace.

WORKPLACE GROUPS

In the years after World War II, the workplace replaced the traditional extended family of earlier times as the primary group for many Japanese, particularly males. Despite the fact that a majority of Japanese workers never held "lifetime" employment and the numbers of those who have this privilege have contracted recently, in a number of companies and government ministries, new employees are treated, at least superficially if not in actuality, like family members. Some companies even have special training programs for new workers that focus exclusively on building loyalty.

Many more Japanese than Westerners still tend to define themselves by their workplace. Typically, when a white-collar employee of a large firm introduces himself, he will say something like "I am Yamato and I work for Toyota," rather than identify whether he is an accountant, an engineer, or an attorney. Japanese white-collar workers are still more likely than their Western counterparts to passively accept transfers to undesirable locations. It is common in Japan for male office workers and managers to be transferred to another part of the country and because their children are in stable school situations, leave their family behind and visit on weekends.

Japanese employees, especially in large companies, tend to put in long hours on the job together, much of which is unpaid overtime. Japanese define "working" a bit differently than Westerners in part because of group expectations and hierarchy. Although most Japanese employees work hard, it is often also a cultural expectation that employees demonstrate group loyalty by being at work at various times of the day, particularly late in the afternoon if the boss has not left, whether they are actually working or not.

It is also common practice in Japanese companies for white-collar employees at various levels, especially males, to socialize together after work on a regular basis. This often entails drinking and dinner and is one to the reasons many Japanese men spend so little time at home. Some company employees will even take "vacations" together at spas or other recreational facilities owned by their firm where they hear motivational speeches and otherwise exclusively associate with fellow employees.

Companies have traditionally been more paternalistic toward employees than is the case in the West. A work associate, particularly an eligible bachelor's superior, might matchmake an employee by introducing him to suitable single women. Although layoffs have increased since the 1990s, they are still more rare in Japan than in Western countries. Also, promotion and pay increases in Japanese companies are still based more on seniority than in the United States. The rationale is that individuals should be rewarded as the amount of time they are loyal to the group increases.

Decision making in the workplace, and other kinds of formal organizations as well, usually reflects the group orientation of the Japanese. Traditionally, Japanese organizations often employ a group decision-making process called *nemawashi*, or "root binding," taken from the gardening procedures used by growers of miniature bonsai trees. As trees are repotted, roots are carefully pruned and positioned to determine future shape. Many times before a decision is made in a Japanese company, leaders will carefully check with many people who could be affected by the decisions, starting with the junior employees. If too many employees have objections, leaders might drop an idea altogether or modify a proposed decision. Even if top management makes a decision contrary to subordinates' decisions, most Japanese consider it important that prior consultation has occurred.

Usually, personal workplace status is based, as noted, on the overall reputation of the organization for which one works. However, one's educational level, gender (males usually have higher status), the particular educational institution from which one graduated, and how long a person has been with the organization also are factors. Although these variables affect one's status with others in virtually all cultures, they have greater effect in Japan than is often the case elsewhere. Except for employees who have equal educational status and joined the company at the same time, most Japanese have very few equals on the job. One's associates usually have either higher or lower status. Even if a person is better at a job than an associate who happens to have been with the company longer, traditionally the less-seasoned employee is expected to be deferential to the senior worker.

Groups in any society require leaders, but Japan's strong group-oriented culture often causes even high-ranking officials or managers to exhibit different behaviors toward their subordinates than is true in more individualistic cultures such as the United States. As is true with Japanese politicians, workplace leaders have been traditionally expected to keep relatively low profiles and certainly not appear to be overly aggressive and autocratic in workplace interpersonal relations.

Japanese often attain leadership positions in an organization not because they are dynamic, decisive, and flamboyant but because they are good listeners and consensus builders. Ideally, top Japanese executives are expected to be the first to sacrifice when hard times arrive. For example, Japanese managers take pay cuts when companies do badly, and sometimes seniors will even resign for a subordinate's misdeed if it is considered serious enough.

SOCIAL CLASS AND MOBILITY

Japan is similar not only to the United States but to Western European countries as well in that between 8 and 92 percent or more of survey respondents from these countries have classified themselves as middle class. Japan is also comparable to other developed nations in the relative percentages of respondents that reported being upper, upper-middle, lower-middle, and lower class (Sugimoto 2003, 36–37).

When Japan, the United Kingdom, and the United States are compared regarding social mobility rates, the opportunity for intergenerational class mobility appears to have become more difficult in Japan compared to the other two nations since the 1970s. From shortly after World War II until that point, a higher percentage of Japanese were getting better jobs than their parents because the great postwar economic transformation of Japan meant that many people who were poor after World War II had increased prospects of getting higher paying jobs because of impressive annual economic growth rates (Sugimoto 2003, 36–37).

How well the educational system functions as an instrument for young people without wealth to advance in society is another indicator of the level of social mobility in a given society. Japan, like other developed countries, has thousands of young people with modest means who every year begin the process of eventually rising to a higher-status job through public school educational success. However, until the 1980s, a substantial number of successful applicants to the nation's most prestigious institution of higher learning, Tokyo University, attended public high schools. By 1993, almost 50 percent of first-year students admitted to Tokyo University were from expensive private high schools, and 21 of the top 30 Tokyo University feeder high schools were private. By 2005, private schools constituted all but one of the top 23 placement high schools (Kelly and White 2006, 69). What is true of Tokyo University is also the case with competition to enter other elite Japanese universities. It appears that at least in the case of admissions to top-ranked universities, public schools are not as much of a vehicle for social mobility as they have been in the past.

Also, like several developed countries including the United States, in Japan the dramatic rise in university graduates over the past two decades means that higher education is no longer an automatic ticket to high status or economic success. However, the type of university one attends in Japan counts for even more than in the United States in determining the individual's later status and income earning potential. The majority of Japanese university students attend private universities, and most are markedly inferior compared to public universities in Japan. As readers of the economics chapter are aware, the growth in part-time and temporary workers in Japan since the 1990s also makes social mobility more difficult for recent high school and university graduates since companies hire fewer full-time employees than in the past.

The larger point here is that Japan is much more similar to than different from other developed countries regarding the existence of socioeconomic classes. In Japan and other developed democratic capitalist countries, average people live far more materially rich lives than earlier generations and have affluence levels that people in developing countries today can only imagine. However, socioeconomic classes are just as much a part of the social fabric of Japan as they are in other advanced societies. This is especially important to remember regarding Japan because many political, media, and educational elites in that country have promulgated the notion that Japan is somehow different in respect to class than other nations. This appeared to be true for almost three decades after World War II, but after Japan reached the status of a highly developed nation, the facts no longer supported the egalitarian myths still believed by some Japanese and foreigners.

PRESSURES TO CONFORM

To return to an earlier point; Japan is different than the West in that group pressure and the vertical nature of society are more powerful elements in social relations. The group orientation of Japan can make organizations effective and nurture individuals who are part of the same group. A clear sense of individuals who are part of an organization about their respective roles, their place in the organizational hierarchy, and who is in charge can also contribute to social stability.

However, groupism and hierarchy also have negative repercussions for many Japanese, especially those who are different from other group members for whatever reason. Ethnic or cultural minority groups, who constitute the fastest-growing segments of Japan's population, find relations with the majority population particularly difficult, as readers will discover later in this section.

The great pressure to conform placed on the individual by the group also has a negative side. There are appropriate procedures for almost any act that Japanese perform if one wants to behave appropriately. This applies to everything imaginable, including the appropriate language, depending on another's age or status; the appropriate placement of shoes by an entrance; and the correct way to wrap a gift. Many Japanese find that close attention must be paid to most verbal and nonverbal communication in order not to risk offending others. Individuals often report that they much admire the direct and open use of language that appears to be part of many cultures' social relations as well as less accentuation on the correct way to do a wide variety of things.

Many Japanese also indicate they respect the greater social freedom to be different that citizens enjoy in other developed countries without the fear of being negatively labeled as unconventional. Japan has not been a society where individuals who dare to be different have traditionally fared well. The old Japanese proverb that the nail that sticks up too much gets hammered down has often meant difficult times for, among others, young people and workers who do not fit in with the group.

The rigidity of Japanese schools is, in part, a direct result of the pressure for conformity. Although this is changing, students who have special learning needs or who have been abroad and out of the educational system for a time were either ignored or bullied in the past. This kind of ostracism and bullying directed at individuals who don't conform to the group also can apply to adults. The late Miyamoto Masao, a Western-trained medical doctor and psychologist with the Ministry of Health, wrote periodical articles and a book exposing the bureaucracies' foibles. Miyamoto reported being told by coworkers in private that even though they admired what he was doing, because he was the target of bullying, they could not afford to be seen with him or to be known as his friend.

Miyamoto's troubles began earlier with his work group when he requested two weeks of vacation—time to which he was legally entitled. Although his superior expressed shock, Miyamoto took the holiday anyway. He then became a pariah among those with whom he worked because many Japanese government bureaucrats don't do such unconventional, individualistic things as take full vacations. Miyamoto argued that Japan's pervasive pressure to conform to group mores is a kind of totalitarianism without an identifiable center. There is no individual, legislative body, judiciary, or committee that specifies these group pressures, but group members usually know full well what is expected of them and most behave accordingly, despite their personal feelings.

Whether deserved or not, Japan has a reputation for not being a particularly creative society. Although the validity of this criticism is certainly open to debate, the Japanese government was concerned enough about the issue that they initiated educational reforms in the early part of the 21st century designed to create better independent and critical thinkers. Many Westerners and Japanese contend that the pressure to conform to group norms in Japanese schools inhibits individual creativity.

The victims of *ijime*, or school bullying, usually have either physical characteristics or mannerisms that set them apart from other student groups. An example is found in the children of Japanese workers stationed overseas. As Japanese companies established foreign branches, the children of the transferred employees attended foreign schools. In such Western countries as the United States and the United Kingdom, this almost always meant a more relaxed atmosphere (Japanese early childhood education excepted) than in Japan. After they returned home, many Japanese young people were subjected to criticism and sometimes harassment from fellow students for their perceived strange foreign ways. There were even cases where Japanese teachers criticized students for being too good in conversational English.

The Japanese government has attempted to respond to this educational problem by helping to establish more than 80 Japanese schools and 187 Japanese supplementary schools for the approximately 52,000 Japanese students now temporarily living in other countries.

The Ministry of Education also sent more than 1,300 Japanese teachers to staff the full-time schools. The Ministry of Education has attempted to accommodate the returnee children through establishing special classes for them in the attached schools of Japan's national universities, conducting training programs for teachers on how to better work with returnee children, and creating special selection processes for returnees who seek admission to competitive Japanese high schools and universities. The two objectives of these broad policy initiatives are to ensure that students who have lived abroad are able to smoothly function in Japanese society and, at the same time, encourage Japanese students and adults to view the returnee young people's international experience as an asset in internationalizing Japanese society. At present, it is difficult to assess the degree of success of these programs.

Students who are gifted and students who have learning problems also traditionally had a very tough time in Japanese classrooms. In the past few years, there has been progress in establishing school-based special education programs. Still, despite an easing of the rigid requirements that prevented accelerated students from skipping grades, few accommodations are made for gifted high school students. Japanese educators, government officials, and members of the public are now experimenting with various ideas, including 21st-century educational reforms that are addressed later in this chapter, to create a better climate for students who are perceived as different from the norm.

As world economic competition becomes more intense, there is mounting evidence that group-oriented business thinking hurts many Japanese companies. Traditionally, Japanese companies have formed keiretsu, or business groups, and purchased materials and products from only member companies, regardless of price. As Japanese manufacturing costs have increased, this strategy is less and less economically defensible. Companies can also lose business opportunities because of the slow decision-making process fostered by a great concern for group consultation. Many times, top Japanese managers or government officials might not be the most competent people in a given organization but have attained their position because of a talent for offending the least number of people. Increasing numbers of young people are also seriously questioning the previously largely unchallenged value that an individual should sacrifice his or her private life for the welfare of the company.

ETHNIC AND MINORITY GROUPS

In large part because of their sense of uniqueness from other cultures, racial homogeneity, and group solidarity, traditionally the Japanese have not particularly related well to minorities in Japan or foreigners in general. The group orientation and the vertical nature of Japanese society, in addition to cultural differences between minorities and the majority population, have resulted in large percentages of cultural and ethnic minorities facing discrimination while languishing in the lower tiers of society.

The Ainu, declared an indigenous people by the Japanese Diet (national legislature) in June 2008 after a long struggle for this classification, are the oldest cultural group on the archipelago who are not ethnically Japanese. The Ainu, who some archeologists argue lived in the archipelago as early as 8000 BCE, are comparable in several respects to Native Americans in their physical features and culture. Ainu homelands originally included southern Sakhalin, the Kurile Islands, northern Honshu, and what is now Hokkaido. The Japanese government used military force, in a manner similar to U.S. policy with Native Americans, to drive the Ainu away from

A member of the indigeneous Ainu tribe. Note the bear on the headdress. Ainu consider the animal sacred. (Corel)

much of their land. By the Tokugawa period, the island of Ezochi attracted the attention of Japanese settlers, who began incursions into the resource-rich area. The Ainu resisted Japanese incursions with force, but by 1789 they had fought and lost their battle.

The Meiji government systematically colonized Ezochi, renaming it Hokkaido. The Japanese government, who used former American Bureau of Indian Affairs officials to help them formulate Ainu policy, was in large part responsible for the destruction of much of the Ainu's traditional culture. Although by the late 19th century the government made efforts to educate and assist a people who had become impoverished because of overhunting and a new dependence on rice and sake, Ainu language was repressed, men had to shave their beards, and women were forbidden to wear ceremonial blue facial tattoos. The Ainu also lost rights to natural resources, and limits were even placed on the annual ceremonial salmon catches. In the 1920s, an Ainu tourist industry developed in response to Japanese demand, and it continues today. Also, by the 20th century Ainu were pressuring the Japanese government for reform. Although the Japanese Diet responded by eventually increasing assistance to the Ainu, and passed legislation in 1997 to promote and preserve traditional Ainu culture, the government still refused to recognize the Ainu as an indigenous people until the summer of 2008.

Because of longtime assimilationist pressures, it is extremely difficult to estimate the actual national Ainu population; estimates vary widely from 30,000 to 300,000 with the more reliable indicating there are probably about 50,000 people who are over half Ainu ethnicity and approximately 150,000 with some Ainu heritage. Despite gradual official Japanese policy and attitude changes toward the Ainu, it remains a serious question as to whether the culture can be preserved since even relatively few Ainu know the spoken language and other traditional customs. In Hokkaido, almost 40 percent of Ainu receive welfare, in contrast to about 25 percent of the general population (Hokkaido is one of Japan's poorer prefectures), and only a fraction more than 17 percent of Ainu attend college.

Burakumin, or "village people," are ethnic Japanese who have been discriminated against since before the Tokugawa period. Although the reasons for this long history of discrimination are debated, Burakumin traditionally engaged in such occupations as butchery, tanning, and funeral work that put them in contact with flesh, which both Buddhist and Shinto religions proscribed. By the Tokugawa period, Burakumin were outcastes who lived in segregated villages. The between 200,000 and 300,000 descendents of Burakumin, many of whom live in the Osaka and northern Kyushu area, still experience some discrimination today. In the Meiji period, an 1871 Emancipation Decree was passed, making the Burakumin commoners instead of an outcaste group, and laws against Burakumin marrying other groups were removed. However, the government also ended monopolies that Burakumin enjoyed with certain trades, depriving them of longtime economic livelihoods. The Meiji also initiated a family registry system that made it easier to identify Burakumin.

Throughout the 20th century, the Burakumin were victims of social discrimination and economic hardship and were usually relegated to low-status jobs. However, Burakumin liberation movements, in existence since before World War II, became powerful enough in the 1960s to pressure the national government into passing substantial legislation beginning in 1969 that provided economic and educational aid to areas with large Burakumin populations. Recent polls of Burakumin indicating that almost two-thirds report they have not been the victims of discrimination constitute evidence of substantial social progress. Still, despite legal equality, Burakumin continue to suffer more than other Japanese from poverty, drug and alcohol abuse, and welfare dependency. Some Japanese families also continue the practice of investigating the prospective spouses of their marriage-age children for Burakumin backgrounds.

Even though Okinawa is today a prefecture of Japan, many Japanese do not consider the approximately 1.37 million people who live there to be Japanese. Also, according to recent polls, a majority of Okinawans consider themselves either Okinawan or Okinawan and Japanese rather than simply Japanese. Okinawan resentments against Japan have a long history. Japan first took over the independent kingdom and then, from an Okinawan perspective, abandoned the islands to yet another foreign power, the United States. The United States returned Okinawa to Japan in 1972. Although a great deal of contemporary Okinawan resentment focuses on the large number of U.S. military bases on the islands, Okinawans resent the Japanese for allowing the military bases to exist on their islands in the first place and for what they see as Tokyo's economic neglect. Okinawa also possesses

Elderly Okinawan couple. Although the situation is dynamic, many people from Okinawa do not consider themselves Japanese. (Corel)

a distinctively different culture from Japan in many respects. The problems between the Japanese mainland and Okinawa are compounded by the fact that Okinawans, although well off by world standards, remain poor compared to most mainland Japanese.

Another ethnic Japanese population, but one, unlike Burakumin, whose culture is markedly different from that of Japan, is the estimated 325,000 recent immigrants to Japan from Latin America; 280,000 from Brazil and the remainder from other Latin American countries. Japanese began to emigrate to Brazil and elsewhere in Latin America in 1908 and continued through part of the 1950s. During World War II, Brazil banned Japanese immigration and closed Japanese schools, which meant that many Japanese Brazilian children lost the ability to speak the language of their grandparents and parents and learned Portuguese in Brazilian schools.

In the 1980s, economic development and smaller Japanese families caused a labor supply problem, and it was also increasingly difficult to get many young Japanese to work in menial and dirty jobs. The Japanese government, because of the ethnic and historical linkages, particularly encouraged young Japanese Brazilians to emigrate to the archipelago, but the newcomers' situations have proven more difficult than either Japanese officials or the immigrants imagined. Many do not accept the immigrants because they don't speak Japanese; prefer Brazilian food, festivals, and carnivals with loud samba music; and allegedly lack affinity with Japanese municipal recycling regulations. There are also problems with frequent school absences, substantially high school dropout rates, and higher instances of crime commission on the part of Japanese Brazilians than the general population. Japanese Brazilians for the most part still have low-paying menial jobs because of language and cultural barriers.

Japanese Brazilians primarily reside in Aichi, Gifu, Gunma, Saitama, and Shizuoka Prefectures, all in Honshu. Japanese Brazilians tend to cluster in the same urban neighborhoods, and a number of urban schools in these prefectures are faced with situations where Japanese is not the native language of a plurality or even a majority of students. Japan now has the largest Portuguese-speaking population of any Asian country. Japanese government officials at all levels are beginning to respond to some of the critical problems Japanese Brazilians face, including offering more university Portuguese-language courses and developing Japanese as a Second Language programs. There also have been attempts by local officials to work with the Japanese Brazilians communities to develop festivals and other cultural events to inform the Japanese public about this immigrant group's unique cultural heritage.

Although the number of Chinese living in Japan exceeded that of Korean residents in 2007, from the early years of the 20th century until that year, Koreans constituted Japan's largest ethnic minority. Their situation in the archipelago, although substantially improved during the last two decades, has been a difficult one indeed. Although there were Koreans in Japan before 1910, that date marked the beginning of Japan's control of a previously sovereign kingdom as well as a steady influx of Koreans to Japan that lasted until the end of World War II. The imperial Japanese government forced many Koreans against their will to work in Japan in mines, construction projects, and other manual labor. Many Koreans were sent to such industrial cities as Kobe and Osaka, and large numbers of Korean Japanese and Koreans live in these areas today.

Although after the war two-thirds of Koreans returned home, today there are almost 600,000 people of full or partial Korean ethnicity in Japan. If Koreans marry Japanese and have children, their offspring are automatically Japanese citizens. However, until 1993 Korean families who had lived in Japan for even up to three generations, but who did not marry Japanese, were considered foreigners and were forced to be fingerprinted. This segment of Japan's Korean population, although no longer subjected to the indignity of fingerprinting and also given special status with such privileges as easier entrance and exit from the country, are still considered aliens.

Today more than 80 percent of Koreans marry Japanese, and a number of Korean Japanese have been quite successful in business and the professions. Not only has fingerprinting ended but also students enrolled in Korean schools are allowed to compete against Japanese schools in sports. Still, since at least the latter part of the Meiji period (1868–1912), Japan has a history of prejudice and discrimination toward Koreans. Many of the Koreans who have been successful in the professions in Japan have intentionally hidden their ethnicity. Other Koreans continue to be highly visible in small businesses, pachinko parlors, and ethnic restaurants but substantially underrepresented in Japan's corporate and business worlds.

OH SADAHARU (1940–)

Before professional Japanese players gained even greater fame by playing in the American major leagues as well as in Japan, there was Oh Sadaharu, who played for the Yomiuri Giants beginning in 1958. For 19 consecutive years, he hit more than 30 home runs a year. He hit 55 home runs in one year and won the Triple Crown for two years in succession in 1973 and 1974. His 868 career home runs are a significantly higher number than American leader Barry Bonds has and is a world record. Originally a pitcher, Oh was from a mixed Taiwanese Japanese family. He later went on to manage in Japan's major leagues after his retirement.

As noted, Chinese in Japan from the mainland, Hong Kong, and Taiwan had, according to the Japanese government, exceeded the number of Koreans by the end of 2007 to become Japan's largest minority group, with 606,889 registered Chinese compared to 593,489 Koreans. Also, recent statistics indicate that the 20,500 Chinese students in Japan constitute two-thirds of all foreign students in the nation. These statistics do not reflect the sizeable percentage of Chinese who are included in the estimated 50,000 illegal foreign workers present in Japan. Because of the relatively close proximity of Japan to mainland China, Japanese authorities allege that Chinese and Japanese gangs have collaborated to smuggle poor people looking for better economic opportunities, particularly from Fujian Province, into Japan. The Chinese tend to be concentrated in Tokyo because of the tremendous demand for unskilled labor in the area, but there are Chinatowns in Yokohama and Kobe as well. Many illegal Chinese immigrants have settled in Osaka.

Demand for more workers due to a shrinking labor supply and young Japanese unwillingness to do dirty, dangerous, or menial jobs has attracted people from many countries. Although the government has responded to this situation by allowing more guest workers, with the exception of a regulation applying only to Japanese Brazilians, Tokyo has refused to grant foreign workers permanent residential status.

Filipinos, the fourth-largest group of foreigners in Japan, are a fast-growing segment of an increasingly multicultural Japan, but there are also newcomers from Iran, Ghana, Pakistan, Bangladesh, Nepal, and a number of other countries. Elements of the Japanese public often blame illegal workers, with some evidential justification, for a disproportionate amount of criminal activity. Still, other Japanese engage in broad negative stereotypes about all foreigners in Japan that are not congruent with reality.

For more than 150 years, Japanese have admired many aspects of Western culture, and Japan is arguably the most Western of Asian nations; however, Americans, Australians, and Europeans occasionally encounter what they consider to be Japanese racial insensitivity. For example, although much less true than in the past,

TSURUNEN MARUTEI (1940–)

Marutei made history in 2002 when he was the first Westerner to become a member of the Japanese Diet. Of Finnish ethnicity, Marutei (his original name was Martti Turunen) as a young child experienced a Soviet attack on his home village in Finland, which helped to shape his lifelong pacifist and ecological beliefs. Marutei came to Japan as a lay Lutheran missionary in 1967. In 1974, he married a Japanese woman and after a long struggle became a Japanese citizen in 1979. Working as a translator and educator in the seaside town of Yugawara in Kanagawa Prefecture, he was elected to the city assembly in 1992 and entered the Diet as a Democratic Party of Japan member in 2002 after a member resigned for whom he was runner-up in the last election. Marutei was directly elected in 2007. He is interested in peace issues, the environment, and building a more multicultural Japan.

Westerners can still sometimes hear themselves referred to as "gaijin" within earshot. The exact Japanese meaning for gaijin is "outside person," which is not the most hospitable of inferences for a visitor. It is also illustrative of what traditionally has constituted the ultimate out-group in Japan—all foreigners.

Despite all this, the Japanese do appear to be becoming more accommodating to diversity. In the last two decades, the plight of minorities has received more and more media and political attention. In 2008, the Democratic Party of Japan began discussions in the Diet about liberalizing immigration law so that more foreigners could attain permanent resident status.

Although many Japanese still embrace the myth of Japan as a homogenous nation, and people who are different, be they Japanese or foreign, often have a difficult time in everyday life, Japan has become a more tolerant society in recent decades due to at least one long-standing government program, the internationalization of Japan's economy, and changing attitudes. In 1987 the Japanese government created the Japan Exchange and Teaching Program primarily to improve students' English-speaking abilities and to help Japan become more internationalized in outlook. Currently, 5,119 relatively young college graduates from 41 countries work either as assistant English teachers in Japanese schools or as international exchange specialists in prefecture and local governments. The tens of thousands of Japanese families who have now either lived in foreign countries because of job assignments or interacted with foreign businesspeople in Japan are having an effect on traditional social relations including excessive groupism and hierarchy and attitudes toward those who are different in other respects.

A case in point is the evidence of changing policies and attitudes toward mentally challenged people. Until the latter part of the 20th century, special-needs students were often treated in negative ways. Families who had mentally disabled or other special-needs children often developed a sense of shame and secluded their offspring. Mentally challenged people were often treated by the larger society as if they didn't exist.

In June 2001, a small town in Nagasaki Prefecture hosted a party that the author attended for a group of American teachers who were doing homestays. The feature entertainment at the party was a rousing performance by a group of *taiko* drummers. Taiko, featuring large drums, riveting rhythms, and colorfully attired enthusiastic drummers, has a long and honored role in Japanese festivals and other social events. This group of drummers, who gave a great performance and were extremely well received by both Japanese and foreigners, was unique in one sense. They were all teenagers who had IQs of between 50 and 75. Before they performed, it was announced that these drummers, who entertain groups throughout the prefecture, were students in a special school. Certainly, in this case, the celebration, instead of suppression of diversity, was quite real and serves as encouraging evidence of progress in tolerance.

The problem of converting Japan into a more multicultural society is now an important element not only to social and ethnic relations and socioeconomic class issues but also to Japan's economic and political future. Multicultural Japan is addressed in more detail in the Contemporary Issues chapter of this book.

REFERENCES

"Ainu People." *Wikipedia: The Free Encyclopedia*. 21 August 2008. http://en.wikipedia.org/wiki/ainu_people.

"Burakumin." *Wikipedia: The Free Encyclopedia*. 21 August 2008. http://en.wikipedia.org/wiki/burakumin.

Ito, Masami. "Diet Officially Declares Ainu Indigenous." *Japan Times*, June 7, 2008. http://search.japantimes.co.jp/cgi-bin/nn20080607a1.html.

"Japanese Brazilians." *Wikipedia: The Free Encyclopedia*. 21 August 2008. http://en.wikipedia.org/wiki/japanese_brazilian.

"Japan Says Chinese Are Now the Country's Largest Minority." *China Post Online*, June 4, 2008. http://www.chinapost.com.tw/asia/japan/2008/06/04/159475/japan%2dsays.htm.

JapanZone. "Tsurunen Marutei." http://www.japan-zone.com/modern/tsurunen_marutei.shtml (accessed August 2008).

Karan, Pradyumna P. *Japan in the Twenty-first Century: Environment, Economy, and Society*. Lexington: University Press of Kentucky, 2005.

Kelly, William and Merry White. "Students, Slackers, Singles, Seniors, and Strangers: Transforming a Family-Nation." In Peter J. Katzenstein and Takashi Shiraishi, eds. Beyond Japan: The Dynamics of East Asian Regionalism. Ithaca, NY: Cornell University Press, 2006.

Lie, John. *Multiethnic Japan*. New York: Harvard University Press, 2004.

Masaki, Hisane. "Japan Stares into a Demographic Abyss." *Asia Times Online*, May 9, 2006. http://www.atimes.com (accessed February 2008).

Millard, Mike. Leaving Japan: Observations on the Dysfunctional U.S.-Japan Relationship. Armonk, NY: M. E. Sharpe, 2000.

Miyamoto, Masao. *The Strait Jacket Society*. Tokyo: Kodansha, 1995.

Moore, Joe, ed. The Other Japan: Conflict, Compromise, and Resistance since 1945. New ed. Armonk, NY: M. E. Sharpe, 1997.

"Number of Chinese Students in Japan Hits New Record High." *The People's Daily Online*. 9 January 2006. http://english.peopledaily.com.cn/200601/09/eng20060109_234012.html.

"Red Army." *Journal of Asian Studies* 48, No. 4 (1989): 724–740.

Reischauer, Edwin O. *The Japanese*. Cambridge, MA: Harvard University Press, 1977.

———. *Japan: The Story of a Nation*. 3rd ed. New York: Alfred Knopf, 1981.

Rice, Richard. "Ainu Submergence and Emergence: Human Rights Discourse and the Expression of Ethnicity in Modern Japan." *Southeast Review of Asian Studies* 28, (2006): 9–24.

Steinhoff, Patricia G. "Hijackers, Bombers, and Bank Robbers: Managerial Style in the Japanese Red Army." *Journal of Asian Studies* 48, No. 4 (November, 1989): 724–740.

Sugimoto, Yoshio. *An Introduction to Japanese Society*. Cambridge, UK: Cambridge University Press, 2003.

Weston, Mark. *Giants of Japan*. New York: Kodansha International, 1999.

Women and Marriage

INTRODUCTION

A few years ago, Arthur Golden's *Memoirs of a Geisha* and the movie on which it was based were major successes in Japan and the West. However, Golden's work, while accurate in many respects about geisha, unintentionally perpetuated a Western stereotype that Japanese women are supplicant creatures that exist to serve men. Today there are only about 1,000 geisha throughout Japan, and even at their height during the Tokugawa years (1600–1868), they were always a tiny minority of Japanese women. The reality of most women's lives in Japan has had little or no connection with geisha. In contemporary Japan, women and their choices are playing major roles in what promises to be societal changes of the greatest importance. Readers will gain a better understanding of actual historical and contemporary concerns of Japanese women through reading this chapter.

WOMEN IN CLASSICAL, EARLY MODERN, AND IMPERIAL JAPAN

Although very little is known about Japanese women's role and status before the Heian period (794–1185) and the scant evidence available is primarily based on Chinese records, some patterns seem to have emerged. Women occupied, if early

Chinese accounts can be believed, a somewhat higher status in the Japanese archipelago than in China. The belief system that came to be known as Shinto featured Amaterasu, a creator goddess, and female shamans were likely. Chinese histories even mention a second-century woman empress, Himiko, although there are no written Japanese accounts from this period or a few hundred years later that verify her existence. While tomb artifacts from the first few hundred years of the Common Era reveal more male- than female-related relics, there is stronger evidence of earlier female subjugation in Chinese culture than in Japan.

As a more sophisticated Japanese state emerged in the late sixth and early seventh centuries, historical evidence indicates that women exercised powerful informal and, at times, formal roles. Empress Suiko (554–628) reigned for 35 years, although during much of this time period Prince Shotoku, whom she outlived, was regent and was responsible, according to the *Nihongi*, for general government control and for specific administrative details. Empress Suiko encouraged Shotoku, a sinophile, to promote Buddhism and injunctions from the Chinese-imported religion as well as Confucian philosophy. Buddhist, Confucian, and Shinto tenets constitute most of Japan's first "constitution," which Shotoku promulgated in 604.

The increasing influence of Buddhism and Confucianism, especially the latter belief system, severely constrained women in many ways. Institutional Buddhism, by and large, never treated women as equal to men and often associated women with corrupting fleshly desires. Confucian teachings went even further and formally relegated women to household work while specifying that only men could engage in work-related activities outside family domiciles. While the foreign belief systems gradually but steadily gained influence during the Heian era, women played profound roles in shaping the fundamental cultural foundations of Japan.

During the years that began with the founding of Japan's third capital, Heian (present-day Kyoto), fewer than 1,000 aristocrats lived in the capital city and politically and culturally dominated Japan. Women were an important part of this group. Although surviving diaries indicate women lived cloistered and often boring lives, women were a vital key to "marriage politics," with a disproportionate amount of females from one family, the Fujiwaras, regularly wedding emperors, thereby keeping this powerful family in control of Japan's government. Women were also influential in other alliances between powerful clans and, unlike later in Japan's history, could inherit property. Very little is known about the lives of ordinary women in Japan's classical or medieval periods since literate people did not often write detailed commentaries on commoners.

Heian aristocratic women played, at least in retrospect, the dominant role in the development of classical Japanese literature. During the Heian years, educated male aristocrats commonly wrote Chinese characters, which were considered the higher-status written language, but aristocratic women, with fewer formal constraints, wrote in the native Japanese kana that had recently emerged. The result was an outpouring of prose by upper-class women that both revealed much about aristocratic lives, especially those of women, and helped to shape elements of traditional Japanese culture. The most important genre was the literary diary, or *Nikki*. "Diary" is in many ways an incorrect term for this prose genre as women tended to include

This woodblock print by 19th Century artist Yoshitoshi depicts one of the Tale of Genji's numerous scenes. The novel has been the subject of many Japanese artists. (Asian Art & Archaeology, Inc./Corbis)

poetry and didn't use the daily entry as a device but took a much more nonlinear approach. Such essayists as Sei Shonagon, Lady Sharashina, and Murasaki Shikibu, among others, wrote about court life, festivals, palace intrigues, and especially romantic encounters. Of all women authors, though, Murasaki Shikibu is by far the most influential in Japan and well known throughout the world. This is not primarily for her diary but because she wrote what literary critics consider one of the world's greatest novels, *The Tale of Genji*.

Murasaki (973–1014) was a noblewoman, who, after her husband died when she was relatively young, served as a lady-in-waiting to the empress in the imperial palace. While there, she composed her famous novel in installments that were circulated among avid readers who were connected to the court. Much of the novel focuses on the life and loves of the protagonist, Prince Genji, and the human feelings and web of human relationships of those who interact with him. Even though the main character is male, the novel is written from a woman's perspective.

Much of Heian women's lives centered on love and courtship. Marriages among aristocrats were political, not love matches, and illicit affairs were common as well as polygamy and concubines. The rituals of courtship included skill in writing and poetry as well as good aesthetic taste, and in a situation where men and women did not regularly see each other during daylight hours, the exchange of notes by prospective lovers revealed innermost feelings through indirect suggestions rather than clear assertions. This indirect style of communication, as well as an appreciation of

IZUMO NO OKUNI (1571–1615)

It is ironic that classic kabuki theater, in which only males can perform, was founded by a woman. Although the dates of her birth are approximate, this most unconventional Japanese woman was first a religious dancer at Izumo Shrine. The young woman learned popular music and attained fame as a dancer and actress when she left the religious life and became a traveling performer. Moving to Kyoto, Okuni went on to form her own female troupe who danced, sang popular songs, and improvised skits for whoever would pay them. Attractive, flamboyant, and bawdy, she used all these attributes to become a sensation. The kabuki that Okuni and others created was street theater in a sense, and the original meaning of kabuki was "to behave unconventionally." Eventually, she moved to Edo, where the new Japanese government was located. She was a sensation there as well but retired at the peak of her popularity and moved back to Izumo. Early kabuki continued to be associated with wild behavior and even prostitution. In 1629 Tokugawa Iemitsu banned women kabuki performers as the result of a much-publicized fight over a dancer.

the beauty of impermanence and the transient, what would later be called *mono no aware*, was a part of aristocratic life. So was a belief that forms were as important as function. These propensities, all associated with feminine proclivities, eventually became part of mainstream Japanese culture and remain so today.

However, during Japan's medieval era (1185–1600), characterized by widespread warfare between rival families for political and economic power and the rise of an aristocratic warrior class, the samurai, influences of Buddhism and Confucianism as well as security issues tended to erode some of the previous privileges women had enjoyed. Women continued to be important in marriage politics, but in general Buddhist tenets consigned them to inferior status even though there was room for women to play a leading role in worshipping Amida Buddha and in paying particular homage to the Lotus Sutra, which condoned salvation for women. In an era when retention of land depended on the power of arms, women saw their right to inherit property become constricted because relatives did not view them as capable of protecting estates.

The continual influence of Confucianism, which culminated in the early 17th century with the Tokugawa shogunate (1600–1868) establishing Neo-Confucianism as the official state ideology, legally placed women in an inferior and vulnerable role relative to men. The samurai code, which applied to women of that class but had ramifications throughout society, based inheritance on primogeniture. A woman had no legal share in her husband's property, although her property became his after marriage. Women could be easily divorced, and fathers as heads of households could send their daughters and daughters-in-law away. Theoretically, women were seen primarily as a means to perpetuate the family line.

Most samurai and a number of commoner women often received some education during the Tokugawa years. However, excerpts from Keibara Ekken's (1630–1714) *Onna Daigaku*, or *Great Learning for Women*, are concrete indications of the low official regard for women. Keibara, a Confucian scholar, physician, scientist, and highly regarded intellectual, wrote that it was even more incumbent for a girl than a boy to revere her parents' instructions since after marriage she would be totally submissive to her father- and mother-in-law. A woman must also "look to her husband as her lord, and must serve him with all worship and reverence" (Jansen 2002, 197). Keibara also opined that the only qualities that were desired in women were gentility, obedience, chastity, mercy, and quietness.

Although women were culturally and legally considered inferior to men, the actual situation, particularly within households and at the workplace, was more complex. In the household, the male head's wife had power over domestic concerns and over children. In non-samurai agricultural, artisan, and merchant families, women often worked alongside their husbands and wielded considerable influence in the workplace. Still, the legal situation did not improve for women with the 1868 Meiji Revolution. The new government made the old samurai codes the basis for family law, thereby perpetuating the legal inferiority of women. During Japan's imperial period until shortly after World War II, nationalization of the old samurai family codes meant the household was an economic unit, the oldest son usually inherited all assets, marriages were often arranged to perpetuate family lines, and women remained legally vulnerable.

Despite their inferior position within the family, the situations for many women radically changed in the late 19th century and first four decades of the 20th century because of industrialization, the influx of Western ideas, and World War II. During the Meiji era, factory representatives and independent contractors recruited girls from rural areas to work in textile and other industries for low wages. The infusion of women factory workers helped the Japanese economy grow and transformed the lives of thousands of women as they became a living part of urbanization, with attendant life style changes. As the cities grew and technology expanded, increasing numbers of women also worked as typists, telephone operators, and ticket collectors as well as other service occupations.

The early part of the 20th century was a period of intense feminist activity in the West, and a Japanese women's movement also emerged in the cities, with women's suffrage its major goal. The effort failed in Japan, and women would not gain the right to vote until the 1947 post–World War II Constitution. It is important to note that as late as 1918, when Japanese women were frustrated in their attempt to gain this political right, only four Western countries—Australia, Sweden, the United Kingdom, and New Zealand—had given women the vote, and American women gained voting rights two years later in 1920.

The complete national mobilization during World War II in Japan meant, as was the case in other warring nations, large numbers of women went to work in factories and in other occupations where men were in short supply. By war's end, many women had already become someone other than a stay-at-home wife.

This depiction of a woman dressed in a kimono is from the mid-17th Century. Men and women normally only wear kimono on special occasions today. (Burstein Collection/Corbis)

WOMEN IN POSTWAR JAPAN

The American occupation and the 1947 Constitution meant unprecedented legal rights for women including suffrage, access to widespread educational opportunities, and, perhaps most important, fundamental changes in marriage laws. Family law now centered on the nuclear and not the extended family. Marriage became a union between two consenting adults and did not depend on the approval of a household head. All children, including girls, were allowed to inherit assets. Men and women also had equal rights to divorce.

As Japan rebuilt its society and economy in the 1950s, new family forms emerged, yet tradition remained an important influence in women's lives. Increasingly, for women the ideal marriage was to a "salaryman," a college-graduate employee of a large company with permanent employment, or to an assembly-line employee who worked for a large firm. Married women, however, often still had the responsibility of looking after their husband's rather than their own parents, who often would be the responsibility of the wives' brothers. Although some married women worked outside the home, the ideal, in a society increasingly dominated by a highly competitive education system, was for a good wife to concentrate on the education of her children, manage the household, and take care of her husband,

KYOIKU MAMA

Kyoiku is the Japanese word for education, and "Kyoiku Mama," a woman who is devoted to her children's education, is now a hybrid Japanese expression. In postwar Japan, a fundamental element of the social structure was a meritocratic examination system where those (mainly young males) who did well on educational entrance examinations and attended the right schools and universities obtained good positions. A middle-class married woman's reputation depended on her children's educational records, and the conventional wisdom was that it was inappropriate for her to concentrate on a career. Japanese society has been changing over the past two decades with ever-larger numbers of university-educated women, more women choosing not to marry, and increases in divorces. "Education mama," while still a valid descriptor of some Japanese women, now explains less about gender roles than was the case in the previous century.

who was putting in long hours at work. Although couples could not be forced into marriage against their wills, many marriages were still facilitated by various third parties including professional matchmakers and employers. Permanent or long-term employment in the private sector was not an option for the vast majority of women because of societal expectations that the right thing to do for a woman was to quit work shortly before marrying or before the birth of her first child and thereafter devote herself to family.

By the 1960s and early 1970s, different expectations became evident among both men and women regarding marriage, as couples, for various reasons, began to value Western notions of romantic love, mutuality of interests, and shared experiences. Still, the long hours Japanese males typically worked served as barriers to married couples developing strong bonds based on shared experiences. As Japan's economy grew, there was increasing demand for women workers, and larger numbers did begin working outside of the home, but often in such part-time employment as cram school teaching or clerking in supermarkets. Women still largely focused on their children's education and, increasingly, on their own personal development through courses offered at cultural or community centers.

By the 1980s, continuing increases in women's educational levels and a persistent feminist movement resulted in changes in employment opportunities for women. Japan signed the United Nations Declaration on Women and subsequently passed the 1986 Equal Employment Opportunity Act. In complying with the law, companies formalized a two-track system that had informally existed for decades, with differing levels of pay and benefits. One track was permanent employment, often leading to management positions and carrying higher pay and benefits, while the second track was reserved for more routine work, nonpermanent employment, and lower salaries and benefits. In theory, the law made gender not a factor

DOI TAKAKO (1928–)

Japan is still very much a political "man's world," but a little over two decades ago one woman's success resulted in more women becoming elected officials. Doi Takako's achievement in becoming the first woman to be elected to the leadership of a major political party in 1986 received national and international attention. Doi grew up in a middle-class family and watched her family home burn in the bombing of Kobe. Doi, who never married, received her undergraduate degree in law from Doshisha University and a master of arts in the same field. She was elected as a socialist to the lower house in 1969, and from 1986 until 1991 served as chair of the Socialist Party. Doi was later lower house speaker in the 1993–1996 coalition government. Doi never forgot her World War II experiences, worked for pacifism, and was a proponent of a strict interpretation of the Article 9 clause of the Japanese Constitution. Although she is no longer in politics, Doi's example encouraged Japanese women of varying ideologies to follow in her footsteps.

in who was hired for what track, but in practice males were almost always hired for the first track with women hired for the second since there were no penalties imposed on companies for noncompliance. De facto discrimination notwithstanding, a combination of the law, a growing economy, better-educated women, political change, and foreign companies in Japan that were less inhibited about hiring women led to a much greater array of jobs for women than in earlier decades. Because of particular expertise associated with their gender, Japanese women dominated or played leading roles in certain businesses and occupations including fashion merchandising, conversational English instruction, and elementary school teaching.

The 1990s brought even more widespread change in the economic and social lives of women. One much-publicized societal phenomenon was a trend whereby Japanese women initiated divorce proceedings against husbands when the men retired from work. Some wives apparently had planned such an action for years, saving their money from part-time work, fulfilling their duties to the children, and then leaving the husband for a new life. News like this in turn probably fueled young women's concerns about the advisability of marrying a husband who would almost never be home during much of their lives. By the 1990s, the burden of proof often lay with young men to convince skeptical young women they would not expect the same kind of lifestyle that had been true of their baby boomer parents. Japanese rural males were even more out of favor because the life of a farm wife or small town wife was viewed as even more onerous than that of the wife of a salaryman. A number of villages, in an effort to stave off plummeting fertility rates because of a dearth of Japanese women, have organized trips to Southeast Asia for rural men in search of wives. Village officials have subsequently arranged group marriages for Japanese farmers and their Filipino brides. There are also marriage agencies in urban areas like Tokyo, some of which have offices abroad, that specialize in finding Chinese and Korean wives for Japanese rural males.

Japan's rapidly aging population also meant more married women would face the additional work of caring for elderly parents. Despite government exhortations for women to have babies and rear children, care for the aged, and, with a shrinking work force, find employment as well, women continued to marry later in life and have fewer children. Many women also showed more reluctance to assume primary or sole responsibility for daily care of elderly parents.

Japan's 1990s economic malaise, a highly competitive globalized capitalism, and more highly educated women with new goals in life all contributed to the rise of two new kinds of workers still in evidence in Japan today: "parasite singles" and "freeters." Although it is difficult to find precise statistics, large numbers of women are parasite singles and freeters. Parasite singles, a majority of whom are probably young women, are unmarried young people who are employed but continue to live with their parents and use much of their disposable income for stylish clothes, an active night life, and foreign travel. Freeters, who are discussed in more detail in a previous chapter, emerged in the 1990s as Japanese companies began to rely much more heavily on temporary workers than had been the case in the past. Freeters work in temporary or part-time positions long enough to support themselves for a few months or more, then quit their jobs, and reenter the work force when they again need income. It is estimated that 60 percent of freeters are women (Imamura 2008, 27).

As the new century approached, the Japanese government made further changes in employment and labor laws in an effort to both increase economic opportunities for women and prevent further population declines. A "Revised" 1998 Equal Employment Opportunity Law created a proviso that the names of companies discriminating against women in the workplace in initial hiring policies, assignments, and promotion be published. Business owners were also mandated to prevent workplace sexual harassment and adjust work schedules accordingly for women before, during, and after pregnancies. Employment chances for women have increased quickly in recent years. However, traditional societal expectations about appropriate roles for women, and recent cuts in available jobs by Japanese companies in order to meet foreign and domestic competition, continue to inhibit women's quest for equal work opportunities.

21ST-CENTURY CHANGES AND CHALLENGES FOR WOMEN

By the beginning of this century, many women were working as part-time employees either voluntarily or involuntarily, others held inferior positions compared to men, and growing numbers of women enjoyed rich professional careers that would not have been earlier available to them because of gender. Since the 1970s, women have been increasingly working outside the home. Currently, a little less than 50 percent of all adult women are in the labor force in some capacity. This massive infusion of women into the workplace has been by no means exclusively caused by

WEDDING PROTOCOL

Whether a wedding ceremony is Shinto, Christian, or secular, usually only family, close friends, and work associates are invited. The reception typically includes a larger number of attendees. The newly married couple sits in the front at the reception, and guests seated closest to the bride and groom are the significant others in their lives who are not family, for example, bosses, influential professors, or teachers. The family members sit furthest away from the bride and groom. People who are or will be important for the couple in their everyday lives are recognized through seating arrangements, as are guests who have significant political or social standings. Traditionally, elected prefectural or national Diet members attend many weddings in Japan.

new opportunities. The 1990s economic malaise, the need to care for elderly parents, rising educational costs, increasing demand for material goods, and decreasing permanent employment for husbands meant that more married women than ever before felt they had to work to help families economically survive.

Marriage and sexual relations seem to be reconceptualized in a number of ways, yet some traditional attitudes remain. As of 2005, the average age a woman first married was 28, compared to 25 in 1980 (*Facts and Figures of Japan* 2007, 38). There are preliminary indications that the average age continues to rise. Highly educated women are often marrying for the first time when they are about 30. Men now first marry when about 30, which is also an increase relative to the past. Women's resistance to conventional marriage patterns and desires to take advantage of new economic opportunities have already been addressed, but the delay on the part of men in marrying seems in large part a result of a changing economy providing fewer permanent employment opportunities. As is the case in most developed countries, Japanese males who do not have regular employment are less likely to marry or more likely to delay marriage than is the case with their steadily employed counterparts. Since men marrying later also affect women, it is difficult to determine what proportions of young women who delay marrying do this because they resent the traditional Japanese wife role, or desire a meaningful career, and what proportions remain unwed because men are delaying marriage.

Marriage is more than ever before viewed as a union based on the free choices of individuals who love each other. The Japanese tradition of a go-between or employer introducing prospective couples seems to be in significant decline while there is growth in both real-time and online dating services. Also, there appear to be significant disagreements among Japanese women about what kind of man constitutes the ideal husband. Despite the much-publicized rejection of traditional salaryman types by some young women, when advertisements for dating services are examined, several of the most prominent of firms tend to accentuate in male profiles the qualities that always make a salaryman attractive: solid educational

WEDDING MONEY

Instead of buying the gifts, it is common practice for wedding guests to give money to the bride and groom. Although there is variation, family members might give the Yen equivalent of between $500 and $1,000 while close friends might give between $200 and $500. Not-so-close friends might give between $100 and $200. The money should be crisp new bills, and it is considered disrespectful to give old bills. The money is given in a congratulatory envelope tied with a special, ceremonial cord. The couple, in return, gives each guest a bag of gifts that might include candy, gift certificates, or towels. There is variation, but typically, each guest gift bag might range from $50 to $300 per guest. When the bride and groom attend one of their guest's weddings, etiquette dictates that they give similar monetary amounts to what they received.

credentials and permanent employment. There is evidence that a number of prospective brides would still like to be stay-at-home mothers but realize that this probably won't be an option because of economic necessity.

Marriages are also becoming more diverse in a number of ways. The traditional Shinto ceremony is often replaced by a Christian wedding even though about one percent of Japanese follow the latter faith. In recent decades, Japanese have married in wedding halls or large hotels, and this practice is common, but "house weddings" are a recent popular trend, especially among older couples. The bride and bridegroom rent a luxurious house, often with a garden, and work with a wedding planner on the event so that guests can mingle in a more friendly surrounding than a large wedding hall. It is estimated that in a recent year 19 percent of all wedding receptions took place in these relatively new venues.

Attitudes about sexual relations before marriage have also changed in Japan. Traditionally, at least the public convention was that it was inappropriate for women to engage in sex before marriage. However, these notions have changed to such a great extent that Christmas Eve is now a much-publicized time for younger, unmarried couples to stay overnight in a hotel. It is a topic of conversation among young women about to which hotels their boyfriends are taking them, hotels advertise special packages, and there is no public outcry. Perhaps not surprisingly, the number of pregnant brides appears also to have substantially increased, and current estimates are that about 25 percent of all Japanese brides are pregnant (Imamura 2008, 27). For a variety of reasons, perhaps most important, Japan's low birthrate, there is little public concern about this trend. However, some in media and government argue that many marriages based on the pregnancy of the bride are not the ideal starting points for successful unions and family environments.

As discussed in other sections of the book, Japan's declining population is primarily due to a birthrate that has been falling for well over two decades. In the

A traditional Shinto wedding ceremony. In the last decade and a half Christian-style weddings have become as popular as Shinto ones. (Dreamstime.com)

most recent year for which data are available, the birthrate was fewer than two children for all women of childbearing age and slightly more than two children for married women. The Japanese government's exhortations for childless women to have babies—and a few prominent politicians, including former prime minister Mori Yoshiro, calling women without children selfish and not worthy of receiving government pensions—appear to be completely ineffective. The government's alternative strategy to pressure employers to create situations where families can better manage work and children may ultimately be more effective. Previous government policies allowing men as well as women to take paternity leave only resulted in less than one percent of fathers doing so, and now the government has mandated that large corporations ensure more male employees take advantage of the policy.

Japanese appear to be facing unprecedented marital pressures. Divorce rates for all Japanese, despite being well below that of the United States and several European countries, have been slowly but steadily rising for at least a decade or more. Historically, Japan's divorce rate has been a fraction of that of the United States. By 2006, Japan's rate had risen to a little over half the American rate (*Facts and Figures of Japan* 2007, 34). Approximately one in four marriages now includes a divorced spouse, and this situation has created new Japanese family dynamics. Divorce seems to have lost much of the shame formerly attached to it in Japan. Also, in 2007 changes in Japan's divorce laws increased the amount of money a

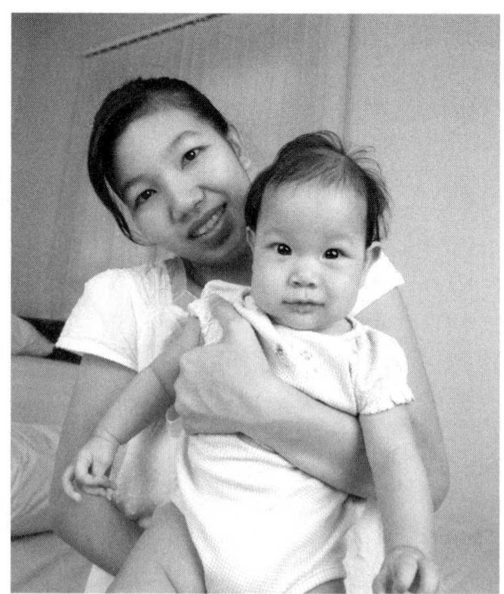

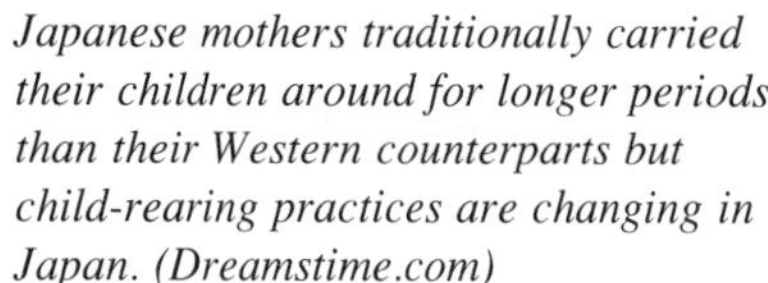

Japanese mothers traditionally carried their children around for longer periods than their Western counterparts but child-rearing practices are changing in Japan. (Dreamstime.com)

divorcée could claim from her husband's pension, thereby increasing the likelihood that rates will continue to rise (Imamura 2008, 27–28).

It is quite possible that women's new aspirations and resultant demands on husbands will change the role of Japanese men in family life as much as that of women. Traditionally, one important difference in Japan and the West is that on average, Japanese men spent much less time at home. Despite some exceptions that seem to have begun in the 1970s, typically, Japanese fathers were seldom involved in child rearing or household chores. According to relatively recent surveys, less than half of Japanese salarymen ate dinner with their families most nights, and at least a third spent fewer than three waking hours a day with their families. In the private sector and in many government institutions, Saturdays are still workdays whether officially counted as such or not. Sundays tend to be the only day that fathers will be involved in any kind of family activities. Japanese women tell a revealing joke about the nature of husband-wife relations; a good husband makes much money and is never home.

However, now women, the government, and perhaps even some employers are putting new pressures on husbands to assume more of a role in child rearing, housework, and family recreation. A men's movement developed in the 1990s to work on such issues as getting males to commit more to fatherhood and to develop parenting skills. As of late, some men's groups have been emphasizing active efforts on the part of males in the cultivation of meaningful relationships with wives in hopes of avoiding divorce. Time will tell whether any of these efforts will bear fruit.

Despite some indications that males might be taking more of a role in child rearing, until relatively recently, the almost universal expectation of a married Japanese woman was that her important role was not marketplace work but child rearing and home management. Although women in most cultures play the leading role in raising children, traditionally, the bond between mother and child in Japan is particularly strong. Mothers sleep with their young for a longer period of time after the child is born than in the West. Studies over the past few decades indicate that on average Japanese women spend more time with their small children than their Western counterparts, although significant increases in the numbers of women in the labor force may lower hours of mother-child contact. Often Japanese children have developed a stronger sense of dependence on their mothers than children in other cultures do.

Young children are treated quite leniently in Japan and are rarely spanked when they misbehave. Instead, the Japanese mother is more likely to forgive the child and make the child feel guilty for not conforming to her wishes. Many sociologists argue that this early development of a sense of shame when one fails to conform to others' expectations helps to create the feeling shared by many adult Japanese of not wanting to let other group members down.

A number of factors including large numbers of women now working outside the home, families having fewer children and often only one child, and rising divorce rates undoubtedly combine to cause modifications in child-rearing practices. Teachers now complain about inattentive parents, latchkey children, spoiled only children, and a general rise in children's disrespect for educators and other adults. Although several of the changes mentioned here are so recent that it is difficult to assess how much traditional child rearing is changing, and recent signs of more male involvement in child-rearing notwithstanding, the primary responsibility for child nurture still falls on mothers.

The aging of Japan's population, addressed in several other sections of this book because it is such a profound social phenomenon, strongly affects the lives of Japanese women. Japan continues to have world-leading life spans for males and females, and by 2013 about a quarter of the Japanese population is predicted to be 65 or older, making Japan the world's "oldest" country. Japan has been and is still heavily influenced by Confucianism, and much more than in the West, married adult women are still viewed as primary caregivers for older parents, usually the husband's, who often live in the home with husband, wife, and children. Currently, although estimates vary, somewhere between 45 and 55 percent of Japanese over 65 live with one of their adult children. The present percentage range has dropped from an estimated 80 percent of Japanese elderly in 1970, and the home in which the elderly live might not necessarily be the husband's, but Japanese wives in this situation still bear the brunt of caregiver responsibilities. Even if elderly parents don't live in the home but nearby—or even in the expanding, but still small by Western standards, nursing home sector—Japanese women relatives are more often than not responsible for significant levels of eldercare.

Despite fewer children in the households, often Japanese women face a situation that David Plath has labeled "the middle-aged Confucian sandwich," in which they simultaneously are taking care of a child or children, the elderly, and the large majority of housework (Kelly and White 2006, 75). There is a related Japanese saying that the woman experiences "the three ages": In her 50s she takes care of her husband's parents, in her 60s and beyond she takes care of her husband, and eventually she must take care of herself. By 2025, the projection is that 46 percent of middle-aged women will provide home care for elderly family members. More than two-thirds of these women will be caring for an elderly person who is bedridden or suffering from senile dementia. Given the decline in marriage rates, there is also a question whether the number of families in the future with whom old people can live will be sufficient to meet the demand for eldercare.

In April 2000, the government passed a public long-term care insurance system offering coverage for both outside, paid home helpers who go to private homes and for more services at care facilities. Every Japanese citizen age 40 and older is covered by the program and is required to pay insurance premiums. If care is needed, it is provided in place of monetary payments. The service is based on level of care needed, and municipal governments are responsible for long-term care program management. Long-term care is a social insurance plan in that one-half of the funding comes from premiums and one-half from government funds. The greater an individual's need for care, the higher the maximum limit on the cost of his or her service. People who use the service are expected to pay 10 percent of total care expenses. Although this policy was a step in the right direction in relieving eldercare pressures on families and particularly women, if the trends of both a rising elderly and a declining general population continue, the government, families, and women will face an increasingly complex problem.

CONCLUSION: WOMEN AND SOCIAL ISSUES

Perhaps at no time in Japanese history have the nation's most pressing social issues been so connected to the position, status, and concerns of women. Furthermore, the issues are linked. Women are having fewer children, so there is a shrinking labor force, which raises new questions about immigration policies. In the absence of a massive influx of new immigrants, a declining tax base means fewer social services, which will probably cause women to bear more of the responsibility of eldercare, work outside the home whether they care to or not, and cope with marital and child-rearing responsibilities. Japanese males, government, and private institutions in turn are facing serious, unprecedented pressures to accommodate contemporary women's lives. Although these challenges are daunting for any society, the Japanese, in large part because of a deeply pragmatic perspective that helps them overcome serious obstacles, will most likely succeed in meeting them.

Although post–World War II changes occurred for Japanese women and their families, similar lifestyles were the norm until the 1990s for a disproportionately large numbers of middle-class women and their families. The appropriate role for a woman was to receive an education that would make her well rounded and competitive in the search for marriage to an educated man with good employment prospects. The woman would then be expected to have two or maybe three children and be responsible for their educations. As readers have learned, several factors including increases in the numbers of highly educated women who have rejected elements of the Confucian "good wife" model, economic changes that have both contracted lifetime employment for males and given women more work opportunities, and exposure to women's lifestyles in other developed countries are drastically altering expectations and options for women and their families in Japan. The extent to which trends that are discussed in this chapter will continue is unknown, but Japanese gender and family relations are now substantially different than was the case less than two decades ago.

REFERENCES

Arntzen, Sonja. "The Heart of History: The Tale of Genji." *Education About Asia*, Vol. 10, No. 3 (Winter 2005): 25–30.

Facts and Figures of Japan 2007. Tokyo: Foreign Press Center, 2007.

Hooker, Richard. "Women & Women's Communities in Ancient Japan." 1996. http://www.wsu.edu/dee/ANCJAPAN/WOMEN.HTM (accessed January 2008).

Imamura, Anne E. "The Japanese Family Faces Twenty-first Century Challenges." *Education About Asia* 8, No. 2 (Fall 2003): 30–33.

———. "Marriage in Japan: Yesterday Today and Tomorrow." *Education About Asia* 13, No. 1 (Spring 2008).

Jansen, Marius B. *The Making of Modern Japan*. Cambridge, MA: Belknap Press of Harvard University Press, 2002.

JapanZone. "Doi Takako." http://www.japan-zone.com/modern/doi_takako.shtml (accessed January 2008).

Kelly, William and Merry White. "Students, Slackers, Singles, Seniors, and Strangers: Transforming a Family-Nation." In Peter J. Katzenstein and Takashi Shiraishi, eds. *Beyond Japan: The Dynamics of East Asian Regionalism*. Ithaca, NY: Cornell University Press, 2006.

Maruyama, Mari. "Japanese Wedding Customs." In Anne Imamura's "Marriage in Japan: Yesterday, Today, and Tomorrow." *Education About Asia*, 13, No. 1 (Spring 2008).

Masaki, Hisane. "Japan Stares into a Demographic Abyss." *Asia Times Online*. 9 May 2006. http://www.atimes.com.

Sumiko, Iwao. "Working Women and Housewives." *Japan Echo* 28, No. 2 (April 2001): 51–53.

Tonkinson, Steve and Lucien Ellington. "Madame Butterfly: A Teacher's Guide." Chattanooga Symphony and Opera. Spring 2005.

Weston, Mark. Giants of Japan. New York: Kodansha International, 1999.

Wilkerson, Kyoko. "Reference Terms for Husbands in Japanese: Sociolinguistic Perspectives." *Southeast Review of Asian Studies*, Vol. 19 (1997): 103–120.

Japan's Educational System

INTRODUCTION

Education has been valued in Japan since Koreans and Chinese first introduced religious and clan leaders on the archipelago to China's writing system, philosophy, literature, political and social thought, and technology more than 1,500 years ago. At first, only a few aristocrats were educated, but the situation changed with the passage of time. By the early 19th century, average Japanese educational levels were comparable with European nations and the United States in many respects. Japan had a national school system solidly in place by 1900. By the 1980s, largely because of Japan's economic success, Japanese schools received widespread attention in the United States and Europe. The very question of the perceived quality, or lack thereof, of Japan's schools became controversial among different groups of Americans. Many Americans developed both correct and substantially erroneous impressions of Japanese education.

In the years since World War II, educational experts concur that Japan's greatest educational achievement is the high-quality basic education that has been provided to most elementary and secondary students relative to that of students in a number of other developed countries. Although recently scores have declined compared to other Asian countries such as Singapore and the Republic of Korea, Japanese students rank high in international mathematics tests when compared to most other developed countries. According to various public- and private-sector sources, more than 95 percent of Japanese are literate, which is particularly impressive since the Japanese language is one of the world's most difficult languages to read and write. Currently, more than 95 percent of Japanese high school students graduate compared to 89 percent of American 18-year-olds (Ellington 2005, 1). Comparable percentages of Japanese and American high school graduates now go on to some type of postsecondary institution, and higher percentages of Japanese university students graduate from college than Americans. Yet as will be discussed, educational reform has now become as important a national issue in Japan as is the case with the United States. Many Japanese are concerned about declines in both basic student knowledge and behavior as well as school quality. Even though comparative evidence indicates that Japan's schools in general experience fewer problems than many of their U.S. counterparts, almost all Japanese realize that in a crowded country largely devoid of natural resources, education is more critically important for national prosperity than elsewhere.

HISTORICAL AND CULTURAL FOUNDATIONS OF LEARNING

The Japanese, as was the case with other East Asians, were profoundly influenced by the principles of Confucius, one of the world's greatest teachers. Education and virtue are inseparable in Confucius' teachings. In Japan's classical and medieval periods, aristocrats and clergy, especially many Zen monks, were highly educated by world standards. Early in Japan's Tokugawa period (1600–1868), the government adopted Neo-Confucianism, with its advocation of not only moral instruction and education in the humanities but also the "exploration of things" in the natural world, as the official state ideology. Samurai, the leading class, were expected to cultivate the "dual way" and both learn the military arts and receive a Confucian-based education. Many attended fief schools, went to higher-level academies, or

PREMODERN EDUCATIONAL EQUALITY SUCH

Westerners such as American Commodore Matthew Perry and the United Kingdom's Sir Rutherford Alcock, who came to Japan in the mid-19th century shortly before the end of the Tokugawa period, were impressed with the general level of education. Samurai had traditionally received Confucian educations in domain and other special schools, but Terakoya, or temple schools, had their roots in 16th-century Japan and educated commoners. These small private schools usually had one teacher—a samurai, Buddhist priest, or learned individual—and a few pupils. Even though the translation of Terakoya ("temple school") leads one to believe that the school is housed in a temple, portions of the teacher's home often constituted the Terakoya. Thousands of Terakoya could be found not only in urban areas but also in small villages throughout Japan. The evidence indicates that instruction was often individualized and that in premodern Japan, a private system had been created that relatively speaking, offered a significant amount of equality of education within a hierarchical society.

were educated by tutors. Although relatively widespread, education was mainly private. The Tokugawa years were peaceful, so samurai, rather than utilizing their military training, used their educations to become government bureaucrats.

Even though a majority of Japanese lived in rural areas, Tokugawa Japan had a vibrant urban culture that helped to stimulate many forms of educational institutions for commoners and members of the middle classes. The several thousand *Terakoya*, or "temple schools," and other schools for the children of merchants, village headmen, and commoners taught literacy and numeracy, such vocational subjects as accounting, and other knowledge useful to business and even farming. By the early 19th century, Japanese literacy rates of 40 percent for men and 15 percent for women were comparable to the United Kingdom and United States. Another sign of Japan's relatively high levels of education by the standards of the day was the flourishing publishing industry that developed in the cities shortly before the 1700s. Books were often published in editions of more than 10,000 copies to satisfy the high demand for particular works (Ellington 1992, 1–22).

With the overthrow of the Tokugawa government in 1868, a public education system was an important objective of the ruling Meiji oligarchs. A key element of the 1868 Charter Oath establishing the new Meiji government was the challenge "To seek knowledge throughout the world" (Duke 1989, 15). Even during the prior relatively isolated Tokugawa years, a group of intellectuals engaged in government-approved "Dutch learning" in order to keep abreast of Western developments in such fields as medicine. Dutch traders were the only Westerners allowed in Japan during the Tokugawa era. The shogunate approved a systematic study of Dutch scientific and technical works and made sure there were Japanese who had Dutch

MODERNIZING JAPANESE EDUCATION (1868–1912)

Japan impressively modernized education during the Meiji period, with the national government placing a high priority on creating a public school system. The new government formally established a three-tier elementary, middle school (equivalent to today's high schools), and university system in 1872, and within four years 26,000 elementary schools were established in Japan. The government's task was made easier by the prior existence of Terakoya as well as samurai (*hanko*) schools, many of which developed into public elementary and middle schools. By 1901, 88.1 percent of children between ages 7 and 12 were attending school—approximately 93.8 percent of boys and 81.3 percent of girls. The attention that Japanese paid to education in the Tokugawa era was probably as important a reason for success as government leadership since local communities absorbed many of the start-up costs to establish schools.

language skills and could act as translators. In the first part of the Meiji years, foreigners, upon government invitation, flocked to Japan to help create schools and universities that included knowledge from the West.

The Meiji government created a meritocratic public school system that was centralized and existed to assist the state in achieving its goal of catching the West economically and militarily. By the beginning of the 20th century, the large majority of children received a basic compulsory elementary education, and the most capable young boys, through top examination performance, were afforded middle and secondary school educations, with less than 5 percent of young men, again through competitive examination, qualifying for imperial universities. Graduates of Japan's most prestigious imperial institution of higher learning, Tokyo Imperial University, as well as those of the other eight imperial universities, went on to run the nation and occupy top ranks in the professions. A few private institutions like Waseda and Keio provided captains of Japan's industries, and the limited opportunities for higher education for women usually existed under the auspices of Christian missionaries and their followers.

Moral education, beginning with Confucian teachings and continuing to this day, has always played a role in Japanese education. Confucian-inspired moral educational principles include respect for teachers, the cultivation of good work habits, and placing the needs of the group before one's individual desires. During the first part of the Meiji period, Confucian teachings were rejected, but by the 1880s, vestiges returned as Japanese leaders reacted negatively to many Western values. State Shinto, adopted by the Meiji government to stimulate patriotism, became a major feature of education and helped to create the nationalism and later militarism that would lead Japan to imperialism and defeat in World War II.

The 1945–1952 American occupation brought about widespread change in Japan's educational system. Education became secular; demilitarized; modeled on the then American 6–3–3 system of elementary, junior, and senior high school attendance; and eventually accessible at higher levels for the entire population. However, earlier legacies remain influential today, including a concern about educating the whole person, a centralized and meritocratic system, and a disproportionately high number of prestigious public rather than private universities.

THE STRUCTURE OF JAPANESE EDUCATION

Japanese public and private elementary and secondary schools, as well as institutions of higher education, are part of a centralized national system headed by the national government's Ministry of Education, Culture, Sports, and Technology (MEXT). Although such centralization is common in most countries, this configuration is in sharp contrast to the United States, where education, despite Washington's significant role, is primarily a state and local responsibility. When Americans contrast Japanese education with their own schools, they often mistakenly think of Japan as a rigidly top-down system where local schools and teachers follow the commands of government bureaucrats. This is a mistaken belief.

Although Japanese students follow a national curriculum developed by MEXT for both required and elective subjects and students study the same topics throughout the country, the curriculum is not as specific as in systems more centralized than Japan's, such as in France. MEXT is a powerful force in Japan's schools, but so are teachers, university faculties, the public, the supplementary school industry, and the Japanese teachers' union. These other groups often either effectively resist MEXT bureaucrats or behave in ways that national educational officials don't anticipate. For example, in 2002 as a result of MEXT reforms, all public schools in Japan adopted the five-day school week. National government bureaucrats implemented this policy to give Japanese youngsters more free time on weekends. However, because entrance examinations, particularly high school entrance examinations, remained important in determining young people's futures, Saturday attendance at private supplemental schools significantly increased.

The Japanese government spends close to 5 percent of the gross domestic product (GDP) on all levels of education, which is approximately 2.5 percent less than the combined U.S. local, state, and federal educational expenditures as a percentage of GDP. However, studies indicate that the average family in Japan spends considerably more on the education of their children than do their American counterparts. More than 90 percent of Japanese children attend preschool, with large numbers attending mostly private kindergartens under the auspices of MEXT and the remainder attending institutions that are mostly nursery schools controlled by the Ministry of Health and Labor. Japan has compulsory education through the ninth grade, and expenditures for elementary and junior high schools are divided almost equally among local, prefectural, and national governments. Presently, more than 90 percent of Japanese elementary and junior high students attend public schools, although there are indications that private junior high attendance is increasing. Even though a larger percentage of Japanese finish high school than in the United States, the national government funds a much lower percentage of high school costs and

A JAPANESE ELEMENTARY STUDENT'S DAY

Although there is some variation, elementary school usually begins at 8:00 A.M., and usually there are four hours of lessons, lunch, and then two more hours of classes in the afternoon. Bandai, a major toymaker, surveyed elementary students about their favorite subjects and found that mathematics is number one, followed by physical education, and then Japanese language. Many students looked on learning math as a kind of game. After the school day, most students spend their time at home or in neighborhood parks. Soccer is now the most popular outdoor sport, and when children are indoors they report their most fun activities are computer games and reading comic books. Twenty-five percent of fourth- to sixth-grade elementary school students attend *juku*, or cram schools, where they mostly study for private school entrance examinations. Students also take swimming, piano, and violin lessons or English language or calligraphy for personal development.

considers upper secondary school funding to be a prefectural and family responsibility. More than 25 percent of Japanese high school students attend private high schools. Until recently, with the exception of the Tokyo-area, private high schools were inferior to public high schools. There are signs that this situation has changed with more affluent families choosing elite private schools.

Japanese students spend at least six weeks longer in school each year than their American counterparts since summer vacation is about half the time of most summer breaks in the United States (Ellington 2005, 1). All Japanese schools from kindergarten through university operate on a trimester academic year, with the school year beginning in April and ending the following March. Japanese students have short winter and spring holidays in addition to summer break.

Japanese students study mostly the same subjects as their American counterparts, but instruction and the amount of class time spent on certain subjects differ in Japan and the United States. The level of mathematics instruction is more advanced in Japan than in the United States. By the end of eighth grade, Japanese students have studied beginning algebra and plane geometry.

Experts consider the Japanese written language to be one of the most difficult in the world to learn. In order to read Japanese, one must learn two different syllabaries, hiragana and katakana, and memorize thousands of Chinese characters, or kanji. Almost all kanji have two or more pronunciations. MEXT has ascertained that before one can read a newspaper, a minimum of 1,945 kanji must be memorized. The latter number is required before a student can complete junior high school. Therefore, an important difference in Japanese and Western education is the greater amount of time students in Japan spend on learning the written language when compared to their counterparts elsewhere.

Beginning in junior high school, virtually all Japanese study English until they graduate from high school, and recently there have been widespread experiments with English language study for elementary students. Japanese students tend to spend much more time learning to read and write English than speaking it, largely because, despite the initiation of a speaking and listening component that some universities require, the examination system assesses knowledge of the written rather than spoken language.

Also, unlike in many American schools, art and music in Japan are part of the course of study for all students through junior high school and are not considered to be "frills." In art class, students study art history and engage in studio art assignments. The national curriculum provides chances for students to learn about and practice both Asian and Western art. The same is true for music curriculum. Students learn music appreciation and how to play such musical instruments as recorders in elementary school. Although in many countries music is taught by specialists, in Japanese elementary schools, classroom teachers also double as music teachers. Japanese elementary teachers are well positioned to handle this duty because each elementary education candidate must pass a rudimentary piano-playing test in order to procure a teaching license.

Japanese students take few electives through junior high school, but beginning in high school, there are different possibilities for young people depending on their interest and abilities. Between 75 and 80 percent of all high school students enroll in academic courses in high schools designed to prepare them for university even though not all of these students subsequently attend four-year universities. Although most students take many of the same courses in academic high schools, there are math/science and humanities/social science tracks that offer students some coursework options. In Japan, a few American-style comprehensive high schools offering different tracks exist, but they aren't popular.

Japanese students who attend vocational high schools enter mostly commercial or industrial high schools, although a few agricultural and fisheries high schools also exist. Vocational high school students take academic and vocational courses. Japanese commercial high school students aspire to work in offices, whereas industrial high school students hope to be considered for manufacturing jobs.

When Westerners think of Japanese education, many imagine such core academic subjects as math, science, and the national language to be the only goal of Japanese schools. This is an incorrect perception because students at all levels spend considerable time in a wide range of activities. Elementary students prepare for and participate in sports and cultural festivals and take field trips. Junior high students spend nearly one-third of in-school time on such subjects as art, music, moral education, physical education, shop, and home economics. Many junior and high school students also spend extensive time participating in school clubs and sports teams. Parents and teachers consider education of the whole child very important, and the amount of time Japanese students spend in these activities mirrors societal beliefs about wholesome child rearing.

Moral education for Japanese children and young people is considered to be especially important, and there are mounting public concerns that traditional Japanese values are not taught as effectively now as in the past. A value most adults are particularly interested in conveying to students is the importance of effort. It is common in Japanese classrooms to see signs exhorting students to try very hard, and teachers often use the verb *gambaru*, meaning "stand firm" or "persevere." This emphasis on trying hard reflects a significant difference between Japanese and American conceptualizations of young people. Many American teachers emphasize such individual differences as IQ whereas most Japanese educators lean toward the perception that people are roughly equal in abilities but those who try the hardest succeed. Respect for the school itself is considered to be another important value. Students and teachers clean the school together on a regular basis, and there are substantially fewer custodial staff in Japan than in the United States.

ADMINISTRATORS AND TEACHERS

Educational institutions are only as effective as the people who work in them. Traditionally, Japanese schools have included substantially smaller ratios of administrators to teachers than is the case in the United States, but this is changing. In smaller schools, there is still only a principal and a head teacher who functions as a vice principal while in schools of more than 1,000 students there is usually a second head teacher. The principal often spends more time working with such external, influential parties as prefectural and MEXT officials than actually supervising the daily school routine. Usually, head teachers teach just one class a day and, along with the faculty, actually run the daily affairs of the school.

One major recent change in nonteaching administrative staff has been the addition of school counselors. In 1995 only 154 schools in Japan had counselors, but because of increased behavior problems, eight years later approximately 7,000 schools had counselors, and the number of schools employing counselors continues to rise. Beginning in April 2008, MEXT initiated the policy of assigning social workers to work with public elementary and junior high schools throughout Japan in response to both behavior problems and the effects of widening income gaps in Japan on more needy families (Japan Times Online 2008).

Japanese teachers have, as a group, traditionally been impressive by world standards. Most were academically at least slightly above average compared to their college classmates who entered other fields. Middle and high school teachers in particular tend to be more active in pursuing their academic specialties than American teachers (Ellington 1992, 80–116). Furthermore, teachers at all levels in Japan take more academic content courses and fewer often less-demanding education courses than their American counterparts. Teacher salaries in Japan are comparable to salaries for pharmacists, middle managers, and other professionals. An international study of developed countries' education systems indicates that Japan ranked as high as 6th in teacher salaries (for lower secondary teachers after 15 years of experience) while the United States ranked 11th out of 28 (OECD 2007).

Because Confucian teachings emphasize education and Confucius was a teacher, the teaching profession is a relatively high-status occupation in Japan, and more applicants seek positions than there are jobs available. Lately, shrinking numbers of school students because of over two decades of declining birthrates have made it even more difficult to obtain a teaching position. Recently, only about 30 percent of education graduates were getting teaching positions, although the percentages vary by quality of educational institution. Prefectural and metropolitan school boards also employ rigorous selection processes, including written examinations and interviews as well as skill and physical fitness tests. Unlike in the United States, Japanese teachers have virtually a guaranteed lifetime position immediately upon being hired, and dismissal of teachers is rare.

Once teachers are hired, their workloads are quite demanding, but in different ways than is the case in the United States and many other developed countries. Japanese teachers at all levels teach fewer classes annually than teachers in comparable developed countries, but they spend the greatest number of hours working at school. For example, Japanese junior high teachers usually teach four classes each day, and their high school counterparts usually teach three daily classes. By contrast, American junior and senior high teachers are responsible for five to six classes a day. Because there are few administrators in Japanese schools, teacher committees assume significant responsibilities. Many Japanese teachers also tutor students in special summer sessions, work in extracurricular activities, and even patrol neighborhoods during summer vacation to make sure students aren't frequenting the wrong kind of places. One innovative but time-consuming Japanese teacher activity is lesson-study development, where small groups of teachers responsible for the same content will spend extensive time jointly preparing, practicing, exhibiting, and publishing accounts of model lessons. Some American public school districts are now experimenting with lesson study.

Concerns for the education of the whole child notwithstanding, Japan's academic expectations of students are on average higher than is the case in many other countries. Part of the reason behind the high academic expectations for students can be attributed to Confucian respect for education and other cultural factors. Another reason for the somewhat rigorous academic expectations is the high school entrance examinations, which virtually all third-year junior high school students take. A much smaller percentage of third-year high school students, those young people who aspire to gain admission to elite Japanese universities, also must successfully negotiate tough academic demands if they are to be successful in university entrance examinations.

ENTRANCE EXAMINATIONS

Virtually all Japanese students take high school examinations in their ninth-grade year, administered in the prefectures. Since a little over half of Japan's high school seniors go on to college, all prospective public and some private university applicants take national standardized university entrance examinations on various subjects. Faculties at some universities also develop additional examinations that prospective entrants must successfully negotiate in order to gain admission.

However, considerably fewer prospective university students than in the past take entrance examinations on a variety of core subjects. Since 1990, in determining admissions requirements, universities have been allowed to pick and choose certain subjects from the national standardized examinations rather than testing students on a wide range of core subjects as was previously the case. Also, in large part because many private universities are in fierce competition for students due to the declining population, a number of institutions rely more on other admissions criteria such as essays, interviews, and prior high school curricular records. Other private universities don't require high examination scores for admission, and some private universities no longer use entrance examinations at all. More than 30 percent of entering first-year university students now are admitted based on other criteria than solely examination performance.

Although now only prospective applicants for elite and higher-tier Japanese institutions of higher learning extensively prepare for university examinations, well over 90 percent of junior high school students spend considerable time preparing for high school entrance examinations. Admission to an academically good high school means a much better chance of later entering a top university. The examination system also affects the nature of instruction in secondary schools. Japanese elementary schools tend to have in many ways relaxed environments, and teachers use a variety of classroom activities. Because teachers in most junior and some senior high schools are under pressure to prepare students for entrance examinations, instruction tends to focus on factual knowledge and to be largely didactic.

High school and university examinations are an important reason that despite population declines, supplementary private educational institutions, or *juku*, remain popular in Japan. About 70 percent of Japanese young people will have taken some kind of private tutoring by the time they complete junior high school. Many elementary juku don't focus on examination preparation but instead enrich students' in-school experiences through supplementary lessons in piano, swimming, or conversational English. Juku that junior high school students or prospective university entrants attend are usually for entrance examination preparation. Although the average juku is quite small, there are also several large corporate, national juku chains that enroll thousands of students. Typically, students preparing for high school or university entrance examinations will attend juku two to three times a week after school or on Saturdays for six months to a year before the examinations. Although juku costs vary, recent average monthly tuitions can range from about US$200 upward, excluding supplementary materials costs (Ellington 1992, 2005).

In the past, Japanese high school seniors who sought admission to such higher-level institutions as Tokyo University often did not succeed on their first try and spent a year, or sometimes more, studying for and attempting the examinations again. Other students delayed taking entrance examinations for a year after high school graduation in order to concentrate exclusively on preparation. Typically in January when national examinations were administered, as many as one-third of those taking the examinations were already high school graduates. In January 2008, only 20 percent of young people taking entrance examinations were not third-year high school students (Japan Times 2008). One reason for this decline is that students who are hoping to get into high-level universities are increasingly attending elite private high schools that specialize in examination preparation. Another reason is that apparently many higher-tier, but not elite, universities are easier to enter than was the case in the past. However, for the most ambitious young people, doing well on university entrance examinations and gaining admission to the right university are still important.

STUDENT LIFE AND BEHAVIOR PATTERNS

As in the United States, in junior and senior high schools, clubs are a regular part of the weekly schedule, and schools offer many of the same competitive sports that are found in the United States, including the highly popular baseball and soccer as well as basketball, even American-style football, swimming, and track. Large numbers of Japanese students also participate in traditional sports including judo, kendo (a form of Japanese fencing), and sumo wrestling. There are also many nonsport extracurricular clubs, including brass band, dance, drama, flower arranging, and tea ceremony. It is a common Japanese belief that extracurricular activities are a form of moral education and enable participants to cultivate important elements of the Japanese "spirit" including respect for senior club and team members, hard work, and learning to be a good team member.

Elementary students in Japan typically learn and play in a relatively relaxed atmosphere, and the requirement to wear uniforms at this level is the exception rather than the rule. The situation changes beginning in junior high, and thereafter virtually all students are required to wear uniforms. Schooling becomes a more

Kendo or "way of the sword" is a martial art that is a part of Japanese junior and senior high extracurricular activities. Some adults continue the practice as a hobby. (Dreamstime.com)

serious business in secondary schools. Many junior high students in particular, as well as their teachers and families, feel the strains of impending high school entrance examinations.

Although students are less likely than their American counterparts to get in trouble in or out of school, in recent years, Japanese youth misbehavior has risen relative to the past and is now a major national concern. During the last two decades, substantial numbers of junior high school students have suffered from "school refusal syndrome" and wouldn't go to school. Also, especially in junior high school, a large number of students report being victims of *ijime*, or bullying, by their peers. More ominous examples of recent Japanese youth misbehavior include increases in violent crime, teenage prostitution, gang activity, and substance abuse. Possible social and educational causes for these rising behavior problems are discussed later in this section.

HIGHER EDUCATION

With approximately 3 million students enrolled in 1,200 universities and junior colleges, Japan has the second-largest higher educational system in the developed world. In contrast to the prewar years and the first several postwar decades, women are now fully participating in higher education, with roughly equal percentages of men and women enrolled in higher education. The old public prewar imperial universities, with Tokyo University at the top, are still the elite institutions of higher learning and the most difficult to enter. A few select private universities, such as Keio and Waseda, and some prefectural public universities are considered prestigious. Most private universities, which constitute the majority of Japanese higher educational institutions, are considered to have lower status. Only about 20 to 25 percent of Japan's university students are enrolled in public institutions. The Japanese government in the postwar years built a substantial number of public universities, but not enough to satisfy increasing demands for higher education. In general, students who aren't admitted to public universities must opt for more expensive, but inferior, private universities. Although there are some signs of change, top government ministries and major corporations still tend to recruit new employees from top-ranking prestigious universities. Higher education governance is partially the responsibility of local institutions, but MEXT also has authority in the process.

For several decades, influential Japanese as well as many of the public and foreign observers have been critical of Japan's universities for several reasons. Until recently, with some major exceptions, Japanese universities have been viewed as mediocre compared to institutions of higher learning in other developed countries. Faculty have been viewed as not particularly interested in undergraduate teaching, and the lack of demands on students have also been a source of criticism. Japanese universities have garnered serious domestic criticism for not having enough graduate and professional programs. Graduate faculty have been under fire for not engaging in enough research that benefits the private and public sectors and society in general, in contrast with much research in European and American universities.

In 2004, the national government initiated sweeping reforms of Japan's 88 public national universities, which account for about 20 to 25 percent of enrollment but

80 percent of the national budget. Faculty and staff no longer have the status of national civil servants with guaranteed jobs for life. The reforms also created a process in which national universities compete with each other for research monies with the hope that the winning university proposals will be those that will bring widespread benefit to society, if successfully completed. Also, systematic efforts are being made through faculty development programs to improve teaching. Both the government and private institutions have in the last few years substantially expanded the number of graduate and post-undergraduate programs. The number of foreign students who come to Japan for graduate work has been increasing during the 21st century. Japan still ranks low among developed countries in expenditures for higher education, however, and lack of academic quality of many private universities remains a serious problem (Arimoto 2007, Eades 2005).

EDUCATIONAL REFORM

The postwar success of Japan's schools notwithstanding, in the 1990s student misbehavior, societal concerns that overemphasis on entrance examinations impeded real education, and Japan's long economic malaise coupled with a fast-changing global economy caused many Japanese to take a critical look at the schools. MEXT education bureaucrats, along with prominent Japanese whom the late prime minister Obuchi appointed to a high-profile ad hoc education committee in 2000, participated in a process that culminated in 2002 educational reforms that officials labeled the most significant since the end of World War II. The reformers responsible for these policies perceived the schools were not teaching students how to be critical and creative thinkers.

The Japanese government eliminated one-third of the national course of study in order to encourage students to be independent thinkers and self-directed learners. Japanese students in grades 3–9 now take Integrated Studies classes, where in collaboration with their teachers they plan projects and field trips. The local environment, local history, and the economy are popular Integrated Studies themes. Students also interact with foreigners and learn conversational English in Integrated Studies. There are no textbooks, and teachers do not give tests relating to Integrated Studies. While elementary teachers and students mostly like Integrated Studies, both the public and junior high teachers take a more negative view of this reform because they are concerned that Integrated Studies will result in less emphasis on preparing students for high school entrance examinations. Many junior high teachers, who are not evaluated on implementing Integrated Studies, ignore the requirements and use the time to help students prepare for high school entrance examinations.

Shortly before and after the 2002 reform attempts, findings from several domestic and international studies caused continued worries about Japanese schools. For example, Japan's first-year high school students who took part in 2006 Organization for Economic Co-operation and Development international tests scored lower in every field than Japanese students who took the same tests in 2003. Japanese students fell from 6th to 10th among 30 industrialized nations in math skills, from 2nd to 6th in scientific literacy, and from 14th to 15th in reading comprehension. Faced with several years of declining international test scores, the Central Education Council of the Japanese government announced a policy in late 2007 to increase core subject area class time in elementary and middle schools by 10 percent. Reports of student alienation from school, the need for more effective moral education, and, for the first time, questionable teacher quality are now widely discussed issues in Japan.

In higher education, despite the already discussed public university improvements, the problem of inferior private institutions of higher learning remains unsolved. Many of these institutions are experiencing declining enrollments and since 2007 have essentially "open door" admissions policies. A few private universities have closed, and more closures are expected. Beginning in the 2008–2009 school year, the national government reduced the required number of integrated studies hours.

Although it is impossible to assess the impact of both scheduled and proposed educational reforms, one thing is certain. Since the Meiji years, the Japanese have placed an extremely high value on education and consistently made it a high national priority. There is absolutely no reason to expect that education will be afforded any less attention as Japan negotiates the rest of the 21st century.

REFERENCES

Arimoto, Akira. "Schooling in Japan" in *Going to School in East Asia*, edited by Gerard A. Postiglione and Jason Tan, 142–169. Westport, CT: Greenwood Press, 2007.

DeCoker, Gary, ed. *National Standards and School Reform in Japan and the United States*. New York: Teachers College Press, 2002.

Duke, Benjamin C. *Ten Great Educators of Modern Japan*. Tokyo: University of Tokyo Press, 1989.

Eades, J. S., Roger Goodman, and Yumiko Hada, eds. *The "Big Bang" in Japanese Higher Education: The 2004 Reforms and the Dynamics of Change*. Melbourne, Australia: Trans Pacific Press, 2005.

"Elementary, Junior High Schools to Be Assigned Social Workers." *Japan Times Online*, January 7, 2008. http://search.japantimes.co.jp/print/nn20080107a3.html (accessed January 8, 2008).

Ellington, Lucien. *Education in the Japanese Life-Cycle: Implications for the United States*. Lewiston, NY: Edwin Mellen Press, 1992.

———. "Japanese Education." *Japan Digest*, September 2005. http://spice.stanford.edu/docs/120 (accessed January 8, 2008).

———. "Japan's 2002 Educational Reforms: The American Experiment" in *Southeast Review of Asian Studies, Vol. XXVII*, edited by Daniel A. Metraux, 187–190. Staunton, VA: Southeast Conference Association of Asian Studies, 2005.

———. *Japan: Tradition and Change*. White Plains, NY: Longman, 1990.

Fukuzawa, Rebecca Erwin, and Gerald K. Letendre. *Intense Years: How Japanese Adolescents Balance School, Family, and Friends*. New York: Routledge Falmer, 2000.

The Japan Exchange and Teaching Program. 2006. http://www.jetprogramme.org (accessed August 20, 2008).

Kelly, William and Merry White. "Students, Slackers, Singles, Seniors, and Strangers: Transforming a Family-Nation." In Peter J. Katzenstein and Takashi Shiraishi, eds. *Beyond Japan: The Dynamics of East Asian Regionalism.* Ithaca, NY: Cornell University Press, 2006.

Kondo, Motohiro. "Controversy Over Japanese Education." *Japan Echo* 34, No. 2 (April 2007): 10–11.

"Lessons from the OECD Tests." *Japan Times Online*, December 18, 2007. http://search.japantimes.co.jp/print/ed20071218a1.html.

Ministry of Education, Culture, Sports, Science, and Technology. "Organization of MEXT." August 19, 2008. http://www.mext.go.jp/english/org/index.htm.

"Number of Chinese Students in Japan Hits New Record High." *People's Daily Online*, January 9, 2006. http://english.peopledaily.com.cn/200601/09/eng20060109_234012.html.

Okada, Shin'ichi et al. Special Section: Educating the Future of Japan." *Japan + Asia-Pacific Perspectives* 4, No. 3 (January 2007): 2–7.

Organization for Economic Co-operation and Development. "OECD Briefing Note for Japan." *Education at a Glance 2007.* http://www.oecd.org/dataoecd/22/2/39317152.pdf (accessed November 2008).

———. "OECD Briefing Note for the United States." *Education at a Glance 2007.* http://www.oecd.org/dataoecd/22/51/39317423.pdf (accessed November 2008).

Rohlen, Thomas P. 1997. "Differences That Make a Difference: Explaining Japan's Success." In William K. Cummings and Philip G. Altbach, eds., *The Challenge of East Asian Education: Implications for America.* Albany: State University of New York Press.

Tanaka, Hideaki, ed. *Japan 2007: An International Comparison.* Tokyo: Keizai Koho Center, 2007.

"Unified Entrance Exams Kick Off Nation-wide." The Japan Times Online, January 20, 2008. http://search.japantimes.com.

Watt, Paul. "Buddhism in Japan." *Asia for Educators.* January 5, 2008. http://afe.easia.columbia.edu/japan/japanworkbook/religion/jbuddhis.html (accessed January 5, 2008).

Wray, Harry. *Japanese and American Education: Attitudes and Practices.* Westport, CT: Bergin and Garvey, 1999.

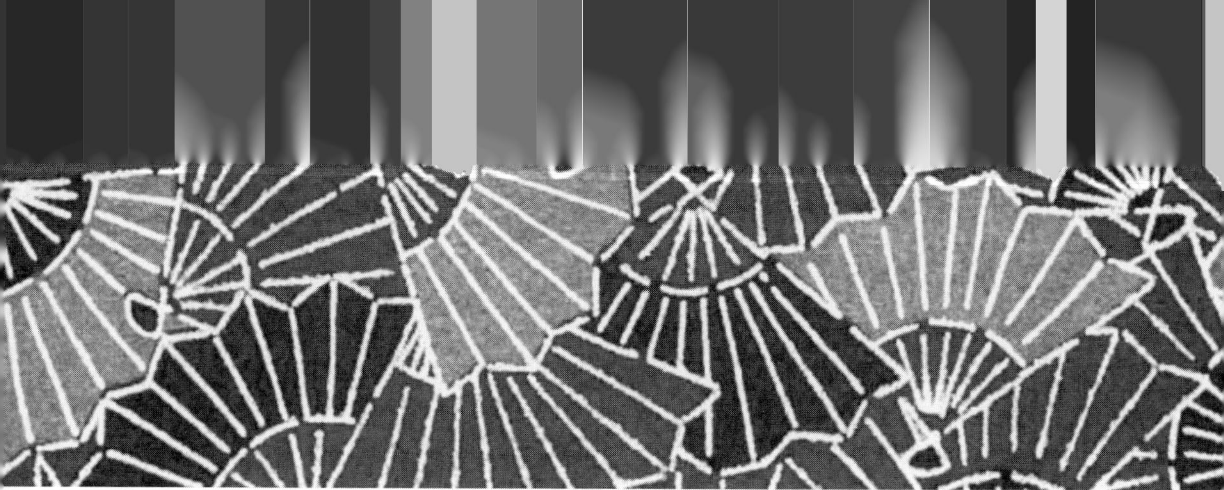

Culture

The Japanese Language

INTRODUCTION

Language has traditionally been a key centripetal force in Japan. Not only is the spoken language unique to Japan, but also estimates are that 95–99 percent of Japanese can read the language as well. The exact origins of the Japanese language have been debated. While many Japanese believe that their spoken language is unique, it is most likely a language originally resulting from the migration of people from the Korean Peninsula, and Japanese and Korean have similar grammatical structures. Although many Japanese words were originally derived from Chinese, spoken Chinese and Japanese are quite different; Chinese is tonal and Japanese is atonal. There are Altaic (continental Asia) and Austronesia (Pacific Islands) components, but the relative physical isolation of the Japanese islands allowed the spoken language to evolve into its own distinct form. However, there are some Western linguistic influences, such as Portuguese, English, and other loanwords that are part of the language. While Japanese is grammatically unrelated to Chinese, the original Japanese written language was adopted from China more than 1,500 years ago. The Japanese already had a spoken language before importing the beginnings of a writing system. Written Japanese is considered one of the world's most difficult languages to learn, but spoken Japanese is relatively easy for an English-speaking person to learn to pronounce and speak.

TABLE A.

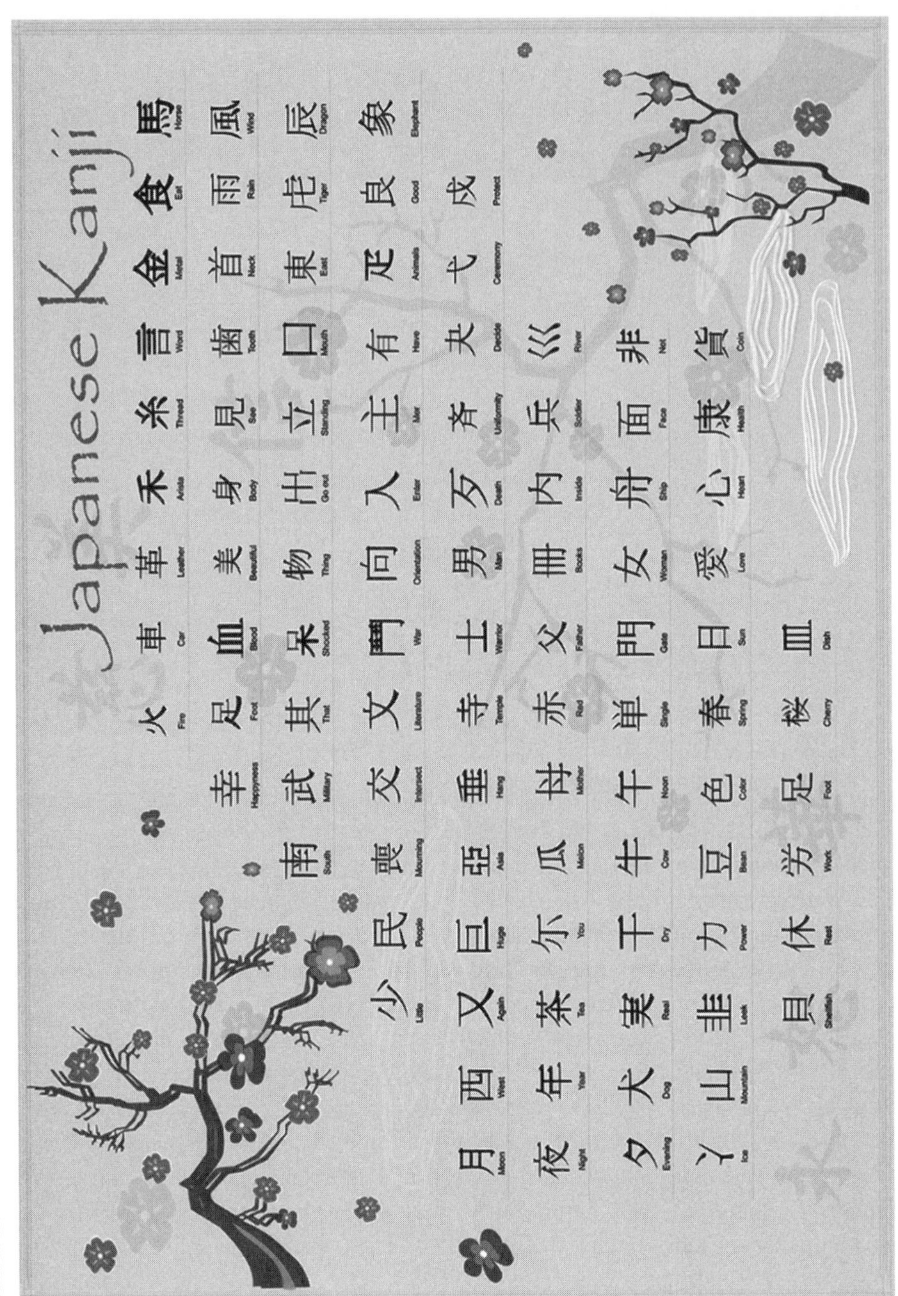

Japanese students spend substantial time memorizing Chinese characters or "Kanji". (Dreamstime.com)

WRITTEN JAPANESE

Written Japanese consists of Chinese characters, or kanji, and two kana or syllabaries, hiragana and katakana. Kanji, which means "Chinese characters," are ideograms or pictorial representations of ideas as well as sounds. Kanji are used in writing the main parts of a sentence such as verbs and nouns as well as names. Although precise dates are disputed, kanji were imported into Japan sometime during the fourth or possibly fifth century CE from China via Korea. At first, the imperial court retained the services of professional letter writers who were Korean to write official correspondence in Chinese. By the seventh century, some of the few Japanese who were literate in Chinese began to use kanji in an attempt to match the Chinese character with Japanese sounds, but this caused major difficulties. Eventually, by the ninth century, Japanese developed the kana, two syllabaries of abbreviated and simplified characters originally based on written Chinese. Often, in newspapers and books other than those for younger children, written Japanese includes kanji and the kana. The typical Japanese newspaper might contain 50 percent kanji, 40 percent kana, and 10 percent other borrowed or modified foreign words and symbols. Although an American must only master 26 letters in the alphabet to have a basis for literacy, Japanese must master approximately 2,000 kanji and two different sets of syllabaries to be in a similar position.

Although there are said to be some 50,000 kanji in existence, today roughly 4,000 characters are commonly used, and a number of these kanji only rarely appear. The Ministry of Education, Culture, Sports, and Technology has identified essential kanji for everyday life, and these are taught to all students in elementary and secondary school. Students must learn 881 kanji by the end of elementary school and a total of 1,945, the number required to become a literate adult, by the time they graduate from high school.

Kanji are, by far, the most difficult written Japanese characters, requiring in some cases as many as 23 strokes. Most kanji also have more than one meaning, and combinations of kanji are used to create even more meanings. Kanji sometimes look like what they mean but usually do not. Table A contains some examples of kanji, along with the most common English meanings.

As mentioned, the kana (hiragana and katakana) developed because, when the Japanese started to use Chinese characters for their own already-existing spoken language, problems emerged. Chinese words are often only one or two syllables, and the Chinese can use a character for each syllable, but Japanese words are frequently polysyllabic. The Japanese developed simplified characters from kanji called kana to indicate a sound without meaning, as is the case with the English alphabet. However, each symbol indicates the sound of a whole Japanese syllable instead of each separate part. For example, in hiragana す is *su*, and つ is *tsu*. Kana are normally easier to read than kanji because they require fewer strokes.

Hiragana and katakana are the two kana syllabaries, and each contains basic symbols representing specific sounds and additional modified symbols. Hiragana is used for inflected endings, grammatical particles, and for Japanese words that were created before the introduction of kanji. Katakana is used for foreign loanwords, usually from the

Table B. Hiragana

あ a ah	い i ee	う u uu	え e eh	お o oh
か ka kah	き ki kee	く ku kuu	け ke kay	こ ko koe
が ga gah	ぎ gi gee	ぐ gu goo	げ ge gay	ご go go
さ sa sah	し shi she	す su sue	せ se say	そ so soe
ざ za zah	じ ji jee	ず zu zoo	ぜ ze zay	ぞ zo zoe
た ta tah	ち chi chee	つ tsu t'sue	て te tay	と to toe
だ da dah	ぢ ji jee	づ zu zoo	で de day	ど do doe
な na nah	に ni nee	ぬ nu nuu	ね ne nay	の no noe
は ha hah	ひ hi he	ふ fu fuu	へ he hay	ほ ho hoe
ば ba bah	び bi bee	ぶ bu boo	べ be bay	ぼ bo boe
ぱ pa pah	ぴ pi pee	ぷ pu puu	ぺ pe pay	ぽ po poe
ま ma mah	み mi me	む mu moo	め me may	も mo moe
や ya yah		ゆ yu yuu		よ yo yoe
ら ra rah	り ri ree	る ru rue	れ re ray	ろ ro roe
わ wa wah		ん n n		を o oh
きゃ kya q'yah		きゅ kyu que		きょ kyo q-yoe
ぎゃ gya g'yah		ぎゅ gyu g'yuu		ぎょ gyo g'yoe

Table B. Hiragana (*Continued*)

しゃ sha yah	しゅ shu yuu	しょ sho yoe
じゃ ja jah	じゅ ju juu	じょ jo joe
ちゃ cha chah	ちゅ chu chuu	ちょ cho choe
ぢゃ ja jah	ぢゅ ju juu	ぢょ jo joe
にゃ nya ne-yah	にゅ nyu ne-yuu	にょ nyo ne-yoe
ひゃ hya he-yah	ひゅ hyu he-yuu	ひょ hyo he-yoe
びゃ bya b'yah	びゅ byu b'yuu	びょ byo b'yoe
ぴゃ pya p'yah	ぴゅ pyu p'yuu	ぴょ pyo p'yoe
みゃ mya me-yah	みゅ myu me-yuu	みょ myo me-yoe
りゃ rya re-yah	りゅ ryu re-yuu	りょ ryo re-yoe

Table C. Katakana

ア a ah	イ i ee	ウ u uu	エ e eh	オ o oh
カ ka kah	キ ki kee	ク ku kuu	ケ ke kay	コ ko koe
ガ ga gah	ギ gi gee	グ gu goo	ゲ ge gay	ゴ go go
サ sa sah	シ shi she	ス su sue	セ se say	ソ so soe
ザ za zah	ジ ji jee	ズ zu zoo	ゼ ze zay	ゾ zo zoe
タ ta tah	チ chi chee	ツ tsu t'sue	テ te tay	ト to toe
ダ da dah	ヂ ji jee	ヅ zu zoo	デ de day	ド do doe
ナ na nah	ニ ni nee	ヌ nu nuu	ネ ne nay	ノ no noe

ハ ha hah	ヒ hi he	フ fu fuu	ヘ he hay	ホ ho hoe
バ ba bah	ビ bi bee	ブ bu boo	ベ be bay	ボ bo boe
パ pa pah	ピ pi pee	プ pu puu	ペ pe pay	ポ po poe
マ ma mah	ミ mi me	ム mu moo	メ me may	モ mo moe
ヤ ya yah		ユ yu yuu		ヨ yo yoe
ラ ra rah	リ ri ree	ル ru rue	レ re ray	ロ ro roe
ワ wa wah		ン n n		ヲ o oh
キャ kya q'yah		キュ kyu que		キョ kyo q-yoe
ギャ gya g'yah		ギュ gyu g'yuu		ギョ gyo g'yoe

Table C. Katakana (*Continued*)

シャ sha yah	シュ shu yuu	ショ sho yoe
ジャ ja jah	ジュ ju juu	ジョ jo joe
チャ cha chah	チュ chu chuu	チョ cho choe
ヂャ ja jah	ヂュ ju juu	ヂョ jo joe
ニャ nya ne-yah	ニュ nyu ne-yuu	ニョ nyo ne-yoe
ヒャ hya he-yah	ヒュ hyu he-yuu	ヒョ hyo he-yoe
ビャ bya b'yah	ビュ byu b'yuu	ビョ byo b'yoe
ピャ pya p'yah	ピュ pyu p'yuu	ピョ pyo p'yoe
ミャ mya me-yah	ミュ myu me-yuu	ミョ myo me-yoe
リャ rya re-yah	リュ ryu re-yuu	リョ ryo re-yoe

West, and for onomatopoeia, words that imitate the sound they represent. The English word "ice cream" is written in katakana as アイスクリーム. Japanese is usually written vertically with columns running from right to left. This means books and magazines begin at what would be the back of their English equivalents. Sometimes, as is the case with the English language, Japanese is written horizontally from left to right. Both hiragana and katakana and their corresponding sounds are illustrated in tables B and C.

As noted earlier, Japanese is one of the most difficult languages in the world to learn to write. The 16th-century Portuguese Jesuit missionary to Japan, Saint Francis Xavier, described Japanese as "the Devil's Language." Although English language study, including language arts or literacy, is a major part of U.S. basic education, in Japan elementary students spend more time on learning to write their national language than on any other subject, and no subject exceeds the amount of classroom hours junior high students devote to Japanese. Students learn their national language through extensive and regular practice. Students do repetitive writing drills and often read aloud entire language passages as a group.

Until about 40 years ago, there were few Westerners who knew Japanese, but with Japan's rise to world prominence by the early 1970s, the situation began to change, and today increasing numbers of foreigners have successfully negotiated Japanese language study.

SPOKEN JAPANESE

Japanese pronunciation is relatively easy for most English speakers. Japanese has no tones, unlike Chinese, and many of its sounds are also found in English. Despite the difficulty of learning written Japanese, there are a number of excellent conversational instructional materials published in the Roman alphabet for foreigners who want to pick up basic phrases quickly.

Japanese vowels may be divided into two types for the purpose of pronunciation. Short vowels' pronunciations are shown in table D. Long vowels are usually pronounced about twice as long as a short vowels, as illustrated in table E. Most consonant sounds are similar to English, with exceptions as listed in table F.

Table D. Examples of Japanese Short Vowels

Short Vowel Sound	Example and Definition
a … as the *a* in father	*akai* (ah-kah-ee) red
e … as the *e* in men	*ebi* (eh-bee) shrimp
i … as the *i* in see	*imi* (ee-mee) meaning
o … as the *o* in boat	*otoko* (oh-toh-koh) male
u … as the *u* in food	*uma* (oo-mah) horse

Table E. Examples of Japanese Long Vowels

Long Vowel Sound	Example and Definition
a … as in father, but lengthened	*bata* (bah-tah) butter
ei … as in men, but lengthened	*eigo* (eh-goh) English
ii … as in see, but lengthened	*iiharu* (ee-hah-roo) insist
o … as in boat, but lengthened	*osama* (oh-sah-mah) king
u … as in food, but lengthened	*yubin* (yoo-been) mail

Unlike English, where the word order is subject-verb-object, Japanese sentence order is subject-object-verb. Rather than saying "I bought this car," Japanese would say something like "I this car bought," or, in Japanese, "*watashi ga kono kuruma o kaimashita.*" Often, Japanese will also omit the subject of a sentence if it is obvious or not considered important. Most Japanese would probably say "*kono kuruma o kaimashita.*" Finally, asking questions in Japanese is even easier than in English. Asking questions that require a "yes" or "no" answer is easy since all that is required is a *ka* at the end of the sentence.

Table G contains some useful expressions for basic conversational survival in Japanese.

LOANWORDS

All languages have loanwords borrowed from other languages, and the Japanese have incorporated a large number of loanwords into their language. This Japanese linguistic tradition goes back to the earliest contacts with the Asian mainland when loanwords came from China and Korea. In the 16th century, the Japanese began to incorporate European words from the Portuguese, Spanish, Dutch, and English into their languages. At a minimum, if both words that appear in dictionaries and words that are in common use but haven't been codified are included, there are probably somewhere

Table F. Pronunciation of Japanese Consonants

Consonant	How to Make the Sound
R	Made with a single flap of the tip of the tongue against the ridge behind your front teeth. The sound is almost a cross between the English *r* and *l*.
F	Before *u*, *fu* is pronounced by releasing the vowel *u* while the lips are held as if you were about to whistle.
G	Always hard as in "good"; never soft as in "gentle."
TS	As the *ts* in cats.

Table G. Survival Japanese Expressions

Japanese Romanization	English Equivalent
Ohayo gozaimasu	Good morning!
Konnichiwa	Hello! (used from about 10:00 A.M. until sundown)
Kombanwa	Good evening.
Sayonara	Good-bye.
O-genki desuka	How are you?
Arigato gozaimasu, Genki desu	Thank you, fine.
Domo arigato gozaimasu	Thank you very much.
Do itashimashite	You are welcome.
Chotto matte kudasai	Wait just a moment please.
Mo ichido onegaishimasu	Once more please.
Hajime mashite	How do you do?
Hai	Yes.
Sumimasen	I am sorry/excuse me.
Tadaima	I am back (said by a person returning home).
Osaki ni	Pardon my going first (before you, when urged).
Gambatte Kudasai	Persevere!

between 35,000 and 40,000 loanwords spoken or written in Japan. However, readers should not get the sense that written or spoken Japanese is simply a derivative language from foreigners. As is the case with other examples of cultural borrowing, the Japanese have often radically changed the foreign cultural form to fit their needs. Foreign words are usually written, pronounced, and spelled differently in their romanized versions than the original words. Furthermore, the meanings frequently change.

Although the Japanese adopted Chinese characters and many Chinese words became part of the Japanese language early in the nation's history, an existing spoken language before contact with China, the early dates of the incorporation of Chinese words, and the fact that meanings changed means there are only a few recognizable Chinese words today. However, a few such as *cha*, the word for "tea," and *san*, the word for "three," are the same in both countries.

Portugal, in the 16th century, was the first European nation to make contact with the Japanese. The name for one of Japan's most famous foods, "tempura," is probably of Portuguese origin. Some other examples of the original Portuguese words, along with the Japanese version and the English translation, appear in table H.

Table H. Portuguese Loanwords with English Translations

Portuguese	Japanese	English
botao	*botan*	button
carta	*karuta*	playing cards
pao	*pan*	bread
tempero	*tempura*	tempura, deep fried fish or vegetables
tobaco	*tabako*	tobacco

Table I. English Loanwords

English	Japanese
gasoline	*gasorin*
pocket	*pocketto*
pink	*pinku*
ballpoint pen	*boru pen*
supermarket	*supa*
word processor	*wapuro*
fax	*fakkusu*
computer	*konpyuto*
door	*doa*

The Spanish, Dutch, and English were also in Japan by the latter part of the 16th and the first part of the 17th centuries. Only a few Spanish and no English loanwords survive from this era. Since the Dutch were the only European people allowed to enter Japan for more than 150 years, there are still at least 40 words that survive. Later during the Meiji period, the French, Italians, Russians, and Germans all contributed a few loanwords to the Japanese vocabulary.

English, however, constitutes the largest single source for loanwords in Japanese, with English words comprising more than 80 percent of the estimated total of originally foreign words used in Japan. Just a few of the many English words in use in Japan are included in table I.

An amusing by-product caused by the major infusion of English-language words into the Japanese language are the various combinations of English-language words that one discovers on signs, sweatshirts, and even cookies in Japan. All Japanese study some English in school and, while the examination system has often been an impediment for the typical Japanese level of English fluency, a large segment of the population finds humor and panache in English-language combinations that make no sense. Many times the typical Japanese is not aware that the expression makes no sense but simply is drawn to the combination of words. Linguist Andrew Horvat noted some typical examples in his book *Japanese Beyond Words*, including "Joyful Bag," "Silhouette Fantasy," "Hello Juicy," and "Gland Hotel" (2000, 92–93).

LANGUAGE AND JAPANESE CULTURE

Japanese, as is the case with any national language, both shapes and reflects cultural values. Traditionally, Japan has been a group-oriented rather than an individualistic society. Social harmony, although certainly not achieved at various junctures in Japanese history, has been valued more than is often the case in the West. Japan also, despite the fact that it is a democracy, has been throughout its history and still is today a more hierarchal society than is the case in the United States or Europe.

Each of these three aspects of Japanese culture has shaped interpersonal communication and language.

As in other East Asian countries, families are considered more important than the individual members, and Japanese write family names first and given names second. Japanese use the personal pronoun "I" much less than is the case in other societies, partially because traditionally it has been considered impolite to call excessive attention to oneself. Generally, self-effacement and praise for others are considered good conversational manners in Japan. A foreigner may learn only a few Japanese expressions, but he or she will often hear the expression "*Anata wa Nihongo ga jozu desu*!" or "You speak Japanese very well!" The Japanese who makes this statement might be highly fluent with English, but it won't be uncommon for him or her to apologize to the native English speaker for poor English. Japanese people extend this self-effacement to their spouses or children when remarking about them to others, so expressions like "my stupid husband" or "my lazy son" are heard more often in Japanese conversation than elsewhere. When a Japanese uses these kinds of expressions, he or she is at one level expressing humility about his or her loved ones and at another level, in a sense, honoring the person who is being addressed.

Highly verbal people and orators have not been as particularly valued in Japan as is the case in the West. Although it is difficult to precisely identify why excessively verbal people are not highly regarded in Japan, some reasons include the structure of spoken Japanese. The speaker often assumes that the listener understands personal pronouns, and verb forms can be easily changed to take broader meanings. For example, in English if one was talking with a friend and wanted to invite the friend to lunch, he or she might say "would you like to go to lunch with me?" In Japanese, this could be said with the expression "*Hiru-gohan ni ikimashoka*" (literally in English "lunch go with me?"). People can use many fewer words to communicate in Japanese than in other languages. In fact, this cultural disregard for rhetoricians is one reason that has been cited for the now-too-low supply of attorneys in Japan. In a group-oriented society, too much talking can be seen as a sign of egotism.

A propensity toward preserving harmony also affects language use, and this causes many Japanese to have a different viewpoint about the purposes of language than what exists in most Western countries. In the United States, for example, the ability to communicate ideas clearly is considered a highly desirable trait in an individual. This is not necessarily true with Japanese. Japanese believe in preserving group harmony, and in order to do this it is important that a person often speak indirectly so as not to offend. For example, if a Japanese person finds a request by an associate impossible to fulfill, he or she often uses a phrase that could be translated into English as "it's very difficult." Most Japanese would consider an out-and-out "no" far too direct, but this is what is almost always meant by this expression. Even an expression, given in response to a request, like "we will study your question" can often mean "no." The Japanese word for "yes," *hai*, is actually often employed to mean "I understand what you are saying" instead of "I agree" because the Japanese word for "no" would be considered too direct and likely to offend. Although Japanese tend to use indirect expressions and circumspectness more than most of the world's peoples, this point shouldn't be overaccentuated since English speakers and other Westerners also use this conversational tactic. Many Japanese who get to know others well, whether they are foreign or Japanese, will become more direct in communications with the passage of time.

One of the greatest differences in Japanese and English is the importance of levels of politeness in Japanese. People in most cultures use honorifics to show respect, but because of both the desire for societal harmony that has traditionally been in evidence and the hierarchal nature of Japanese society, a number of conversational forms are used in Japan. Which one a person uses depends on such variables as class, gender, in-groups, and out-groups as well as specific situations. There are polite and everyday forms of Japanese conversation, with different verb forms and particles depending on the form.

There are also honorific and humble forms of address. A person will speak quite differently depending on the person he or she is speaking to or about. Both forms and words, including verbs, nouns, pronouns, and adjectives, often change depending on the status of the person to whom one is talking. A person will use different words for "mother" or "father" when speaking to his or her own parents than when speaking about them to someone else. Polite greetings are a standard form of honorific. Consider the English meaning of a common first-time greeting, *dozo yoroshiku, onegai shimasu*, or "Please, I beg your indulgence," and the high level of politeness for honorific conversational forms in Japan begins to be sensed. The widely used Japanese word for "excuse me," *sumimasen*, also means "I'm sorry," which is another indicator of how often Japanese use honorifics to help promote what many in Japan consider to be appropriate human relations. The suffix *san* is perhaps the most famous honorific in the Japanese language. It is a gender-neutral equivalent of Mr., Mrs., or Miss and is placed at the end of the family name of a person being addressed (e.g., Tanka-san). One of the most basic rules of polite Japanese conversation is that one should refer to other adults as *san* but never to oneself. "Sensei," the honorific Japanese word for "teacher," may also be used for certain other people of intellectual accomplishment, including physicians. As is the case with *san*, sensei should never be used by the speaker as a self-referent.

The prefixes *o* or *go* are nouns (or adjectives) referring to certain people or things to indicate respect. For example, *mizu* ("water") and *cha* ("tea") each have special status in Japanese society, and polite conversation includes the expressions *o-mizu* and *o-cha*. Generally, *o* is used with words of Japanese origin while *go* is attached to words that were originally Chinese in origin. Nowhere is the use of different language forms to show respect more indicative of the nature of the Japanese language than when the familial terms for one's own family and others' families are contrasted. Table J contains important information for those readers who want to learn some conversational Japanese.

Traditionally, Japanese women tended to use different personal pronouns than men, and their speech assumed specific forms including using more polite forms and using polite conversational forms more frequently. Japanese women engaging in polite speech around men often appear markedly submissive in both language

Table J. Terms for Japanese Family Members

English	Familial Terms for Talking to Others About One's Own Family	Familial Terms for Talking to Others About Members of Their Family or Someone Else's Family, or to Members of One's Own Family
Grandfather	*Sofu*	*Ojiisan*
Grandmother	*Sobo*	*Obasan*
Uncle	*Oji*	*Oji san*
Aunt	*Oba*	*Oba san*
Father	*Chichi*	*Otosan*
Mother	*Haha*	*Okasan*
Elder brother	*Ani*	*Oniisan*
Younger brother	*Ototo*	*Ototo san*
Elder sister	*Ane*	*Oneesan*
Younger sister	*Imoto*	*Imoto san*
Sons	*Musuko*	*Musuko san*
Daughters	*Musume*	*Ojosan*

and manner of speech. However, as sexism has receded in a number of important ways including access to higher education and Japan has experienced increasing internationalization, many women are challenging the expectation that they engage in *onnarashi*, or respectable feminine speech.

Despite challenges to gender-based differences in language, the still-prevalent concerns in Japan about the status of others and how to communicate with someone whom they've just met in the most appropriate manner manifests itself in the widespread use of *meishi*, or business cards. One reason business cards are much more common in Japan than in the United States is that it is a quick way for someone who meets another person to obtain an idea of a stranger's status and adjust language accordingly in initial interactions. It is much more common in Japan than in the United States for university graduates who are employed in a wide range of occupations to have business cards. School teachers are also a good example since Japanese educators almost all have business cards while this is usually not the case in the United States.

LEARNING JAPANESE LANGUAGE

Although learning to read and write Japanese takes a sustained period of focused effort, the expansion of Japanese courses in the West makes it much easier to study the language than in the past. There are also excellent Japanese language programs at a number of universities in Japan that are especially designed for foreigners. The existence of a wide range of romanized conversational-language self-study materials means that those who plan to spend time in Japan but are not able because of other time demands to learn to write Japanese can develop a relatively high level of oral fluency without learning to read kanji and kana. Also, many university and community college continuing education programs in the United States offer conversational Japanese courses. If further time is spent in Japan and familiarity with the kana and a few kanji is developed, Japan becomes an easy country in which to travel.

REFERENCES

Akiyama, Carol, and Nobuo Akiyama. *Learn Japanese the Fast and Fun Way*. 2nd ed. Hauppauge, NY: Barron's Educational Series, 1999.

Association for Japanese-Language Teaching. *Japanese for Busy People*. Tokyo: Kodansha International, Ltd., 1984.

Horvat, Andrew. *Japanese Beyond Words: How to Walk and Talk like a Native Speaker*. Berkeley, CA: Stone Bridge Press, 2000.

Imaeda, Kazuko. *Breeze into Japanese: Practical Language for Beginners*. Boston: Cheng & Tsui Co., 2004.

Menton, Linda. "Borrowing Words: Using Loanwords to Teach About Japan." *Education About Asia* 6, No. 2 (Fall 2001): 28–30.

Rowthorn, Chris and Ray Bartlett, Andres Bender, Michael Clark, and Matthew D. Firestone. *Lonely Planet: Japan*. 10th ed. Oakland, CA: Lonely Planet Publications, 2007.

Tym, Alice L. "Centripetal Forces in Japan." *Japan Teaching Module*. University of Tennessee at Chattanooga. October 8, 2007. http://www.utc.edu/asia/teaching (accessed October 2007).

Yoshida, Yasuo, ed. *Japanese for Today*. Tokyo: Gakken, 1973.

Etiquette in Japan

INTRODUCTION

Knowledge of any society's expected conventional rules of behavior in various settings helps an outsider both better understand that culture and successfully negotiate it as a visitor. Since language, culture, and etiquette are impossible to separate, readers who intend to travel to Japan are urged to read both the preceding section on language and most, if not all, of the preceding chapter on society. In this section, a brief description of a few deeply held, traditional, and commonly shared cultural beliefs that influence daily Japanese interpersonal interactions will be followed by a more specific discussion of the most important rules of etiquette any traveler to Japan needs to observe much of the time.

However, two caveats are in order. Although Japan remains one of the world's more homogenous major nations, generational differences, social class, increased cultural and economic globalization, and a small but increasingly diverse collection of minorities mean there are situations where people don't follow what are considered to be conventional rules. Still, the wisest course of action for the traveler to Japan is to assume that what is suggested in the discussion of important rules of etiquette applies in all interactions with people whom the visitor does not know relatively well. The second caveat is that those readers who are planning a stay in Japan that is a month or longer should read one of the recommended references on etiquette included at the end of the chapter.

CULTURAL BELIEFS AND ETIQUETTE

Long-held beliefs that still permeate Japanese culture make the rules of etiquette more extensive and probably complex than is the case in the West. Part of the basis for the greater accentuation most Japanese place on etiquette than Westerners is rooted in the differences in respective religious traditions. The Judeo-Christian traditions tend to emphasize what is viewed in those traditions as universal moral rules that then become a theoretical foundation for subsequent individual interpersonal relations with others. The Ten Commandments are a leading example of the Western tradition. The set of spiritual injunctions are specific, and the individual's subsequent personal conduct should be based on the religious "laws."

Shinto has no moral code equivalent to the Ten Commandments, Buddhism's Eightfold Path is certainly less specific than the Ten Commandments, and although Confucianism stresses individual virtue, associated moral injunctions are presented within a secular framework. Although Japanese learn general ethical precepts through their belief systems, in contrast to the West, there are no specific written religious codes in Japan that theoretically are the cornerstone for individual morality and actions toward others. Probably, the most important unwritten ethical injunction that Japanese learn is to interact with others to preserve group harmony. Inculcation of this belief from early childhood, and the fact that Japan is relatively ethnically homogenous, means that similar rules of etiquette that have evolved through practice become expected "Japanese" behavior.

Since traditionally Japanese believe that an individual owes his or her very existence to others, if a complex code of etiquette is needed to preserve human relations, so be it. This means that the Japanese even have such terms as *tatemae* and *honne* for situations that individuals encounter where there are discrepancies or conflicts between expected public behavior and true feelings. Tatemae means what is expected of an individual engaging in a particular social behavior, as opposed to honne, the individual's true feelings about the social situation or other person. For example, a Japanese company employee might bow deeply to the president even though the employee feels that the CEO is incompetent. Westerners are more likely to look down on individuals coping with this kind of situation by being formally polite. In contrast, many Japanese are more forgiving since they think it is inevitable that one will face these kinds of situations. Americans, for example, are much more likely to condone actions based on true feelings. More Japanese tend to first consider their obligations or duties to others and often suppress their true desires. None of this implies any moral superiority or inferiority on the part of Japanese relative to Americans but rather illustrates the greater demands placed on Japanese to follow general widely practiced outward behavioral forms than is the case in the West.

Rank, status, and hierarchy are also closely related to perceptions of public behavior in Japan. Despite being a stable democracy, the desire to preserve good group and societal relations means that rank and status matter more in Japan than in Western countries with similar political situations. For example, there is more of a propensity on the part of Japanese than Westerners to wear uniforms. Almost all Japanese secondary school students wear uniforms as well as larger numbers of workers in a variety of jobs. This cultural proclivity to wear uniforms, like the widespread use of business cards, is a form of etiquette in that it allows others to recognize individuals' statuses and treat them accordingly.

In contrasting the United States and Japan, there is a much-repeated saying about the difference in rules of conduct in the two countries: In the United States anything is permitted unless it is explicitly forbidden, while in Japan anything is forbidden unless it is explicitly permitted. Although there are many exceptions to this generalization, when etiquette and manners are concerned there is much truth in the adage. Japanese are bound by many etiquette expectations. However, foreigners can take much solace in the fact that except for a few notable exceptions, Japanese are quite forgiving of outsiders. Educated Japanese recognize how complicated etiquette can be in their culture and are truly tolerant of foreigners' mistakes.

Before turning to specific recommended behaviors, another way to summarize the effects of a dense array of etiquette "dos and don'ts" is that the large number of unwritten rules causes many Japanese to take a relatively conservative perspective on expectations about how people should behave in public. This is perhaps best illustrated by the report to me from a Japanese friend whose family hosted their first American college student homestay guest. When I asked her what her mother and father felt about the young man, she reported that they thought that while he was a nice young man in general, he had some weird behaviors. When she asked for an example, her mother exclaimed that on at least two occasions the guest had walked by the refrigerator, opened it, and just looked around for a couple of minutes. When the young man arrived, he had been told to make himself at home, and by trolling for a snack he certainly was behaving like a typical young American family member, but many Japanese would consider this informal behavior on the part of a stranger eccentric or unacceptable.

SURVIVAL ETIQUETTE

Part of good etiquette is understanding the role of oral conversation in good manners. Even travelers who are in Japan for a week or less should take a little time to learn a few simple greetings and how to say "thank you." Also, Japanese who speak English, in attempting to honor guests, will often make statements that appear somewhat strange or even duplicitous to foreigners. Additional information about both of these language-related topics is included in the previous section of this chapter.

Shoes Off before Entering Certain Buildings Perhaps the worst breach of etiquette foreigners can make is to not take off their shoes when entering a Japanese home, school, temple, or certain other buildings or rooms in buildings. Although said to be originally associated with Shinto and concepts of purity, the practice also is indicative of Japanese respect for the private space of the home that is apart from the hurly-burly outside world and the spiritual importance of the temple or school. For what it's worth, Japanese also have a much easier time keeping their houses clean as a result of this practice, and a few Westerners are so impressed that they adopt the custom as well.

Virtually all Japanese homes have a *genkan*, or entranceway, with a space where visitors take off their shoes and step up onto the actual floor of the house. It is

Almost all Japanese remove their shoes when entering houses. Shoes are left at the entrance or "genkan." (Dreamstime.com)

important to arrange your shoes neatly by the step as well, and the custom is to have the toes facing the door. Normally, people wear slippers inside the house except when they enter a tatami ("bamboo mat") room, and then they leave their slippers outside the room. Since Japanese tend to have smaller feet than many Westerners, those American or European travelers who know they will be staying in private homes for a few days or more might want to take a relatively new pair of bathroom slippers that comfortably fit.

Tatami mat rooms are also a feature in traditional Japanese inns, or *Ryokans*, and other traditional settings, and the same rules about shoes apply. Also, special slippers for Japanese toilets are placed outside toilet entrances in homes and schools, so when using the toilet, change from regular to WC (water closet, or restroom) slippers, and change again upon leaving the toilet. Although what follows may seem obvious, since the author has suffered embarrassment on a few occasions, great care should be taken by the traveler in advance that his or her socks or stockings don't have holes. Every pair should be checked.

Bowing Although foreigners now frequently get handshakes, bowing is still the typical Japanese form of greeting or parting. It is also common to bow when apologizing, requesting a favor, or expressing thanks. Although techniques differ, traditionally in Japan it is more polite to bow from the waist rather than just nod the head. The higher the status of the person one is greeting, the deeper one is expected to bow. However, the deep bowing, as some Westerners might have seen Japanese

Although they might shake hands with foreigners, bowing is a more common practice when Japanese meet or see each other. (Dreamstime.com)

do in Hollywood movies, would be considered bizarre, so avoid the deep bow in most circumstances. Occasionally, one may be in the situation of bowing in a tatami mat room, and this is usually done on the knees since Western-style chairs are not used in tatami rooms.

Bows also occur simultaneously. Japanese men usually bow with their hands at their sides while women bow with their hands in front of them. It is important to remember that the polite thing to do in Japan is to bow, and if a Japanese offers a handshake, a slight bow to the person while shaking hands is a good idea. Bowing is, to a certain extent, an art form, and it is sometimes difficult for foreigners to get it exactly right. However, Japanese are quite forgiving about foreigners and bowing, but they do appreciate when non-Japanese make the gesture.

Business Cards Having an ample supply of business cards, or *meishi* in Japanese, is particularly important for those travelers to Japan who wish to establish longer-term relationships with businesses or organizations. If possible, it is recommended that travelers have double-sided cards printed with Japanese and the traveler's language. Meishi use and proper business card etiquette demonstrate to Japanese contacts that the traveler is serious about cultivating relationships and understands something of Japanese culture. Typically, business cards have a person's position, organization, and various addresses. Business cards have multiple uses in Japan and their own set of attendant rules. First and foremost, they are a quick way for people to judge each other's status, thereby allowing both parties to act accordingly. Business cards also serve as invaluable sources of business and professional information. In a society where personal connections are most important, recipients of an influential person's business card may very well find many new opportunities.

Business cards are exchanged at the beginning of a meeting, and one should stand if presenting the card to someone who has a higher position. When presenting meishi to someone, the polite way to do it is to use both hands, bow, and present the card so that the person to whom you are giving it can read it. Never deal a meishi as if it were a playing card. It is also considered impolite to stuff a business card in one's back pocket or to take a meishi from a back pocket and then present it to someone else. Most Japanese will have cardholders for their own and other people's meishi. When sitting at a table, arrange the meishi you've been given in the order of people sitting across from you if possible so you can better remember names and positions. Travelers to Japan are also advised to take more meishi than they think they need, and the same advice applies when attending any meeting.

Meetings Although there are definitely exceptions, traditionally Japanese who are contemplating business arrangements or other formal associations with outside parties will often attempt to get to know prospective future associates in social settings in order to get some sense of what they are like as people. This could very well mean an initial social situation, usually in a restaurant and not a private home, with plenty of food and alcohol and conversation that does not relate to possible business arrangements. This is difficult for many Westerners, who are accustomed to more fast-paced, direct, and impersonal relations. Generally, patience is the rule of thumb for the Westerner. When more formal meetings occur and all parties are seated, if

In contemporary Japan, some Japanese and many foreign tourists remain interested in the tea ceremony. (Corel)

the meeting is at a company or educational institution, guests are usually served Japanese green tea or coffee. Guests should wait until the host encourages them to drink before doing so. Then, even if green tea is not a favorite, if it is served it is a good idea to take at least one sip so that the host will not possibly be offended, although foreigners will often be given a choice of beverages. Japanese appreciate a lower-key verbal approach and are often instinctively negative toward outsiders who seem too verbose or too self-centered in their interpersonal communications, so if possible keep this in mind during discussions.

Traditional Sitting Although Western furniture is now used throughout Japan, most travelers to Japan will encounter situations where they will be sitting on the floor, including when any tatami mat is used for a function. *Seiza*, or the formal way to sit, is done through kneeling with legs underneath, but this is painful for foreigners. Japanese are understanding on this matter and usually make an effort to keep the amount of time the Westerner is on the floor minimal or not be offended if he or she must stand occasionally or stretch out the legs when sitting. If this is the case and the legs must be extended, be sure not to point the feet directly at another person. In more casual situations, usually Japanese men will sit cross-legged while women will sit on their knees or place both legs on one side. Formal sitting is declining in Japan because it is painful for many younger people.

Seating and Standing Etiquette Tatami mat rooms often have a *tokonoma*, an alcove that features beautiful calligraphy, pottery, or a traditional Japanese ikebana flower arrangement. The most important person is seated near the tokonoma.

In any room, the most prominent individual is seated furthest away from the entrance, a practice that apparently has historical roots in that the highest-ranking person was given the most security from possible attackers. In traditional Japanese meal seating arrangements, the highest-ranking guest and the host will be seated opposite each other at the center of the table, with others seated to the left and right of the two principals depending on their status. It is good manners for guests to wait until the host seats them. When entering a room, traditionally the highest-ranking person as a rule is in front and seated first, with other people following by age or rank.

In cars, the most important person, and the most prominent guest is usually treated as the most important person, enters the car first and sits in the backseat behind the driver on the right side since, as in the United Kingdom, steering wheels are on the right side in Japan. The least important person will sit in the front seat with the driver.

Japan is not a "ladies first" society. When a Westerner waits for a woman member of a group to enter a car or building first, this can cause confusion.

Etiquette on Trains and Subways Japan has the best long train system in the world and extensive subway systems in major and medium-sized cities. Japanese trains and subways are, with rare exceptions, famous for being on time. There are vertical lines by each designated train car stop, and those who wish to board line up, wait for passengers to disembark, and then get into the train car. One major etiquette mistake for Westerners to make in Japan is to travel with oversized heavy suitcases. Although many younger people seem to be changing, most Japanese are light travelers for a variety of reasons, and the crowded conditions on trains is perhaps the most important one. Also, because Japanese are typically slighter of build than the typical Westerner or American, the overhead spaces where luggage is generally stored on trains are small. Travelers to Japan should thus carry a modest amount of luggage and avoid the use of hard and large plastic suitcases. Also, it is a good idea when approaching a stop to carefully get the luggage down from the storage area before the train reaches the station because there are only a few minutes allocated for passenger embarkation and disembarkation.

Women travelers in particular should be aware that in overcrowded subways, groping can be a problem. If confronted with this action, act quickly and be direct and demonstrative if the identity of the perpetrator is known. Usually, speaking with a raised voice to the perpetrator (or in the direction of the perpetrator) in any language will solve the problem since the miscreant will be afraid of attracting further attention.

Japanese Punctuality Traditionally, the notion of being fashionably late does not exist in Japan. Although obviously people are sometimes late, it is usually due to planning errors or traffic congestion. Social events and previously arranged meetings between representatives of different organizations begin and end precisely on announced times. The best possible advice for visitors to Japan, especially first-time visitors who may have more difficulty negotiating Japan, is to plan on arriving a few minutes early so as not to be late. A common mistake Americans make in Japan at large formal parties is to be somewhat shocked when, even though everyone seems to be having a good time, the Japanese in charge thanks everyone for attending and announces the party is over. This is a common procedure in Japan and does not in any way mean that Japanese did not enjoy themselves. This kind of conclusion of an evening does not usually happen in more informal settings.

Clothes Notions of acceptable dress in Japan, including business dress, are becoming less formal, and former Prime Minister Koizumi even suggested that men dispense with neckties in the summer so as to avoid high air-conditioning costs. Despite these developments, it is important to remember that Japan is still more conservative on the question of what constitutes appropriate dress than most Western countries. Shorts on adult men and women are not nearly as common in Japan as in many Western countries. Loud, garish clothing among most adults is still the exception rather than the rule.

Business travelers should dress conservatively, especially when first meeting Japanese counterparts. If the business traveler is wearing a jacket at a meeting and the Japanese host is not wearing one, after greetings and when everyone is settled, politely ask the host if it is permissible to take off the jacket. Women who are in Japan for business should dress as if they were attending a board meeting and take care to avoid too much jewelry or makeup. Japanese are less accustomed to management-level meetings with women than is the case in the West, and foreign women should choose dress with the objective of being taken seriously by the host and not primarily admired for other reasons.

Gift Giving Japan is very much a gift-giving society, and when visiting a Japanese home, a workplace, or office on business or pleasure, it is very good etiquette to bring a gift. Although there is no iron-clad rule of thumb, gifts are usually given at the beginning or near the end of a meeting or homestay. The appearance of the gift is quite important, so while gifts need not be expensive, they should be as neatly wrapped as possible. Since Japanese typically pay more attention than Westerners to appearance, it is important to wrap a gift. However, this can be a problem for the visitor to Japan who is staying in one place for a short period of time and has a structured travel schedule that involves a number of meetings. Two strategies are recommended. Either pack the wrapping material in luggage and wait until the day of the meeting or the night before to wrap the present or presents, or pack attractive gift bag material and use that option if neatly wrapping presents is not a talent. It is also considered bad form, unless one grants you permission, to open the gift in the presence of the giver. It is indicative of good manners to show appreciation for the gift and, if allowed to open it, to show that one likes the gift. Don't give a gift that contains four objects since the Japanese pronunciation for the word "four" and the word "death," *shi*, is the same.

Japanese particularly appreciate gifts that are representative of one's region or specific locale, so the assumption is that foreigners will purchase gifts in their home countries before visiting Japan. Local art objects, company or school paraphernalia, or small books containing photographs of home and family members are good examples of appropriate gifts. Name-brand liquor is also usually appreciated in business circles. If meeting with representatives of a business or organization, it is a good idea to give the senior person at the meeting a somewhat nicer gift than the subordinates since it is a sign of respect to honor the person in charge.

Excessive and Loud Talk Japanese distrust overly verbal people and dislike excessive loudness. Japanese can often be quite comfortable with silences when around other people. This doesn't mean that a visitor to Japan should be silent and withdrawn, but being too verbose is more unacceptable in Japan than in the West. Excessively loud people are also considered rude. This can be a real problem for Americans, who unintentionally are often the loudest people on a Japanese train or in a commercial establishment. The author has taken a number of American groups to Japan and at least once on every study tour has needed to remind his travel companions about this matter of train etiquette.

Compliments In group-oriented Japan, it is considered good manners to be self-effacing while being very complimentary of the other person. Foreigners who know very few Japanese phrases are often told, sometimes in flawless English, that they speak such good Japanese. Expect to be complimented on a variety of attributes. Your Japanese friend or acquaintance is not being duplicitous but is only attempting to be polite. If you compliment a Japanese, he or she is most likely to respond that they don't deserve the compliment. This same response on your part is appropriate when you are complimented in Japan.

Directness and Opinions Because they are taught to preserve group harmony, most Japanese are somewhat indirect when asked questions and often shy away from giving opinions. For example, if asked whether one likes a particular food, it is considered rude to simply answer "yes" or "no." Especially if in a home, the hosts might very well have gone to some trouble to procure the food. The polite alternative to "no" would be the equivalent of "I like it a little," which lets the host know, in a polite manner, that one really does not care for the dish. Many Japanese tend to have, because of their socialization to be indirect in delicate matters, a hard time telling another person "no" in response to a request. If, upon making a request, one hears the phrase "it is very difficult," it is best to interpret the answer as "it is impossible."

Appropriate Conversation Topics Although there are exceptions, Japanese often avoid asserting direct opinions, particularly if the subject is controversial. It is probably best to avoid extensive discussion about World War II, politics, or international relations unless one knows his or her Japanese conversant well. As is the case with conversation anywhere, common sense is in order. Many Japanese are curious about visitors' families and, in turn, enjoy talking about their families. Other Japanese for whatever reason don't find this topic of interest. If a question from the visitor doesn't elicit an extended response, then another topic should be pursued. When people from differing cultural and language backgrounds interact, jokes, which usually don't translate well, should as a rule of thumb be avoided. If you are an American, try to avoid interjecting the expression "uh" between expressions since it apparently has a harsh sound to many Japanese and is confusing.

With young people, asking questions about *anime*, *manga*, sports, school, clubs, especially if the young person is in middle or high school, or hobbies is a good icebreaker. Traditionally in Japan, many adults have taken pride in a particular hobby, so this subject can be a good icebreaker. Baseball is a popular sport in Japan, and many Japanese, especially males, feel great pride in the accomplishments of famous Japanese baseball stars in the United States, so related questions can often elicit conversations.

If the visitor wants to learn more about traditional culture, he or she might ask Japanese adults their opinions about kabuki, noh, or haiku (further information about these topics are located elsewhere in this book). Although contemporary movies and popular culture interest typical Japanese more than the topics just mentioned, asking about these or similar venerated art and literary traditions shows an interest on the foreigner's part in Japan's heritage. Since American film is common in Japan, asking about favorite U.S. movie stars is another conversational possibility.

Adult readers who will be in social situations in Japan where alcohol is consumed should be aware that many Japanese share the belief that it is not a breach of etiquette when drinking to be more candid and talk about subjects that would be unacceptable if alcohol were not being consumed. How the visitor responds to a more candid or direct comment than he or she expected is entirely dependent on the specific situation.

Patience One problem many foreigners encounter in Japan is that when making requests, they expect an immediate answer. Always keep in mind that Japan is still in many ways a group-oriented society, and often when a request by an outside party is made, consensus among several people must be first sought. The best strategy is simply to expect more time to pass before receiving an answer to a request. The positive side of this cultural trait is that once Japanese make decisions, because there is consensus, they tend to carry out the decision very expeditiously.

Hierarchy Japan is influenced by Confucian teachings, and great emphasis is placed on age and status. As readers have probably already understood, when dealing with several Japanese it is important to defer to the oldest or highest-ranking person. This extends even to families, and there are words in the Japanese language for older or younger siblings and children. Many Americans who don't speak another foreign language are quickly impressed by others who are fluent in more than one language. A common mistake the author has observed that first-time visitors make when meeting with Japanese where an interpreter is present is that they pay him or her more attention than they do the senior official who is also present. Make sure with body language and other nonverbal communications to avoid this mistake.

Forms of Address When addressing adults, one should normally use the honorific *san* after the person's family name, for example, Yamato-san or Yamane-san, regardless of whether the person is male or female. *Never* refer to yourself as "san"! When addressing an educator or other person who has higher status because of wisdom or knowledge, the Japanese term for teacher, "sensei," is polite. Use sensei after the person's family name: for example, Suzuki-sensei. Almost all Japanese address each other by family names; given names are rarely used. Children are an exception. San should not be used with them, and it is appropriate to use a given name. Relatives and close friends often add *chan* after a child's name as an endearing alternative to the more formal san: for example, Junko-chan.

Bathing and Toilets Japanese baths also have their own etiquette rules. The typical bath has a partitioned area with a shower, such washing implements as soap and shampoo, and a deep tub. If one is a guest in a home, the hosts will have already filled the tub. Japanese wash *before* they get in the tub. It is imperative that one follow this custom, using soap and shampoo and rinsing off before getting into the tub. The experience of a Japanese bath is similar in many ways to hot tubs in the United States. The purpose is to relax in the water, which is usually very hot. After soaking in the water, one can use soap again, rinse off again, and get back in the water for more soaking. Never let the water out of the tub when you are done if you are a guest in a Japanese home. Most likely, other people will be using the water after you.

Toilets are separate from baths in Japanese homes, and throughout Japan there are two types of toilets, Western and Japanese. The latter toilets are mounted, and any good guide book has more detailed instructions about how to use Japanese toilets. Although many public facilities have both kinds of toilets, this is not always the case, so familiarity with how to use a Japanese toilet is critical. Since toilet paper is not freely provided in many public facilities such as train stations, it is a good idea to always have tissues.

Public Displays of Affection Although there are increasing exceptions, particularly among younger people, hugging and kissing in public are not Japanese propensities. When one says good-bye to a Japanese host family, for example, it is probably best not to initiate public displays of affection; of course, it is quite appropriate to respond if the Japanese take the initiative.

Impolite Personal and Conversational Mannerisms It is considered extremely rude to blow one's nose in public, and this should be avoided. When one must sneeze, turn to the side, cover the face, and, if using a handkerchief or tissue, don't put it away immediately. Japanese restrooms often don't provide paper towels or tissue paper, and many restaurants don't have paper napkins (instead, a hot towel often is provided at the beginning of the meal), so it is a good idea to bring disposable tissues and/or a handkerchief with you while visiting Japan. Crossing the legs should be avoided and in particular having a knee above a table in a meeting. Leg-crossing in public is traditionally considered to be a sign of disrespect.

Eating Etiquette In direct contrast to the United States, it is considered perfectly normal to make noise, for example, to slurp noodles, while one eats. When eating in Japanese homes and often elsewhere, it is common for all at the table to enthusiastically say *Itadakimasu* before beginning, and never begin eating until this has occurred. Itadakimasu is a blessing of sorts. The translation is "I gratefully partake," and it is the polite equivalent of "I eat" and "I receive." After eating, the appropriate phrase spoken by all is *Gochiso sama deshita*. The literal translation is "It was indeed a feast," so one is in effect is saying, "Thank you for the lovely meal."

Chopsticks have their own special rules. One should not pass food to another person using chopsticks. Nor should chopsticks be stuck upright in any food. This is especially true of rice since sticking chopsticks in rice at the altar is a custom at Japanese funerals. It is fine to pick up a small dish (many Japanese foods are served in small dishes) and hold it under one's chin in order to avoid spillage. Most Japanese eat soup by using chopsticks for the food in the soup and then drinking the broth. It is important to try and eat everything one is served if having a meal in a private home. It is considered impolite to fill one's own glass and good manners to fill other diner's glasses. If one has had enough to drink, it is best to leave the glass full and indicate by a polite refusal or a hand gesture.

When everyone has finished eating, it is considered good manners to leave all dishes in the same positions they were in when served. Replace lids on bowls and put chopsticks back in holders if this is applicable.

CONCLUSION: JAPANESE TOLERANCE AND A CHANGING JAPAN

As noted earlier, those readers who visit Japan should definitely pay attention to these etiquette tips because they represent the most essential codes of interpersonal contact that most Japanese still respect and admire. There are visible signs, however, that a substantial number of Japanese young people are deviating from what has traditionally been considered appropriate etiquette. Travelers who remain in Japan for any length of time will have little problem seeing exceptions to the recommended behavior described here.

It should be reiterated that Japanese realize their conventional rules of human interaction are extensive and in some aspects rather complex. Thus, they tend to be quite forgiving, with certain exceptions like wearing shoes into a house, when foreigners make mistakes. Also, if this section seems intimidating to some readers who will be traveling to Japan, take heart that one of the most important rules of etiquette in Japan is to treat a guest so well that he or she feels like royalty. There is a long-held Japanese sentiment that all a house guest needs to do is pick up his or her chopsticks. In fact, sometimes it is considered a little rude for guests to even offer to help with housework! Rest assured that most short-term visitors find Japan one of the most delightful countries in the world in which to sojourn.

REFERENCES

"A Guide to Living in Japan." *ELT News*. 2008. http://www.eltnews.com/guides/living (accessed March 2008).

Bergenthal, Kenneth. "Guide to Japan." *Executive Planet*. October 2007. http://www.executiveplanet.com/index.php?title=Japan (accessed March 2008).

"Etiquette." *Japan Guide*. http://www.japan-guide.com/e/e622.html (accessed March 2008).

"Etiquette and Manners." *JGuide: Stanford Guide to Information Resources*. http://jguide.stanford.edu/site/etiquette_manners_2114.html (accessed March 2008).

"Honorifics." *Answers.com*. http://www.answers.com/honorifics (accessed March 2008).

Itasaka, Gen, ed. "Etiquette" in *Kodansha Encyclopedia of Japan*, 232–234. Vol. 2. New York: Kodansha International, 1983.

Rowthorn, Chris, et al. *Lonely Planet: Japan*. 10th ed. Oakland, CA: Lonely Planet Publications, 2007.

"Seating and Standing Protocol." *Travel Savings Today*. 2006. http://www.traveltst.ca/index.php?pageId=66-20k (accessed March 2008).

Japanese Literature

INTRODUCTION: UNDERSTANDING PEOPLE AND CULTURE

Literature both entertains and offers profound insights about particular cultures and, most important, about individuals and their lives. Japan has a literary tradition that dates back to the 8th century CE with the publication of both the *Kojiki*, a history of the archipelago that also included mythical accounts of Japan's creation, and the

Man'yoshu, or *Collection of Ten Thousand Leaves*, a collection of more than 4,000 Japanese poems. From these beginnings until the mid-19th century, Japanese writers worked with a variety of literary genres including the novel, drama, various kinds of poetry, and essays that collectively reflect the archipelago's rich traditional culture. Then, as Japan entered a new period of its history characterized by extensive interactions with foreigners from Western countries, literature changed as profoundly as the rest of Japanese culture.

The world of Japanese literature is much too vast for comprehensive treatment in the short space afforded it in this volume. Perhaps Japan's greatest literary gift to the world, Murasaki Shikibu's *The Tale of Genji*, because of its importance in understanding the Heian period (794–1156) and the birth of traditional Japanese cultural values, is addressed in the history chapter and the women's section of the society chapter. Japanese drama as a performing art is included in the art section of this chapter.

What follows is an attempt to provide readers with a sampling of Japan's rich and ongoing literary tradition through a series of sketches of some of Japan's greatest literary figures and their works. Although lovers of literature and prose are encouraged to read the works of numerous other superb Japanese authors, those included here are all known worldwide because their writings, in a variety of ways, inform all of us about both Japanese culture and the human experience. The authors profiled in the narrative also all share the distinction of withstanding the test of time or, in the cases of Kawabata Yasunari and Oe Kenazaburo, winning the world's most prestigious prize for literature. Japanese literature before the 20th century constitutes the first portion of this section. The 20th century, the years when the world discovered Japan's literature, is then afforded extensive treatment.

JAPAN'S LITERARY TRADITION: PRE-20TH-CENTURY AUTHORS

As described elsewhere in this book, it was aristocratic women, writing in kana in the 10th and early 11th centuries, who wrote the first works whose style and insights later made them world classics. Murasaki Shikibu's novel, *The Tale of Genji*, completed sometime in the first decade of the 11th century, constitutes a window into values that would later become part of Japan's culture. However, Murasaki was only one of several Heian-period (794–1156) aristocratic women who left written nonfiction works including diaries and personal memoirs.

Sei Shonagon (966?–1026?) is also considered one of the greatest authors in the history of Japanese literature. Shonagon's *Pillow Book* is a combination of seemingly random recollections of various events, anecdotes about herself and people she knows, descriptions of life at the imperial court, expressions of likes and dislikes, and lists. Little is known about Sei Shonagon. She was from an aristocratic family who had only minor influence at court but included respected poets and scholars. Shonagon was highly educated in both Chinese and Japanese and was reputed to have been involved in an unhappy marriage. Sei Shonagon became a lady-in-waiting for Empress Teishi during the last few years of the 10th century and

A Tokugawa era woodblock print by Kigugawa Toshinobu Eizan of the Heian writer Sei Shonagon. Her work is second only to Murasaki Shikibu in its lasting importance. (Bridgeman Art Library)

probably wrote the *Pillow Book* in the beginning of the millennium. In addition to this work, a few of her poems survive from other sources. Although unproven, some scholars assert that she later entered a nunnery and died in poverty.

Even though the facts of the author's life are scarce, readers of the *Pillow Book* encounter a woman who is confident, quick-witted, opinionated, reflective, and sometimes shocking, as when she writes of common people. Although she inhabited a culture of more than 1,000 years ago, readers of the *Pillow Book* will vicariously get to know an individual whose personality would stand out in any time and any era. Consider these excerpts from lists in the *Pillow Book*:

> **Things That Cannot Be Compared**
>
> Summer and winter.... Youth and age. A person's laughter and his anger.... Love and hatred.
>
> Things That Have Lost Their Power
>
> A large boat which is high and dry in a creek at ebb tide.
>
> A woman who has taken off her false locks to comb the short hair that remains....
>
> A man of no importance reprimanding an attendant.
>
> (Asia for Educators, "The Pillow Book" n.d.)

Things People Look Down On

The north side of a house.

A person with a reputation for excessive good nature.

A very old man.

A loose woman.

A crumbling earthen wall around an establishment. (McCullough 1991, 165)

The timelessness of great literature can often be measured in how it speaks to young people. Many American professors and high school teachers who use Sei Shonagon report animated discussions of sections of the *Pillow Book*, with some students always remarking on how much of the prose is both genuine and, at times, almost contemporary.

The feminine-dominated literature of the Heian years largely reflected a time of peace, but as the state crumbled and powerful armed clans began to fight each other for control of territory, Japan often was a place of war and misery during its medieval periods (1156–1600). Readers gain deep insights about these troubled times through a genre of war tales, the most famous of which is *The Tale of the Heike*. This epic chronicles the bloody Gempei War fought by two powerful clans, the Taira or Heike and the Minamoto, over who would control Japan.

The Tale of the Heike tells the story of the rise and fall of the Taira clan, who are eventually defeated and hunted down one by one by the victorious Minamoto, who establish a military government that controls Japan from Kamakura. Readers encounter political intrigues, heroic deeds, and tragic lovers in this most famous of medieval war novels. *The Tale of the Heike* also imparts a sense of Japan's unique warrior culture that later would be embodied in the samurai. The most important themes of this masterpiece are Buddhist; all human affairs and actions are impermanent and transient.

The development of *The Tale of the Heike* is as fascinating in many ways as the story. The war was so significant that an account of it was first written by a minor noble in the 13th century, but the manuscript was lost. However, traveling groups of Buddhist monks, accompanied by the *biwa*, a lute-like instrument, chanted the stories of the Gempei War throughout Japan. Akashi no Kakuichi (1300?–1371), the most famous of these performing monks, was both a monk and scholar who lost his eyesight as a young man. Akashi, who became one of the most renowned performers of this celebrated oral tradition, specialized in the Heike tales. Three months before he died in 1371, Akashi dictated the tales in their entirety to a faithful disciple. During the later Tokugawa period, *The Tale of the Heike* was published as a book. In both its development and subject matter, this Japanese literary classic evokes thoughts of Homer's *Iliad*. Readers can get an understanding of the Buddhist themes that permeate the book by considering these famous opening lines:

In the sound of the bell of the Gion temple echoes the impermanence of all things … The proud ones do not last long, but vanish like a spring night's dream. And the mighty ones, too, will perish like dust before the wind.

Japan's warrior class was not only expected to exhibit martial skills but also to prefer death to capture and to be literate enough to compose a death poem before committing ritual suicide. Yorimasa, a warrior about to be captured, asks his loyal retainer to cut off his head after he has committed seppuku ("stomach cutting"), but first Yorimasa turns to the west, joins his palms, and chants "Hail Amidha Buddha" 10 times in a loud voice. Then he composes this poem:

Like a fossil tree

Which has borne not one blossom

Sad has been my life

Sadder still to end my days

Leaving no fruit behind me. (*The Tale of the Heike* passages from Asia for Educators)

Just as readers of the *Iliad* can go back thousands of years and grasp ancient beliefs, readers of the most outstanding work of Japanese medieval war literature can gain clearer understandings of cultural values that might, if simply described in nonfiction narrative, be difficult to imagine.

The transition from classical to medieval Japan and the warfare that accompanied it produced yet another kind of literature—that of the recluse who grows weary of the turbulence of the world and lives a life of spare but modest and cultured tranquility. Kamo no Chomei's *An Account of My Hut* epitomizes this literary genre. Chomei (1156–1216) was from a family of aristocrats and priests and distinguished himself foremost as a poet but also as a literary critic and musician. Chomei was known at the imperial court and in Kamakura, where the second shogun who headed the military government was a devotee of poetry. However, Chomei lost any desire for further worldly success when the retired emperor failed in his attempt to make Chomei a priest at the Shinto Kamo Shrines. Chomei took Buddhist vows in 1204 and in 1209 moved to a mountain south of Kyoto near Uji and constructed a small 10-foot-square hut. Chomei lived quietly there and penned an essay about five years after the move that has become his greatest work.

Chomei writes about political upheaval, such natural and man-made disasters as an earthquake and famine, and the temporary nature of human life. However, the author also includes discourses on the simple pleasures of viewing surrounding scenery, observing religious rituals, writing and playing the koto in solitude, and enjoying an occasional companion. This short but elegant ode to simplicity and tranquility in troubled times has influenced subsequent Japanese literature as well as philosophy.

Beginning in the 17th century, Japan during the Tokugawa years (1600–1868) developed a rich urban culture, numerous private schools and academies, a critical mass of literate people, and a publishing industry. Although a variety of literature ranging from kabuki drama to comic novels flourished, haiku poetry, perfected by Matsuo Basho (1644–1694), is known today throughout the world. What was originally a Japanese creation has attracted the attention of a wide variety of people ranging from famous authors like Richard Wright and Ezra Pound to elementary school children.

YOSHIDA KENKO (1283–1350)

Yoshida, a poet, was a figure in the imperial court who chose to withdraw from the powerful and take Buddhist vows. Yoshida's *Tsurezuregusa* (the title is available in English translated as *Essays in Idleness*) is a collection of observations and stories similar in form to the Heian period's *Pillow Book*. However, Kenko concentrated on different themes than Sei Shonagon. He manages to write about the transience of existence without being morbid and convey a deep love of the past in preference to the present without being tiring. Kenko's prose is both beautiful and direct. This author's accessible work of introspection is often read abroad for its literary value and the window it provides into a particular kind of educated Japanese in the medieval period.

Haiku, which was developed from longer linked verse, consists of 17 syllables arranged in three or four lines. The purpose of this short poetry form is to directly evoke feelings, thoughts, and images in the reader, whose imagination is then free to fill in mental details. Traditional Japanese haiku always includes direct or indirect nature or seasonal references, but contrary to one popular misimpression, haiku is not simply nature poetry. Although many haiku have spiritual and religious implications, all haiku are focused word pictures.

Basho was born of a minor samurai family in a town near Kyoto, moved to Edo, and became a recognized poet and teacher in his lifetime. In his latter years, Basho was increasingly influenced by Zen Buddhism and published travel literature that combined poetry and prose. The best way for readers to understand Basho's, or any, haiku is to experience it. The following are two haiku of Basho. Most haiku lovers feel that commentary on specific haiku hinders its appreciation rather than enhancing understanding:

as I clap my hands
with the echoes, it begins to dawn—
the summer moon

housecleaning day—
hanging a shelf at his own house
a carpenter (Asia for Educators, "The Poetry of Basho")

Japanese authors and the works they produced were influenced by China and Korea or were based on indigenous aspects of Japan's culture until the last half of the 19th century. During the decades of the Meiji period (1868–1912), Japanese literature began to reflect sweeping cultural changes as such authors as Natsume Soseki and Shimazaki Toson in their novels articulated traditional values, Western ideas, and the conflicts that intercultural contacts produced. This process enhanced rather than diminished Japanese literature as authors emerged in the 20th century

NATSUME SOSEKI (1867–1916)

Natsume Soseki, who majored in English literature at Tokyo Imperial University and studied in the United Kingdom, is considered to be one of Japan's greatest modern novelists. His haunting *Kokoro* helps readers understand such universal themes as human isolation, and the feelings of reflective Japanese who were seeing their society drastically changed by Western modernity, through this account of a friendship between a student and an older intellectual who has withdrawn from the world. *Kokoro* is often assigned in university and high school literature courses in the West as well as Japan. Soseki's first novel, *I Am a Cat*, originally serialized and also read outside of Japan, is an often humorous satire. The protagonist, a cat, makes fun of a variety of people, including his own schoolteacher owner.

who would both introduce the world to Japanese culture and vividly describe how that culture was changing through global influences.

GIANTS OF 20TH-CENTURY JAPANESE LITERATURE

By the latter decades of the 20th century, Japanese literature was recognized as not only representative of one culture but an outstanding genre of world literature as well. Several of Japan's literary giants either combined international and indigenous cultural influences in their work, went through periods where they appeared to be exclusively influenced by foreign work, or, in contrast, primarily focused on capturing the essence of traditional Japanese culture. These personal tensions, coupled with individual genius and the desire to write, resulted in some of the best world literature of the century.

Tanizaki Jun'ichiro (1886–1965) ranks as one of the most versatile writers in Japan's literary history. Tanizaki produced finely crafted short stories of varying length on a wide range of contemporary and historical topics, autobiography, poetry, drama, essays on aesthetics and literary criticism, and outstanding novels including his masterpiece, *The Makioka Sisters.* Although he exhibited talent in all these genres, Tanizaki is probably best remembered as a superb storyteller.

Born to a prosperous merchant family in Tokyo, Tanizaki's father was an unsuccessful businessman whose failures eventually left the family in dire economic straits, and they were reduced to what was for them humiliating poverty. Tanizaki's mother was renowned for her beauty, and according to Tanizaki, she and other relatives pampered him as a child. Tanizaki showed early brilliance as a student, reading avidly, mastering English and Chinese, and, according to boyhood contemporaries, discussing the works of Kant and Schopenhauer by ages 11 and 12. Despite increasing family poverty, Tanizaki received a first-rate education at top middle and high schools and entered the literature department of Tokyo Imperial University, Japan's most impressive institution of higher learning, but dropped out before graduation.

As a young man, Tanizaki lived a Bohemian lifestyle and was heavily influenced by Western writers including Edgar Allan Poe and Oscar Wilde. One of his best early published short stories, "The Tatooer," which established his reputation as an outstanding writer, is similar to works these two authors might have written. During his first years as a writer, which ended in the early 1920s, the young author developed, at least at a superficial level, a condescending attitude toward his own culture, appeared to focus on the West, wore flashy neckties, developed a passion for Western dancing, bragged that he never took his shoes off during the day, and moved to the Western section of Yokohama. It was also reported that Tanizaki was planning to leave for Europe and perhaps permanently reside there. Then an event occurred that changed the young writer's life forever, the great Tokyo earthquake of September 1, 1923.

Tanizaki, who was on a bus when the earthquake occurred, survived unharmed and at first rejoiced that since Tokyo would be rebuilt virtually from the ground up, it would become a Western city. However, he moved to the Osaka area while Tokyo was being rebuilt and began to turn away from and even be repulsed by Westernization, while increasingly embracing traditional elements of Japanese culture, including Buddhism, history, aesthetics, and *The Tale of Genji*, which he attempted to translate into English. By most accounts, when Tanizaki focused his attention on his own culture, he transformed himself from a good to a great writer. The caveat should be added that even though Tanizaki concentrated on Japanese culture, he never abandoned using a variety of stylistic influences that he learned from Western writers.

Perhaps the best introduction to Tanizaki's work is *Seven Japanese Tales*, which combines a variety of stories including the aforementioned "The Tatooer," about an obsessed artist and his woman subject, as well as short historical fiction, a tale of a young man accused by fellow students of being a thief that was later made into a movie, and the story of a blind masseur who cares for a noblewoman. Several of the stories in this work have mysterious, ambiguous, and bizarre endings that are characteristics of Tanizaki's style. *Capitan Sugimoto*, set in sixth-century Japan and in part based on accounts of earlier events that appeared in Heian writings, is perhaps the best example of Tanizaki's longer historical fiction. Particularly compelling is an excerpt from the novella that tells of a young boy following his aged father, who meditates over a rotting corpse at night in a Buddhist-inspired effort to rid himself of the attachment to a younger wife who has left him. Tanizaki was forced to stop writing his great epic, *The Makioka Sisters*, which he began before World War II in serialized versions, because of wartime censorship. He completed the book after the war. *The Makioka Sisters* chronicles the declining fortunes of four women in an aristocratic Osaka merchant family in the 1930s. The novel has been compared to Margaret Mitchell's *Gone with the Wind*.

Kawabata Yasunari (1899–1972), who in 1968 became the first Japanese writer to win the Nobel Prize for Literature since Rabindranath Tagore in 1913, was also propelled by a combination of deep affinity for Japanese culture and mastery of

Western stylistic techniques. The circumstances of Osaka-born Kawabata's early life were tragic. He lost both parents by the age of 3, his grandmother and sister at age 9, and his grandfather when he was 15. Much of Kawabata's work would be tinged with sadness, and the Japanese concept of *mono no aware*, an awareness of the transience of things, permeated his writing. Kawabata entered the English department at Tokyo University but after a year changed his major to Japanese literature and graduated in 1924. Nevertheless, Kawabata was influenced by such modernist Western writers as James Joyce.

Kawabata first gained fame for the publication in 1926 of the short story "The Izu Dancer," which was partially based on a trip the author took on the Izu Peninsula while a college student and allegedly after the end of a romance. In the story, the protagonist falls in with a group of traveling entertainers, is greatly attracted to a young dancer, and when he realizes she is too young for him, is both saddened and relieved. Kawabata, as was the case with many Japanese writers, wrote short stories as well as serialized works for magazines that were later published as novels. Kawabata also created short short stories that he called "*tanagokoro no shosetsu*," "stories that fit into the palm of your hand," which are miniature masterpieces of fiction. Kawabata has been praised by literary critics as evoking emotions in readers that are similar to those that good haiku poets manage to stimulate in their work: sudden awareness of beauty, a sense of motion and stillness, and

Kawabata Yasunari (1889–1972) became, in 1968, the first Japanese novelist to win the Nobel Prize for Literature. (Bettmann/Corbis)

ARIYOSHI SAWAKO (1931–1984)

Ariyoshi successfully wrote popular books covering a wide range of topics including a number of best sellers that effectively used fiction to give voice to the real-life concerns of women. From a wealthy business and landowning family who lost everything in the aftermath of World War II, she graduated from Tokyo Women's Christian College, supported herself before she gained fame as an author through working in management and production in a kabuki troupe, had a lifelong interest in Japanese history, and wrote both contemporary and historical fiction. She deeply researched the topics that constituted her fiction. Ariyoshi had many successful books, some of which were made into movies. Her better-known novels include *The River Ki*, the story of three generations of Japanese women; *Not Because of Color*, which is the story of a Japanese woman who marries an African American soldier; *The Twilight Years*, which examines the topic of senility and the disproportionate burden it places on adult women caregivers; and *Kabuki Dancer*, a historical fiction focusing on the actress who allegedly created this now traditional Japanese art form.

indelible images of nature. Critics also give Kawabata accolades for his ability to write about women and in particular to make them believable in their actions and perceptions. Both of these talents just described are evident in the novel that is considered his masterpiece, *Snow Country* or, in Japanese, *Yukiguni*. The memorable first paragraph of the novel that the author began in 1934, originally serialized in portions in magazines, and finally completed in 1947 captures the spare beauty of Kawabata's prose: "The train came out of the long tunnel into the snow country. The earth lay white under the night sky. The train pulled up to the station" (Kawabata 1957, 3).

The author tells the story in *Snow Country* of an ill-fated relationship set in a hot spring resort area in the northern mountainous part of Honshu between Komako, a country geisha, and Shimamura, an urban dilettante who slips away to the area for trysts. Shimamura, although sophisticated, is superficial. He has a minor reputation as a critic of Western ballet but has never seen a performance. Komako, although an obscure geisha, is a powerful character. A third more shadowy, yet intense woman, Yoko, also captures Shimamura's attention, and he is drawn to her and away from Komako. The male protagonist seems to be able to appreciate the attributes of women but to be unable to love a woman as a person. The climactic scene in the book that involves an indoor fire in a building where a movie is being shown evokes Buddhist images of the illusionary and transient nature of sensory pleasures. The novel's prose also conjures up dreamlike images.

Kawabata, who was also fascinated with *The Tale of Genji* and took consolation during World War II by immersing himself in the literary classic, was a productive writer whose career spanned the pre- and postwar years. Other of Kawabata's

Mishima Yukio (1925–1970) became internationally known as a novelist and playwright. Mishima incorporated both Western and Japanese traditions in his fiction. (Bettmann/Corbis)

best-known works include *The Master of Go*, whose origin may be traced to nonfiction pieces Kawabata wrote covering a famous match of this traditional East Asian game; *The Old Capital*, whose plot focuses on the daughter of Kyoto kimono business owners who discovers she is adopted and has a twin sister in a village to the north of the city; and *The Thousand Cranes*, which tells the story of a young man in his late twenties who becomes involved with his dead father's mistress, who is also a teacher of the Japanese tea ceremony. The protagonist of *The Thousand Cranes* goes on to interact with another of his father's former mistresses, who is also attracted to the tea ceremony.

Although by the 1950s Kawabata came to epitomize much of traditional Japanese culture, he was active in PEN, the international writer's association; organized a conference in Japan; and employed Western stylistic techniques throughout his career. Kawabata died in 1972 in what was most probably a suicide by gas in an apartment he rented near his Kamakura home. Only two years earlier, a younger writer, Mishima Yukio, whom Kawabata considered to be an exceptional literary talent, also committed suicide.

Mishima, whose real name was Hiraoka Kimitake (1925–1970), is one of 20th-century Japan's most talented and prolific authors whose work is known worldwide. Mishima also lived a stormy and colorful life that ended in a ritual seppuku that attracted international attention. He was born in Tokyo of a government official father and a school principal's daughter. Mishima's paternal grandmother, who had been raised in aristocratic and samurai circles, reared the child until he was about 12. She influenced the child's literary development but also virtually sequestered him from other children. After tumultuous relations with his father, who disliked the boy's affinity for literature, and an education at the prestigious Peer's School, where he graduated first in his class and was honored by a silver watch from the emperor, Mishima was excused from military service by a misdiagnosis of tuberculosis, which he did not contest. After the war, Mishima studied law at Tokyo University and worked for a brief time in the Finance Ministry before becoming a full-time author.

In 1949 Mishima published his first major work, the quasi-autobiographical *Confessions of a Mask.* Mishima was a prolific author who produced 40 novels as well as plays, poetry, essays, and drama. He possessed an extensive knowledge of both classical Western and Japanese literature and deftly used themes from Japanese noh plays, Greek tragedy, and romance to write modern dramas. Mishima's novels repeatedly deal with beauty and its decay, dying young, the mystique of bushido, and traditional Japanese notions of the emperor and patriotism. Many of these themes, particularly an almost obsession with and glorification of death, are often repeated in his work, but Mishima had such a range of talent that he could write engaging novels about a variety of topics. *The Sound of Waves* takes place on a contemporary remote Japanese island but is based on the classical Greek tale *Daphnis and Chloe. After the Banquet* is about an aging politician who falls in love with a middle-aged woman, attempts a comeback, and is defeated in a mayoral election. Mishima seemed to have no conflict with being a self-avowed defender of traditional Japanese culture and a writer who was markedly influenced by Western classicism. He could combine the two in his writings and create unique works through the force of his personality and great talent.

Mishima has a number of major works, some of which have been made into movies, as has the story of the author's life. The subject of his 1956 novel, *The Temple of the Golden Pavilion*, is a real-life event—the sensational arson of the famous Kyoto temple, Kinkakuji, by a deranged monk. Many of the themes of Mishima's work are in evidence in the book. The protagonist of the novel, a young man named Mizoguchi, is physically ugly and migrates to Kyoto from a rural area in northern Honshu, eventually serving in the Golden Pavilion. Mizoguchi, who idealizes the temple since childhood, eventually sees it as the epitome of a beauty that he will never personally possess and resolves to burn it down and die in the fire. The disturbed monk succeeds with the former objective but fails in his suicide. The novel also has Zen-like elements. A "koan," or Zen riddle, receives differing interpretations in the work.

As his career unfolded, Mishima increasingly became controversial because of his political positions, which were rooted in beliefs in traditional Japanese virtues including a pure form of emperor worship. Mishima's position on the emperor alienated both the Japanese political Left and the Right since he was condescending about the Showa emperor as an individual but honored the emperor as a god who epitomized Japanese traditions. Bullied as a child and an adolescent, Mishima successfully engaged in rigorous bodybuilding as an adult. He increasingly glorified samurai values and called an introduction that he wrote to a historic samurai manual, *Hagakure*, the greatest of his writing.

Mishima became increasingly disillusioned about modern Japan and hostile both to political Leftists and a government and Self-Defense Force that he saw as timid in challenging them. In a bizarre chain of events, Mishima formed a private army, the Shield Society, of about 100 men and with a few companions took over the

HARUKI MURAKAMI (1949–)

Haruki Murakami, has, as of the publication of this book, sold more novels in translation than any other Japanese author. A Waseda University graduate and former owner of a jazz coffee house, Murakami quickly captured critics' and fans' attention for publishing three novels, *Hear the Wind Sing* (1979), *Pinball 1973* (1980), and *The Wild Sheep Chase* (1982), the so-called Rat Trilogy. *A Wild Sheep Chase*, the most popular seller of the three in the United States, has been described as a mock detective tale and involves such characters as a burned-out Japanese yuppie, his girlfriend with eye-stopping ears, a mystical sheep, and a right-wing hoodlum. Some of his other titles include *Norwegian Wood, Hard-Boiled Wonderland and the End of the World, Dance, Dance, Dance, A Wind-up Bird Chronicle,* and *Kafka on the Shore.*

Tokyo-based eastern headquarters of the Self-Defense Forces on November 25, 1970. The purpose of the action was to initiate a coup d'état to restore imperial power, but when this failed, Mishima committed ritual suicide. There is powerful evidence that he knew the political action would fail, and he had all of his personal affairs in order the day he died.

In 1993, Oe Kenazaburo (born in 1935) became the second Japanese author to win the Nobel Prize. Although Oe praised the ambiguity of Zen in his Nobel acceptance speech, unlike the other 20th-century authors he writes less about traditional Japanese culture and has been profoundly influenced by literary postmodernism and topics that are considered contemporary global concerns.

Oe was born in a very remote Shikoku mountain village and was a child during World War II. While a young boy and after his father's death during the war, Oe's literary imagination was stimulated by his mother, who provided him with a wide variety of Western and Japanese books. Oe entered Tokyo University in 1954, where he studied French literature and did his major undergraduate work on Jean Sartre's novels. Although Oe had attracted the attention of critics when he was still a university student, the young author won his first literary prize in 1958 for a novella set at the end of World War II, *The Catch*, that tells the story through a child narrator of a downed American airman in a small, isolated Japanese village. He published his first novel, *Nip the Buds, Shoot the Kids*, in 1958, which is an account of 15 reform school children who are taken to a village where the residents abandon them when a plague occurs. The book ensured Oe's reputation as a novelist, and he also became a relatively high-profile Left-wing intellectual.

In 1963, Oe fathered a mentally disabled son, who has been an influence on his writing and thinking. He was also significantly influenced by a visit to Hiroshima. Oe won the Shincho Literary Prize for his novel *A Personal Matter*, published in 1964, which tells the tale of Bird, a young man in his late twenties, who has dreams, including of going to Africa, that are interrupted when his son is born with a herniated

BANANA YOSHIMOTO (1964–)

Daughter of a famous poet, philosopher, and critic, Yoshimoto's given name is Mahoko, but she adopted the pen name "Banana" while a student at Nihon University. Yoshimoto, who has legions of devoted fans in Japan and throughout the world, claims two of her major themes are what it is like to be a frustrated young person in Japan and the impact of traumatic events on personal lives. Her first novel, *Kitchen*, was a quick major success and has enjoyed world-wide sales, been made into two movies, and been anthologized. Other Yoshimoto titles translated into English include *Asleep*, *Goodbye Tsugumi*, and *Hardboiled and Hard Luck*.

brain. One of Oe's masterpieces is considered to be *The Silent Cry*, which was first published in 1967 and won the Tanizaki Prize but attracted criticism as well as praise. The novel's main characters are two brothers in the early 1960s who have returned to a family estate, and its themes are postmodernist in that they deal with manufactured realities, historical parallels that go back to 1860, and suicide. Oe addresses a variety of themes in his writing, including postwar Japanese alienation, issues of cultural identity, the dangers of nuclear weapons, the developing world, and environmental issues. He has written a wide range of essays, short stories, and novels. Other well-known works include *An Echo of Heaven*, *The Treatment Tower*, and *A Quiet Life*.

Banana Yoshimoto is a popular Japanese writer who now has an international following. (Corbis)

CONCLUSION: JAPANESE LITERATURE AND THE 21ST CENTURY

In this century, the Japanese writers and works described in these pages continue to gain popularity throughout the world. Young people interested in Japan seem just as intrigued by contemporary culture as by traditional Japan, if not more so. Haruki Murakami is a leading, internationally selling author, and Banana Yoshimoto is establishing herself as well among readers around the world. Although it is uncertain at this point whether these younger authors' works will prove as enduring as the literature of Murasaki, Basho, Tanizaki, or Mishima, Japanese poetry and prose gives every indication of remaining vibrant and influential for the indefinite future.

REFERENCES

Asia for Educators. "Japanese Literature." http://afe.easia.columbia.edu (accessed April 2008).

———. "*The Pillow Book*: Reading." n.d. http://afe.easia.columbia.edu/japan/japanworkbook/literature/pillow.htm (accessed April 2008).

———. "*The Poetry of Basho*: Reading." n.d. http://afe.easia.columbia.edu/japan/japanworkbook/literature/basho.htm (accessed April 2008).

———. "*The Tale of the Heike*: Reading." n.d. http://afe.easia.columbia.edu/japan/japanworkbook/literature/heike.htm (accessed April 2008).

Intute: Arts and Humanities. "Japanese Literature." http://www.intute.ac.uk/artsandhumanities (accessed April 2008).

Isataka, Gen, ed. "Heike Monogatari" in *Kodansha Encyclopedia of Japan*, 124–125. Vol. 3. New York: Kodansha International, 1983.

The Japanese Literature Home Page. http://www.jlit.net (accessed April 2008).

Kawabata, Yasunari. *Snow Country*. Tokyo: Tuttle Publishing, 1957.

Keene, Donald. *Five Modern Japanese Novelists*. New York: Columbia University Press, 2003.

———, ed. *Modern Japanese Literature: From 1868 to the Present Day*. New York: Grove Press, 1956.

Kitagawa, Hiroshi, and Bruce Tsuchida, trans. *The Tale of the Heike*. Tokyo: University of Tokyo Press, 1974.

McCullough, Helen Craig, ed. *Classical Japanese Prose: An Anthology*. Palo Alto, CA: Stanford University Press, 1991.

Miller, Barbara, ed. Masterworks of Asian Literature in Comparative Perspective: A Guide for Teaching. Armonk, NY: M. E. Sharpe, 1994.

Richie, Donald (Arturo Silva, ed). *The Donald Richie Reader: Fifty Years of Writing on Japan*. New York: Stone Bridge Press, 2001.

Ruch, Barbara. "The Other Side of Culture in Medieval Japan." In John W. Hall, ed., et al. *The Cambridge History of Japan*. Vol. 3. Cambridge University Press, 1990.

Tanizaki, Junichiro. *Childhood Years: A Memoir*. Translated by Paul McCarthy. New York: Collins, 1990.

———. *The Makioka Sisters*. North Clarendon, VT: Tuttle Publishing, 1971.

———. *Seven Japanese Tales*. North Clarendon, VT: Tuttle Publishing, 1969.

Varley, H. Paul. *Japanese Culture: A Short History*. New York: Praeger Publishers, 1977.

Weston, Mark. *Giants of Japan*. New York: Kodansha International, 1999.

Japanese Art

INTRODUCTION

Art that Japanese created has profoundly affected the archipelago's peoples, Asia, and the world for a long time. Small children in various countries throughout the world are inspired by origami, the Japanese art of paper folding. Two of the world's greatest creative geniuses, Vincent van Gogh and Frank Lloyd Wright, both discovered new ways of perceiving color, light, the environment, and humans' role within it because of Japanese creative arts. As with any culture, Japanese arts are influenced by such factors as geography, spiritual practices, history, and foreign contacts.

Even before Japanese written records existed, what we know today as the Korean Peninsula, China, and parts of South Asia had left indelible cultural footprints in the archipelago. For example, the Koreans introduced Japanese to the process of creating elaborate gold ornaments, and Koreans, Chinese, and even South Asians brought a wide range of Buddhist-inspired art to the archipelago. Yet archeological evidence also exists that indicates a particular set of Japanese aesthetic perceptions were already taking shape. These proclivities that constitute a foundation for Japanese art will be addressed throughout this section.

The human's place in the natural world is perhaps the paramount underlying traditional aesthetic notion that has continually influenced Japanese perceptions. Many

Origami swan. Origami, the Japanese art of paper folding, has become part of the elementary curricula in many U.S. schools. (Dreamstime.com)

Japanese see humans as beings who are impermanent but part of a much larger natural world. As Japanese began to communicate essences of nature through the medium of the arts, they accentuated the individual artist's important role in not only communicating this essence but also actively helping to create the natural world while working. These perceptions of humans as so integrated into the natural world are unlike the dominant perspective of our own culture, where people are often viewed as separate from nature. A related traditional Japanese aesthetic has been the preference for harmony between humans and the natural environment. Religious sites, dwellings, tableware, and a variety of other material creations were often fashioned to harmonize with the natural surroundings. Subsequently, it became difficult to clearly define art, since from early on Japanese created functional products that were also intended to evoke moods and feelings, particularly about the natural world. Also, Japanese preferred the evocation of emotion through art but placed little emphasis on art forms that were "pretty" yet decorative and static.

As time passed, in Japan the belief emerged that when an artist wishes to evoke strong human emotions in others, often this can be more effectively done by taking a minimalist approach; for example, one flower tastefully arranged is more striking than an entire field to the seer. Such Japanese aesthetic perceptions as harmony between human and environment and minimalism were not created in a vacuum. Throughout Japan's history, successive waves of foreigners exerted great influence on the arts, but over time the Japanese took selected outside influences and modified them to fit their own perceptions of the world around them.

Since the larger culture both shapes and is shaped by art, readers particularly interested in the topic of this section are advised to also read the history, religion, literature, music, leisure, and women's sections of this book. In the remainder of this section, the development of classical Japanese art forms will be addressed. Particular emphasis is given to what is distinctively Japanese and the interplay between Japan and foreign cultures in artistic developments. Although the section encompasses a wide range of time, those Japanese arts that have both survived the test of time and continue to exert national and international influence today are particularly emphasized. Although this survey cannot possibly be complete because of limited space, readers will gain a basic understanding of the beauty and distinctiveness of Japanese art and its now-global influence. With the exception of brief discussions of noh, kabuki, bunraku, and the rise of Japanese cinema, what follows is primarily devoted to visual arts, although some topics addressed—architecture, the tea ceremony, and such crafts as sword making—are considered art forms but don't fit into these two rather rigid categories. Readers interested in learning more about noh and kabuki should consult the portions of the book addressing, respectively, history and music.

THE ARTS: PREHISTORIC TO HEIAN (11,000 BCE–794 CE)

Both of the names of the first two periods of Japanese prehistory, Jomon (11,000 BCE–300 BCE) and Yayoi (300 BCE–250 CE), have pottery associations. Jomon clay pots were created by hand, and cords were used to impress the pottery with simple exterior designs. Earlier examples of surviving artifacts resemble other Neolithic

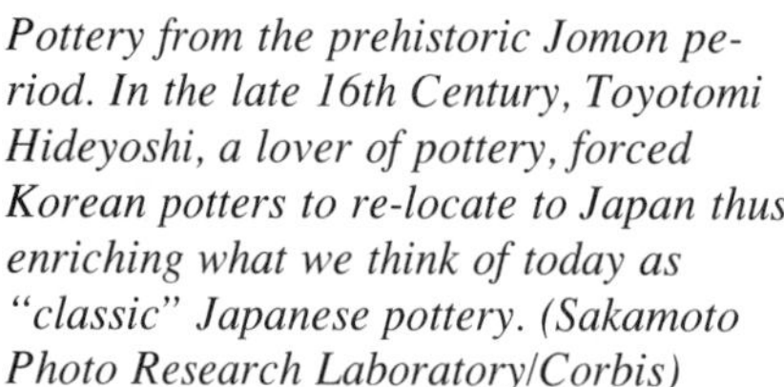

Pottery from the prehistoric Jomon period. In the late 16th Century, Toyotomi Hideyoshi, a lover of pottery, forced Korean potters to re-locate to Japan thus enriching what we think of today as "classic" Japanese pottery. (Sakamoto Photo Research Laboratory/Corbis)

cultures. The Jomon were a pastoral people, gathering, hunting, and fishing. However, during the middle and latter Jomon years, surviving artifacts became more complex, and there is evidence of intercultural contact, although with precisely whom it is difficult to know. Human figurines with elaborate cord-impressed designs and enormous insect eyes have been unearthed. Stems, possibly as part of oil lamps, have been found as well as stone circles used as burial pits that are similar to what was utilized in Siberia during prehistoric times.

Yayoi, the name for the culture of the subsequent people who apparently drove away the Jomon, is derived from the wheel-thrown pottery uncovered at the Yayoi site near Tokyo. The artifacts of this period reveal a society that many scholars consider the first Japanese civilization. Some members of Yayoi culture were probably recent immigrants from the Korean Peninsula and other parts of the Asian mainland. In addition, rather sophisticated pottery including tableware as well as bronze- and iron-handled cups and swords remain from this period. There was contact with Korean kingdoms and Han China. Korean jewels have been found that date from this period as well as Han dynasty bronze mirrors and other objects. Wet rice cultivation meant that Yayoi culture became one that featured settled communities, which, in addition to foreign influences, resulted in the creation of more sophisticated artifacts. Also, despite being a much more sophisticated culture than their Jomon predecessors, artifacts that can be identified as Yayoi in origin, including pottery and figurines, show much less adornment than foreign artifacts, even though there is a high probability the latter Yayoi people could have created more decorative objects. This is some of the first evidence of the Japanese preference for the purity of the simple.

By the latter Yayoi period and for several hundred years afterward during the Kofun and Yamato eras, as the young Japanese state was birthed, Asian continental influences were causing significant changes in the Japanese islands. Still, the indigenous collection of practices and beliefs known as Shinto were reinforcing notions of humans as part of nature and of the beauty of simplicity. Beginning with the reign of Emperor Temmu (r. 672–686 CE), the famous Shinto shrine at Ise in present-day Mie Prefecture is one of Japan's most famous cultural assets. This center of Shinto and other larger shrines has had a timeless influence on secular Japanese aesthetics and architecture. The Ise Shrine buildings are made of soft-textured, unpainted cypress. The wooden structures are rebuilt every 20 years to preserve their pristine natural harmony with nature. They appear simple and include raised floors, thatched roofs, and cross-ended rafters. Much use is made of horizontal space and Ise, like a number of larger Shinto shrines, is located in a beautiful forest grove. The visitor to these types of Shinto shrines often will work through such natural settings as groves of trees to get to the shrine buildings. He or she can look up from the grounds and see a vast expanse of sky, which evokes different kinds of feelings than those one experiences when visiting most Christian churches or Islamic mosques. Humans often feel more a part of the natural world when visiting Shinto shrines than is the case with other sacred spaces. Spare elements in shrine design also create powerful feelings of harmony with the natural.

Early Asian continental artistic influences came primarily from Korean kingdoms that transmitted Chinese characters and Buddhist-inspired art including sculpture, temple architecture, and mural paintings. The use of Chinese characters as originally the only writing system was significant since written characters have had an artistic impact on the Japanese (as is the case with other East Asians) that far exceeds that of written alphabets on other cultures. In the seventh century CE, the primary direct external Asian influence on the Japanese was Korean, but by the mid-eighth century, during the Nara period (710–794), Japan had more direct contact with China. A famous emperor, Shomu, also made Buddhism a state-sponsored religion. The emperor started a temple-building program throughout Japan, and this policy exposed educated upper classes to the art of the imported religion. The Buddha statues in these temples took on a more sensuous and full-bodied appearance, unlike the earlier, leaner Korean Buddhas—a style modeled after Tang dynasty China. Temples were also constructed along Chinese lines: symmetrical, grand, and imposing. However, Japanese depictions of people in various temple murals and sculptures were more likely to depict human emotions than Chinese art, where often humans were depicted as inconsequential relative to the landscapes in which they were encompassed. Depiction of emotion when humans were subjects would remain a constant in Japanese art.

Although Japan was mostly influenced by China and Korea, there are examples from the seventh and eighth centuries of Indian and Persian artistic knowledge transmitted to Japan either first to continental East Asia via the Silk Roads and then to the archipelago, or in the case of Persia possibly through a northern trade route that bypassed China. A portable Shinto shrine that was of Japanese manufacture, produced in the seventh century and housed in a Buddhist temple, features a Persian

CALLIGRAPHY

Shodo, or "the way of writing," which is the Japanese word for calligraphy, is indicative of the longtime deep appreciation that the Japanese hold for the art of writing. Using Chinese characters and, at times, the kana has never been just about written communications. Ever since the introduction of Chinese characters to the archipelago, artful calligraphy is considered essential for educated and refined people. A traditional belief is that the quality of one's calligraphy is indicative of character. Calligraphy writing materials include a brush, ink and an ink stone, and a water container. Calligraphy includes many styles and is now appreciated around the world.

four-color oil painting technique. By the advent of the Heian period, Japan's aristocracy was both affected by continental notions of beauty and related artistic manifestations and influenced by native Japanese aesthetic propensities.

ART AND HEIAN JAPAN (794–1185)

The famous British historian of Japan, the late Sir George Sansom, once asserted something to the effect that the small group of aristocrats who constituted the imperial court in the city of Heian (present-day Kyoto) centered their lives to such a great extent on standards of artistic taste that art was almost a religion and religion an art. One's calligraphy, notions of color coordination in clothing, and even the kind of paper used for writing love notes were all viewed by aristocratic peers as signs of the individual's worth.

During this period, considered to be an era when many elements of what we think of today as Japanese culture were born, the novels and diaries of a few aristocrats, mostly women, reflected and shaped culture as well as providing themes that would be part of Japanese visual arts. Japanese, more than people in other cultures, focus on the seasons in a variety of ways ranging from opening conversations about the weather to including seasonal nuances in visual displays of food. This propensity is not new and is partially rooted in classical prose and poetry. Surviving paintings from folding screens and sliding doors from the Heian era often depict courtiers enjoying the varying seasons. Hand-painted scrolls, or *e-maki*, that combined visual art, poetry, and calligraphy were a product of this age. The first surviving e-maki, completed sometime between 1120 and 1130, depict a famous scene from *The Tale of Genji*. Bird's-eye indoor views are used and do not distinctly feature individual facial features, but the presumption of the artist was that viewers of the scrolls knew the story and the paintings communicated subtle but powerful emotional messages. Also, in e-maki and other venues, Japanese script, or kana, developed shortly before the period to expand a too-narrow writing system that was previously solely based on imported Chinese characters, began to appear as an art form in itself.

> ### KIMONO
>
> Kimono, the most famous type of Japanese traditional dress, is considered an art form. Kimono are wraparound garments that both men and women wear. However, women's kimono are more widely known and feature an array of colorful patterns. The fabrics used for formal women's kimono may be hand painted or dyed using traditional Japanese dying methods. Formal kimono can cost many thousand yen. Kimono are usually worn only for ceremonies, weddings, and funerals since Japanese wear Western-style clothing in their daily lives.

The Heian age was a Buddhist one for the aristocracy. Byodo-in, the former Fujiwara residence near the capital, was converted in 1053 into a temple. Byodo-in draws visitors today from all over the world and is an architectural masterpiece. The temple is a superb example of how Japanese elites combined Chinese design patterns with their own indigenous preferences. Although Chinese-style pillars and walls were used in building the main hall and associated buildings, the combination of the complex's relatively small size, the raised eaves, the construction of the buildings approximately a foot from the ground, and the reflection of the main building in the small artificial lake in front of it make it a distinctive Japanese art

Love affairs between Japanese aristocrats, as depicted in this print, constitute a major part of Murasaki Shikibu's Tale of Genji. (Library of Congress)

form. The total effect of Byodo-in is a sense of space, light, and harmony with the natural environment.

Since Japanese aristocrats, particularly in the first part of the Heian era, regarded China as the superior culture, often particularly the exteriors of public buildings were constructed in more formal Chinese styles. However, in their private quarters, elites, including emperors, preferred Japanese designs that were much more austere than Chinese interior arts, which tended to be more ornate. Exteriors of aristocratic dwellings of the period were constructed quite similarly to Byodo-in's structures, which were partially styled after Chinese buildings. The main living quarters of the family head faced south, with usually three secondary buildings facing in the other three directions. All the buildings were raised about a foot off the ground and connected by covered corridors. Heian private gardens, like Byodo-in, were built in front of the main building and featured a stream-fed small lake with a small artificial island in the middle.

MEDIEVAL ARTS (1185–1600)

While fundamental elements of Japanese aesthetics manifested themselves in such art forms as calligraphy, architecture, and painting during the Heian era, these ideas about beauty were illustrated by additional new artistic forms that emerged during the often-turbulent medieval period. Swordsmiths, garden designers, tea masters, and potters vastly expanded Japanese art and often received the support of powerful shoguns. Much of the original stimulus for the new art forms came from increased contact with China, particularly with Ch'an (Japanese Zen) monks. However, the Japanese radically transformed such art forms as gardens and tea ceremonies to better fit their own changing culture.

Medieval Japan, particularly during the beginning and end of the era, was the scene of civil disorder in which contending factions fought for control of the country. These events were reflected in the e-maki and screen and sliding-door paintings depicting battles, and in the elevation of sword making to an art form that would be prized both in Japan and elsewhere. Japanese sword makers wore pure white to symbolize that they were working with a spirit in the metal as they engaged in creating swords. They worked with two layers of iron and steel, and the process involved repeated folding and beatings. Even a casual visit to a museum today or observation of photographs of medieval Japanese sword blades will quickly indicate why Japanese swords were, and are still, considered art forms as well as weapons.

During the medieval years, Japanese gardens took on many of the characteristics that today foreigners consider "Japanese" when they consider gardens. Influenced by Zen, but also by Japanese aesthetic notions about nature and simplicity, gardens began to be created, Ryoanji in Kyoto being the most famous example, where the most basic elements were used in construction. The Zen belief that a narrow focus can often result in an expanded consciousness meshed well with the Japanese idea that less is more. Ryoanji and other dry rock gardens are radically minimalist in that only rocks, sand, and space were utilized in an attempt to narrow and enrich the viewer's perspective.

Dry rock gardens, as is the case with other classical Japanese gardens, are carefully manicured to look "natural." The famous tea master and garden designer Sen

SEN NO RIKYU (1522–1591)

The Japanese tea ceremony of today is one of the most eclectic art forms ever devised. It blends architecture, interior design, flower arranging, gardening, ceramics, and other crafts. Most of all, even though practiced as a secular art form today, it is imbued with the spirit of Zen Buddhism. Sen no Rikyu is the individual most responsible for the art form that survives in Japan today. Sen no Rikyu, reared in affluence, became wealthy at 18 when his father died but had begun to study the tea ceremony and excel in it as a younger teenager. In an era when the tea ceremony was used by elites to display their grand works of art, Rikyu was an effective advocate of *wabi*, or "poverty" tea, that demonstrated to participants the beauty of the commonplace. Sen no Rikyu also was a serious student of Zen even when he became prominent, but the tea master was so honored even his personal Zen teacher studied tea with Sen no Rikyu. The fierce warlords Nobunaga and Hideyoshi were captivated by Sen no Rikyu's steely determination and artistic ability, as was the emperor to whom Sen no Rikyu served tea. For reasons that are not completely clear, Hideyoshi, who reportedly would suffer no real or imagined affront, ordered the tea master to commit "seppuku," or ritual suicide.

no Rikyu once carefully raked all the fallen leaves in his garden, then went to a tree, shook it, and exclaimed after the leaves fell that the garden now appeared natural. Readers might recall a basic Japanese aesthetic that humans are an active part of nature. They are not simply passive onlookers but help to create the natural world since they belong to it. A related notion, present in the concept of the Japanese garden and other art forms as well, is that first the artist perceives the essence of stone, rock, or many other materials ranging from clay to iron and then frees, through his or her effort, that essence for others to grasp. This spirit permeated and unified a number of artistic pursuits. Landscape artists also designed gardens, and garden designers, particularly Sen no Rikyu, were active in creating the now famous Japanese Way of Tea.

The Chinese literati had engaged in tea parties where appreciation of fine celadon cups and other expensive tea utensils were as much a part of the culture as the conversation and the beverage. At first, Japanese elites copied the Chinese in establishing the custom of the tea party. However, in the late 15th century, Shuko, a devoted Japanese student of Zen, made the imported custom into both a different experience and a classic art form. Sen no Rikyu, in the middle and latter part of the 16th century, expanded on Shuko's effort. Japanese aesthetic notions of minimalism, harmony with nature, and appreciation of beauty in the aged or humble object permeate the tea ceremony.

The Japanese tea ceremony involves a few people in quiet, natural surroundings. The object of the tea ceremony is to slow down time and forget worldly cares, but what participants visually experience is an important part of this process. The classic Japanese tea ceremony takes place in a natural setting, perhaps in a grove of trees where a small tea house is located within a garden. Often visitors must bend over to enter the hut. In the entrance to the tea house, a single calligraphy or one flower might serve as the only decoration. The visitors carefully watch every practiced and measured move of the tea master as he or she prepares the beverage. Tea utensils such as cups are asymmetrical, characterized by such earth colors as burnt orange or pale green, and the opposite of ornate and symmetrical pottery or lacquerware. Beauty is found in the seemingly mundane and simple.

The gardens and the Way of Tea, although originally rooted in Zen Buddhism and intermingled with older Japanese perspectives about humans and nature, became secularized and part of the larger Japanese culture. Sen no Rikyu is important not just for his art but also because of his class. He was from a wealthy merchant family rather than a noble clan. By the 15th century, affluent merchants were acquiring tastes in art and aesthetics that were previously limited to aristocrats. The same was true of powerful military and political leaders who were in no way effete elites. Both Oda Nobunaga and Toyotomi Hideyoshi, two of the three military leaders whose actions resulted in the unification of Japan, partially because they wanted to be perceived as patrons of culture and also because of genuine enthusiasm, embraced the artistic cult of tea. Today, Japanese pottery, characterized by the features described of the ware employed in the tea ceremony, is internationally famous. Hideyoshi, in the midst of a military invasion of Korea marked by brutal fighting, took the time to notice and admire Korean "peasant style" pottery. He invited and in some cases forced some of Korea's most prominent potters to move to Japan, thereby expanding the production of what we know of today as a classic Japanese art. Hideyoshi did this because of his involvement with tea.

The medieval period also witnessed the birth of the performing art of noh. Noh is a theatrical performance that uses a script that is essentially a dramatic poem concerned with historical events and almost always contains Buddhist themes. Noh is performed by one lead dancer, who is usually masked, and several lesser characters, a chorus who reveal parts of the story, and a musical ensemble. Noh actors are also musicians and dancers. Although the historical and musical aspects of noh are discussed elsewhere in this book, there are important artistic elements of noh that relate to Japanese aesthetics that deserve attention in this section. The noh stage is largely devoid of scenery, and the only elaborate visual physical features of noh are the masks and costumes. Yet noh has powerful dramatic effects for audiences who have even a rudimentary understanding of this performing art. It is a clear manifestation, like the tea ceremony, of the Japanese aesthetic notion that powerful effects can be obtained from minimalism—that less is more. In medieval times, noh was theater for the elites, and those contemporary lovers of noh tend to be still particularly well-educated and cultured Japanese.

As the medieval period reached its conclusion in the 16th century, Europeans landed in Japan and the Jesuits introduced Western styles of visual arts to some Japanese, most notably painting and illustrations for books. However, the Tokugawa government's persecution of Christians and expulsion of all Europeans except

KATSUSHIKA HOKUSAI (1760–1849)

Most famous as a ukiyo-e artist, Hokusai worked in a variety of art mediums including painting and drawing. He produced 15 volumes of sketches including thousands of scenes of everything from Buddhas to fish. Hokusai also published a popular book on drawing. Born illegitimate, he was adopted into a family of artisans, began to paint when he was 6 years old, and was eventually apprenticed to a prominent ukiyo-e artist. Hokusai became well known (he painted for the shogun) in his lifetime, and affluent, but his fortunes suffered both because of sporadic declines in demand for his art and an 1839 fire that destroyed much of his work. Despite business setbacks and the personal tragedy of having both of his wives die, Hokusai continued to paint. During his seventies, he prayed for more life so that he could perfect his craft.

the Dutch in the early 17th century suppressed almost all Western artistic influence until the subsequent century.

TOKUGAWA JAPAN (1600–1868): "CLASSIC" JAPANESE ARTS AND WESTERN CONTACT

As more extensively described in the history chapter, literacy and commerce flourished in the Tokugawa era (1600–1868) as these years, when Japan had limited contact with most of the rest of the world, were generally peaceful and prosperous. Although a majority of people lived in the countryside, a rich urban culture also developed in Edo (present-day Tokyo) as well as in several other cities. Not only elites but bourgeoisie as well had the time and money for leisure activities. Urban prosperity and leisure resulted in an expansion of the arts. Ironically, the most well-known arts that became prominent and are today considered classic Japanese art forms, ukiyo-e and kabuki, were part of popular cultural entertainment and communications during the Tokugawa years.

In earlier times, the Chinese experimented with wood-block print technology in which artist, wood-block carver, and printer collaborated to produce large numbers of copies of one illustration. Wood-block printing had existed in Japan since the Heian period but was largely limited to Buddhist institutions. Ukiyo-e, the Japanese name for wood-block printing, literally means "pictures from the floating world," a Buddhist expression illustrating the impermanence of what is generally considered to be everyday life.

Tokugawa urbanization spawned a pleasure industry of actors, artists, gamblers, and prostitutes. The shogunate permitted what they considered to be necessary evils to satisfy the public but regulated their practice to specific sections of cities. Ukiyo-e depicting famous courtesans and kabuki actors began to appear as advertisements

Kabuki theater appealed to a variety of people in the Tokugawa era but today is considered a classical Japanese art form. (Corel)

accompanying other printed communications about the "floating world." Further ukiyo-e production, on topics that had nothing to do with the pleasure industry, was also stimulated by the growth of literacy rates and the attendant need to illustrate a variety of genres of books.

Originally, ukiyo-e technology was limited to the production of black-and-white prints, but by 1745 the art had developed to the point that two colors could be introduced, and by 1764 full-color ukiyo-e was possible. It should be again emphasized that ukiyo-e, like contemporary visual advertising, was common and certainly not considered to be great art. Although some ukiyo-e artists such as Utamaro (1754–1806), Hokusai (1760–1849), and Hiroshige (1797–1858) attained fame in their lifetimes, they and other practitioners were not from the elite classes. Utamaro was typical of earlier ukiyo-e artists in that his paintings were of famous floating-world characters, but later Hokusai and Hiroshige created new types of wood-block prints. Hokusai's still influential *The Great Wave off Kanagawa* is his most famous work, but the prolific artist addressed a wide range of subjects in his art.

Hiroshige, who began his adult life as a firefighter, also painted a variety of types of ukiyo-e but is now celebrated for his 19th-century travelogue *The Fifty-Three Stages of the Tokaido*. This series of prints that are now considered masterpieces are not only beautiful landscapes but also invaluable to historians and others interested in Tokugawa Japan. They provide rich detail about the everyday life of a

ANDO HIROSHIGE (1797–1858)

Although he could not leave his hereditary fireman's job until the age of 26, like Hokusai, Hiroshige became well known in his lifetime. In 1830 Hiroshige gained recognition through a series of landscape prints and was invited to accompany an official procession the shogun sent to Kyoto via the Tokaido road with a gift of horses for the emperor. The Tokaido was a major national highway, and Hiroshige was able to complete a series of ukiyo-e based on his journey and attain national prominence. The most well-known travel and landscape artist of his day produced several similar travel series including *Famous Places in Kyoto* and *Eight Views of Omi.*

variety of people, what they wore, their occupations, and even the buildings where they lived and worked. Today, ukiyo-e is prized throughout the world.

Kabuki and bunraku, also briefly addressed in the history and music portions of the book, flourished as entertainment for a wide range of urban residents during Tokugawa times. Kabuki has an operatic format similar to Beijing opera. Although the subject matter can be serious and often reflects some Shinto and Buddhist themes, the plays are secular with dramatic action accompanied by dances, music, and off-stage sound effects. While kabuki owes a debt to noh, its origins also lie in traveling troupes of performers. Kabuki stories, featuring limited scripts but plenty of drama, were based on historical tales and fables and on the lives of ordinary Edo people. The subject matter ranged from adventure to thwarted romances and love suicides. Noted historian of Japanese culture Donald Keene has defined bunraku as "a form of storytelling, recited to a musical accompaniment and embodied by puppets on a stage" (Keene 1965, 31). Several kabuki playwrights wrote for bunraku as well, and themes of plays were rooted in popular histories and legends. Although there was more emphasis on the story in bunraku than in kabuki, both performing arts are distinctively Japanese. Unlike Western theater, they are presentational rather than representative. To put it another way, the extensive narratives that recreate detailed reality in Western plays in a similar format to cinema are not characteristic of the classic Japanese performing arts. Although noh is the most spare in visual and story characteristics of the three dramatic forms, kabuki and bunraku both share the less-is-more philosophy that is so much a part of Japanese arts.

By the latter part of the 18th century, despite the earlier repression of Western ideas, interest was growing in "Dutch Learning," and this had some impact on artists. Medical books with illustrations were translated from Dutch to Japanese as well as illustrated books on a variety of other topics. By the 19th century, groups of scholars and intellectuals existed whom the shogunate either authorized to keep up with Western knowledge or who independently sought it on their own. A few artists even began to experiment with Western-style portrait painting, and most notably, paintings by Watanabe Kazan clearly indicate interesting Japanese and Western syntheses. Western influence on Japanese arts would dramatically expand with the 1868 opening of Japan by the new government.

NEW DIRECTIONS AND GLOBAL ARTS (1868–PRESENT)

In an effort to modernize so as to be on equal footing with Western powers, the Meiji government dramatically changed the Tokugawa seclusion policies, and Japanese interacted with foreigners in a broad array of fields including the arts. For the first decade and a half after this abrupt societal change, large numbers of Japanese even considered many of their own art forms to be backward. Fortunately, this trend did not last long, and both Japan and the world have benefitted. By the late 1870s and early 1880s, thoughtful and creative Japanese and Westerners both recognized the immense beauty of Japan's traditional arts but also understood that exposure to the finest Western art forms was culturally enriching as well.

Kuroda Seiki, who studied in France for seven years and was named the first professor of Western arts at Tokyo Imperial University, is now considered the father of Western arts in Japan. However, because he had learned in depth about another culture's art, Kuroda better understood and valued Japanese art. He produced some impressive fusions of the two styles using Western oil painting as a medium but depicting Japanese themes. Important Western voices also spoke for traditional Japanese arts. Former President Grant witnessed a noh performance when in Tokyo and was so impressed with its power that he urged top Japanese political leaders to ensure noh's survival as an art form (Metraux 2006, 42). In Europe, impressionist and postimpressionist painters including Vincent van Gogh were influenced by traditional Japanese art and helped to create interest in it in the West. Van Gogh was particularly moved by Japanese wood-block prints that featured striking integrations of bold colors in subjects ranging from mountains and rice fields to famous geisha and actors.

One of the most influential advocates of Japanese art in Japan was Ernest Fenollosa (1853–1908). Fenollosa, a Harvard graduate who came to Japan to teach philosophy at Tokyo Imperial University, was passionately moved by what he considered to be the spiritual nature of Japanese arts. He and a former student, Okakura Tenshin, managed to get the Meiji government in 1889 to create the Tokyo Art School, which focused exclusively on Japanese and Asian arts.

Japanese architecture was particularly affected by contact with the West. After concentrating on copying Western buildings in the latter part of the 19th century, in the first two decades of the 20th century, Japanese architects revisited and gained renewed admiration for their own cultural heritage. In the first few decades of the 20th century, they began to concentrate on how to combine traditional tastes with Western techniques.

As this problem was being addressed in Japan, Frank Lloyd Wright, who was becoming one of the world's most famous architects, was keenly interested in Japanese aesthetics. Wright had first marveled over, and then intensely studied, the Japanese Phoenix Villa on display at the 1892 Chicago World's Columbian Exhibition.

Wright profoundly admired the traditional Japanese propensities to both accentuate functionalism in design and to make structures of all types a natural part of the larger environment. He visited Japan as early as 1905, acquired an extensive Japanese art collection, and worked in Japan designing the famous Imperial Hotel in Tokyo. The building, completed in 1922, incorporated outstanding elements of Japanese and Western design.

Ironically, although traditional architectural techniques are still used in Japan, when the nation hastily rebuilt after World War II, much construction was done so quickly that any artistic aspects were ignored. However, the works of the great architect Tange Kenzo, who designed the Peace Memorial Hall at Hiroshima and the 1964 Tokyo Olympics Sports Arena, powerfully reaffirm the artistic principles that Wright loved.

One of the outstanding creative achievements of postwar Japan was the development of world-famous cinema. The first foreign movie was shown in Japan in 1894, and by the 1920s a film industry existed. Although for the first few years shallow action thrillers were the norm, even before World War II creative directors were communicating longtime Japanese cultural issues to movie audiences. *Shukin Geki*, or "home dramas," emerged as a film genre appreciated by domestic audiences before the war. Although from a Western perspective nothing much happened in these films and they tended to be about the lives of ordinary lower-middle-class people, the themes of interpersonal relations among families and how people in primary groups behave toward one another in other kinds of small groups echo the content of much of classical Japanese literature.

Ozu Yasujiro (1903–1963) worked on a variety of films of this genre before World War II. After the war, he became internationally famous for depicting the lives of ordinary people and in particular focusing on the conflicts between tradition and modernity in a rapidly changing Japan. One biographer of Ozu has written, "In the future when people want to see what Japanese life was like before and after World War II, they will watch the movies of director Ozu Yasujiro" (Weston 1999, 303). Kurosawa Akira (1910–1998) is even more internationally famous than Ozu. Kurosawa's subject matter was incredibly broad. His most famous works include films based on Japanese history, remakes of Shakespeare's works in a Japanese context, penetrating critiques of Japanese bureaucrats, and action-packed samurai movies. However, Kurosawa's films are never superficial, and they provide evidence of what critics agree to be incredible attention to cinematic detail. Thanks to the work of Ozu, Kurosawa, and a few other directors, Japanese cinema became world famous in the latter part of the 20th century.

CONCLUSION: JAPANIZATION AND WESTERNIZATION

Today, examples of Japanese art, architecture and gardens are present in many parts of the world. Japanese film, manga, and anime have global aficionados including many young ppeople. The architectural influences of Japanese minimalism and harmony with nature can be also ascertained in planned communities in Europe, the United States, and elsewhere. Japan is often described as the Asian nation that has incorporated the largest amount of foreign influence yet retained its own distinctive culture. Nowhere does this argument seem to be more powerful than in the visual and performing arts. Traditional Japanese gardens, kabuki, and calligraphy as well as their modern variants remain viable art forms along with foreign cinema, sculpture, and architecture. The world strongly influences Japan in the arts as does Japan the world.

REFERENCES

Eleftheriotis, Dimitris and Gary Needham. *Asian Cinemas: A Reader and Guide*. New York: University of Hawai'i Press, 2006.

"Japanese Art." *Intute: Arts and Humanities*. http://www.intute.ac.uk/artsandhumanities (accessed April 2008).

Hiroshige. *The Fifty-Three Stages of the Tokaido*. Nagoya: The Tokai Bank Foundation, 1984.

Itasaka, Gen, ed. "Kabuki" in *Kodansha Encyclopedia of Japan*, 90–97. Vol. 4. New York: Kodansha International, 1983.

Itasaka, Gen, ed. "No" in *Kodansha Encyclopedia of Japan*, 23–29. Vol. 6. New York: Kodansha International, 1983.

Keene, Donald. Bunraku: The Art of the Japanese Puppet Theatre. Tokyo: Kodansha, 1965.

Metraux, Daniel. "The Mikado, Guranto Shogun, and the Rhapsody of US-Japan Relations in Early Meiji." *Education About Asia* 11, No. 3 (Winter 2006): 39–44.

Richie, Donald (Arturo Silva, ed.). *The Donald Richie Reader: Fifty Years of Writing on Japan*. New York: Stone Bridge Press, 2001.

Stanley-Baker, Joan. *Japanese Art*. London: Thames & Hudson, Ltd., 1984.

Varley, H. Paul. *Japanese Culture: A Short History*. New York: Praeger Publishers, 1977.

Weston, Mark. *Giants of Japan*. New York: Kodansha International, 1999.

Japanese Music

INTRODUCTION: WORLD MUSIC

Beginning in the 1980s, U.S. consumers wishing to buy music were able to find a category titled "world music" in stores where recordings could be purchased. Although this title is a bit misleading since much of "American music" has European or African origins that go back to the colonial period, U.S. consumers could better find indigenous music of other cultures in stores after the advent of the world music category. It is paradoxical that Japan, with a relatively homogenous population by world standards, has been so open to music from other places. It is a country where world music is not just for aficionados of foreign music. Certain genres

THEME BARS

Because of wide exposure to foreign and particularly American television, various groups of Japanese love different aspects of American and Japanese foreign culture and music. In big cities, particularly Tokyo, one can find a variety of bars where themes constitute the major foci. On the musical front, there are bars that celebrate the Grateful Dead, reggae, blues, bluegrass, and a variety of other musical genres. There are also bars that attract fans of different foreign popular cultural traditions. For example, there is at least one American-style country-and-western bar in Tokyo that not only features music but also has mechanical bulls and roping contests and whose patrons dress up like cowboys. The Jodo Buddhist sect even has a theme bar in Tokyo where monks chant and pour drinks.

of foreign music enjoy widespread sales in Japan, and many Japanese play or perform music whose origins can be traced to a number of different cultures.

A quick sample of contemporary Japanese music reveals a rich tapestry of genres. Beethoven's Ninth Symphony is wildly popular as a live performance and in recorded form, and Vivaldi's *The Four Seasons* is another national favorite. Western-style choral groups permeate the nation's schools along with a massive number of adult amateur choruses. Jazz has been popular in Japan since the 1920s. Visitors to Yoyogi Park in Harajuku in Tokyo or to nightclubs throughout Japan can find a wide range of rock, punk rock, hip-hop, reggae, and jam band music. There is also what musicologist Bonnie Wade calls "niche music" (Wade 2004, 137), each with devoted and skillful followers. Bluegrass, Bavarian folk songs, salsa, and blues are just a few examples.

Japanese traditional music and associated instruments coexist with the imported music of other cultures and often either directly or indirectly influence what are considered to be non-Japanese musical forms. *Gagaku*, the oldest and most elite form of Japanese music, is itself an import from eighth-century Tang China. However, this musical genre died more than 1,000 years ago in China but remains vibrant in Japan. Japan's major traditional performing arts—Noh, bunraku, and kabuki—all rely on particular forms of traditional music, as do Japanese Shinto shrines. Such Japanese instruments as the samisen, shakuhachi, *taiko* (*taikyo*), and koto are integral parts of the nation's traditional musical heritage that since 1868 seemed in serious decline. However, after World War II, such internationally famous modern composers and musicians as Takemitsu Toru and Toshiko Akiyoshi incorporated these instruments into compositions, arrangements, and performances. Today, a variety of Japanese traditional and contemporary Western-influenced and indigenous popular music has devoted fans in Asia and around the world.

The objectives of the subsequent portion of this section are to introduce readers to traditional Japanese music and to describe how such musical genres as jazz, choral music, and European-style classical music now constitute an integral part of

Japanese music as well. Japanese cultural propensities are one explanation of the latter phenomenon. Vivaldi's *The Four Seasons* is an illustrative example. Among European classical compositions, *The Four Seasons* ranks second only to Beethoven's Ninth Symphony in popularity in Japan. Readers of the sections of this chapter on literature and art are aware that seasonal changes constitute a perennial theme in the creation of both fiction and nonfiction and in the performing and visual arts. Thus, Vivaldi's masterpiece had a special cultural resonance with the Japanese.

Although what follows is chronologically organized, the linearity present in other portions of this book won't be as neat in the music section. This is because in some cases either the musical forms or the instruments used for a particular musical genre, or both, were first intended for elites but with the passage of time became popularized, shakuhachi music being one example. Also, decades after many Japanese were attracted to European music and grew less familiar with their own traditions, contemporary composers, arrangers, and musicians began to revisit Japan's musical heritage and either incorporated elements from the past into new music or introduced Japanese to past musical forms that brought people back to the original traditions.

It is also important to consider that even more so in Japan than in other cultures, the lines between literature, the performing arts, and music are often blurred. Readers who desire to better understand the role of traditional Japanese music in culture should read the sections of the book where history, religion, literature, and art are addressed.

MUSIC IN EARLY AND MEDIEVAL JAPAN

Even before the creation of a Japanese state, archeologists have found that during the late Jomon and then the Yayoi periods, clay figures of musicians existed. As was the case with other aspects of culture, Japan was a latecomer in development in East Asia compared to China or the Korean Peninsula. The first written records of music go back to 453 CE, when 80 Korean musicians from the Silla kingdom visited what is now Japan. Music, musicians, and musical instruments reached early Japan from Korea, Manchuria, and China as well as indirectly from South Asia through the Silk Roads into continental East Asia and then Japan. There were also early songs and dances associated with Shinto shrines that developed independently of continental influences.

All of these musical influences, but most notably imported music from the imperial court of the Chinese Tang dynasty (617–906 CE), resulted in the creation in Japan of "gagaku," or music that was played at the emperor's court. Gagaku's literal meaning is "elegant music," and the Chinese compositions in particular were in part installed as a formal aspect of the Japanese state to create more of an aura of elegance that could be associated with the sovereign.

The builders of Japan's new government during the Nara (710–794 CE) and Heian (794–1156) periods were trying to transform the emperor from a mere sovereign into a heavenly ruler similar to the Chinese emperor so that Japan's imperial court could be as glorious as the Tang's. Gagaku, with its often ethereal sound, was one such tool. Confucian teachings, then highly influential among Japanese elites, also stressed the importance of court rituals for societal order and harmony, so gagaku played a role in reiterating the Chinese philosophy that was so influential in the formation of the early Japanese state. However, Shinto ritual music and ancient Korean music, both of which existed in Japan before the importation of Tang court music, also became part of gagaku.

Gagaku and *bugaku*, the latter term being used for court music accompanying dances, is played by an ensemble of musicians seated on the floor, and different instruments are used depending on what form of music is performed. However, the common gagaku instruments are flutes; *Hichiriki*, a double-reeded instrument similar to an oboe; such percussion instruments as *taiko*, or drums; a *shoko*, or gong; a *togaku*, or small mouth organ; and two-stringed instruments: the koto, a 13-stringed zither, and the biwa, a 4-stringed lute. The wind instruments, and in Shinto songs human voices, carry the melodies.

By the Heian period, gagaku was performed by nobles and by hereditary groups of musicians who were organized in guilds. Gagaku was performed at court and in a variety of aristocratic social events including horse racing, archery contests, and cockfighting. Gagaku is mentioned on a number of occasions in *The Tale of Genji*. The music's tempo, unlike today, when it tends to be performed slowly, varied quite a bit depending on the venue. During medieval and early modern Japan, gagaku's influence lessened, but some aristocrats, the guilds, and Buddhist temples kept the tradition alive.

Shortly after the 1868 Meiji Restoration, the tradition of gagaku performance in the imperial court was revived and continues today. Numbers of musicians who do court performances are descendants of the families that constituted the guilds who performed at court more than 1,000 years ago. Modern composers have incorporated elements of gagaku compositions and instruments into contemporary, European-style classical music as well as jazz.

Gagaku music as a genre was, and is still, considered music for the upper classes, but it had effects on popular music after its rise and decline at court. Although some common people had been exposed to biwa music, particularly in Kyushu when the instrument first reached Japan, this gagaku instrument became a staple in the 13th and 14th centuries, when it was used by storytellers as accompaniment to chanting and singing the epic *Tale of the Heike* and other warrior sagas. Takemitsu Toru (1930–1996), Japan's most famous and prolific modern composer, wrote music for biwa.

While Confucian ideals, Tang court music, and Shinto rituals all influenced gagaku, Buddhism is a major influence in noh, Japan's oldest continual musical dance-drama. Although forms of noh existed earlier, the theatrical genre that came to full fruition in the 14th century was heavily influenced by Zen Buddhism. The plays, as is discussed elsewhere in this book, often have Buddhist themes, and musically noh actors and the chorus were also influenced by earlier traditions of Buddhist chanting. Other Japanese traditions such as gagaku and bugaku music, as well as music from Shinto shrines, also influenced noh.

Nonmusical aspects of noh are described in more detail elsewhere in the book. Noh features all male actors and choruses who sometimes narrate and sometimes speak for actors; an ensemble of two or three drums, depending on the play; and one flute. Noh music consists of singing or chanting by the chorus or actors. The drum and flute music is not background music but an important component in giving noh its power. The music is used with entrances and exits, for dances, and with some scenes that call for music and chants. The spare nature of noh music, as is true of other elements of a performance, powerfully communicates the Japanese aesthetic of *ma*—the notion that sound can only exist in conjunction with the power of silence. Modern jazz composers in Japan and elsewhere—for example, John Cage in the United States—have consciously incorporated this concept into their music. In contemporary Japan, noh has devoted followers and is an active theatrical art form. UNESCO has recognized it as an intangible cultural heritage.

MUSIC IN TOKUGAWA JAPAN

Although popular forms of music existed in Japan since before written history, the growth of other musical genres and urban development in the years between 1600 and the 1868 Meiji Restoration resulted in an increase in varieties of music and instrumentation. The shakuhachi, a vertical bamboo flute with a notched mouthpiece and five finger holes, can be heard in contemporary Japan in the two traditions that developed in early modern Japan, but also in later Japanese folk music as well and in jazz and classical music, both in Japan and throughout the world. The popularization of shakuhachi music has Zen Buddhist roots. Originally during the medieval period, wandering groups of beggar-minstrels, or *komoso* (the Chinese characters for the term mean "straw mat priests"), played the shakuhachi. By the Tokugawa period, although all *komoso* never were primarily focused on religion, the group of players had become a serious zen sect and traced their beginnings to the ninth-century Chinese priest Fuke.

A number of samurai, particularly masterless samurai, or "ronin," were part of the Fuke Zen sect. In part because of this development, the first Tokugawa shogun, Ieyasu, granted the group a monopoly on playing the instrument and the right to wear the identity-hiding basket-type hat. The Meiji government would later end this monopoly in the late 19th century when it abolished traditional guilds.

Over time, two shakuhachi musical divisions developed. One was the *honkyoku*, or "original pieces," that focused on Zen traditions. However, in the latter years of the Tokugawa period and through the imperial and post–World War II years, a secular tradition emerged in which players joined ensembles with koto and samisen musicians. After the advent of Western music, music for the shakuhachi drew on European classical, jazz, and avant-garde influences. Still, the most famous shakuhachi music consists of such spiritually oriented compositions as "Koku," or "Empty Sky." As was the case with Noh theater music, the aesthetic influence of *ma* is present in some of the more famous traditional shakuhachi music. Silence is used to great effect in opposition to the lonely flute.

In addition to the shakuhachi, during the Tokugawa period, the koto and samisen also began to be played and heard by groups of people other than elites. The koto, like a number of traditional Japanese instruments, was developed from a related instrument that came to Japan from China. Although there are now variants that have more strings, typically the koto is a 13-stringed, wooden half-tube, semicylindrical zither. The koto player sits in front of the instrument as is the case with an American steel guitar or dobro player. Koto musicians use the left hand to manipulate movable bridges for each string and use the right hand with picks to pluck the strings. Originally, an early version of the koto had been part of imperial gagaku. After the demise of that form of music and the rise of a warrior medieval government, its playing was limited to a few aristocrats and Buddhist priests.

However, by the 1600s, people other than educated males played the koto, and the instrument was often combined with the popular samisen. Although the koto declined in popularity in the late 19th century after the arrival of European music, such innovative musicians as Miyagi Michio (1894–1956) and Sawai Tadao (1937–1997) revived interest in the traditional instrument by composing and performing traditional works that blended European influences, therefore helping to internationalize interest in koto. Koto music remains a living part of Japan's culture today.

The samisen, a three-stringed plucked lute with a long neck and an unfretted fingerboard, arrived in Japan from the Ryukyu Islands about the middle of the 16th century. It was an instrument for often-blind, wandering minstrels and also became associated with the Edo pleasure quarters. Samisen music became essential to bunraku, the puppet theater that thrived in the Edo period, and was the melodic instrument for kabuki, perhaps the most famous of all Japan's theatrical genres.

Kabuki originated as theater for commoners even though samurai also attended on a regular basis in urban centers during the Tokugawa period. However, kabuki never lost its reputation as theater for a variety of people, and the stories and music represent this diversity. Unlike noh, there is more heterogeneity in kabuki music. Samisen, percussion instruments, and a flute (both the latter instruments borrowed from noh) are a regular part of kabuki performances, but koto music may be employed as well in a wide range of songs and dance. One of several differences between kabuki and noh is that kabuki actors don't sing in plays; this function is performed by professional singers.

Unlike noh, kabuki often has musicians offstage who play both compositions and sound effects that are representative of such sounds as bird calls and temple bells or designed to fulfill a number of functions: accompaniment of stage action, mood setting, weather conditions, character identification, and even the establishment of social class identity. For example, the sound of koto music usually indicates a refined cultural environment. Kabuki patrons learn that the sound of a slow beat of a large drum usually indicates an impending suicide. There are old popular songs that if accompanied by subtle percussion, indicate that a scene will take place in a geisha house.

The offstage music is usually played from a small room in the stage-right corner, and musicians can watch events on stage while not seen by the audience. Onstage music featuring samisen, flute, and one or two drums is usually played to accompany dances. Again, kabuki and the music that is an integral part of this theatrical form are less formulaic than noh. Some plays feature rows of samisen players and singers, other plays have both backstage and onstage music, and a few plays do not employ backstage music. Although kabuki declined during the Meiji period and again shortly after World War II, a resurgence in its popularity began in the late 1960s, and today this unique Japanese performing art has received international recognition. As a result, kabuki music remains a living part of Japan's cultural heritage.

ENCOUNTERS WITH WESTERN MUSIC: 1868–1945

Although Japanese encountered such variants of Western music as the pipe organ and some Western instruments in the 1500s, the expulsion of Europeans made initial Japanese interest in European music short lived. Even though the Dutch were present in Kyushu in small numbers during most of the Tokugawa period, the only tangible musical product of this interaction was the establishment by Takashima Shuhan, a student of "Dutch learning" in the 1830s, of a fife and drum corps that had imitators in other domains. The forced opening of Japan by Americans and Europeans and the new Meiji government brought an end to the heretofore limited musical contact Japanese had with the West.

At first, the Meiji government, despite its thirst for Westernization, always contained powerful factions, who were Confucian in philosophical outlook, wanted to control the entry of "unwholesome" Western music. However, brass bands that played robust military marching songs were quite congruent with Japan's new policy of building a strong army and navy. By 1869, Englishman Edwin Fenton had formed the first Japanese brass band. Brass band development continued as other Europeans helped to create army and navy brass bands. Performances of brass bands became popular, and even today in Japan there are substantial school and amateur brass bands. As was the case with other aspects of Western culture, Japanese began to be sent or to go abroad on their own to study music. In 1875, Izawa Shuji was sent to study in Massachusetts for four years and after his return formed an organization that would go on to become the Tokyo Music School and what is today the Tokyo University of Fine Arts. Izawa and his associates also helped to design the new public school music curriculum and in doing so attempted to fuse European and Japanese music. This attempt often failed because of the different natures of the musical forms. Also, in Japan even more than in Europe or the United States, certain musical genres were rigidly associated with specific social classes. However, there was one particular specific success and a more general long-term achievement based on these efforts of Izawa and others.

Choral music featuring Western musical techniques but lyrics that contained Confucian notions of filial piety were popular in Meiji Japan. Choral music in Japan went on to develop into a musical genre that enjoys a high degree of contemporary popularity. According to Japan specialist and musicologist Bonnie Wade, today "hundreds of thousands, if not millions of Japanese sing in choruses, whether a children's chorus, teen chorus, mothers' chorus, young women's chorus, men's chorus, mixed chorus, PTA chorus, or business chorus" (Wade 2004, 146). The author had the chance in 2008 to hear the entire Mie University–attached middle school eighth grade perform two folk songs from Okinawa in preparation for a field trip to Japan's newest prefecture and was moved by the power and talent of 200 13-year-olds. When asked

In Japan, music and art are both required of all elementary and junior high school students. (Courtesy of Lucien Ellington)

why Japanese like choral music so much, the school principal, who had been involved in various choral groups since his own high school days, gave an answer that is corroborated in scholarly works. Japanese are particularly attracted to choral music because of the cooperation required for excellence, the harmony that is apparent when the music is well sung, and the intrinsic beauty of the music.

The early efforts to create a public school music curriculum succeeded in a more profound general way. Despite periods of time when Japanese music was given short shrift, followed by the 1930s and early 1940s when the militarist government unsuccessfully attempted to repress Western music (except for the music of their allies, Germany and Italy), the Japanese school curriculum today provides students with an organized music education where they learn both Western and Asian music. Also, since the beginning of Japan's modern educational system in the 1970s, unlike the case in many schools in the United States, the Japanese have considered music an important part of the school curriculum and not a frill that is subject to cuts during economic hard times.

European classical music also became popular in Japan not long after 19th-century contact with the West. European specialists began to arrive in Japan to teach in late Meiji, and increasingly the best Japanese students were sent to Germany to study classical music in the nation that had one of the strongest reputations in the West for excellence in this genre. World War I and its aftermath would also serve to boost European classical music's popularity in Japan.

During that conflict, Japan was allied with the Western powers and opposed Germany, particularly in the German holdings in Tsingtao China. Japanese forces captured 4,600 Germans, and large numbers of them were transported to a POW camp on Shikoku in Japan, where they remained until the signing of the 1919 Versailles Treaty. German prisoners formed a camp orchestra in which a number of Japanese amateur musicians also played. Beethoven's Ninth Symphony was the most popular rendition in the camp and from those beginnings is now the most popular classical music composition in Japan and is played throughout the nation at the end of the year. Given the propensity of a group-oriented culture to enjoy choral singing, readers should bear in mind that this particular symphony marked the first time that a symphony composer called for a chorus as well as an orchestra.

A more general effect of World War I's aftermath was a substantial increase in the number of Russian musicians, many of them White Russians forced out by the Bolsheviks, who came to Japan and played and performed. By the 1920s and 1930s, Japanese love of European classical music, which remains today, solidified and Japanese and foreign symphonies were organized or performing on guest tours. Also, European and American record companies created subsidiaries in Japan, and by 1937 Japan was the world's largest market for classical records.

However, Western popular music also grew in popularity in Japan during the latter part of the 19th and first few decades of the 20th century. Many Japanese had interactions with Christian missionaries or, in the case of the upper-middle class, sent children to Christian schools. As a result, Christian hymns and portable organs became popular.

Also, expanding private enterprise in Japan resulted in a boom for Western-oriented popular music and a demand for new instruments with which to play the music. The piano was a rare but highly treasured instrument in late-19th-century Japan, but portable organs were more affordable. The 1890 birth of the company producing pianos and organs that would become Yamaha helped to create more of a demand for these Western instruments. Instrument makers also featured instruction in an effort to sell their products. Eventually piano lessons for children in Japan would become something that first wealthy families and then many middle-class parents desired for their children's cultural enrichment.

Commercial brass bands, stimulated by Mitsukoshi Department Store's free training program for young musicians who couldn't afford formal training, also became popular in the first two decades of the 20th century. The department stores then used the bands for various advertising and store promotions. As band members left the military, they created another private business. *Bandoya*, or "bands for hire," were popular early in the century. *Bandoya* played music for silent films in movie theaters as well as doing promotions for businesses and playing at parties.

In the 1920s, the Japanese experienced a jazz boom, and jazz bands, often led and populated by Filipino musicians who had learned jazz from Americans, became popular. Today, Japanese rank among the world's most sophisticated jazz audiences, and several Japanese jazz musicians and composers have international reputations. As mentioned, during the war years there was an attempt to suppress most Western music and interest in it. American-style jazz was replaced with something called "light music," and the saxophone was censored as a decadent instrument. However, this trend lasted only as long as the militarists, and after World War II the Japanese continued their love affair with various forms of Western music while often also rediscovering some variants of music that existed on the archipelago before the mid-19th century.

POST–1945 JAPAN: WORLD MUSIC FLOURISHES

Traditional Japanese music had suffered at the expense of foreign imports for much of the time since the late 1800s, but several important postwar developments stimulated new-found interest in Japan's musical heritage. As mentioned, Japan's leading composer, Takemitsu Toru, incorporated parts for traditional instruments into his music. In 1955 the national government created "Living Cultural Treasures," and the naming of a shakuhachi and *taiko* drum master as well as Kabuki actors for these awards increased public interest in traditional Japanese music. In 1966, the National Theater of Japan was created (now the National Arts Council) with performance venues in Tokyo and later other parts of Japan where kabuki, noh, and bunraku are performed with associated music. This in turn created a demand for new compositions, arrangements, and performances of traditional music.

Also, shortly after the war ended, filmmaker Kurosawa Akira released a movie titled *Men Who Step on the Tiger's Tail*, based on a well-known noh performance that then became a kabuki play about the flight of Yoshitsune and his faithful warrior monk retainer, Benkei, from Yoshitsune's jealous brother and Japan's first shogun, Yoritomo. The movie version of the story featured an array of traditional Japanese and Western music, further exposing the public to the former. Kurosawa and other Japanese filmmakers incorporated other elements of traditional Japanese music into their work. Foreign interest in Zen Buddhism in the 1950s led to a larger interest in traditional Japanese culture, including music that both created world interest and attracted new attention among younger Japanese to some genres of traditional music.

One traditional Japanese instrument, the taiko drum, became internationally popular during the postwar years through the efforts of such masters as Oguchi Daihachi and Tanaka Seichi as they created ensembles of drummers who drew on indigenous traditions and foreign influences in playing a variety of different-sized drums that thrilled audiences in the United States, Europe, and Japan with electrifying and transformative rhythms. Estimates vary, but there are currently somewhere between 150 and 200 taiko groups in North America alone.

Japan today, in addition to having avid practitioners and fans of the niche music described earlier, also has larger followings devoted to several indigenous and foreign popular music forms. *Enka* music is a type of Japanese popular music that dates back to before World War II. Typically, enka songs are ballads and other slower numbers that have soulful themes and tend to be nostalgic. Enka is often about long-lost loves, missed opportunities, and other emotional topics. The music bears some resemblance to American country or blues ballads but is definitely a product of Japanese culture. Women enka singers almost always wear kimono, and men singers wear either Western or Japanese attire. A form of enka is also popular in the Republic of Korea, and there is some debate about whether the Koreans or

Drums have been used in a variety of settings throughout Japan's history but taiko ensemble drumming has become popular throughout the world in recent decades. (Corel)

the Japanese started this musical genre. Older Japanese who came of age in the 1940s and 1950s are enka's largest audience today.

In addition to enka, teenagers in particular were influenced by American 1950s and 1960s rock and roll. Gradually, a musical genre developed that had several temporary names but by the early 1990s began to be called "J-pop." J-pop has many more fans than enka and is similar to Western pop music except most of the lyrics are in Japanese, although English-language expressions may also be included in particular songs. Because of anime, video games, and other media, particular popular artists have fans all over the globe. Younger people are usually fans of new musical J-pop stars. As is the case with the popular music of other countries, contemporary Japanese pop music permeates movies and television programs in Japan. Television plays a big role in creating J-pop stars. One common route to stardom is for a singer to get a chance to sing on a commercial and, if a good response is obtained, appear on a television program. If a potential audience for the singer appears likely, then he or she will be invited to make a CD.

Other specific genres of popular music have enjoyed large followings in Japan, with some Japanese artists becoming globally popular. This is true of the pop/punk/garage band Shonen Knife. Formed in late 1981 by two sisters and a girlfriend, the band, who listed the Ramones as one of their influences, has been through many changes but has a large cadre of fans. Japan is now home to internationally popular heavy metal groups and experimental music bands, and the country is now considered by many to be at the forefront of alternative music. Also, much of these new music genres are now influencing composers of such video games as Dragon Quest and Final Fantasy.

Japanese hip-hop has roots that go back to the early 1980s with the emergence of bands and artists like Rock Steady Crew Japan and DJ Krush. By the 1990s, there was teen-oriented J-rap music, and hip-hop entered the mainstream. However, even though the format of the Japanese variant is similar to what emerged from African American urban environments, the lyrics reflect Japanese, not American, culture. Hip-hop is not the music of often-poor urban people as is the case in the United States, but the lyrics do reflect social tensions within Japanese society. Some themes of lyrics stress a battle against pressure for overconformity and are about feeling estranged from society because of different family arrangements or atypical parents.

Japanese music is already being affected, though, by recent immigrants who have brought their own musical traditions to Japan. As is discussed in other parts of the book, significant numbers of Brazilian Japanese, who are ethnically Japanese but culturally Brazilian, have been moving to Japan since the 1990s and are bringing their Latin American culture, including music, with them. Brazilian Japanese have already held media-publicized festivals in such places as Gifu Prefecture, where a large concentration has settled, and their music has been a part of what transpired at these events. Filipinos have also been moving to Japan in large numbers over the past two decades for work opportunities and bringing their own music to the archipelago. These two groups constitute the third- and fourth-largest ethnic groups in contemporary Japan, ranking behind Chinese and Koreans. While most of the Korean population has been in Japan for 50 years or longer and recent Chinese immigrants have direct connections through their own media to mainland culture and music, Brazilian Japanese and Filipinos will probably take Japan's larger musical culture in new directions.

CONCLUSION

Japan is ethnically a relatively homogenous culture by world standards, but most people on the archipelago have positively responded to foreign music without abandoning their own traditions. When asked why people in the late 1800s responded so enthusiastically to Western brass bands or Christian hymns, or why Japanese young people developed their own form of hip-hop in the 1980s and 1990s, some Japanese observers mention a national love of the new and exotic while other commentators opine that the Japanese are particularly connected to music. Whatever the reasons for the adaptation of such diverse musical genres, the fact is that there is indeed a vibrant world music present everywhere in the Japanese archipelago.

REFERENCES

Atkins, Taylor. "Edifying Tones: Using Music to Teach Asian History and Culture." *Education About Asia* 8, No. 3 (Spring 2003): 17–20.

Barbara's New Enka Site. May 27, 2008. http://www.technogirls.org/enka/index.htm (accessed August 19, 2008).

Itasaka, Gen, ed. "Biwa" in *Kodansha Encyclopedia of Japan*, 157. Vol. 1. New York: Kodansha International, 1983.

———, ed. "Gagaku" in *Kodansha Encyclopedia of Japan*, 1–2. Vol. 3. New York: Kodansha International, 1983.

———, ed. "Shakuhachi" in *Kodansha Encyclopedia of Japan*, 75–76. Vol. 7. New York: Kodansha International, 1983.

———, ed. "Shamisen" in *Kodansha Encyclopedia of Japan*, 76. Vol. 7. New York: Kodansha International, 1983.

Miyazaki, Sophia. *Koto World*. August 18, 2008. http://www.kotoworld.com (accessed August 18, 2008).

Varley, H. Paul. *Japanese Culture: A Short History*. New York: Praeger Publishers, 1977.

Wade, Bonnie C. *Music in Japan: Experiencing Music, Expressing Culture*. New York: Oxford University Press, 2004.

Food

A CULTURAL AND SOCIAL HISTORY

A complex array of geographical, economic, and cultural forces determine the foods of any culture. Food also helps to shape cultures. Any discussion of food and the Japanese begins with rice. When cultural meanings of food are explored in the West, the starting point is bread. Bread is often the food people share when they eat and has symbolic meanings in Christianity, the dominant Western religion. Expressions like "breadwinner" and "breadline" are part of Americans' vocabulary. Rice occupies an even more central place in Japanese culture and life than is the case with bread among Americans and Europeans.

"Asia" was a term invented by the ancient Greeks, and the peoples who inhabited this region only really began to consciously think of themselves as Asians about the early part of the 20th century. Today, there is substantial discussion among intellectuals about whether the region of the world we call Asia has common and centripetal elements. Rice is one such centripetal element. Although not all Asians eat rice, Asians constitute the majority of the world's people for whom rice rather than bread is the staple food. For most Asians and for the Japanese in particular, rice is much more than a food.

Wet rice paddy cultivation first reached Japan from the Asian mainland in the fifth century BCE. It is featured in the *Kojiki*, or *Record of Ancient Matters*, one of two compilations of the real and imagined past written by officials struggling to establish a Japanese identity. The *Kojiki* has several references to rice deities. Amaterasu, the sun goddess who founded Japan, is reported as being the mother of a grain deity who in turn is the parent of Jimmu, the legendary first emperor. Jimmu is sent from heaven to the Japanese islands to transform the archipelago into a land of succulent ears of rice. The imperial family has been associated with rice since the beginnings of that institution. Rice had early religious significance for Japanese, who acquired the power of deities through participating in rituals during rice

Traditionally, rice is served at the end of a Japanese meal. (Dreamstime.com)

planting and harvesting times and by eating rice. Even today, New Year's and agricultural ceremonies feature rituals where sake and *mochi*, or rice cakes, are offered to deities and then consumed by humans.

Rice remained both an important food and a symbol of Japan throughout later history. Rice paddies were cultivated by groups of families who had to effectively work together to grow the treasured crop. Some anthropologists even assert that the Japanese propensity to seek harmony, or *wa*, and group consensus had its primordial beginnings in rice paddies. *Gohan*, the Japanese word for "steamed rice," is also the word for "meal" in Japan. In order to differentiate between meals, the prefixes *asa* (morning), *hiru* (noon), and *ban* (evening) are added to *gohan*.

Rice has long been associated with what it means to be Japanese at some level. Rural Japan with its verdant green rice paddies has represented notions of traditional Japanese purity when contrasted with impersonal urban environments. During Tokugawa times, such famous wood-block print artists as Hiroshige and Hokusai created rice paddies with Mount Fuji in the background in their work. Expressions like "eat from the same rice bowl" denote close group associations while "eat cold rice" has the opposite meaning. Even though rice consumption has declined by over half of what was consumed in the 1960s, it remains a culturally important food. It is usually served in the home once or more each day. Rice or rice products are used as offerings to ancestors in small home shrines and, as noted, in ceremonies and holidays. Japanese eat sticky short-grain rice, which is different from the long-grain rice common to China. Even though an identical variety to what the Japanese grow is also harvested in California, many Japanese continue to be suspicious of foreign rice.

Sake, a brewed alcoholic beverage made from fermented rice, appeared early in Japanese history and is deeply associated with Japan's history, culture, religious beliefs, and economy. The first written accounts of sake consumption in Japan date back to around the third century CE, and detailed instructions for its manufacture exist from as early as the eighth century CE. Sake drinking was most probably first associated with religious rites that celebrated the planting or harvesting of rice, and the beverage became connected with Shinto shrines early in Japanese history as well as with the imperial family and the aristocracy. Even today, large kegs of sake may be seen piled outside of temples and shrines, and the beverage continues to play an important role in many ceremonies and festivals. As time passed, sake eventually became a popular beverage. The upper classes drank filtered sake that had been strained through cloth, and common people consumed a rougher unfiltered variety.

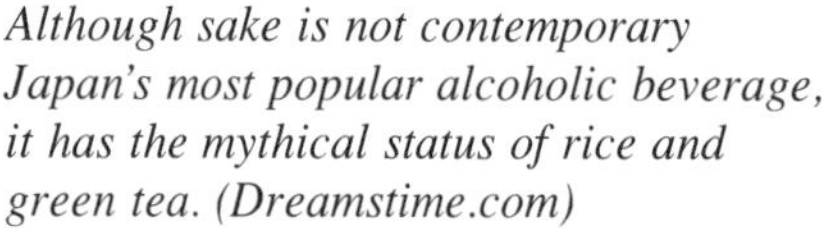

Although sake is not contemporary Japan's most popular alcoholic beverage, it has the mythical status of rice and green tea. (Dreamstime.com)

Beginning around 1200 CE, sake manufacturing increased in Japan. Although governments passed laws against drinking or manufacturing sake from time to time, none of the edicts had much effect. By the 14th century, taxes were collected on sake, and the beverage was traded as a commodity sometime shortly afterward. By the 1500s, many of the same processes that are used today to manufacture sake had been perfected. By the Tokugawa period, sake manufacture played a prominent role in Japan's economy and contributed to rural prosperity. Because of bountiful agricultural harvests through most (but not all) of the Tokugawa years, many peasants had more food than they could consume. The more enterprising peasants used their surplus rice harvests to make sake, and a few successful sake manufacturing families would go on to found important businesses and factories.

Tea, like sake, is more than just a beverage in Japan. Although today some Japanese drink Chinese tea, which is fermented, from the beginning in Japan unfermented tea was consumed and favored. O-cha, or Japanese green tea, which has this coloration because it is not fermented, remains today the drink of choice for millions of Japanese. Tea's history and use are associated with Japan's debt to China and the eventual development of uniquely Japanese religious and aesthetic practices. Although there are different accounts about how tea arrived in Japan from China, it is most likely that from the beginning tea drinking was intimately associated with Japanese Buddhism, particularly with the Zen sect. Chinese Ch'an Buddhist monks first used tea as an aide in remaining awake for meditation. In the late 12th century, Japanese Buddhist monks were traveling to China to study in Ch'an monasteries. After a few or many years of study, the Japanese returned to their homeland, transmitted Ch'an teachings about enlightenment, and founded the Japanese sect based on these teachings, known as Zen. Drinking and growing of tea arrived along with religious knowledge. The most creditable accounts of tea's Japanese beginnings indentify Eisai, a prominent figure in the development of Zen, with introducing tea to Japan in 1191 by bringing seeds home from his China studies.

Although it remained a drink of the elites, tea became popular among aristocrats as well as Buddhist clergy, and there were tea-tasting contests in Japan's medieval period among the former accompanied by festivities and much sake drinking. Zen monks at first performed a tea ritual dating back to their Tang dynasty Chinese Ch'an counterparts. By the 15th and 16th centuries, a "way of tea," or *chado*, developed in Japan that was shaped by religious and lay tea masters. Chado is known in the West as the tea ceremony. Sen no Rikyu, the most famous chado master in Japanese history, simplified the practice and accentuated Zen influences in the way of tea. This ritual, which emphasizes the appreciation of the moment, the beauty of the simple, and the promotion of tranquility, became both a part of Japanese Zen and the larger culture. Tea huts were constructed at Zen temples and elsewhere expressly for the ceremony, and tea utensils and the pottery used for tea became an art genre. Today, secular forms of the tea ceremony are considered part of traditional culture, and almost any foreigner who visits Japan will be invited to participate in a tea ceremony. There are several tea ceremony schools of practitioners, and Japanese junior high schools often have tea ceremony clubs.

Even though tea drinking and culture long constituted an integral part of the lives of elite Japanese, it was not until after the beginning of the 20th century that technology made possible the mass consumption of the beverage. Today, the consumption of green tea is a constant backdrop for daily life, and most Japanese and foreigners consider green tea to be both the nation's drink and a part of traditional culture.

It is also important in the cultural and social history of food in Japan that for many centuries the government prohibited the consumption of meat. This dietary restriction was first imposed in 675 CE, a little more than 100 years after Buddhism reached the archipelago, since a major tenet of the religion was that killing animals was wrong. Eating the flesh of animals was also considered unclean in Shinto. There was apparently substantial popular resistance to the early restrictions since records indicate that various emperors felt compelled to issue antimeat edicts. By the 10th century, meat eating had mostly ceased in Japan.

This Japanese popular cultural pattern was different than the situation in China and the Korean Peninsula. In these cultures, Buddhist priests and nuns were not allowed to eat meat or fish, but the restrictions did not apply to ordinary people. Japanese prohibitions against meat extended only to mammals. Although wild birds were eaten, early on chickens and roosters were considered messengers of Shinto kami, and their meat and eggs were not consumed until the 15th century. The Ainu and Japanese who lived in isolated mountainous areas hunted and ate wild animals, and there were no restrictions on eating seafood, including whales, which were considered to be fish. Chinese, Japanese, and Koreans all shared the practice of not drinking the milk of animals or consuming dairy products. The long prohibition on eating meat caused Japanese cuisine and its preparation to take on different forms than was the case in other East Asian countries.

Traditional Japanese cooking, with its reliance on vegetables and fish, emphasized serving fresh food in as close to its natural form as possible and keeping human manipulation of the cuisine at a minimum. Ideally, according to traditional Japanese beliefs, humans should not overdo food preparation. Even though the practice of eating sashimi, or mouth-sized slices of raw fish, came relatively late in Japan's history, sashimi especially appeals to Japanese because it is the quintessential underdone food. Traditional Japanese beliefs about food that accentuate the emphasis on the natural, the simple, and the understated are in harmony with a wide range of distinctive aesthetic forms including Zen gardens, the tea ceremony, traditional Japanese architecture, and haiku.

Although some foods, such as bread and sukiyaki, were introduced during the first period of European contact in the 16th century, foreign influences on Japanese food culture became much more substantial with the 1868 Meiji Restoration, which opened the archipelago to a wide variety of Western practices. Meiji political leaders decided that Japanese diets, at least the diets of those directly involved in the military and industry, needed to be changed if the country was to achieve its dual goals of military and economic parity with developed nations. Japanese were smaller than their Western counterparts, and the Meiji government promoted the addition of meat and diary products to the traditional diet in an effort to increase the size and strength of ordinary people. Even though meat dishes were adopted, their seasonings and modes of preparation were changed to better fit Japanese culture. Soy sauce and other Japanese seasonings were used to make meat taste better with rice. Since the Japanese used chopsticks, meat needed to be cut in smaller pieces than in the West when it was being prepared for the table.

After World War II, Japan's cuisine became even more internationalized with the introduction of meat dishes from China and the Korean Peninsula as well as the importation of food from every corner of the globe. In contemporary Japanese cities, numerous Chinese and Korean restaurants, French bakeries, and ethnic food from throughout the world are present. A variety of American fast-food restaurants—such as Baskin-Robbins, Dunkin' Donuts, McDonald's, and Wendy's—are in evidence in both cities and small towns. The Japanese also have their own varieties of fast-food chains. Even if the Western traveler is not inclined toward fast food, it is an interesting intercultural experience to visit at least once a Japanese Kentucky Fried Chicken or McDonald's to observe the similarities and differences in the Japanese varieties of these eateries.

Traditional Japanese cuisine is also much appreciated, and as will be evident later, some foreign dishes are now considered part of "traditional" food offerings. Traditional Japanese food is quite healthy and contains a small amount of red meat and fat. Some traditional dishes often taste very different from American or other Western cuisines, and many foreigners tend not to be neutral about Japanese food. They either like it a great deal or prefer to avoid many dishes.

Rice still retains, and will probably always retain, a special place in both Japan's food and its larger culture. However, as noted, rice consumption has steadily fallen. Also, rice's place in a typical meal has changed. Before the years of high economic growth, for many Japanese rice was often the main dish, and a few side dishes such as miso soup and pickled vegetables were also served. Today, rice is a regularly served but constant side dish.

Although many Japanese foods and beverages are still largely confined to Japan, recent globalization and extensive interactions between Japan, the United States, and Europe have dramatically increased the popularity of Japanese food and beverages elsewhere. Sushi and sashimi and Japanese restaurants are common in most of the United States and many European countries. Green tea is now one of the more trendy beverages in the United States, and both imports from Japan and Americanized versions are increasingly common. Ramen is particularly popular with young people and can be found in any American supermarket.

FOOD AS ART

The preparation, presentation, and serving of food are art forms at some level in many cultures, but this is particularly true in Japan. Display of both food and utensils is important as well as functional in eating. Traditionally, Japanese ate with chopsticks, and their use is still prevalent in Japan, although silverware is a common feature in Western-style restaurants. Traditionally, Japanese food is served in a variety of small dishes that come in various sizes and shapes and are made from different materials. Historically, Japanese homes did not have chairs, and people sat on the floor to eat, so it was important that tableware be small enough to fit the hand, making it easier to hold the bowl or plate close to the mouth to avoid spillage. Since men have larger hands than women or children, families will often have different-sized tableware for various members. Each family member generally has his or her own rice bowl; chopsticks, or *hashi*; and tea cup. Pottery, porcelain, lacquerware, wood, or glass is used and fits the occasion. In summer it is more pleasing to hold a smooth porcelain cup; during hot weather the cup is of less density and is often used for cool drinks. In winter the more substantial feel of pottery is appreciated, and heavier pottery better retains the warmth of a beverage without burning the hand of the one who holds the cup. Traditional Japanese cups do not have stems and are designed to be grasped by the whole hand. Bowls that contain food are not completely filled so that enough room is left for people to appreciate the artwork.

Serving seasonal foods and maintaining the connection between freshness, the seasons, and eating are recurring themes in Japan's food culture. In the fall, a platter of seafood and vegetables might be garnished with decorative autumn leaves to accentuate the season. Another general rule in culinary presentation is the selection of foods that present combinations of five colors commonly found in nature: greens, reds, yellows, browns, and black. In traditional Japanese meals, the cumulative visual and tactile effects of appropriate tableware and the carefully arranged presentation of an entire meal evoke striking impressions among both Japanese and foreigners.

Japanese have a reputation of being a practical people, and food is prepared and arranged for the convenience of eaters. Most meats and fruit are cut into small pieces that are easy to consume with chopsticks. Food is arranged on a table so that the cut pieces can be managed easily from left to right with the chopsticks in the right hand. Food is piled higher at the back of a plate than in the front also to make the food easier to negotiate with chopsticks. As in Europe, fish are served with the heads, but a whole fish will have the head to the left on a plate and the dorsal part away from the eater so that the head can be controlled by the left hand and the fish more easily eaten with the chopsticks in the right hand. It is customary to serve sashimi in odd numbers, which are considered lucky, and servings of five sashimi are common. Thus, the small flat dish in which the soy sauce comes is large enough, but not too large, for one sashimi at a time.

EATING IN RESTAURANTS AND HOMES

Although eating is both a life-sustaining and a social activity in any culture, the Japanese are particularly well known for going to great lengths in preparing and sharing meals. Eating in restaurants is even more popular in Japan than in the United States. A few years ago, the results of one study indicated that although Japan had less than half the population of the United States, the country contained almost as many restaurants. Because Japanese homes are substantially smaller than their U.S. counterparts, it is much more common for such social events as birthday and anniversary parties to occur in restaurants in Japan.

Japanese restaurants often specialize in particular dishes, and it is not uncommon for people who go out to eat to have one dish at a particular restaurant and then go to several more and enjoy other specialties. There are restaurants where a variety of dishes may be obtained as well. The most common kind is the *shokudo*, which may be found around train stations and in shopping areas. Shokudo serve both Western and Japanese dishes, and they often have set lunches that are available at good prices. Japanese pubs, or *izakaya*, usually specialize in such tasty snacks as grilled fish, soybeans, and meat kabobs called "yakitori." There are also specialized yakitori restaurants. The consumption of beer and sake is just as important as the food in yakitori restaurants. As already noted, during the high-growth years sushi bars became popular all over Japan and remain so today.

More formal traditional Japanese restaurants also serve a variety of dishes. The typical traditional Japanese restaurant will serve a large meal of many courses including both cooked and raw fish; a variety of vegetables, often served cold; some meat, egg, or tofu; a variety of sauces and condiments; soup; and rice. Beer, sake, and tea are the usual beverage accompaniments. *Kaiseki* restaurants that had their beginning as an adjunct to the tea ceremony, are elite traditional Japanese restaurants that are largely, but these days not entirely, vegetarian, and dining is often in private rooms.

In upscale establishments, and particularly when eating in a Japanese home, it is wise for the visitor to carefully examine how the food is arranged. As noted earlier in this section and elsewhere in the book, Japanese place as much emphasis on form as function and often take an artist's approach to food as a visual display. Although appropriate conduct at meals is discussed in the etiquette section of this book, visitors should be aware that tipping is not done in Japanese restaurants. If one leaves money on the table, there is a good chance it will be returned. It is a good idea to practice with *hashi* before going to Japan. Although many restaurants and homes have Western cutlery, visitors to Japan may also often find themselves in situations where only chopsticks are available.

COMMON JAPANESE DISHES

Confections Japanese confections tend to be beautiful but rarely appeal to Western tastes. Many, such as *manju* and the gelatinous *yokan*, are made with a sweet bean paste. They should be tried at least once, though, if possible accompanied by hot tea, and certainly admired for their visual beauty.

Curried Rice Curried rice, or *kare raisu*, in Japanese, is now a standard food in Japan but has international roots. Curried rice is an Indian dish that reached Japan via the United Kingdom. The dish can be found in or around virtually every train station that has a restaurant in Japan, and there are even chain curried rice establishments. Curried rice can be served in a variety of ways but is topped with beef or pork and a curry sauce thickened with flour, then garnished with pickled vegetables. The dish is served with varying levels of curry depending on the individual's tolerance for spicy food. Curried rice is a favorite with foreigners as well as Japanese.

Daishi *Daishi* is a commonly used stock that gives much Japanese food its distinctive light taste. The key ingredients in daishi are *konbu*, a tasty form of seaweed, and dried bonito fish flakes. Mountainous areas near the sea constitute the most desirable production areas for konbu since the humus of decayed deciduous tree leaves that reach the ocean are vital nutrients for the konbu. Daishi is used for miso soup, clear soups, stews, and a number of other dishes.

Miso Soup Along with rice, miso soup is a dish that will always be served with a traditional Japanese meal and is often eaten at breakfast as well. Miso (a fermented paste) is produced by steaming soybeans, then salting and crushing the beans. *Koji*, a mold that acts as the fermenting agent, is then added to the mixture. Miso is aged for several months to one or two years. Miso, which also can be made using barley or rice, is used as flavoring for a number of Japanese foods. Miso soup contains miso broth, tofu, and "wakame," a stringy dark-green seaweed.

Natto These sticky fermented soybeans are eaten mixed with chopped green onion and soy sauce and used as a topping for boiled rice. This nutritious traditional Japanese food is made by adding a rice straw bacteria that promote the fermentation process. Many foreigners have more difficulty eating natto because of its unusual smell and taste than is the case with other Japanese foods.

Miso soup is one of many ways that Japanese utilize the soy bean. US farmers benefit. (Dreamstime.com)

Niku-jaga The Japanese Imperial Navy developed this British-influenced dish in the late 19th century when it was attempting to feed sailors food that would make them stronger. Beef, potatoes, and onions are cooked in a broth flavored with soy sauce.

O-bento O-bento is not a food, but any visitor to Japan should know the term. O-bento are box lunches that are widely available, particularly at train stations. They normally consist of rice, chicken, or seafood and pickled vegetables. O-bento are usually tasty and nutritious. They can be simple or quite elaborate.

Okonomiyaki This has been described as a Japanese pancake, but forget the Western taste connotations—it's actually more akin to an omelet or frittata. Usually available at restaurants by the same name, okonomiyaki consists of meat or seafood and vegetables cooked in a cabbage and vegetable batter. A special sauce somewhat similar to American barbecue is poured over the concoction.

Ramen These are big bowls of wheat noodles in a meat broth. Ramen is served with a variety of toppings including sliced pork.

Sashimi and Sushi Both sashimi and sushi are raw fish cuisines. The practice of eating raw fish began in Japan only in the 19th century and was not widespread until after World War II when improvements in refrigeration, hygiene, and transportation made enjoyment of this now international cuisine pervasive in Japan. Sashimi is sliced raw

Sashimi are thin strips of a variety of raw fish served on rice. Preparing sashimi is a culinary art form. (Dreamstime.com)

fish that is dipped into a small bowl of shoyu (soy sauce) and wasabi, a type of hot horseradish. Standard accompaniments are steamed rice and *gari*, or pickled ginger. It is an extremely healthy food and is always served very fresh. Tuna, salmon, carp, squid, octopus, shrimp, and a variety of other seafood are used for sashimi. As a rule of thumb, however, such larger fish as tuna are more generally good for sashimi and sushi than smaller fish. The original word "sashimi," which formerly meant any sliced food, provides a hint of the importance of correctly slicing sashimi in its preparation.

In order to make sushi, the chef cuts a small piece of raw fish into a strip and serves it on a little rice canapé. The rice served with sushi has a bit of rice wine vinegar mixed into it, and a smidgen of wasabi paste often is nestled between the fish and rice. Sushi and sashimi, often consumed at sushi bars, now appear to be a permanent part of Japan, and world, food culture. There are an estimated 15,000 sushi bars in Tokyo alone, sushi bars are now found worldwide, and sushi and sashimi are available in the United States in a wide range of establishments including convenience stores and supermarkets.

Shabu-shabu This dish consists of thin beef slices and vegetables that are cooked by first dipping them in a light broth and sauces and then preparing them in a pot over a fire at the table. A seafood version is also available. Many restaurants in Japan specialize in shabu-shabu.

Shoyu (Soy Sauce) It is difficult to conceptualize a Japanese meal without soy sauce. It is used in seasoning a variety of soups and broths and in simmering other foods. It is also almost always on the table and sprinkled directly on food. Soy sauce is made with soybeans, salt, and water and then fermented for several months with *koji* mold. The liquid is then extracted from the mash.

Soba and Udon Soba is a thin brown buckwheat noodle. Udon are thick white wheat noodles. Both are served in a broth in cold and hot versions.

Sukiyaki Although sukiyaki was also not originally indigenous, the Japanese now claim it. The dish consists of a broth with various vegetables, clear noodles, and thinly sliced beef. Individual bites of sukiyaki are usually dipped into raw beaten egg, then eaten with rice. Sukiyaki is cooked at the table in a shallow iron pot that then is used as the common serving dish. Sukiyaki became a common dish in the 19th century after the Meiji Restoration due in part to government encouragement of meat consumption in an effort to increase the strength of Japanese.

Tempura The Portuguese originally introduced tempura, but the Japanese call it their own. Tempura consists of vegetables, fish, or shrimp lightly coated with batter and fried. It is eaten with special sauce and tends to be a favorite Japanese food for many Westerners.

Tonkatsu Tonkatsu is a deep-fried breaded pork cutlet served with a tangy brown sauce and raw shredded cabbage. It is now sometimes available made with chicken. Although this dish might sound basic, many Japanese and foreigners think it is delicious.

Tsukemono These are vegetables such as cucumber, eggplant, and daikon (Japanese radishes) that are pickled with various substances including miso paste, salted rice bran paste, soy sauce, and vinegar.

Unagi Unagi, or eel, is a popular although expensive Japanese delicacy. It is cooked over hot coals and coated with a special mixture of sake and soy sauce. Eel-liver soup, pickled vegetables, and rice are often served with unagi.

Yakitori These are kebabs of chicken or pork, sometimes with vegetables. They are eaten with a special sauce. Yakitori tends to be a favorite Japanese snack food.

COMMON BEVERAGES

Alcoholic

The consumption of alcoholic beverages is even more of a common part of business and social life in Japan than in the United States. Although some Japanese adults don't drink alcohol, as is the case in Europe, there are almost no Japanese who object to alcohol consumption on moral or religious grounds, as is the case with some Americans. Westerners often associate Japan with sake and are sometimes surprised to find that beer is as popular, if not more so, than the oldest and most famous Japanese alcoholic drink. During the Meiji Restoration, the Japanese learned beer brewing techniques from the Germans, and Japanese beer has a reputation for high quality. Recently the variety of brews available has expanded, and there are small breweries featuring specialty beers available in Japan. Sake, or rice wine, is the traditional Japanese alcoholic beverage and is also quite popular. Sake is part of traditional Japanese culture and is often served at celebrations and festivals. There are several types of sake, which is served hot in small cups or, increasingly during hot months, cold. *Shochu* is a quite potent distilled spirit made of sweet potatoes and has become more popular in recent years. Domestic and imported liquors are also available in Japan, and in recent years both imported and domestically produced wine has become increasingly popular.

Nonalcoholic

Japanese green tea is the most pervasive nonalcoholic drink in Japan and comes in several varieties, including roasted versions. Although it contains caffeine, several studies have indicated that green tea may be a quite healthy beverage. It contains vitamin C and may have properties that inhibit certain cancers. The Japanese drink it hot and cold and have a certain sense of national pride in O-cha because of its links with religion, cultural aesthetics, and literature. Chinese dark tea (oolong) is also widely available in Japan.

Coffee has been popular in Japan since Europeans and Americans introduced the beverage. Coffeehouses have, over the past 60 years, become a part of the Japanese urban landscape and were widespread in Japan when they were largely confined to major American cities. Coffeehouses often serve as meeting places for friends, business contacts, and company employees who want to escape for a respite from the office. Usually breakfast is available at coffeehouses as well, and Starbucks found fertile ground when franchises began to open some time ago. Japanese coffee tends to be stronger and richer than mainstream American coffee, and there usually are no free refills. Iced coffee has been more popular in Japan for much longer than in the United States and is available in coffeehouses, restaurants, and vending machines.

The Japanese enjoy a variety of soft drinks, and fruit-based drinks are in plentiful supply at vending machines and convenience stores. Drink vending machines are more a part of Japan's cultural landscape than is the case in the United States and can be found everywhere, including bus stops in remote rural areas. For further information on Japanese food, consult the Annotated Bibliography of Recommended Works on Japan.

REFERENCES

Komei, Tsuchiya. "Japanese Meals with International Roots." *Nipponia* 36 (March 2006): 18–19.

Koyama, Hirohisa. "Eat It Raw: How to Prepare Sushi and Sashimi." *Nipponia* 36 (March 2006): 20–23.

Moore, Richard. "The Japan Rice Paradox." *Education About Asia* 9, No. 3 (Winter 2004): 10–13.

Mutsuda, Yukie. "An Appreciation of Fermented Foods." *Japan+* 4, No. 12 (April 2007): 40–45.

Naomichi, Ishige. "Food: Another Perspective on Japanese Cultural History." *Nipponia* 36 (March 2006): 5–7.

Ohnuki-Tierney, Emiko. "Rice as Self: Japanese Identities through Time." *Education About Asia* 9, No. 3 (Winter 2004): 4–9.

Otani, Hiromi. "Tempting Arts: Tableware and Food Presentation." *Nipponia* 36 (March 2006): 8–11.

Rowthorn, Chris, Ray Bartlett, Andres Bender, Michael Clark, and Matthew D. Firestone. *Lonely Planet: Japan*. 10th ed. Oakland, CA: Lonely Planet Publications, 2007.

Sanada, Kuniko. "Intriguing Tastes, Naturally." *Nipponia* 36 (March 2006): 16–17.

Torikai, Shin-ichi, and Kuniko Sanada. "Traditional Seasonings for Today's Tables." *Nipponia* 36 (March 2006): 12–15.

Sports and Leisure in Japan

ASOBI

Asobi is the Japanese term for both "play" and "playing." Contemporary Japanese pursue an amazing variety of recreational activities. However, many forms of sports and leisure in Japan are combinations of variants of indigenous activities that existed since the dawn of time, recreational pursuits borrowed from early China, and Western games and leisure that have been modified to fit Japanese needs.

OTAKU

This term, which originally was a polite and formal way of saying "you," became over the last three decades a word that media and social critics as well as young people themselves employed to define a person who tended to be extremely knowledgeable about minutia relating to a specific hobby. Originally, otaku were involved in anime and manga but have broadened their interests to include everything from video games to pop music stars to fantasy play. Otaku are the object of much criticism in Japan because they are viewed as antisocial and wasting their lives on trivialities. The otaku phenomenon is now global as young people elsewhere, particularly those obsessed with manga and anime, proudly call themselves otaku. *Cosplay*, or the hobby of dressing up in costume, has become a big part of Japanese otaku culture, as has the practice of meeting with like-minded peers.

Uniquely contemporary Japanese forms of fun also exist that have been exported elsewhere. Today, Japanese popular recreational culture has drawn global aficionados, most of whom are young.

More than two decades ago when this author first began to study and teach about Japan at the university level, most students interested in Japan were motivated by an admiration for Japan's economy. Today, "interest in Japanese culture" is one of the most frequent answers young Japanophiles cite for their fascination with the country. What young people usually are referring to is an attraction to Japan's vibrant popular culture. *Japan Times* columnist Roger Pulvers has labeled this global fascination "MASK," or love of manga, anime, sushi, and karaoke.

How have Japanese amused themselves through history, and what does it tell us about Japanese culture? What are popular sports and leisure activities in Japan today? Although what follows can only be a somewhat superficial preview of this broad topic, this section of the book will provide readers with some sense of how Japanese have played through the ages as well as today.

TRADITIONAL SPORTS AND LEISURE: PAST AND PRESENT

Like other societies, many of Japan's earliest forms of sports and leisure first developed in conjunction with either religious rites or festivals. A good example is sumo wrestling, whose origins could go back as far as 2,000 years, yet the sport remains popular today. The earliest sumo matches, as was the case with horse racing, tug-of-war, and archery matches, were originally held as part of religious rites either thanking the gods for a good harvest, attempting to please the divinities, or even trying to foretell the future. Later, the focus changed from human interactions with kami to an emphasis on the individual competitors and the sport.

Sumo is a duel between two gigantic men wearing only loincloths that usually quickly ends when the first wrestler loses by touching the ground with any part of the body or being forced out of the ring. Every year there are six major professional tournaments, each lasting 15 days. Thousands attend sumo tournaments, and a much larger audience watches the events on TV.

Even though sumo is now a modern sport with about 700 professional wrestlers and many amateurs, sumo's links with its ancient origin remain. Grand champion–ranked wrestlers, who enter the ring for opening ceremonies, wear a special cloth around their waists that is of the same configuration as the twisted straw ropes that are often seen in Shinto shrines. The cloth is a symbol of the sacred rank the wrestler has attained. Before wrestlers crouch to go into action, they throw salt on the ring, purifying it.

Eventually, rites associated with Shinto and local deities or kami developed into festivals, or matsuri, that are addressed elsewhere in this book. However, festivals as well as holidays (see the section on holidays in this book) throughout history and today give people the chance to dress in costumes, dance, get out of the workday routine, and generally have a good time. During matsuri, revelers carrying the heavy portable shrine, or *mikoshi*, which houses the local kami, run through crowds, adding to the general euphoria.

Shinto also emphasized the beauty and divinity of nature. This indigenous Japanese cultural proclivity was enhanced in the dawn of the Heian period and even before that era through the importation of sophisticated Chinese cultural pursuits. Heian aristocrats had ample time for leisure since they were freed from work. These elites engaged in poetry contests celebrating nature, flower and cherry blossom viewing, and flower contests in where participants vied to see who had produced the most beautiful varieties of particular flowers. The basic Buddhist tenet of transience was particularly appreciated by Japanese and has been long epitomized by the short-lived but much-celebrated cherry blossom. Later in Japanese history, women would come to wear special kimonos for cherry blossom time, and dancing, singing, drinking, and eating characterized the spring ritual. Today, many Japanese still enjoy cherry blossom viewing festivals in the spring as well as moon and flower viewing.

Heian aristocrats adopted other Chinese imports including indoor board games similar to checkers. Dice, believed to have been first developed in the ancient Indus River valley civilizations, probably came to Japan via China as well. There are early written references to gambling, which is still a popular leisure activity. Other Chinese forms of recreation included music and art that Japanese often changed to fit their tastes.

Later periods of Japanese history brought new forms of physical activities, some of which are still practiced. *Budo*, or "the martial way," is a good example. What we know in the West as the martial arts began in Japan during the later part of the Heian period with the rise of the class that would subsequently become samurai. Originally used in combat, by the Tokugawa period (1600–1868) seven martial arts—swordplay (known today as kendo, or "the way of the sword"), archery, spearmanship, horseback riding, jujutsu (now known as judo), firearms, and military strategy—constituted, along with academic subjects, the required education of the samurai.

During the Tokugawa period, martial arts were almost never used in combat since most of the era was peaceful. However, learning the martial arts constituted more than acquiring physical skills since training encompassed a philosophical foundation influenced by Buddhism, Confucianism, and Daoism. Typically martial arts students learned meditation techniques that ideally resulted in a calm, detached demeanor while engaging in these physical activities. By the early 20th century, kendo and judo were taught in the public schools, and kendo and judo student and adult clubs are still popular throughout Japan. Karate, perhaps the most high-profile self-defense art associated with Japan in the West, though popular today, was not a traditional Japanese martial art. Allegedly begun in India, it was transmitted to China and evolved into a practice that later came to Okinawa. Okinawa became a part of Japan, and the sport had reached the main islands by the 1920s. Karate's popularity declined for a bit after World War II but began to grow again in the mid-1950s and is again popular in contemporary Japan.

Tokugawa urban culture also brought such new forms of literature and poetry as kabuki theater and haiku, which are addressed elsewhere in this book. Even before the Tokugawa years, markets developed around temples and shrines that contained stalls and later shops selling unusual or colorful goods. Today, the Japanese are becoming more famous each year throughout the world for their avid pursuit of shopping, but this affinity is not new. Also, there were travel booms during the Tokugawa years that centered on pilgrimages to famous Shinto shrines, and Edo (now Tokyo) inns even sold passes that customers could use to stay at other inns outside Japan's largest city.

By the mid- and late 19th century and early 20th century, a wide variety of Western amusements—such as tennis, baseball, golf, soccer, jazz, Western classical music, and movies—all reached Japan. Today, the Japanese have one of the widest ranges of traditional, imported, and indigenous contemporary ways to "play" as people anywhere in the world.

CONTEMPORARY JAPAN: SPORTS

In addition to traditional sports, Japanese engage in a wide variety of sports ranging from marathon running to basketball, volleyball, and even American-style football. Volleyball is particularly popular at the school and university levels, and there is a professional league, which is also the case with basketball. However, presently baseball is the most popular sport in Japan, but soccer is challenging it in popularity, and golf is a high-profile sport as well.

Baseball is now so popular in Japan that it is considered part of the culture and not viewed primarily as an American import. In the early 1870s, Horace Wilson, an American teaching in Japan, introduced the sport. By the 1930s, American all-stars were visiting the country and playing against Japanese teams. Although baseball was suppressed during World War II, it came right back during the American occupation. There are a host of reasons given for the resilience of baseball in Japan ranging from the aesthetics of the beautifully ordered baseball diamond to the importance of form in practice. Japanese baseball players are sometimes compared to

COFFEE HOUSES

The Japanese enjoyed the first Western-style coffee house when one opened in 1889 in Tokyo and have loved them ever since. Coffee is a great favorite of the Japanese, and coffeehouses have evolved over the years into places of refuge from work where customers can linger over coffee and light breakfasts. Some coffee houses specialize in certain kinds of music, particularly jazz, and many also have a relaxed atmosphere where customers can leisurely read manga or other kinds of magazines. There are Japanese chains and independent coffee houses, and Starbucks has been a successful import as well.

egoless, Zen-influenced samurai. Although academics and other experts hotly debate this comparison and the related subject of exactly why baseball is popular in Japan, there is little question the sport will always have a significant following. It is played at all levels, beginning with little league.

The National High School Baseball Championship is the most viewed amateur sports event in Japan. Every August, after a series of regional tournaments, 49 teams, one from each of Japan's 47 prefectures, and an extra one each from Hokkaido and Tokyo prefectures, fight each other for the right to be national upper secondary

Baseball is popular in Japan as in the US. Crowds are typically more lively at a professional Japanese game than is the case in the US. (Courtesy of Lucien Ellington)

THE AMBIENCE OF JAPANESE BASEBALL

Japanese baseball crowds and their enthusiasm make their American counterparts look asleep. There are large cheering sections complete with flags that maintain continual cheers when their team is at bat. A larger variety of noisemakers are sold in the stadium, which add to the constant high energy level that is present during Japanese baseball. Japanese particularly like souvenirs, and the range of choices inside and outside the stadium equals or exceeds what is found at major league stadiums in the United States. More Japanese teams seem to have cute cartoonlike characters as mascots, for example, the Yokohama Bay Stars, than is the case in the United States. Also, the range of food and drink, everything from Johnny Walker Scotch to sushi to popcorn, is available not only at concession stands but often through vendors in the stands. The fundamentals of the game are the same in the United States and Japan, but in general, the high energy level is a distinct feature of Japanese baseball.

school champions. The single-elimination tournament is held in the venerable Hanshin Koshien Stadium near Kobe and Osaka, and the final round of games is nationally broadcast on television and followed by millions. The high school players who advance in the Koshien tournament have traditionally been idolized by many, and a number of traditions surround the tournament, including team members collecting small amounts of "sacred dirt" from the stadium immediately after their elimination. The tournament is also seen as a gateway to Japanese professional baseball, and some of Japan's biggest stars—such as Ichiro Suzuki, Hideki Matsui, and Daisuke Matsuzaka, who have become U.S. stars—first rose to prominence in this legendary sporting event.

Japan has two professional major leagues as well as minor league teams, and a Japan series occurs each fall to determine the national major league champion. Although baseball is played essentially the same way in Japan and the United States, one need only watch Japanese baseball on television or attend a game to quickly observe some significant cultural differences on and off the field. Although this is changing because of the influence of foreign players, Japanese teams tend to approach the game in a somewhat more conservative manner than is the case in the United States. A batter is even more likely to sacrifice bunt with a runner at first and less than two outs in Japan than in the United States.

Regardless of whether there is or isn't a "samurai ethos" permeating the game, Japanese players, especially pitchers, tend to put in more hours practicing than is often the case in the United States. Off the field, the cultural contrasts are even more striking. The atmosphere at a typical Japanese professional baseball game much more resembles that of an American football than baseball game. There are organized cheering sections that seem to engage in nonstop exhortations for their team, and the crowd has the intensity level of American football fans.

This scene is of a cheering section at professional baseball game in Japan. The cheering sections remind some Americans of what might be heard at a college football game. (Courtesy of Lucien Ellington)

Because of the group solidarity the Japanese feel about such homegrown international stars as Ichiro Suzuki, Daisuke Matsuzaka, and Hideo Nomo, often American games in which these players participate are broadcast live in Japan despite the time differences. Recently, however, another sports import, soccer, is becoming more and more popular and, some report, at baseball's expense.

Japan appears to be going through a serious soccer boom that all started with the creation of a professional league, the J. League. The first match on May 15, 1993, in Tokyo National Stadium drew 59,626 fans, and growth has been steady. The J. League started with 10 clubs; now there are teams on the four major Japanese islands, and a second division began in 1995. In a recent year, 8.5 million fans attended J. League games, making Japan well within the top 20 in the world in professional soccer attendance. Soccer interest has mushroomed at all levels. Japan participated in its first World Cup in France in 1998. In 2002, Japan and the Republic of Korea cohosted the World Cup, and this event received enormous media attention in both countries. Japanese government statistics now indicate that among middle school boys, soccer has eclipsed baseball in popularity, and the sport is also gaining in popularity among women. A semiprofessional women's league now exists.

Golf has come along way since the first Westerners opened the Kobe Golf Club in 1903 with about 120 members. Golf, while less popular as a spectator sport in Japan than baseball or soccer, has been a favorite of Japanese salarymen for several decades. Japan's lack of usable space has made golf enormously expensive compared to the United States. In the late 1980s at the peak of the Japanese economic bubble, memberships at the best private clubs could be as high as $4 million, and groups of investors who bought private golf clubs as investments further drove up prices (Rowley and Tashiro 2006). Although private memberships have plummeted in the last decade and a half, they are still quite high, from close to $700,000 in the most elite clubs to lower private membership fees that range from $8,500 to $25,000 or more (Rowley and Tashiro 2006). Public courses also exist in Japan, but it is problematic getting reservations, especially on weekends, and people wait for months.

Many new private courses are dispensing with expensive membership-only stipulations and fees to attract casual players, especially during the week. Typically, private clubs feature expert women caddies, ornate club facilities, and in many cases hot baths, which drive up costs. In traditional clubs, making a hole in one has meant that the "lucky" golfer was obligated to buy presents for hundreds of members, and insurance companies have even offered "hole-in-one" coverage. This corporate culture is slowly changing as more diverse kinds of people are now taking up golf.

Despite the costs, more than 11 million Japanese play golf, and there are indications that the diversity of those who take up the sport is increasing (Rowley and Tashiro 2006). Although men are much more likely to play golf than women, there are indications that more women are taking up the game. One reason might be the graying of Japan's population, many of whom are relatively affluent. At any rate, with the end of Japan's more than decade-long economic malaise, golf seems to be making a comeback. Although there are conflicting data, some surveys indicate that over 10 percent of adults rank golf as their favorite sport to play, making it the most popular adult-participant sport in Japan. However, many of the respondents, maybe even a majority, infrequently actually play a course but instead go to public driving ranges that may be found throughout the country. They are often large multiple-story constructions with rows of cubicles on each floor, allowing relatively large numbers of people to hit balls into the gigantic green nets that cover the sides of the driving ranges.

MAJOR POPULAR CULTURE PURSUITS: "MASK" AND MORE

As noted earlier, when people around the world, especially young people, experience Japanese culture these days, usually the object of attention and experience will be on manga, anime, sushi, or karaoke. Three out of four of these now-global popular cultural icons are discussed at length in this section. Sushi (thin strips of raw fish embedded in a rice canapé) and its variant, sashimi (sliced raw fish), are discussed in detail in the food section of this chapter.

However, both of these delicacies deserve a brief note in this section for two reasons. Sushi bars, almost all of which serve sashimi as well, permeate Japan. Going to sushi bars with friends is a leading example of the Japanese propensity, even more than people in many other cultures, to pass leisure times in eating establishments. Sushi and sashimi are also important because perhaps more than any other Japanese cuisine, they've become such a part of global popular culture. Many younger aficionados in various countries don't even associate it with Japan. Before manga, anime, and karaoke are highlighted, two subjects are addressed that aren't part of global leisure activities, but help us better understand what Japanese do for fun, deserve attention: the role of hobbies and pachinko.

Many Japanese consider it somewhat abnormal for an individual not to have a hobby. Typically, one of the first conversational expressions after greetings that Japanese language students learn is "*Anata no shumi wa nan desuka*?" or "What is your hobby?" Japanese pursue hobbies that range from such traditional practices as tanka or haiku poetry, ikebana (flower arranging), and tea ceremony to playing bluegrass music and engaging in Jung discussion clubs. Clubs of like-minded enthusiasts are particularly popular in Japan, and in the late 1960s several national newspapers started cultural centers in large cities where hundreds of people could gather on Saturdays and in the evenings to take classes ranging from kimono sewing to underwater photography. These cultural center students often go on to form their own clubs with fellow enthusiasts or take part in the large number of established organizations and clubs that promote a particular leisure activity. There are also town halls, women's centers, and special classes for the elderly, all of which receive public funds and provide opportunities for many Japanese to pursue a wide range of hobbies. Japanese people engage in a wide variety of other kinds of leisure activities including enjoying television, playing video games, engaging in both domestic and international travel, and playing pachinko that might or might not be considered by the practitioner or others as a "hobby." Pachinko is largely unknown outside Japan but is so popular with Japanese that it warrants similar in-depth treatment as the more famous and now-global leisure pursuits.

PACHINKO

The most controversial and, to many foreigners and Japanese nonaficionados, incomprehensible Japanese popular cultural phenomenon of all may be pachinko. Pachinko began in the United States in the 1920s as a children's toy that was called the "Corinthian game." The game was a primitive form of pinball. Players would shoot little balls through a slot on the right side of the board and try to get the balls past barriers and into little holes. The game was introduced to Japan in the 1920s and became popular in candy stores. Because adults liked it too and there were crowds in the little shops containing the machines, someone had the bright idea of placing the game machine in a vertical position.

In the years after World War II, pachinko parlors began to sprout up like mushrooms on the Japanese landscape. Today one can find colorful and somewhat garish pachinko establishments in rural villages that don't even have movie theaters. There are an estimated 14,600 pachinko outlets in Japan, according to police estimates, and approximately 16.5 million players throughout Japan (Shimizu 2007). A visit to brightly adorned, neon-covered pachinko parlors for the novice is usually a truly bizarre experience. There are rows and rows of electronic machines emitting

ONSEN

Hot springs are a recreational pastime that Japanese have enjoyed for centuries and, given Japan's mountainous topography, are numerous. Onsen have grown into a major industry, and Japanese use them for recreation and for allegedly medicinal purposes. Often, famous onsen have inns and are located amid beautiful scenery. The routine is to bathe before entering the onsen; sit and soak, often before a picture window with beautiful scenery outside; get out, use cool water, and have a beverage; and then repeat the process, often several times. Onsen are enjoyed collectively, usually, but not always, in segregated baths for men and women.

incredible levels of noise. People sit transfixed for hours in front of the machines, feeding them little silver balls, and if some of the balls end up in the right holes, the machines make noise and spit out numbers of additional silver balls. Pachinko is considered adult entertainment rather than gambling, but winners who collect large numbers of balls can trade them in for such gifts as ashtrays, lighters, perfume, golf balls, and coffee beans. Successful players can then take their booty right outside to a small shop and sell their prizes for cash. In a recent year, the industry earned revenues including those from related "pachislot" slot machines that totaled approximately 27.50 trillion yen, or about US$275 million (Shimizu 2007). This is considerably more money than the annual revenues of vehicles produced by Japanese domestic automobile manufacturers.

Pachinko was once patronized for the most part by middle-aged men, but the industry has successfully expanded its consumer markets, and Japanese of all ages and both genders now play the game. There are pachinko cable TV stations, and players can learn through cell phones and other technology up-to-the minute reports of locations of machines that are yielding the most balls. Japanese critics of pachinko are numerous and vocal, and they constantly berate players for the hours they spend in front of the machines.

Government authorities have tightened regulations on parlors because of the heavy debts incurred by many players. An even more serious problem with pachinko relates to national security. An estimated 3,000 parlors are operated by Koreans living in Japan with links to the North Korean government, and although it is almost impossible to estimate accurately, reliable sources indicate that annually approximately 200 billion yen illegally reach North Korea as a result of pachinko (Shimizu 2007). However, the industry, despite declines in patrons and revenues over the last few years, is a huge one as evidenced by the above earning and player statistics. Although more famous outside Japan than pachinko, Zen meditation has never even begun to attract the number of adherents as this most peculiar recreational pursuit.

MANGA

Manga, literally translated as "whimsical pictures," are Japanese comic books. Although most popular in Japan, manga are becoming part of global popular culture. If American or other Western readers of this book wonder what the big deal is about comic books, they should visit large chain bookstores in their own countries and examine the manga sections because this Japanese popular culture hit is now available in more and more countries. Although more manga are sold in Japan than in all the world's countries combined, recent annual statistics for manga sales in the United States were estimated at $200 million (Wiseman 2007).

The roots of Japanese fascination with cartoons go far back in history to 12th-century paintings that depict cartoonlike characters. By the late 19th century, cartoons had become a regular feature in magazines, with serialization often occurring. Manga really took off after World War II. Japanese-style manga are very thick, often running to hundreds of pages, and are available in a wide variety of places including bookstores, train kiosks, and coffeehouses. The most popular manga are also serialized and can be published for years if there is consumer demand. In addition to the great length of manga and the long runs of the most popular series, another characteristic that separates manga from the comic books of other nations is the incredible number of topics encompassed in the genre. Girls' manga, adult women's manga, science fiction manga, mahjong manga, historical manga, business manga, action manga, and pornographic manga are all circulating throughout Japan.

Much, if not most, manga does not address complex issues, but some of the most high-profile series, for example, *Vagabond*, based on the life of the historical swordsman Minamoto Musashi, explore such themes as how life transcends those who live it and the process of subjugating a more powerful foe than oneself. Often manga stories will take a slice-of-life approach addressing real issues in Japanese society. Moyoco Anno's long-running *Hataraki Man*, or *Working Man*, is a good example as it depicts the trials and tribulations of a hard-working woman magazine editor and her interpersonal relations amid real-life office situations. Anno, a woman, has created a product that has been in part responsible for the sale of approximately 1.8 million copies of the magazine in which it is serialized, and now there is an anime based on her character (Okada 2007, 5).

Although children and young people consume most manga, as can be gathered from the diversity of topics mentioned the genre appeals to people of all ages. It is quite common to see salarymen on trains and subways wearing Brooks Brothers suits and reading manga. Famous serialized manga characters and plots have included *Ashita No Joe* (*Tomorrow's Joe*), a young Tokyo working-class boxer who battles his way to the top; *Doraemon*, a children's manga featuring a robotic cat from the future who befriends a 10-year-old (also the subject of very popular movies and a TV show); and *Fireball*, a science fiction story in which a superpsychic battles a megacomputer. *Dragonball* and *Pokemon* are other examples of children's manga that have become popular in foreign countries including the United States.

The artists who draw and write manga are now becoming cult heroes in many countries. Probably the most famous manga artist of all is the late Tezuka Osamu, a

KAWAI ("CUTE")

Kawai translates as "cute" and originally was much closer to the English meaning but now has broader connotations in Japan and is certainly a part of the leisure life of the country. Sumo wrestlers, cartoon characters, comedy teams, fashion models, pop stars, Tokyo Disney Land, and, of course, Hello Kitty can all earn the label kawai. Pop culture historians date the expansion of the meaning of the word back to the 1980s. Since then, an entire kawai industry has emerged. Kids are inundated with kawai toys. Although the term is bandied about much more by adult women than men, a man wearing a Mickey Mouse tie could be complimented for being kawai. Kawai became a fashion statement years ago in Japan.

physician who in his 44-year career produced everything from a multiple volume series on the Buddha to an examination of the Nazi era. He was also a pioneer in the development of anime. The most popular manga will often end up as anime or in video game format. Manga sales, however, despite totaling $4.1 billion annually in Japan for the most recent year when statistics are available, have slumped compared to the 1980s, and artists are even creating cell phone manga to keep the industry vibrant (Wiseman 2007).

ANIME

Anime, which is an English loanword, are Japanese animated videos and movies characterized by highly stylized colorful art. The Japanese were wild about Walt Disney animation from the time it first appeared in the country, but anime is a much more extensive popular culture trend in Japan than Disney cartoons are in the United States. Although anime is popular with children, there is a large adult market for Japanese animation. The variety of subjects that end up as anime far surpasses the range of animated cartoons produced in the United States. Fantasy, history, mythology, religion, and science fiction–related topics intended for adult audiences end up as anime in Japan. Retellings of Japan's ancient myths such as the creation of the archipelago, a four-hour epic about a demon terrorizing Tokyo in the 1920s, and a science fiction film about an archeologist searching for God's last message to humanity constitute just a smattering of the wide-ranging subjects included in this genre.

Japanese anime has developed an international following in a number of foreign countries, particularly among teenagers and college students. Throughout the United States, anime clubs exist in universities, high schools, and even public libraries. One example is Hayao Miyazaki's *Spirited Away*, whose protagonist, a 10-year-old girl named Chihiro, never liked to travel or explore anything new. Then, when she is with her parents and they are taking a shortcut to their new home, Chihiro ends up being transported to a spirit world and encounters situations reminiscent of Lewis Carroll's

Alice's Adventures in Wonderland. This anime, which was popular in the United States, won its creator the first academy award for an anime in 2003. However, anime had been popular in the United States for more than a decade by this time. Several anime that became popular in the U.S., including the early 1990s *Sailor Moon* television series, begun as manga shortly before being produced as anime.

KARAOKE

Karaoke's literal meaning is "empty orchestra." This musical leisure pursuit that provides people the opportunity to sing their favorite song accompanied by a stereo-quality musical sound track originated in Japan in the early 1970s and is now an indispensable part of the nightlife there and throughout other parts of the world. In karaoke, patrons sing their favorite songs while an automated machine plays the music, and the lyrics are available on video prompters. At first, karaoke was a feature in nightclubs, but increasingly in Japan, parties of 5 to 10 people will rent karaoke boxes, bring food and refreshments inside, and sing to their hearts' content in relative privacy.

Daisuke Inoue, its inventor, was a musician who started playing with a band in 1970 in Kobe clubs, backing up salarymen who sung their favorite songs. One patron who owned a small company and liked to sing with Inoue's band was going on an overnight trip to a hot springs and wanted Inoue to accompany him and play music so that he could sing. Inoue, who had another engagement, provided the businessman with a sound track of his favorite song and was paid for his services. Inspired, Inoue and his friends made 11 karaoke boxes equipped with tapes and amplifiers and leased them to local clubs. Although larger companies, rather than karaoke's inventors, ended up making huge profits, Inoue changed Japanese and world popular culture. Karaoke is a worldwide industry that produces approximately $10 billion in annual revenues. There is an international karaoke competition that was represented in a recent year by candidates from 20 countries. The Karaoke Channel on digital cable and satellite TV; karaoke tracks for cell phones, computers, and iPods; and even karaoke taxis in Bangkok are just small parts of the movement. In Japan, an estimated 280,000 karaoke establishments cater to estimates that run as high as more than 53 million people (Iyer 1999).

CONCLUSION: CELL PHONES

Although many contemporary Japanese continue to pursue some of the sports and leisure activities that have roots in the early history of the country, at the same time, the archipelago today seems to be on the cutting edge of some of the world's most unusual leisure activities. One recreational trend that is becoming pervasive in Japan and makes such popular culture pursuits as anime or manga, which seem avant-garde in the West, appear somewhat traditional, is the creative use of cell phones for fun. Not only do Japanese text message their friends, negotiate pachinko, download manga, and play anime-based games on their cell phones, but now thousands of primarily young women are writing cell phone novels.

Of the 10 best-selling novels in Japan in 2007, five were originally written on cell phones. Although people have been able to download classic novels and read them on their cell phones for some time, the cell phone novel boom took off in 2004 when Japanese providers began to offer unlimited text messaging as part of a flat monthly fee for users. A number of young women began to upload their works in progress to Maho i-Land, an already-existing community Web site that made it possible for users to upload novels from their cell phones for other readers' comments. Writers aren't paid for their work, but a few have earned money and fame when publishers have reproduced the novels as original books. Maho i-Land now has 6 million users and more than 1 million "mobile" novels at its site (Kane 2007).

The novels, which are almost all about love and other interpersonal relations issues, employ simplified language peppered with expressions, simile, and musical notes that are often fully understood only by this particular subculture. Cell phone authors typically only use their first names. The number one 2007 novel in Japan, *Love Sky*, authored by Mika, was, according to the owners of the Web site where it was downloaded, read by 20 million people on cell phones or computers and then sold 1.2 million hard copies and was made into a movie (Kane 2007). The plot, about a boy who breaks up with his girlfriend to ease her future pain of watching him die of cancer, is a typical plot in the genre. Rin, who wrote a novel titled *If You* about tragic love between two childhood friends, did so during her senior year in high school while commuting to a part-time job over a six-month period. Her work was first voted the number one cell phone novel and then was published in book form and sold 400,000 copies, making it Japan's fifth-leading novel of 2007. Rin's mother didn't believe her when she told her parent she was coming out with a novel.

Although literary critics are shocked and bemoan the lack of setting, simple language, and exclusive focus on love in the cell phone novels, authors of this genre almost all mention how they grew up using e-mail and cell phones and, significantly, reading substantial manga. So one form of popular culture recreation, with the aid of technology, is now birthing another form.

As mentioned at the outset, this section is only an introduction to how the Japanese engage in asobi, or play. However, hopefully readers realize what interesting options exist for asobi in a culture that for much of its almost 2,000-year history has been integrating its own traditions with what is most attractive from the outside world.

REFERENCES

"Golf." *Japan Guide*. June 9, 2002. http://www.japan-guide.com/e/e2082.html (accessed February 2008).

"Golf, Japanese Style." *Japan Golf Tours*. 2005. http://www.japan-golf-tours.com/japan-golf-tour-information.html (accessed February 2008).

Hayford, Charles. "Samurai Baseball vs. Baseball in Japan." *Japan Focus*, April 4, 2007. http://japanfocus.org/products/details/2398 (accessed February 2008).

"History of Anime." *Anime Sekai*. 2005. http://www.animesekai.net/history.html (accessed February 2008).

Itasaka, Gen, ed. "Karate" in *Kodansha Encyclopedia of Japan*. Vol. 4. New York: Kodansha International, 1983.

———, ed. "Martial Arts" in *Kodansha Encyclopedia of Japan*. Vol. 5. New York: Kodansha International, 1983.

Iyer, Pico. "Daisuke Inoue." *Time Asia* 154, No. 7/8 (August 23–30, 1999). http://www.time.com/time/asia/asia/magazine/1999/990823/inoue1.html (accessed February 2008).

"Japanese Golf Slump." *Nightly Business Report*, January 9, 2006. http://www.pbs.org/nbr/site/research/educators/060106_08a (accessed February 2008).

J. League: The Official Site. http://www.j-league.or.jp/eng (accessed April 2008).

Kane, Yukari Iwatani. "Ring! Ring! Ring! In Japan. Novelists Find a New Medium." *The Wall Street Journal Online*. 26 September 2007. http://online.wsj.com/public/article/SB119074882854738970.

Kondo, Hisashi. "Interview: Roger Pulvers." *Japan +*, Vol. 4, No. 11 (March 2007): 36–39.

"Koshien Stadium." *Wikipedia*. 2008. http://en.wikipedia.org/wikipedia.org/wiki/Koshien_Stadium.

Mitsukuni, Yoshida, Tanaka Ikko, and Sesoko Tsune, eds. *Asobi: The Sensibilities at Play*. Tokyo: Cosmo Public Relations Corp., 1987.

Okada, Shin'ichi, et al. "Manga Mania." *Japan+* 4, No. 11 (March 2007): 2–21.

Rowley, Ian, and Hiroko Tashiro. "The Golf Bug Is Biting Japan Again." *Business Week*, October 23, 2006. http://www.businessweek.com/magazine/content/06_43/b4006102.htm (accessed February 2008).

Sanchez, Frank. "History of Anime." *Anime Info*. 2003. http://www.animeinfo.org/animeu/hist101.html (accessed February 2008).

Schilling, Mark. *The Encyclopedia of Japanese Pop Culture*. New York: Weatherhill, 1997.

Shimizu, Kaho. "Pachinko Seeks to Shed Shady Image as Market Shrinks." *Japan Times Online*, September 25, 2007. http://search.japantimes.co.jp/cgi-bin/nn20070925i1.html (accessed February 2008).

"Sports." *Kids Web Japan*. 2007. http://web-japan.org/kidsweb/explore/sports/index.html (accessed February 2008).

"Sumo." *Kids Web Japan*. 2007. http://web-japan.org/kidsweb/virtual/sumo/sumo01.html (accessed February 2008).

Suzuki, Daisetz T. *Zen and Japanese Culture*. Rutland, VT: Charles E. Tuttle Co., 1959.

Tsutsui, William. "Nerd Nation: Otaku and Youth Subcultures in Contemporary Japan." *Education About Asia* 12, No. 3 (Winter 2008): 12–18.

Wiseman, Paul. "Manga Comics Losing Longtime Hold on Japan." *USA Today Online*, October 18, 2007. http://www.usatoday.com/news/world/2007–10–18-manga_N.htm (accessed February 2008).

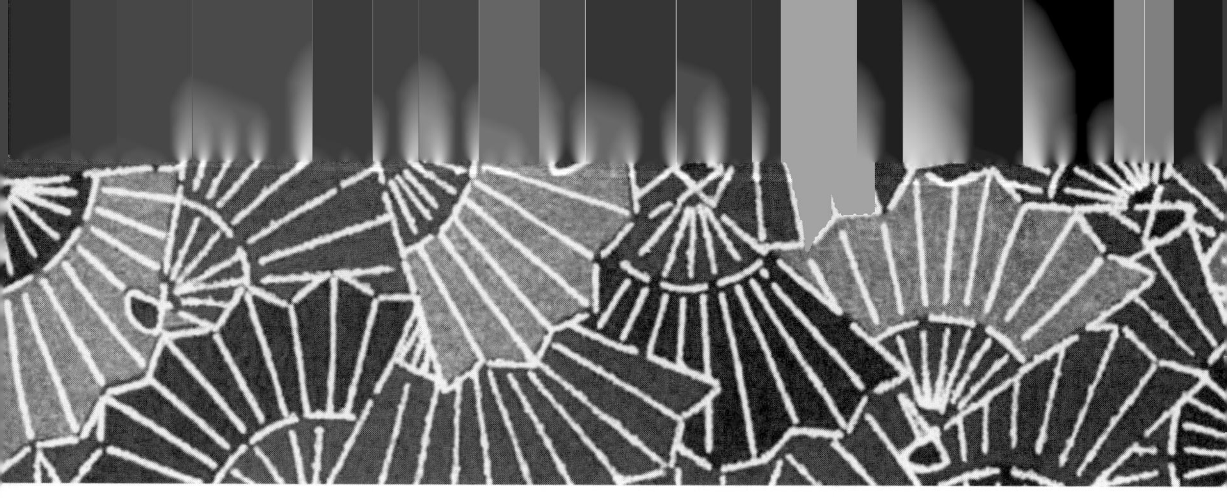

Contemporary Issues

INTRODUCTION: IS JAPAN FACING MASSIVE CHANGES?

In the months following the end of World War II, only a tiny number of people—Douglas MacArthur and Yoshida Shigeru are examples—were able to even partially conceptualize what Japan could be like in the foreseeable future. These two leaders envisioned a prosperous country allied with the United States and one where people were free to live outside of the control of militarists. As the first decade of the 21st century ends, contemporary Japan has risen to much more than even these policy makers envisioned. Japanese live in a free and prosperous society. Through in large part the hard work of its people, Japan has one of the world's leading economies. The country has a parliamentary democracy. Japanese have some of the world's highest literacy rates and the longest life expectancies for both sexes of any major nation.

Yet the history of the archipelago, contemporary geopolitics, the scarcity of natural resources, and even the enviable achievement of long life spans all make most Japanese realize that the nation is more vulnerable to substantial reverses of fortune than many other developed countries. Because of external challenges, Japan now is at a point where a foreign policy approach that has worked for more than six decades is undergoing substantial change. Furthermore, the need to maintain a vibrant, productive workforce will probably result in cultural changes that heretofore the Japanese did not anticipate. Although hopefully these changes will not be accompanied by an event as traumatic as World War II, most probably the problems Japan now faces cannot be addressed without major change. In the remainder of this chapter, key contemporary geopolitical and domestic issues the Japanese face are examined. However, readers who are interested in gaining a deeper understanding of the nature of Japan's contemporary issues are strongly advised to also read the chapters in this work on geography, history, government, economics, and society for essential contextual understanding of what follows.

JAPAN'S FOREIGN POLICY AND CHINA: "A MIDDLE POWER?"

Japan's contemporary foreign relations with regional neighbors and other Asian countries are affected by history, the actions of political leaders, and the public in both Japan and elsewhere. Two of the most critical problems Japan must solve, relations with China and North Korea, also involve the United States. Throughout most of the last 50 years of the 20th century, Japan usually simply followed the Cold War foreign policy lead of the United States. This policy, known as the Yoshida Doctrine, allowed Japan to concentrate its resources and brainpower on domestic economic development. Although the Japan-U.S. alliance is still strong, domestic and external factors are moving Japan toward a substantially more independent foreign policy than existed in the decades following the end of World War II.

Relations with the world's largest nation, China, have a complex history and are the subject of much current discussion in Japan. Positions on how to approach China, as is the case in the United States, often transcend party lines. Throughout Japan's long history, Chinese culture was honored, and although some political elites attempted to pose as ruling a society equal to China, generally the Japanese people respected China as the oldest and most prominent East Asian power. This all changed during the Meiji period and for much of the 20th century. Particularly after Japan's easy victory in the 1894–1895 Sino-Japanese war, political leaders and much of the public began to think of China as a failed and inferior nation. Also, Japan began to actively seek domination of Chinese-controlled territory by carving out spheres of influence on the mainland. In the 1930s, the Japanese army engaged in large-scale actions including the takeover of Manchuria and the 1937 clash with China that began World War II in the Pacific. The brutal actions of the Japanese army in China during World War II deeply affected Sino-Japanese relations.

Many analysts and scholars believe that memories of Chinese and Koreans about Japan's wartime atrocities were compounded by American occupation policies that allowed the Japanese to retain the emperor. Those who hold this perspective argue that the U.S. policy allowed Japan to avoid taking responsibility for instigating the Pacific War. By contrast, in addition to clear public statements of remorse, the Germans went to great lengths to atone for war guilt, and during the immediate postwar years former Nazis were removed from various government positions. The Germans also held their own war crimes trials in addition to the Allied war crimes trials. Although American officials removed Japanese militarists from many positions during the early part of the occupation, a number of these individuals regained influence once the Cold War began and the United States became more focused on real and potential communist aggression than on past Japanese actions. Even though the Japanese government has subsequently both engaged in public apologies and financial compensation and aid to China (and South Korea), the issue of war responsibility remains contentious in East Asia.

Japan's alliance with the United States in the Cold War and Mao Zedong's hostility also kept Sino-Japanese relations negative until after his death in 1976. Deng Xiaoping, who began to liberalize the Chinese economy, welcomed Japanese investment in China and brought about what seemed to be a new era in Sino-Japanese relations, which lasted well over a decade. However, beginning in the late 1980s, a host of factors caused Sino-Japanese relations to decline to the point that by 2005 the situation had become critical in many ways.

The Japanese share some of the responsibility for this bilateral decline. For years, Japanese school textbooks had avoided much discussion of World War II. Textbook treatment of imperial military World War II actions improved when in 1997 the Japanese Supreme Court ruled in favor of author Saburo Inega and against the Ministry of Education over its censorship of his accurate description of Japan's wartime atrocities. Then in 2001, the ministry allowed the publication of a little-used but controversial Japanese middle school text that depicted Japan's role in the Pacific War in a relatively positive light. The text and its 2005 second edition sparked demonstrations and the destruction of Japanese property in China and became a symbol of all that was negative about Japan in the eyes of many Chinese. Also, Prime Minister Koizumi Junichiro's and other prominent Japanese politicians' visits to the Yasukuni Shinto shrine dedicated to imperial war dead sparked substantial media attention and protest, not only in China but in the Republic of Korea (ROK) as well.

Still, by the 1990s and afterward, a number of unrelated contemporary Chinese foreign policy developments and policy stances were increasingly worrying Japanese and American political leaders as well as the Japanese public. The Chinese government increased military spending by double digits annually, threatened Taiwan at various times, and sent naval vessels into Japanese waters and aircraft into Japanese airspace. Beijing began asserting sovereignty over the tiny but potentially oil-rich Senkaku Islands near Okinawa, which Japan had claimed since 1895 and developed over a period of years (the Chinese have older historical records in which the islands are mentioned by their Chinese name). The Chinese government also did not stop its citizens from violating Japanese intellectual property rights and, through often-violent repression of dissidents and minority groups, angered large numbers of Japanese political leaders and the public, who valued democratic freedoms and who were critical of China's one-party authoritarian rule. Furthermore, large numbers of younger Japanese adults feel that they have nothing to do with World War II and that the Japanese government has apologized enough for its actions. The younger generations are tired of receiving Chinese blame for the war.

The Chinese Communist Party (CCP), faced with a situation in which virtually nobody believed in Marxism and CCP leaders who pursued capitalist policies could only claim economic growth as a reason they should remain in power, kept anti-Japanese sentiment alive among the public and in some cases intensified the rhetoric relative to the past throughout the 1990s and later. This was done both through the media and through the increase of anti-Japanese education in China's school curriculum. It has been effective. A 2006 *Pew Global Attitudes Project* poll of Chinese feelings about Japanese yielded typical negative results with 70 percent of Chinese adults having unfavorable opinions of Japan and only 21 percent holding favorable attitudes (September 21, 2006).

By the early 21st century, the Japanese public was becoming more negative toward China than was the case a few years before. In 2003, survey data by the Japanese cabinet office on foreign policy issues indicated that roughly equal numbers of respondents (approximately 48 percent each) answered that they felt either an affinity at some level or little or no affinity with China. By 2004, and the public trend continues as of the publication of this book, the same polls indicated that approximately 60 percent of the Japanese public felt little or no affinity with China. The 2006 Pew poll cited earlier revealed that only 28 percent of Japanese were favorable toward Chinese. The percentage of Japanese in the cabinet office polls who think the bilateral relationship is not going well has risen from about 48 percent in 2003 to close to approximately 70 percent in 2008 (Harris 2008, 46).

Paradoxically, the strengthening of economic ties continued through most of this recent period of political discord and ill feelings. As of 2008, China was third behind the United States and the Netherlands worldwide as a home to Japanese direct investment, and Chinese imports accounted for more than 20 percent of total Japanese imports—more than any other nation (Harris 2008, 47). However, political leaders in both countries have recently feared that fallout from the worsening bilateral situation would affect the economic relationship that is important for both China and Japan.

It is widely believed that former Chinese president Jiang Zemin, who even when he visited Japan in 1998 called for more sincere apologies about World War II after Japanese leaders had issued several, used anti-Japanese rhetoric to strengthen Chinese nationalism. However, China's president did not anticipate that the situation would go so far as to help bring about anti-Japanese riots in Chinese cities. Among key Japanese political leaders, at least the situation has improved since both Zemin and Koizumi left office in 2002 and 2006, respectively. Although Japanese Prime Minister Shinzo Abe's tenure was short lived, he helped to bring about a more positive tone in Beijing by selecting China as the first foreign country for an official visit. His successor, former Prime Minister Fukuda Yasuo, was an advocate of improving relations with China, and Chinese President Hu Jintao seems predisposed to reciprocate. Aso Taro, the Liberal Democratic Party (LDP) prime minister who assumed office in late September 2008, moved quickly to stress the importance of Japan's economic relationship with China.

In May 2008, Hu became the first Chinese president to visit Japan since Zemin's ill-fated trip in 1998. Along with other positive developments of the visit, including Hu's assurances that Japan's and China's territorial disputes in the East China Sea can be resolved, the president also asserted that "post-war Japanese financial aid played a positive role in the construction of modern China" (Iinuma 2008, 7). Despite these hopeful signs on the part of Japanese and Chinese political leaders, public opinion polls in both Japan and China conducted before the visit indicated that roughly two-thirds of the public in each country didn't like the other nation (Iinuma 2008, 8).

Japanese political leaders not only face the problem of influencing public opinion in more positive directions about China but also must grapple with the problem of how to deal with China on substantive issues, remain an ally of the United States, and not get sucked into a confrontation between the great powers. At one level, there is agreement that transcends parties. Both LDP and Democratic Party of Japan (DPJ) leaders want to continue the U.S. alliance. Not only do the United States and Japan share common political values, but also one of the remaining vestiges of the old Yoshida Doctrine is that Japan is still the recipient of an alliance with the world's largest superpower, which strengthens Japan's security in light of an ever-growing Chinese military power. Also, at varying levels of agreement, elected officials, members of the Foreign Ministry bureaucracy, and political analysts all realize that Japan must develop an independent foreign policy course relative to the Cold War past. In the near future, the United States could very well be less of a force in the region because of other international commitments and a lack of economic resources to commit to East Asian regional security.

Although the LDP conservative contingent is larger, both the LDP and the DPJ have elected officials, associated academics, and pundits who share differing beliefs about China's intentions and how to deal with this emerging world power, regardless of what independent foreign policies are pursued. Both parties have hardliners who don't trust China, given its military buildup, and think the Japanese Self-Defense Forces (SDF), already among the world's five-largest militaries in terms of spending, should be strengthened and that the U.S. alliance should be made even stronger. There is also a large group of elected officials, as evidenced by the 345-member bipartisan Japan-China Friendship Diet Committee, who favor more engagement with China. Finally, increasing numbers of political leaders and policy advocates, many of whom are skeptical about China and many of whom are more reconciliatory toward the People's Republic of China (PRC), believe Japan should pursue a middle-power course of action toward China.

"Middle power" is an international relations term and refers to countries that aren't great powers on the world stage but that still have influence and some international leverage. Middle-power advocates believe that the Japanese government should actively work with other middle-power nations—such as Australia, various Southeast Asian countries, and South Korea—to collectively develop coherent strategies that ensure their own joint national interests. These middle powers might cooperate with China or the United States, depending on particular circumstances, but avoid being completely a part of one superpower camp or the other. This notion is hotly contested within Japan but seems to have some traction with the public. Generally, the Japanese public, like people all over the globe, are more concerned with such bread-and-butter issues as the economy and taxes and don't normally assign a high priority to thinking about foreign policy. However, such external events as the Chinese anti-Japanese riots early in the 21st century, or various ongoing actions by the Democratic People's Republic of Korea (DPRK, or North

Korea), often galvanize public beliefs about a particular international situation or policy toward a foreign power.

JAPAN AND THE KOREAN PENINSULA

Japan's relations with both countries that currently exist on the Korean Peninsula are, as in the case with China, influenced by contacts that go back before the beginning of the Japanese state. However, late-19th- and 20th-century Japanese imperialism and aggression have left bad memories among many Koreans. Korea was a Japanese colony from 1910 until the end of World War II, and the Japanese were often brutal rulers. Yet at the same time, the Japanese created fissures in Korean society by co-opting numbers of Koreans through providing them educational opportunities and economic benefits in return for service to Japan's empire.

Even though the Japanese government has apologized for its ill treatment of Koreans, particularly during World War II, and paid reparations to young women who were forced to sexually service imperial Japan's army, Japan's relations with its ally, the ROK (South Korea), have been difficult on a number of occasions throughout the postwar period. To cite one of many examples, publication of a middle school Japanese textbook in the early part of the 21st century that cast the Japanese-instigated Pacific War in neutral and positive terms resulted in a public outcry in South Korea and official government condemnation. Japan and the ROK also have a long-running dispute over ownership of the tiny Dokdo Island that lies

2002 Korean comfort women protest. One of the reasons for South Korean ill-feelings toward Japan is a perception by many Koreans that the issue of the "comfort women" (women forced into sexual servitude by the Japanese Army during World War II) issue has never been resolved. (AP/Wide World Photos)

between the two countries, and recent polls indicate that only a little more than one-third of Japanese have favorable opinions toward the ROK, with lower percentages of Koreans reciprocating in a favorable way toward Japanese. At times, it seems only the presence of the United States, who is allied with both countries, preserves stability between the two nations. However, the current ROK-Japan situation has substantially improved since the first few decades after the conclusion of World War II. Japan and the ROK successfully cohosted the 2002 World Cup soccer games, a situation that would have been impossible a few years earlier. Now that the ROK has a democratic government, there are at least shared political values.

Relations are far worse between Japan and the North Korean government. Despite a few attempts at normalization, the DPRK has consistently been both a destabilizing influence in Japanese society for most of the postwar period as well as the greatest clear security threat the Japanese currently face.

In 1998, North Korea tested a missile capable of carrying a nuclear warhead by firing a projectile that violated Japanese airspace before falling into the Pacific Ocean. Then, in July 2006, in an even more provocative action, the North Koreans test-fired another missile that splashed down in the Sea of Japan. In the most serious action to date, in October 2006 the North Korean government exploded what it claimed was a nuclear device. This was later confirmed to be a small plutonium atomic bomb. Although the latest incident is especially chilling, it and the two missile tests described earlier are only part of a series of actions by North Korea that are threats to Japan's security and social stability.

In 2002, North Korean dictator Kim Jong-Il, after years of denial, admitted to DPRK abductions of at least 13 Japanese citizens against their will from their homeland so that they could teach Japanese language and culture to North Koreans, who would then spy in Japan. However, the families of those kidnapped in a number of cases do not know whether the abductees are dead or alive. In at least one case, the North Koreans claimed that one of the abductees was dead and produced false DNA as evidence.

North Korea's Yongbyon nuclear facility is seen in this satellite image taken on March 2, 2002. Japan is probably the country most impacted by the North Korean regime's possession of nuclear weapons. (DigitalGlobe/Getty Images)

The Japanese and American governments also confirmed that the North Koreans have obtained large amounts of revenues from Japan through illicit drug trafficking and counterfeiting. Japanese authorities monitor the huge pachinko industry, which recently accounted for almost one-quarter of all service industry revenues, because many of the operators are reputed to be North Korean sympathizers and large amounts of revenue are smuggled to the DPRK. In 2001, Japanese military forces sunk their first ship since World War II—a North Korean spy vessel in Japanese waters.

Although because of the PRC's size and global power, long-term relations with China probably constitute a more complex problem for the Japanese, the North Korean government is presently much more of a clear and present danger to Japan's national security. A brief elaboration on why this is the case is in order. North Korean dictator Kim Jong-Il has virtually unlimited power in the nation. The DPRK, with a population of more than 23 million, currently has more than 1 million military personnel, the largest percentage of citizens under arms of any of the world's nations. Males are drafted to serve in the military beginning at age 17, and enlistments can last for 10 years or longer. The DPRK military is amply supplied and fed in an economy that is so poor that there are intermittent famines, electricity is not dependable, and computers and paper are scarce.

In addition to arms sales and drug trafficking money, much of DPRK revenues come from famine relief aid, since government economic policies often result in food shortages. The government divides the population into favored, ordinary, and hostile classes, and the latter are in the countryside and often have little food. The government controls all media, and where there is electricity houses are wired to receive regular government announcements and citizens are monitored at weekly meetings to be sure they are listening. The DPRK government blocks the borders to keep citizens from leaving the country, and it constantly engages in propaganda messages to citizens that Japanese and Americans are rapists and murderers and that the South Koreans are their lackeys. The DPRK ranks at the bottom or near the bottom regarding every category of freedom in international comparisons.

North Korea is still technically at war with South Korea since an armistice and not a treaty was signed in 1953. The demilitarized zone on the Korean Peninsula between the two countries is home to one of the largest concentrations of military personnel and weapons in the world. Japan, allied to both the United States and the ROK and an immediate neighbor of North Korea, is unavoidably involved in one of the world's great foreign policy conundrums: how to deal with the DPRK. With the possible exception of South Korea, Japan probably has more to lose because of geographical proximity than any other nation if war erupts on the Korean Peninsula. Unlike China, whose border is contiguous with the DPRK, Japan has been the object of substantial North Korean condemnation since the founding of the DPRK.

As of the publication of this book, Japan is a member of six-party diplomatic talks (along with China, Russia, the ROK, the United States, and the DPRK). The general objective of the talks that began in August 2003 is to end the DPRK's nuclear program in return for a number of concessions to North Korea, including access to economic aid from the other nations and security guarantees from the

United States. However, each of the nations involved in the talks with North Korea also has specific objectives. In Japan's case, safety for Japanese cities that are easily reachable by Korean missiles is a paramount concern, as well as resolution of the Japanese abduction problem. Japan's objectives are that an outcome of the talks will be the return of any Japanese held in the DPRK against their will and full disclosure by the North Koreans of the fate of all Japanese who were kidnapped.

There is no guarantee of final success of the six-party talks, although they have led to North Korea's promise to dismantle its nuclear weaponry program and to cooperate in external verification efforts to assess that it has lived up to the agreements. Many foreign policy observers are skeptical the North will give up all nuclear weapons since the DPRK has spent billions of dollars over the course of at least two decades developing them, and the North Korean government has consistently violated its past formal agreement pledges regarding this issue. Many experts hope that even if the North Koreans retain a few nuclear bombs, the talks can result in the DPRK giving up all weapons-grade plutonium, thus refraining from developing more weapons and stimulating nuclear proliferation elsewhere through the export of plutonium-related nuclear technology. The problem is compounded by the difficulty of obtaining intelligence on how many nuclear weapons the North Koreans currently possess, although experts now believe the number of bombs ranges between six and eight.

The Japanese government, as of 2008, was moving toward engaging the North Korean government again after a hiatus caused in part by little progress in the abduction issue since Prime Minister Koizumi's historic 2002 visit to North Korea and the resultant formal agreement with Kim Jong-Il to begin the process of normalizing relations. The Japanese public continues to distrust North Korea and to worry about whether an eventual reconciliation between the two Koreas might pose new dangers to Japan. Also, given the distrust that still exists between Japanese and South Koreans, many Japanese political leaders as well as the public wonder whether the ROK will be a dependable ally if the DPRK directly threatens Japan. Some Japanese share concerns as well about the reliability and judgment of Japan's most powerful ally, the United States.

JAPAN, THE UNITED STATES, AND CONTEMPORARY INTERNATIONAL CHALLENGES

As readers of the History and Government chapters are aware, in 1945 Japan and the United States began a transformation from a war that Japan specialist Michael Green described as "the most violent in either nation's history" (2007, 28) to a relationship that for more than six decades has been largely mutually beneficial to each country's economy and national security. Furthermore, the institutionalization of Japanese democracy means that as several U.S. presidents and Japanese prime ministers have recognized, the two nations now share deep commitments to core economic and political freedoms. The late Mike Mansfield was perhaps the most popular U.S. ambassador to Japan, and his oft-quoted description of the alliance as "the most important bilateral relationship in the world, from the standpoint of the

United States" (Foley 2001) is in many ways accurate from an American perspective.

Japan was a solid American asset during the Cold War, and the United States was able to use it successfully in strategically countering the Soviet Union through operating from a country in close geographic proximity to the USSR. At the same time, Japan helped the United States maintain relative stability in East Asia through the volatile Mao years and despite a consistently antagonistic North Korea. A brief period of calm ensued for a few years after the Cold War ended, but new international challenges emerged in the form of a global struggle against Islamic extremist terrorism and the emergence of a potential future superpower—China. Japan has been, given the constraints of its constitution, a reliable U.S. partner through the entire postwar period and in the American-led war on terrorism.

Japan has probably benefited even more from the postwar American partnership than the United States. Despite the existence of three hostile Cold War neighbors with political and economic systems that were the antithesis of what the Japanese were developing, U.S. military protection was, in all likelihood, the single most important reason that there was no armed confrontation that directly affected the Japanese archipelago. Given the country's geographical location, it is difficult to imagine the continuance of a free prosperous Japan without American military deterrence during those critical years.

The benefits for both countries continue today. The threat posed by the current North Korean regime requires continued Japan-U.S. joint deterrence. There is no consensus in Japan or in the United States among political leaders and foreign policy elites whether a rising China will constitute a serious security threat to either or both countries. Still, given China's substantial increases in military spending that now span two decades, the majority of Japanese and U.S. leaders have found the continuing American military forces in Japan essential. There has been no serious political movement in either country to change the status quo.

Still, Japan and the United States are different countries that share fundamental points of agreement but also have contrasting cultures and self-interests. Foreign policy problems both nations face where they must interact with each other are in some ways more complex than those of the Cold War. However, old mutual concerns that date back to the Cold War and even earlier among some leaders and the public in each country still influence contemporary relations. Throughout the Cold War and even today, many Japanese are concerned about American unilateralism, as evidenced by the middle-power movement discussed earlier. In the 1970s, President Richard M. Nixon took the United States off the gold standard, fixed exchange rates, and in a separate policy action made his historic trip to the PRC. In both cases, Japanese leaders were stunned that they did not receive serious American consultation before these events, which had major impact on Japan, occurred. As of 2008, feelings existed in Japan that President George W. Bush struck a deal with Pyongyang in the six-party talks without adequately consulting Japan.

The Japanese also remember the first Bill Clinton administration, when the president implied that Japan was an economic threat to the United States, unsuccessfully tried to negotiate managed trade, and seemed to focus exclusive, favorable attention on China while ignoring the Japan relationship. Although Clinton later moved completely away from his first-term "economic threat"–based policies and paid much more attention to the strategic Japan relationship when problems developed with China over Taiwan, the Japanese still took note of an unprecedented eight-day 1998 Clinton visit to China, during which a stop in Tokyo was omitted.

Legitimate Japanese concerns about U.S. mistakes in the joint relationship have also been clouded by incorrect perceptions about the United States. There is a perception in Japan that Republican administrations are friendly and Democratic administrations are hostile. What actually exists in the United States among foreign policy elites are pro-China and pro-Japan factions that can affect policy but transcend party lines. Also, in the 1980s, a number of influential Japanese leaders decided that the United States was a broken society with an economy that was beyond repair and went public with their assertions.

This work is quite naturally more about Japan than the United States. However, it is important to glimpse American attitudes that influence the relationship. Even before the end of the Cold War, as Japan's economy grew impressively, Japanese politicians and bureaucrats used informal trade barriers to keep out many American goods and services. This legitimate American concern about unfair trade fed the incorrect notion that despite all foreign direct investment, accounting at the time for substantially less than 10 percent of the total value of the U.S. world-leading economy, the Japanese were economically taking over the United States. An arguably more legitimate American concern was that Japan benefited more than the United States from American military forces. However, this point was often misunderstood in the United States. Many Americans believed that the Japanese had no military forces and were getting a completely free ride while ruining the U.S. domestic economy.

With the alliance's achievements and misunderstandings, what are the attitudes of Japanese political leaders and the foreign policy establishment toward the alliance and problems concerning it that might change the postwar status quo or must be negotiated?

Barring future unforeseen, dramatic events that would be unprecedented in scope since 1945 and change current opinion, Japan's political leaders by and large believe maintaining the relationship is critical. In addition to the real North Korea threat and the ambiguity of China's intentions, Japan and the United States share a commitment to a neoliberal worldview that accentuates economic and political freedom. Currently, the two most powerful political parties, the LDP and the DPJ, are closer together on the importance of the alliance than the LDP and the Socialist Party were in Cold War days.

However, within Japanese political circles there are important differences in approaches to the United States coexisting with a common overall majority opinion. Advocates of the middle-power approach want to keep strong but more distant relations with the United States. Many middle-power adherents tout the United Nations (UN) as a vehicle to achieve Japan's foreign policy aims. Those LDP and DPJ members who support a strong alliance with the United States worry less about the danger of Japan being drawn into a great power confrontation and more about the dangers of the East Asian region and how it might affect Japan. Where most political leaders agree is in the view that external events and history mean that Japan must be more assertive in the exercise of independent foreign policy.

The majority opinion is so true that some of Japan's most influential political leaders have been described by the media as the "Heisei Generation." The Heisei period began with Emperor Hirohito's death in 1989 and is the current name for the era of Emperor Akihito's reign. However, pundits use it to describe the generation of Japanese politicians who were born after World War II, came to power after Hirohito's death, and think that Japan has apologized enough for its wartime actions. They also believe Japan should be a normal nation with an assertive foreign policy. There are Japanese political leaders who would prefer Japan not to make its own foreign policy decisions and long for the old Yoshida Doctrine, but even they see that external events probably make this impossible. During the Cold War, foreign diplomats gossiped that Japanese representatives had the reputation of smiling, sleeping, and smoking at international meetings, meaning they simply followed the United States' lead on critical issues. That was a different time.

In addition to key contemporary foreign policy issues affecting both countries that have already been discussed, the specific Japan-U.S. issue that must be resolved relatively soon concerns American military bases in Japan: the location of troops, the structure of command, and Japan's role in changes that will occur. Currently, 75 percent of the 37,000 American troops stationed in Japan are in Okinawa. The Okinawans, although many economically benefit from this situation, have for decades been unhappy with the presence of such a large contingent of foreign troops.

Their anger is directed both at Tokyo, which is viewed as unfairly making Okinawa the site of this deployment after the particularly brutal fate of civilians, mainly caused by the Japanese army, in the ferocious World War II battle of Okinawa, and at the U.S. military, which expropriated land for bases shortly after the war. In 1995, the situation became more emotional in a much-publicized case in which three American servicemen in Okinawa were accused of raping a 12-year-old girl. They were convicted the following year.

Although the American military has been in general exemplary in Japan, in 2008 a U.S. sailor arrested for allegedly robbing and murdering a taxi driver near Tokyo also brought condemnation from the Japanese media and public. National resentment about this incident also brought to the surface a longtime resentment on the part of many Japanese that the U.S. military, with self-contained American bases under U.S. command, is less of an ally and more of an occupying foreign presence, despite polls indicating that the public does not oppose an American military presence in Japan. A number of defense analysts assert that this current base arrangement is also a practical command structure problem since many strategists argue that U.S. and Japanese forces would be more effective if the command structure were more integrated.

In May 2006, the Japanese and U.S. governments attempted to address both these problems through reaching final agreement on the realignment of U.S. forces in Japan. Incrementally, co-basing command structures are being created with the integration of SDF and U.S. forces command and functions and of American troops on Japanese bases. In the same agreement, a redeployment of 8,000 marines from Okinawa to Guam by 2014 was announced. The American side in negotiations argued that redeployment to Guam would also give U.S. forces more flexibility to respond to crises outside of East Asia while still being in position to operate in the latter theater. A key part of the agreement is that Japan agreed to pay for a large portion of realignment of troops and to pay $6 billion, or almost 60 percent of the costs, of relocating the marines. The cost-sharing issue represents a challenge for Japanese politicians and one that they have creatively already began to solve. However, eventual Japanese public reaction to the amount of money expended on Japan's part for the relocation, and an expansion of SDF responsibilities with base reorganization once the process unfolds, is uncertain.

The Yoshida Doctrine is crumbling, but not dead. The Japanese never received American military protection for nothing, but they have managed to keep their own defense costs nominally around one percent of GDP. Most Japanese political leaders know that increased American security commitments globally mean the probability of less of an American presence in the future. When completed, the Guam deployment will result in less of an immediate American military presence in Japan. Many Japanese elected officials and bureaucrats also understand that the independent foreign policy they prefer means greater utilization of human and economic resources.

The force realignment expenses, estimated as close to $20 billion, apparently will not be counted as military expenses. Already the Japanese Coast Guard expenditures are not counted as military expenses since the coast guard is a part of the Ministry of Land, Infrastructure, and Transportation. Japanese political leaders allow these somewhat misleading situations because they realize that although their country must bear greater responsibility for its security, the notion of a "pacifist nation" is still embraced by much of the public; other Japanese expect the Americans to provide production with minimal amount of Japanese resources needed. The question of what Japan can constitutionally do, as readers of the Government and Politics chapter are aware, is another overarching issue that will be discussed in the scheduled constitutional revision debates of 2010.

JAPAN AND THE WORLD

Japan's foreign policy is obviously going to be profoundly different in some ways than was the case in the last 50 years of the 20th century and the beginning of the 21st century. Interestingly enough, the interrelated problems of an aging population and a lack of births commensurate with Japan's need for productive adults have also become a global as well as a domestic issue for the nation. Japan is not only crafting foreign policy in new directions that might or might not have positive future results but also quickly becoming a multicultural nation in the face of the economic and social ramifications of too few babies and large numbers of elderly. These issues are addressed in the final section of this chapter.

THE VIEWS OF TWO FOREIGNERS

Donald Richie is an American who first came to Japan in 1947 as a young soldier during the occupation and has lived there almost all of his adult life. Richie, a journalist and critic, is famous for introducing Japanese film to the world but also is admired both in Japan and internationally as an astute observer of his adopted nation's culture. Michael Zielenziger was the Tokyo-based bureau chief for Knight Ridder newspapers from 1997 to 2003 and has written extensively on social, economic, and political developments in Japan and East Asia. Both of these astute outside observers are illuminating about traditional Japanese attitudes and their strengths and weaknesses as the archipelago's people attempt to adjust to a rapidly changing world.

Richie and Zielenziger, like the many foreigners who admire Japanese culture, recount in their writing important traditional attitudes they find admirable. Richie describes a personal late-1940s experience that made a lasting impression. He was walking down the street and observed workmen building a wall around a house that would intersect with a large tree branch. Rather than cutting down the tree, the workers built a hole in the wall for the branch. Richie was struck by this example and many similar ones indicating the ease and harmony with which ordinary Japanese coexisted with the natural world. Although many physical manifestations of these attitudes would subsequently disappear from urban and rural Japan in the development booms that followed, this admirable cultural spirit lives on in Japan and globally in the many people who admire traditional Japanese aesthetics. Zielenziger has written about attributes of the traditional Japanese appreciation of beauty of the sparse rather than the overabundant and how this positively affected a view of people and the environment that is helping to make Japan a world leader in a number of environmental initiatives, including efforts to reduce greenhouse gases. The Japanese conception of beauty in nature and its spiritual and aesthetic ramifications have inspired poets, theologians, novelists, architects, artists, and ordinary people all over the world for a long time. Notions of humans and the environment and what constitutes beauty are just two pieces of a mosaic of positive traditional Japanese beliefs and cultural propensities; others include inculcation of the value of effort and perseverance, frugality, modesty, and teamwork.

However, Richie, Zielenziger, and other analysts both within and outside Japan are also aware of negative attitudes that are more prevalent in Japan than is the case in many countries—a sense of cultural uniqueness and a disdain for foreigners because they are not Japanese. Although it is difficult to identify exactly when the profound sense of Japanese uniqueness from other cultures became pervasive in society, evidence of it exists from the 1880s until the end of World War II in government pronouncements and state education as well as in Japanese attitudes and actions toward other Asians and foreigners in general.

Japan's experience with immigration during the imperial period was primarily one in which foreigners served a useful purpose for the state, but there was little or no attempt to integrate them into the larger society. The Meiji government paid handsome salaries to Americans and Europeans with expertise in a variety of fields to help the country modernize, but by the late 1880s it abruptly ended the practice when Westerners had fulfilled their functions. When Korea became a Japanese colony in 1910, Japan's government imported Korean workers for menial tasks. These policies were significantly expanded during World War II, and the government forced Koreans to come to Japan and work in factories, mines, and construction. At the end of the war, there were more than 2 million Koreans in Japan, and half a million returned home. When Japan regained independence in 1952 with the end of the occupation, the government officially declared the remaining Koreans and Taiwanese (who were also brought to Japan as workers) to be foreigners.

In the decades after the war, an entire genre of writing, *Nihonjinron*, or "theories about the Japanese," became popular in Japan. *Nihonjinron* authors asserted that the Japanese had a completely unique culture from any other in the world. The genre, which still has a following today, is broad and includes such contentions as Japanese intestines and brains are different from other humans' and claims that Japanese cultural propensities can be found nowhere else in the world. Although *Nihonjinron* appears to have declined in popularity, in part because of this body of work many Japanese at one level or another think Japan is so different from the rest of the world that social conventions and customs that are found elsewhere could never be applicable to the Japanese.

Ironically, while Japanese have long been fascinated with sampling foreign cuisine and customs in safe environments, the prevailing Japanese attitude has traditionally been to keep foreign people at arm's length. Many outsiders who spend time in Japan often agree with the maxim that Japan is a wonderful country to visit but a difficult one in which to live if one is not Japanese. Two decades ago, it was common for foreigners to openly hear Japanese use the term gaijin, or "outside person," in their presence.

Although the unself-reflective use of a potentially insulting term like gaijin is more rare today, many Japanese still have mixed feeling at best about people who are ethnically different. As was noted in the Society chapter, strong traditional notions about what it means to be Japanese—for example, conformity to the group and repression of individual desires—mean that Japanese who don't conform to these precepts often have as many problems fitting in as foreigners.

Japanese insularity regarding foreigners and lack of responsiveness to their cultural differences is now, because of demographics, a serious potential threat to the nation's continued prosperity. As discussed earlier in the book, Japan has one of the highest life expectancies in the world and a fertility rate that has been in decline for more than two decades. If these longevity and birthrate trends continue, barring substantial increases in immigration, Japan's population is expected to drop from its present 127 million to about 95 million by 2050. Such a situation, if not addressed, will result in lower standards of living for Japanese and an unprecedented strain on public-sector social welfare programs because of too few taxpayers and too many recipients of government services.

Improvements in labor productivity and more efficient use of the education and skills of women in the workplace can partially address this problem, but UN estimates are that the country needs about 400,000 new immigrants annually if Japan's current economic development levels are to be maintained. Statistics for the most recent year available indicate that 228,784 foreigners were admitted to Japan with permission to work, a much smaller number than recommended in the UN study. Furthermore, the large majority of those foreigners had temporary resident status with little chance of becoming naturalized citizens under present immigration laws.

CAN JAPAN BECOME A GENUINE MULTICULTURAL SOCIETY?

Not only does Japan need workers from outside the archipelago to keep productivity levels high enough that tax revenues will be adequate, but also the rapid changes characteristic of a global, knowledge-oriented economy demand fresh thinking and such approaches to cutting-edge businesses as information technology (IT) that highly skilled, educated outsiders often bring. Key Japanese business leaders are aware of this critical point. In a recent speech Okuda Hiroshi, president of the Japanese Business Federation, called for more efforts to recruit skilled immigrants and noted that the 1990s IT revolution in the United States, which led to years of impressive economic growth, was in part fueled by the admission of approximately 1 million foreigners a year.

Japan's reticent, at best, attitudes toward foreign immigration, have, in the opinion of several economic and business analysts, already hindered the nation's chances for achieving greater success in an increasingly demanding global economy. Prospective immigrants with highly skilled backgrounds view the United States, Europe, and even such regional competitors as South Korea and China as more hospitable homes for immigrant brainpower than Japan because of the difficulty that non-Japanese who plan to live there often encounter. Michael Zielenziger thinks Japan's extended malaise of the 1990s and early part of this century can at least be partially attributed to the negative results of traditional attitudes toward outsiders who challenge the collective status quo. In his words, "A nation that cuts the feedback receptors, that diffuses the power of the individual inside collective systems, that puts harmony over friction and stability over competition eventually loses its dynamism and its ability to adapt" (Zielenziger 2006, 294). Bringing new perspectives and ways of approaching work and problem solving is one of the advantages gained from an infusion of (particularly well-educated) outsiders. Zielenziger also writes of the differing respective attitudes toward foreigners in South Korea and Japan during the 2002 World Cup that the two nations jointly hosted. The residents of Seoul eagerly embraced the large influx of foreigners, and there were a variety of social interactions between Koreans and visitors. In contrast, the Japanese media warned citizens about the potential rowdy behavior of foreign soccer fans, and in Japanese cities where matches were held, some restaurants and inns closed their doors rather than cater to large numbers of foreigners.

A much-publicized discussion has been occurring in Japan for some time on the question of whether to significantly accelerate the already growing number of foreigners and, if so, how to go about doing it. Government panels, the Japanese Business Federation, and now even elected officials realize the demographic fate of not

JAPAN'S CRIME RATE

Although Japan's crime rates have increased in some categories relative to the nation's past rates, Japan remains one of the safest countries in which to live when international comparisons are considered. According to UN statistics in a comparison of 20 countries, Japan ranked last in percentages of citizens who were victims of assault, robbery, and property crimes. Japan ranked 19th out of 20 in the percentage of citizens who were victims of rape. The Japanese were last in the same study in the number of citizens victimized by any kind of crime. In comparison, the U.S. international ranking was as follows; assault (10th), robbery (17th), rape (14th), and property crimes (7th). The United States ranked 15th out of 20 countries in the percentage of victims of any kind of crime.

enough workers to Japan's future and are calling for liberalization of immigration policies. Although none of the plans put forward thus far call for the same high levels of immigrants as the UN study, in 2008 a group of elected officials headed by an LDP Diet member put forth a plan calling for an increase of 10 million immigrants in the next 50 years. This increase will eventually constitute 10 percent of Japan's population if the final goal is achieved. The plan, which will be discussed in some detail later, calls for substantially higher numbers than a 2006 government panel's recommendation of increases that would eventually total no more than 3 percent of Japan's population.

The number of total foreign legal immigrants in Japan has steadily risen to more than 2 million people, excluding a large number of illegal immigrants. Estimates are that legal and illegal immigrants now constitute about 1.6 percent of the population, and newcomers are already beginning to change Japanese society. Future increases in the numbers of newcomers to Japan will bring about even more change.

Opposition to future increases exists within government bureaucracies and among the public on two major grounds. Many Japanese believe that foreigners are responsible for a disproportionately high number of crimes given their relatively low numbers compared to the general population. Government statistics partially support public opinion. Criminal arrests of foreigners have risen 296 percent between 1990 and 2006. However, the numbers of foreigners in Japan have steadily increased as well over this same time period. Also, despite an increased emphasis on proposed immigration policies for substantially increasing the numbers of highly educated immigrants moving to Japan, to date, the largest number of immigrants are unskilled workers who are recruited for low-level jobs, which would account for some of the increases in criminal arrests. Typically, the jobs are classified as temporary or part-time and lack any benefits. Some employers have recruited foreign workers for criminal activities. For example, in a recent year, approximately 40 percent of all Filipinos who were admitted to Japan were listed as "entertainers"

JAPAN'S POLICE SYSTEM

Japan's police system combines separate prefectural police departments guided by the National Police Agency. Each one of the prefectural forces is also administratively responsible to a prefectural public safety commission. The National Police Agency, who also reports to a National Public Safety Commission, is responsible for supervising police training programs, compiling crime statistics, procuring equipment, and providing national criminal identification services. In the most recent year for which statistics were available, 288,451 people were employed in all of Japan's police forces combined. There were 7,524 employees of the National Police Agency. Despite Japan's relatively low crime rates, the ratio of citizens to police in Japan is high compared with that of most developed nations, but the police have an efficient system consisting of 6,328 neighborhood police boxes or *koban,* which are small offices where two to four policemen have rotating duty. The latest statistics indicate that on average police reach a crime scene seven minutes and three seconds after it is reported.

on their visas. Authorities claim many of these workers in this category are women who are involved in prostitution.

More generally, opponents of increased immigration argue that if Japan admits the large numbers of foreigners that are proposed, Japanese cultural core values will be threatened. Many Japanese take a negative view of neighborhoods populated by Chinese, Japanese Brazilians, and Filipinos, claiming that there is too much noise and garbage. In the small city of Himeji, for example, repeated complaints from Japanese about some of the city's approximately 1,000 Vietnamese littering, not respecting parking laws, and staying up late at night singing karaoke resulted in some housing complex administrators setting a 10 percent limit on Vietnamese residents. There are also social scientists who are not emotionally attached to these general Japanese concerns about foreigners but based on their work believe that Japan is currently incapable of effectively accommodating the foreigners already present because of too few facilities and services for foreigners in such important institutions as schools and social service agencies.

The problems that many foreign residents in Japan currently face can be divided into three areas: legal-political, infrastructural, and cultural. Tsurunen Marutei, an ethnic Finn who is a naturalized Japanese citizen and a Diet member, has asserted that "Japan does not have a comprehensive immigration policy" (Caryl and Akiko 2006). The overwhelming majority of naturalized citizens are still Korean or Chinese. Over the last two decades or so, immigration authorities in response to labor market needs have granted guest worker visas to a much more diverse population, including Iranians, Bengalis, Filipinos, Indians, Nepalese, and Vietnamese.

Unless an immigrant is granted an exemption from the requirement, admission to Japan for work is contingent on securing employment in advance. Although there are some cases where highly educated workers have been recruited—Indian IT workers are an example—in the past most workers were granted work visas that ranged from six months to three years (although visas can be renewed). If the holder of a work visa becomes unemployed, when the visa expires he or she is considered an illegal immigrant.

Although in 1989 the government reorganized immigration procedures to facilitate skilled worker entry and to end situations in which immigrants remained with expired visas, large numbers of unskilled workers have entered Japan by receiving "trainee" status from employers. While some trainees were in legitimate skills development programs, this new category resulted in abuse from employers who were simply looking for sources of cheap labor and included no human capital development training. Guest workers must pay into Japan's pension system like the rest of the workforce, but upon leaving Japan they receive a lump sum equal to only 36 months of employment. The system has been incentivized to create a temporary guest worker program despite the fact that such temporary programs have tended to fail in other countries. There is also residential status with no restriction on employment made available to Brazilians of Japanese descent as well as other people who have family connections to Japanese nationals. Brazilian Japanese now constitute Japan's third-largest immigrant population because of this policy.

Japan could probably improve on its record of granting political asylum to foreigners. Compared to other developed countries, Japan continues to be closed to foreigners who are the victims of oppressive political regimes. In a 22-year period that began in 1982 and ended in 2004, only 330 of 3,544 applications were approved, and Japan continues to maintain tough policies toward asylum seekers. The Japanese government has used the excuse of lack of living space, and political analysts also cite reluctance on the part of Japan's leaders to alienate nations that have repressive governments but are also major energy suppliers to Japan. However, liberalization of this policy will probably be more feasible in the future given Japan's declining population and its need for productive workers. Liberalization of political asylum policies for foreigners is also consistent with Japan's commitment to free democratic institutions.

Currently, Japanese institutions, particularly schools and social service agencies, are having problems accommodating existing immigrant populations. In the case of schools, immigrants' lack of knowledge of the Japanese language is a major problem. The overwhelming majority of Brazilian Japanese, for example, come to Japan with little or no understanding of the nation's difficult language. As of the publication of this book, Japanese educational institutions are just beginning to plan Japanese as a Second Language programs. Although more Japanese universities in areas where large concentrations of Brazilian Japanese live are offering Portuguese, the supply of university classes does not match the number of Japanese educators who need some knowledge of the native language of the children whom they are attempting to educate. Currently, Japanese Brazilian students typically spend a large amount of time in Japanese language classes rather than in science or history classes, do not do well in school because of a combination of lack of language and content knowledge, and often drop out.

The 2008 plan that LDP elected officials submitted to the prime minister's office calls for special monies to strengthen Japanese language education for foreign students in elementary and junior high schools. These levels of schooling are compulsory in Japan and therefore receive significant national funding. The plan also calls for future immigrants and those immigrants who are already in Japan to receive similar social welfare services that Japanese citizens now enjoy. The rules for granting foreigners permanent and long-term resident status will be liberalized if the Diet and government approve. A proposed antiracism law is part of the package as well. The plan is receiving serious consideration, although immigrant quotas and the antiracism law, among other provisions, require legislative action that could take up to three years. Other parts of the proposal such as the liberalization of the immigrant admissions system, particularly the contraction of the visa program and the expansion of more permanent or long-term status approvals for immigrants, can be implemented within months if the prime minister and cabinet approve.

Regardless of what new immigration policies the Japanese government eventually adopts, and despite substantial opposition, Japan is likely to become much more ethnically heterogeneous in the next few decades than any time in its history since possibly the migration from the Asian mainland to the archipelago before the birth of the Japanese state. The difficult goal is to make Japan more multicultural as well as ethnically diverse. Despite the traditional resistance to foreigners described earlier, in the last three decades there have also been significant positive developments toward acceptance of diversity on the Japanese archipelago.

As readers of the social classes and ethnicity portion of this book are aware, such long-suffering minorities as Ainu, burakumin, and Korean residents have made unprecedented legal gains in their treatment by the larger society. The Japan Exchange and Teaching Program is over two decades old and has resulted in more than 5,000 bright young foreign college graduates interacting with teachers, students, local government officials, and citizens throughout Japan. The Japanese government has made a sustained effort to attract foreign students, and the numbers have risen annually from approximately 54,000 in 1997 to more than 117,000 in 2005. Although the percentage of foreign students in Japan is still lower than that of the United States or major Western European nations, the longitudinal trend has been for the most part positive since the government adopted this policy.

Individual Japanese have taken action independently of the government that is resulting in more grassroots diversity. Marriages between Japanese and non-Japanese have been consistently rising and comprised 5.5 percent of all marriages in the most recent year for which data are available. Foreigners who have conducted business in Japan for a decade or longer almost always concur that the breadth and depth of interactions between Japanese and foreigners that has occurred since the 1980s has resulted in much more cosmopolitanism on the part of Japanese and foreigners alike in business interactions.

Historically, no society has ever become more diverse without conflict, often misguided policies, and, unfortunately, bloodshed as well in many cases. However, some of the most successful nations on earth have managed to achieve success at multiculturalism and retain, at the same time, core values that make citizens and residents of these societies distinct and serve to strengthen the countries as well. Japan has many assets including a hard-working and highly educated population who live in a free society and have a culture that has influenced the world in many positive ways. The task of creating a more diverse society will be difficult but far from impossible for the Japanese.

REFERENCES

Bach, William. "Drugs, Counterfeiting, and Arms Trade: The North Korean Connection." U.S. Department of State. May 20, 2003. http://www.state.gov/p/inl/rls/rm/21044.htm (accessed June 2008).

Caryl, Christian and Kashiwagi Akiko. "This Is the New Japan: Immigrants Are Transforming a Once Insular Society." *Japan Focus*, November 8, 2006. http://www.japanfocus.org/_c_caryl_and_a_kashiwagi-this_is_the_new_japan__immigrants_are_transforming_a_once_insular_society (accessed June 2008).

Chanlett-Avery, Emma. *North Korea's Abduction of Japanese Citizens and the Six-Party Talks* (CRS Report for Congress RS22845). Washington, DC: Federation of American Scientists, 2008. http://www.fas.org/sgp/crs/row/RS22845.pdf (accessed June 2008).

Debito, Arudou. "The Coming Internationalization: Can Japan Assimilate Its Immigrants?" *Japan Focus*, 2006. http://japanfocus.org/products/details/2078 (accessed June 2008).

Ennis, Peter. "Bush vs. Kim: Standoff Continues: White House Keeps North Korea on Terrorist List." *Oriental Economist* 76, No. 8 (2008): 9–11.

———. "US, Japan Off Base: Futenma, Okinawa, Highlight Alliance Tensions." *Oriental Economist* 76, No. 5 (2008): 9–10.

Facts and Figures of Japan 2007. Tokyo: Foreign Press Center, 2007.

Foley, Thomas. "East Asia Through the Prism of the U.S.-Japan Relationship." U.S. Department of State. May 24, 2001. http://fpc.state.gov/fpc/7488.htm (accessed).

French, Howard W. "Insular Japan Needs, but Resists, Immigration." *New York Times*, July 24, 2003. http://www.nytimes.com/2003/07/24/international/asia/24JAPA.html?ei=5007&en=53c7315175389e69&ex=1374379200&partner=USERLAND&pagewanted=all&position= (accessed June 2008).

Goodman, David G. "Japan: Confronting the Challenges of the 21st Century." *Illinois International Review* (2007): 1–2.

Green, Michael J. "The US-Japan Alliance: A Brief Strategic History." *Education About Asia* 12, No. 3 (2007): 25–30.

Grilli, Peter. "Dialogue on Japan: Conversations with Donald Richie." *Education About Asia* 12, No. 1 (2007): 5–11.

Harris, Tobias. "Japan Accepts Its 'Middle-Power' Fate." *Far Eastern Economic Review* 171, No. 6 (2008): 45–49.

Iinuma, Yoshisuke. "The Big Thaw: Hu Jintao's Historic Visit to Japan." *Oriental Economist* 76, No. 6 (2008): 7–8.

"Japan Tracks Suspected Spy Ship." *BBC News*, September 5, 2002. http://news.bbc.co.uk/2/hi/asia-pacific/2237988.stm (accessed June 2008).

Kashiwazaki, Chikako, and Tsuneo Akaha. "Japanese Immigration Policy: Responding to Conflicting Pressures." *Migration Information Source*. November 2006. http://www.migrationinformation.org/Profiles/display.cfm?ID=487 (accessed June 2008).

Katz, Richard. "Japan in Transition: Richard Samuels and Kenneth Pyle Discuss Japan's Foreign and Defense Policies." *Oriental Economist* 75, No. 9 (2007): 7–10.

———. "Red May Be Blue: Are Republicans Better for Japan?" *Oriental Economist* 76, No. 2 (2008): 13–15.

———. "US Military Bases in Japan: 'Co-basing is the Key.'" *Oriental Economist* 76, No. 4 (2008): 9–10.

Kawashima, Shin. "The History Factor in Sino-Japanese Ties." *Japan Echo* (October 2005): 16–22.

Kawashima, Yutaka. *Japanese Foreign Policy at the Crossroads*. Washington, DC: Brookings Institution Press, 2003.

Matsutani, Minoru, and Jun Hongo. "Helping Hand for Immigrants: Hope Seen in Plan to Promote Japanese-Language Education." *Japan Times Online*, August 16, 2008. http://search.japantimes.co.jp/cgi-bin/nn20080816f1.html (accessed September 2008).

"North Korea." *CIA: The World Factbook*. August 21, 2008. https://www.cia.gov/library/publications/the-world-factbook/geos/kn.html.

Oh, Kondgan. "North Korea: The Nadir of Freedom." *Footnotes: Foreign Policy Research Institute* 12, No. 16 (2007). http://www.fpri.org/footnotes/1216.200705.oh.northkorea.html (accessed June 2008).

Pew Global Attitudes Project. "Publics of Asian Powers Hold Negative Views of One Another." September 21, 2006. http://pewresearch.org/pubs/249/publics-of-asian-powers-hold-negative-views-of-one-another (accessed March 2009).

Savada, Andrea M. *North Korea: A Country Study*. Boston: DIANE Publishing Co., 1995.

Worsley, Ken. "More on Foreign Workers in Japan: What Is Keidanren After?" *Japan Economy News*, April 20, 2007. http://www.japaneconomynews.com/2007/04/20/more-on-foreign-workers-in-japan (accessed June 2008).

Yoshihide, Soeya. "Diplomacy for Japan as a Middle Power." *Japan Echo* (April 2008): 36–41.

Zielenziger, Michael. *Shutting Out the Sun*. New York: Nan A. Talese, 2006.

Zissis, Carin. "The Six-Party Talks on North Korea's Nuclear Program." *Council on Foreign Relations*. June 28, 2008. http://www.cfr.org/publication/13593.

Glossary

Ainu These are indigenous people who historically inhabited northern Honshu and Hokkaido. Their original ethnicity and culture were different than Japanese.

anime (animation) Although the Japanese didn't invent animated movies, Japanese anime is probably the most famous form of animation in the world today as fans in many cultures enjoy full-length anime movies and television series.

asobi This is a form of the Japanese term for the verb ''play.'' However, the word has broader connotations than the English term, which is usually associated with children. *Asobi* encompasses forms of sports and leisure in which people of all ages might engage.

Basho Matsuo (1644–1694) Basho, a celebrated poet in his own lifetime, is credited with being a leader in establishing haiku as a poetic form. Basho, who was heavily influenced by Zen in his later life, also wrote memorable journals about his travels.

bowing This Japanese custom upon meeting someone else, whether for the first time or many times, continues even though many Japanese will shake hands with Westerners. The polite bow is from the waist rather than just a nod of the head.

Buddhism This world religion that originated in South Asia and spread to China and the Korean Peninsula, was introduced by Koreans to the emerging Japanese nation in 552 CE. Buddhism profoundly changed Japan's cultural and religious landscape.

Burakumin The term translates as "hamlet" or "village" people but in Tokugawa Japan was the categorization of an outcaste group of ethnic Japanese who worked in occupations that involved flesh, such as butchery, undertaking, and tanning. Discrimination against burakumin, although legally eliminated, still sporadically occurs.

***chado* (chanoyu)** This term, meaning "the way of tea," is the Japanese name for the Zen-inspired tea ceremony that dates back to Japan's medieval period. The major objective of this practice is to reach enlightenment through the appreciation of the smallest details that accompany the preparing and serving of tea.

Confucianism Confucius (551–479 BCE) lived and taught in China. Confucianism spread from China to the Korean Peninsula and later Japan. The belief system still has major influence in East Asia today. Key beliefs of Confucianism include loyalty to family, respect for tradition and ritual, a focus on education, and knowledge of one's place in the social system.

Diet The Diet, Japan's bicameral legislature, was first established in the 1890 Constitution. The lower House of Representatives has the most powers of the two houses in the contemporary Japanese parliamentary democracy, but the upper House of Councilors has more powers than the British House of Lords, making the Diet a genuine two-house legislature.

Doi Takako (b. 1928) In 1986, Doi Takako earned the distinction of being the first woman to become the leader of a major political party—the Socialist Party of Japan. She later went on to become the lower house speaker in the 1991–1993 coalition government. An academic, Doi was first elected to the Diet in 1969 and worked for pacifist causes during her entire political career.

domo arigoto gozaimasu This polite form of thank you is used when another has done one special favors. "*Domo arigato*," "*arigato*," and "*domo*" are used for less significant situations.

Edo (present-day Tokyo) This sleepy fishing village was part of Tokugawa Ieyasu's ancestral lands, and he made it the capital shortly after unifying Japan in 1600. Edo and Tokugawa are both used as descriptors of the era between 1600 and 1868 that encompasses early modern Japanese history.

freeter This Japanese term is a loanword combining the English word "free" and the German word "*Arbeiter*." Although freeter does not have a precise definition, in general, it describes Japanese young people, some of whom have technical skills, who work part-time or temporarily for a company, save money, quit, enjoy extended leisure time until they need more resources, and then find a similar position and repeat the cycle.

gagaku "Elegant music" is the literal translation of gagaku. This now traditional Japanese genre was originally Chinese Tang dynasty (617–906 CE) imperial court music that was imported to Japan to give the new imperial system more status. Gagaku ceased being played in China more than 1,000 years ago but survives in Japan, where it is performed today. The music features an ensemble of reed and stringed instruments and percussion.

genkan This is the Japanese term for the entrance to a home. The *genkan* usually includes a raised horizontal floor and a space preceding it to take off shoes and step up into slippers.

gochiso sama When Japanese finish a meal, the appropriate phrase all use is *gochiso sama.* The literal translation is "it was indeed a feast," so in effect one is saying, "thank you for the lovely meal."

gohan This Japanese term for cooked rice also in traditional Japan was a synonym for "meal." *Asa gohan*, *hiru gohan*, and *ban gohan* still translate as breakfast, lunch, and dinner.

Great Kanto Earthquake This September 1, 1923, earthquake and subsequent series of fires destroyed most of Tokyo and almost all of Yokohama. The worst natural disaster in recorded Japanese history, this calamity resulted in more than 110,000 deaths.

hai Technically often mistranslated as "yes" in English, *hai* can mean yes, but it also has a more ambiguous meaning of "I understand what you are saying."

haiku This now world-famous short poetry featuring 17 syllables and three lines was developed from longer poetic forms in the 17th century. The purpose of haiku is to evoke a mood or feeling. Although traditional Japanese haiku employs seasonal references, contrary to popular opinion, haiku is not nature poetry.

Heian period (794–1156 CE) During this period of Japanese history, a few aristocrats in the imperial court in the city that is now Kyoto developed what is considered to be the basic elements of traditional Japanese culture.

Hiroshige Ando (1797–1858) This wood-block print artist's most famous series was *The Fifty-Three Stages of the Tokaido.* Hiroshige, the son of a fireman, also practiced that trade until he could make his living as an artist, did other travel ukiyo-e, and attained fame in his lifetime.

Hiroshima This present city of more than 1 million people had a population of 255,000 on August 6, 1945, when the United States dropped the first atomic bomb ever used in wartime. Although casualty estimates vary wildly, somewhere between 66,000 and 100,000 people died from the bombing immediately and a few days afterward.

Hokkaido Japan's most northern island, its 32,247 square miles constitute about one-fifth of Japan, but only 5.7 million people, or about 5 percent of the nation's population, live in Hokkaido.

Hokusai Katsushika (1760–1849) This artist who worked in a variety of mediums rose from humble origins to become one of Japan's most prolific artists.

Hokusai is most famous for his ukiyo-e and his celebrated *Great Wave off Kanagawa*.

Honda, Soichiro (1906–1991) The founder of Honda Motor Corporation made the company a major international corporation. Honda was highly unusual in the Japanese corporate world because he enjoyed talking with the press, raced cars and motorcycles, and had only an elementary education.

honne This Japanese word defines what one really feels about a given situation or person. Maintaining *wa*, or harmony, is an important objective in Japan, so traditionally Japanese are taught as children that it is often appropriate behavior to suppress one's true feelings.

Honshu Japan's largest island with approximately 89,000 square miles, Honshu also is home to approximately 80 percent of Japan's people and some of its biggest cities, including Tokyo, Yokohama, Osaka, Nagoya, Kobe, and Kyoto.

ikebana (flower arranging) This is a traditional Japanese art form that is highly influenced by Zen Buddhism and Japanese aesthetics. In ikebana, practitioners work to arrange one flower, rather than a number of flowers, in an attractive and natural way.

imperial system Although myths mark the date as much earlier, the system may have started in the 5th century CE with perhaps Emperor Ojin as the first ruler. Japan now has one of the longest continuous histories of an imperial system of any of the world's countries. From at least the 10th century, emperors tended to reign and not rule, and the American occupation–imposed constitution clearly defines the emperor as the symbol of the state with no political power.

itadakimasu When Japanese eat, it is customary for everyone to say *itadakimasu* before beginning. The translation is "I gratefully partake," and it is roughly equivalent to a blessing.

Kabuki This form of popular theater—the Chinese characters mean "song, dance, and skill"—originated during the Tokugawa period. Although it had its roots in wandering minstrels and appealed to a variety of classes, today kabuki is considered part of traditional Japanese culture.

kana Because Chinese characters alone proved inadequate for both writing and pronouncing an already existing spoken language on the archipelago, the Japanese developed simplified characters called "kana." The kana, hiragana and katakana, each contain 51 basic symbols representing specific sounds. Hiragana is used primarily for Japanese words and grammar, while katakana is used for foreign borrowed words.

kanji Kanji is the Japanese term for written Chinese characters. Chinese characters were imported into Japan from Korea sometime in the fourth century CE and are used in writing nouns and verbs in a sentence. Students are responsible for learning 1,945 kanji before graduating from high school.

Kanto This region, located in the eastern part of central Honshu, has an area of 12,504 square miles, is the most densely populated part of Japan, and contains Tokyo. Plains encompass more than half the region.

Kawabata Yasunari (1892–1972) Kawabata is considered one of Japan's finest novelists and was the first, in 1968, of two Japanese to date to win the Nobel Prize for Literature. *Snow Country* is the author's most famous work. Although trained in Western literature, Kawabata wrote vivid descriptions of traditional Japanese culture.

kendo (way of the sword) Kendo was one of the principal martial arts that samurai were required to learn. Today sticks are used instead of swords, and kendo clubs are popular in junior high schools.

***komban wa* (good evening)** This is a greeting Japanese use when seeing each other at night.

***konnichi wa* (good day)** This is a greeting that Japanese use when seeing each other during the day but not in the morning.

koto This (usually but not always) 13-stringed, wooden half-tube, semicylindrical zither had its origins in a related Chinese instrument but is now considered an integral part of Japanese traditional music. The player sits in front of the instrument and uses the left hand to manipulate moveable bridges and picks in the right hand to pluck the strings.

Kurosawa Akira (1910–1998) Akira Kurosawa is considered one of the greatest filmmakers in the global history of cinema. He made movies on a variety of subjects, and his cinematic techniques inspired filmmakers in other cultures. While maintaining a Japanese cultural perspective, Kurosawa addressed universal themes in his work.

Kyushu Japan's most southern main island has an area of 17,000 square miles and a population of close to 15 million people. Major cities include Fukuoka, Kitakyushu, Kumamoto, and Nagasaki.

MacArthur, Douglas (1880–1964) Although some scholars disagree, most analysts of the American occupation of Japan give General Douglas MacArthur considerable credit for overseeing a peaceful reconstruction of Japan from a militarily aggressive authoritarian state to a peaceful and prosperous parliamentary democracy.

manga (comic books) Japanese adults, young people, and children read manga, and the variety of topics included in manga dwarfs the range of Western comics. Just a few examples of manga include history, business, science fiction, biography, sports, and pornography.

matsuri This is the Japanese term for Shinto festivals that medium-sized and larger shrines often sponsor. The mostly annual events are colorful as revelers carry the local kami about in a portable shrine.

Meiji period (1868–1912) The young emperor who cooperated with the small group of leaders who overthrew the Tokugawa shogunate titled his reign Meiji, or ''Enlightened Rule.'' The period marked the modernization of Japan and its entry on the world geopolitical and economic stage.

***meishi* (name cards)** Business cards are absolutely essential in Japanese business culture, and professionals have them as well. In a hierarchal society, they help establish respective status when two people meet.

***mono no aware* (pathos of life)** This difficult-to-translate term with Buddhist connotations has come to define a traditional Japanese cultural propensity to find a sad sense of beauty in the transience of life.

Mount Fuji Located on the border between Shizuoka and Yamanashi prefectures in Honshu, this 12,385-foot dormant volcano is a universal symbol of Japan. Fuji was so highly regarded in Japanese history that it was given the honorific *san*.

Murasaki Shikibu (late 10th–early 11th centuries) Murasaki is the most famous woman novelist in Japan's history, and she authored *The Tale of Genji*, considered to be the world's first psychological novel. She wrote her masterpiece while serving as a lady-in-waiting for the empress.

Nippon (or Nihon) As the Japanese nation was developing, political elites, in an effort to gain status for the new state, took the Chinese characters for ''source'' and ''sun'' and named the country. This has evolved into such translations as ''land of the rising sun.''

Noh This traditional form of Japanese theater originated in the 14th century and is heavily influenced by Buddhism. Actors wear masks, and the performing art is as much dance as theater.

O-bento *O-bento* are box lunches with seafood or chicken, rice, and vegetables that are either prepared at home for school or work or available for purchase at train stations and department stores. *O-bento* boxes, especially the ones made of lacquer, are illustrative of the Japanese propensity for art in everyday objects.

***O-cha* (green tea)** Although a variety of teas are available in Japan, green tea is by far the most popular tea and has now attained global attention because of its possible healthful effects. *O-cha* is drunk hot or cold.

***O-furo* (bath)** This is a traditional Japanese bath. The whole custom of bathing in Japan includes more than just cleanliness and has an element of relaxation and release from the cares of the outside world. In Japan the custom is to clean oneself outside of the bath and then soak in the bath's hot waters.

***ohayo gozaimasu* (good morning)** This is a greeting that Japanese use before 10:00 A.M. *Ohayo gozaimasu* is the polite form, and *ohayo* is less formal.

pachinko This form of pinball, which millions love, features a vertical machine where the player attempts to manipulate falling silver balls into holes. Pachinko is a major service industry that accounted in a recent year for about one-quarter of all earnings in that entire sector of the economy. Successful players can trade in large numbers of winning balls for small prizes.

prefecture After the Meiji Restoration, the new government abolished the old administrative units and replaced them with prefectures. Today, Japan has 47 prefectures. Although similar to U.S. states in many ways, prefectural governments have less power than their American counterparts in interactions with the national government.

Pure Land Buddhism This popular form of Buddhism, based on the worship of the Amida Buddha of Infinite Light, who was part of the Buddhist pantheon in various Asian countries, became popular in late classical and early medieval Japan. Today, the two major Pure Land sects encompass the largest number of self-professed Japanese Buddhists.

Ryoanji Rock Garden This austere garden consisting of 15 rocks and white gravel surrounded by low walls was built in 1450 and is part of a small Zen temple. It is one of Japan's most famous cultural sites, and some believe it epitomizes the spirit of Zen.

sake Even though beer is now an even more popular alcoholic drink in Japan, sake, a rice wine, is not only widely consumed but is a national cultural symbol. Its roots go back to antiquity.

samurai This warrior class was in some ways, particularly during the Tokugawa period, equivalent to feudal European knights. By the 1600s, they were the only class allowed to bear arms and were given an education in both Confucian teachings and the martial arts.

san This is a Japanese honorific similar to the English Mr., Ms., or Mrs. However, *san* is used after a person's name and can be used in reference to a person of either gender. *San* is not used when referring to children.

sashimi Sashimi is sliced raw fish that is dipped into a small bowl of soy sauce and wasabi, a type of spicy horseradish. Standard accompaniments are pickled ginger and steamed rice.

sayonara This Japanese word means ''good-bye'' and is used if two people won't see each other for a long time or perhaps never again. Other terms such as ''*ja mata*'' are used if people are parting but will see each other again soon.

Shikoku The smallest of Japan's four major islands, Shikoku has an area of 7,262 square miles and a population of well over 4 million people. Major cities include Tokushima and Takamatsu.

Shinto Translated as ''way of the kami,'' the collection of spirit worship beliefs that later came to be known as Shinto constitutes Japan's only national indigenous religion.

shodo The literal meaning is the "way of writing," and it indicates the deeper meaning that Japanese place on calligraphy than simply a means of written communication. Calligraphy is considered an art form, and in the past it was believed that the quality of one's calligraphy was indicative of one's character.

Shogatsu (New Year's) The most popular holiday in Japan is celebrated, as is the case in the West, on January 1. During Shogatsu and the next two days, Japanese clean their houses, settle accounts, and visit friends. Millions of people visit Shinto shrines on Shogatsu.

shogun After Minamoto Yoritomo had gained control of Japan, in 1192 he manipulated the emperor into appointing him shogun, or "barbarian-suppressing general." Japan would be actually or nominally ruled by shoguns until the 1868 Meiji Restoration.

Shotoku Taishi (574–622) As the new Japanese state was taking shape, this prince who ruled as regent for 20 years was influential in disseminating advanced Chinese knowledge in the culture. He also issued a series of moral injunctions, largely based on Confucianism and Buddhism, that have been called, somewhat inaccurately, Japan's first "constitution."

Showa period (1926–1989) Although Emperor Hirohito selected Showa, or "Enlightened Peace," for his reign name, the 1930s and the first half of the 1940s were marked by Japan's militarist accession to power and World War II, but the emperor lived to see the Japanese "economic miracle."

sumimasen This Japanese word has a variety of meanings including excuse me, pardon me, I'm sorry, and thank you. It is one of the most useful Japanese words a foreign traveler can learn.

sumo This traditional Japanese sport featuring two large wrestlers who try to throw each other out of a small ring goes back to Japanese antiquity and harvest festivals. It remains a popular sport in Japan today.

sushi These are small rice canapés that contain bits of raw fish or vegetables. Sushi is usually wrapped in seaweed.

tatemae This Japanese term means what a person actually feels inside as opposed to the facade he or she might present to others. Japanese are part of a society that places special importance on the group, so there is more of a need to present an appearance that won't potentially offend people in Japan than is the case in many countries.

tempura Tempura consists of vegetables, fish, shrimp, or vegetables lightly coated with batter and fried, and it is eaten with a special sauce. Today it is considered a traditional Japanese food, but it was introduced by the Portuguese in the 16th century.

torii (gate) This is the gate to a Shinto shrine (*jinja*). The gate marks the dividing point between the physical and the spiritual. It is traditionally constructed of three pieces of wood.

Toyota (originally Toyoda) Toyota Motor Corporation is Japan's most famous and prestigious corporation. The company was founded by Toyoda Sakichi as a spinning and weaving company in 1918, and Toyota began automotive operations in 1933. Today, Toyota and GM vie for world leadership in automobile production and sales.

ukiyo-e (''pictures of the floating world'') This is now the Japanese term for wood-block print, and the original reference referred to the subjects of the prints, who were mostly courtesans and actors. The ''floating world'' reference has Buddhist connotations implying transience. Although wood-block printing was practiced in China, during the Tokugawa era such Japanese masters as Hokusai and Hiroshige created what is now a world-famous art form that is considered a quintessential part of traditional Japanese culture.

Yamamoto Isoroku (1884–1943) The innovative and highly intelligent Japanese admiral planned the Japanese attack on Pearl Harbor. It is ironic that Yamamoto admired the United States and had worked and studied there, including at Harvard. He reluctantly planned the operation after attempting to discourage Japan's political leaders from going to war with the United States.

Yoshida Shigeru (1878–1967) Diplomat and politician, Yoshida served as prime minister during much of the occupation period. He was a forward-thinking conservative who managed to work with the Americans to create a situation where Japan could count on U.S. military protection and have the freedom to concentrate on rebuilding the nation's economy.

Zen This Buddhist sect that originated in China and spread to Japan and Korea emphasizes meditation. Zen has a profound influence on traditional Japanese arts including the tea ceremony, kendo, and Japanese gardens.

Facts and Figures

The following tables present facts and figures about contemporary Japan. These statistics begin with basic facts about the country and continue with the country's demographics (including population, ethnicity, and religion), geography, economy, communications and transportation, military, and education. Following these basic facts and figures, more detailed data of interest are presented as a series of tables, charts, and graphs.

COUNTRY INFORMATION

Table A.1. Country Information

Location	Comprises the Japanese Archipelago in Northeast Asia, situated between the Pacific Ocean to the west and the Sea of Japan to the east, and several smaller islands and islets, including the Ryukyu Islands to the southwest of the main archipelago
Name	Nihon
Government	Constitutional monarchy with parliamentary legislature
Capital	Tokyo
Weights and measures	Metric system
Time zone	13 hours ahead of eastern standard time
Currency	Japanese yen
Head of state	Emperor Akihito

(*Continued*)

Table A.1. Country Information (*Continued*)

Head of government	Prime Minister Aso Taro
Legislature	Bicameral; National Diet of Japan consists of House of Representatives (lower house) and House of Councilors (upper house)
Major political parties	Liberal Democratic Party (LDP, Jiyu Minshuto), Democratic Party of Japan (DPJ, Minshuto), New Komeito Party (NKP, Komeito), Japanese Communist Party (JCP, Nihon Kyosanto), Social Democratic Party (SDP, Shakai Minshuto), People's New Party (PNP, Kokumin Shinto), New Party Nippon (NPN, Shinto Nippon), New Party Daichi (NPD, Shinto Daichi)

DEMOGRAPHICS

This table features information about the people of Japan, including statistics on population, religion, language, and voting.

Table A.2. Demographics

Population	127,288,419 (2008 est.)
Population by age	(2008 est.)
0–14	13.7%
15–64	64.7%
65+	21.6%
Median age	(2008 est.)
Total	43.8 years
Males	42.1 years
Females	45.7 years
Population growth rate	– 0.139 (2008 est.)
Population density	873 people per sq. mile (2008 est.)
Infant mortality rate	2.8 deaths per 1,000 live births (2008 est.)
Ethnic groups	Japanese (98.5%), Chinese, Korean, Other (2004)
Religions	84% Shinto, 70% Buddhist, 2% Christian; 8% belong to Shinshukyo (''New Religions''), including Tenrikyo, Aleph, Mahikari, Shinreikyo, the Church of World Messianity, and Seicho no ie. *Note: Shinto is commonly practiced by adherents of other faiths, particularly Buddhists.*
Majority language	Japanese
Other languages	English is a common second language; small populations speak Ryukyuan languages (Amami, Miyako, Okinawan, Kunigama, Yaeyama, Yonaguni); the Ainu language is nearly extinct, spoken by only a handful of people
Voting age	20 years
Voter participation	

TABLE A.2. Demographics (*Continued*)

	58.6% in 2007 House of Councilors election; 67.5% in 2005 House of Representatives election
Literacy	99% (2002)
Life expectancy (average)	82.1 years (2008 est.)
Fertility rate	1.2 children per woman (2008 est.)

GEOGRAPHY

The following table provides general facts and figures on the geography of Japan.

TABLE A.3. Geography

Land area	145,877 sq. miles
Arable land	13%
Irrigated land	10,008 sq. miles (2003)
Coastline	18,487 miles
Natural hazards	Volcanoes, earthquakes, tsunamis, typhoons
Environmental problems	Air pollution, acid rain, acidification of freshwater resources, overfishing
Major agricultural products	Rice, vegetables, sugar beets, pork, poultry, eggs, milk, citrus fruit, fish
Natural resources	Fish, swift rivers, few mineral resources
Land use	12% cropland, 2% permanent pasture, 67% forests and woodlands, 19% other
Climate	Temperate, humid throughout the year

ECONOMY

This table offers basic economic information for Japan, including financial, labor, trade, and industrial statistics.

TABLE A.4. Economy

Gross domestic product (GDP)	$4.4 trillion (2007)
GDP per capita	$35,651 (2007 est.)
GDP by sector	Agriculture, forestry, hunting, and fishing: 1.4%; mining, manufacturing, and utilities: 22.6%; construction: 6.1%; wholesale and retail trade, hotels, and restaurants: 13.3%; transportation and communication: 6.6%; finance, insurance, real estate, and business services: 18.3%; government services, education, and health care: 5.5%; other services: 22.6% (2005)

(*Continued*)

Table A.4. Economy (*Continued*)

Exchange rate	118 yen = US$1 (2007)
Labor force	Agriculture, hunting, forestry, and fishing: 4.3%; manufacturing, resource extraction, and utilities: 19.3%; transportation and communication: 6.2%; construction: 8.8%; government, community, and social services: 22.6%; commerce: 37.8%; other: 1.1% (2006)
Unemployment	3.8% (2007 est.)
Major industries	Motor vehicles, electronics, semiconductor devices, machine tools, steel and nonferrous metals, chemicals, pharmaceuticals, textiles, shipbuilding, processed foods
Leading companies	Toyota Motor, Nippon Telegraph & Telephone, Honda Motor, Mitsubishi, Sumitomo, Mitsui, Nissan Motor, Sony, Canon, Nikon, Toshiba, Hitachi, Sanyo Electric, Panasonic, Japan Tobacco, Nippon Steel, Nintendo, Takeda Pharmaceutical, Denso, KDDI, Nippon Oil, Sojitz, Shin-Etsu Chemical, Astellas Pharma
Exports	$646.8 billion (2006)
Export goods	Machinery, motor vehicles and parts, consumer electronics, cameras and photographic equipment, scientific instruments, watches, electronic and telecommunications equipment, chemicals, metals
Imports	$578.7 billion (2006)
Import goods	Petroleum, coal, natural gas, metals, machinery and equipment, food, chemicals, textiles, raw materials
Current account balance	$210.5 billion (2007 est.)

COMMUNICATIONS AND TRANSPORTATION

The following table features facts and figures on Japan's communications networks and transportation.

Table A.5. Communications and Transportation

Electricity production	1.025 trillion kWh (2005)
Electricity consumption	974.2 billion kWh (2005)
Telephone lines	51.2 million (2007)
Mobile phones	107.3 million (2007)
Internet users	88.11 million (2007)
Roads	743,781 miles (2006)
Railroads	14,586 miles (2006)
Airports	176 (2007)

MILITARY

Since World War II, the Japanese military has been officially limited to self-defense activities although troops have been deployed overseas in limited roles a number of times. The following table outlines some basic military statistics.

Table A.6. Military

Defense spending (% of GDP)	0.8% (2006)
Active armed forces	239,900 (2004)
Manpower fit for military service	22,963,000 males; 22,134,127 females (2008 est.)

EDUCATION

The Japanese educational system is well known and respected around the world. The following table presents some basic statistics about education in Japan.

Table A.7. Education

Estimated literacy rate (estimates vary 95–97%)	98–99%
Students in high school	97.7% of age cohort
Female high school graduates in college	51%
Male high school graduates in college	56.6%
High school graduates in vocational school	17.8%

Sources: ABC-CLIO World Geography database; *CIA World Factbook* (https://www.cia.gov/library/publications/the-world-factbook); U.S. Department of State, *Japan: International Religious Freedom Report 2008* (http://www.state.gov/g/drl/rls/irf/2008/108408.htm); U.S. Department of State, *Background Notes: Japan*, September 2008 (http://www.state.gov/r/pa/ei/bgn/4142.htm).

Source: *Facts and Figures of Japan 2007* (Tokyo: Foreign Press Center, 2007).

PRIME MINISTERS OF JAPAN, 1885–PRESENT

Since the adoption of the 1889 constitution, Japanese prime ministers have been chief executives in a parliamentary system although many prime ministers have only exercised limited political power.

Table B. Prime Ministers of Japan, 1885–Present

Prime Minister	Took Office	Left Office	Party
Ito Hirobumi	December 22, 1885	April 30, 1888	None
Kuroda Kiyotaka	April 30, 1888	October 25, 1889	None
Sanjo Sanetomi	October 25, 1889	December 24, 1889	None

(*Continued*)

Table B. Prime Ministers of Japan, 1885–Present (*Continued*)

Prime Minister	Took Office	Left Office	Party
Yamagata Aritomo	December 24, 1889	May 6, 1891	None
Matsukata Masayoshi	May 6, 1891	August 8, 1882	None
Ito Hirobumi	August 8, 1892	August 31, 1896	None
Kuroda Kiyotaka (acting prime minister)	August 31, 1896	September 18, 1896	None
Matsukata Masayoshi	September 18, 1896	January 12, 1898	None
Ito Hirobumi	January 12, 1898	June 30, 1898	None
Okuma Shigenobu	June 30, 1898	November 8, 1898	Constitutional Party (Kenseito)
Yamagata Aritomo	November 8, 1898	October 19, 1900	None
Ito Hirobumi	October 19, 1900	May 10, 1901	Friends of Constitutional Government (Seiyukai)
Saionji Kimochi (acting prime minister)	May 10, 1901	June 2, 1901	None
Katsura Taro	June 2, 1901	January 7, 1906	None
Saionji Kimochi	January 7, 1906	July 14, 1908	Seiyukai
Katsura Taro	July 14, 1908	August 30, 1911	None
Saionji Kimochi	August 30, 1911	December 21, 1912	Seiyukai
Katsura Taro	December 21, 1912	February 20, 1913	None
Yamamoto Gonbei	February 20, 1913	April 16, 1914	Imperial Japanese Navy
Okuma Shigenobu	April 16, 1914	October 9, 1916	Kenseito
Terauchi Masatake	October 9, 1916	September 29, 1918	Imperial Japanese Army
Hara Takashi	September 29, 1918	November 4, 1921	Seiyukai
Uchida Kosai (acting prime minister)	November 4, 1921	November 13, 1921	None
Takahashi Korekiyo	November 13, 1921	June 12, 1922	Seiyukai
Kato Tomosaburo	June 12, 1922	August 24, 1923	Imperial Japanese Navy
Uchida Kosai (acting prime minister)	August 24, 1923	September 2, 1923	None
Yamamoto Gonbei	September 2, 1923	January 7, 1924	Imperial Japanese Navy
Kiyoura Keigo	January 7, 1924	June 11, 1924	None
Kato Takaaki	June 11, 1924	January 28, 1926	Constitutional Party (Kenseikai)
Wakatsuki Reijiro (acting prime minister)	January 28, 1926	January 30, 1926	Kenseikai

Table B. Prime Ministers of Japan, 1885–Present (*Continued*)

Prime Minister	Took Office	Left Office	Party
Wakatsuki Reijiro	January 30, 1926	April 20, 1927	Kenseikai
Tanaka Giichi	April 20, 1927	July 2, 1929	Seiyukai
Hamaguchi Osachi	July 2, 1929	April 14, 1931	Constitutional Democratic Party (Minseito)
Wakatsuki Reijiro	April 14, 1931	December 13, 1931	Minseito
Inukai Tsuyoshi	December 13, 1931	May 16, 1932	Seiyukai
Takehashi Korekiyo	May 16, 1932	May 26, 1932	Seiyukai
Saito Makoto	May 26, 1932	July 8, 1934	Imperial Japanese Navy
Okada Keisuke	July 8, 1934	March 9, 1936	Imperial Japanese Navy
Hirota Koki	March 9, 1936	February 2, 1937	None
Hayashi Senjuro	February 2, 1937	June 4, 1937	Imperial Japanese Navy
Konoe Fumimaro	June 4, 1937	January 5, 1939	None
Hiranuma Kiichiro	January 5, 1939	August 30, 1939	None
Abe Nobuyuki	August 30, 1939	January 16, 1940	Imperial Japanese Army
Yonai Mitsumasa	January 16, 1940	July 22, 1940	Imperial Japanese Navy
Konoe Fumimaro	July 22, 1940	October 18, 1941	Imperial Rule Assistance Association (IRAA, Taisei Yokusankai)
Tojo Hideki	October 18, 1941	July 22, 1944	Imperial Japanese Army
Koiso Kuniaki	July 22, 1944	April 7, 1945	Imperial Japanese Army
Suzuki Kantaro	April 7, 1945	August 17, 1945	Imperial Japanese Navy
Prince Higashikuni Naruhiko	August 17, 1945	October 9, 1945	None
Shidehara Kijuro	October 9, 1945	May 22, 1946	None
Yoshida Shigeru	May 22, 1946	May 24, 1947	Liberal Party (Jiyuto)
Katakama Tetsu	May 24, 1947	March 10, 1948	Japan Socialist Party (JSP, Nihon Shakaito)
Ashida Hitoshi	March 10, 1948	October 15, 1948	Japan Democratic Party (JDP, Nihon Minshuto)
Yoshida Shigeru	October 15, 1948	December 10, 1954	Jiyuto
Hatoyama Ichiro	December 10, 1954	December 23, 1956	JDP; after 1955 merger with Jiyuto, Liberal Democratic Party (LDP, Jiyu-Minshuto)
Ishibashi Tanzan	December 23, 1956	February 25, 1957	LDP
Kishi Nobusuke	February 25, 1957	July 19, 1960	LDP
Ikeda Hayato	July 19, 1960	November 9, 1964	LDP
Sato Eisaku	November 9, 1964	July 7, 1972	LDP
Tanaka Kakuei	July 7, 1972	December 9, 1974	LDP
Miki Takeo	December 9, 1974	December 24, 1976	LDP
Fukuda Takeo	December 24, 1976	December 7, 1978	LDP

(*Continued*)

Table B. Prime Ministers of Japan, 1885–Present (*Continued*)

Prime Minister	Took Office	Left Office	Party
Ohira Masayoshi	December 7, 1978	June 12, 1980	LDP
Ito Masayoshi (acting prime minister)	June 12, 1980	July 17, 1980	LDP
Suzuki Zenko	July 17, 1980	November 27, 1982	LDP
Nakasone Yasuhiro	November 27, 1982	November 6, 1987	LDP
Takeshita Noburo	November 6, 1987	June 3, 1989	LDP
Uno Sosuke	June 3, 1989	August 10, 1989	LDP
Kaifu Toshiki	August 10, 1989	November 5, 1991	LDP
Miyazawa Kiichi	November 5, 1991	August 9, 1993	LDP
Hosokawa Morihiro	August 9, 1993	April 28, 1994	Japan New Party (Nihon Shinto)
Hata Tsutomo	April 28, 1994	June 30, 1994	Japan Renewal Party (JRP, Shinseito)
Murayama Tomiichi	June 30, 1994	January 11, 1996	Social Democratic Party of Japan (SDPJ, Shakai Minshuto)
Hashimoto Ryutaro	January 11, 1996	July 30, 1998	LDP
Obuchi Keizo	July 30, 1998	April 5, 2000	LDP
Mori Yoshiro	April 5, 2000	April 26, 2001	LDP
Koizumi Junichiro	April 26, 2001	September 26, 2006	LDP
Abe Shinzo	September 26, 2006	September 26, 2007	LDP
Fukuda Yasuo	September 26, 2007	September 24, 2008	LDP
Aso Taro	September 24, 2008	n/a	LDP

LEGENDARY AND HISTORICAL EMPERORS OF JAPAN, 660 BCE–PRESENT

Although Japan's imperial institution is the world's oldest, scholars don't agree on who was the first historically verifiable emperor. Cases are made for Sujin (97 BCE–30 CE) and Ojin (270–310 CE).

Table C. Legendary and Historical Emperors of Japan, 660 BCE–Present

Emperor/Empress[1]	Beginning of Reign[2]	End of Reign[2]
Jimmu[3]	660 BCE	585 BCE
Suizei[3]	581	549
Annei[3]	549	511

TABLE C. Legendary and Historical Emperors of Japan, 660 BCE–Present (*Continued*)

Emperor/Empress[1]	Beginning of Reign[2]	End of Reign[2]
Itoku[3]	510	476
Kosho[3]	475	393
Koan[3]	392	291
Korei[3]	290	215
Kogen[3]	214	158
Kaika[3]	157	98
Sujin[3]	97	30
Suinin[3]	29 BCE	70 CE
Keiko[3]	71 CE	130
Seimu[3]	131	191
Chuai[3]	192	200
Jingu[3]	201	269
Ojin	270	310
Nintoku	313	399
Richu	400	405
Hanzei	406	410
Ingyo	411	453
Anko	453	456
Yuryaku	456	479
Seinei	480	484
Kenzo	485	487
Ninken	488	498
Buretsu	498	506
Keitai	507	531
Ankan	531	535
Senka	535	539
Kimmei	539	571
Bidatsu	572	585
Yomei	585	587
Sushun	587	592
Suiko	592	628
Jomei	629	641
Kogyoku[4]	642	645
Kotoku	645	654
Saimei[4]	655	661
Tenji	661	672
Kobun	672	672
Temmu	672	686
Jito	686	697

(*Continued*)

TABLE C. Legendary and Historical Emperors of Japan, 660 BCE–Present (*Continued*)

Emperor/Empress[1]	Beginning of Reign[2]	End of Reign[2]
Mommu	697	707
Gemmei	707	715
Gensho	715	724
Shomu	724	749
Koken[5]	749	758
Junnin	758	764
Shotoku[5]	764	770
Konin	770	781
Kammu	781	806
Heizei	806	809
Saga	809	823
Junna	823	833
Ninmyo	833	850
Montoku	850	858
Seiwa	858	876
Yozei	876	884
Koko	884	887
Uda	887	897
Daigo	897	930
Suzaku	930	946
Murakami	946	967
Reizei	967	969
En'yu	969	984
Kazan	984	986
Ichijo	986	1011
Sanjo	1011	1016
Go-Ichijo	1016	1036
Go-Suzaku	1036	1045
Go-Reizei	1045	1068
Go-Sanjo	1068	1073
Shirakawa	1073	1086
Horikawa	1087	1107
Toba	1107	1123
Sutoku	1123	1142
Konoe	1142	1155
Go-Shirakawa	1155	1158
Nijo	1158	1165
Rokujo	1165	1168
Takakura	1168	1180

TABLE C. Legendary and Historical Emperors of Japan, 660 BCE–Present (*Continued*)

Emperor/Empress[1]	Beginning of Reign[2]	End of Reign[2]
Antoku[6]	1180	1185
Go-Toba[6]	1183	1198
Tsuchimikado	1198	1210
Juntoku	1210	1221
Chukyo	1221	1221
Go-Horikawa	1221	1232
Shijo	1232	1242
Go-Saga	1242	1246
Go-Fukakusa	1246	1260
Kameyama	1260	1274
Go-Uda	1274	1287
Fushimi	1287	1298
Go-Fushimi	1298	1301
Go-Nijo	1301	1308
Hanazono	1308	1318
Go-Daigo	1318	1339
Kogon[7]	1331	1333
Komyo[7]	1336	1348
Go-Murakami	1339	1368
Suko[7]	1348	1351
Go-Kogon[7]	1351	1371
Chokei	1368	1383
Go-En'yu[7]	1371	1382
Go-Kameyama	1383	1392
Go-Komatsu[8]	1382	1412
Shoko	1412	1428
Go-Hanazono	1428	1464
Go-Tsuchimikado	1464	1500
Go-Kashiwabara	1500	1526
Go-Nara	1526	1557
Ogimachi	1557	1586
Go-Yozei	1586	1611
Go-Mizunoo	1611	1629
Meisho	1629	1643
Go-Komyo	1643	1654
Go-Sai	1655	1663
Reigen	1663	1687
Higashiyama	1687	1709
Nakamikado	1709	1735

(*Continued*)

Table C. Legendary and Historical Emperors of Japan, 660 BCE–Present (*Continued*)

Emperor/Empress[1]	Beginning of Reign[2]	End of Reign[2]
Sakuramachi	1735	1747
Momozono	1747	1762
Go-Sakuramachi	1762	1771
Go-Momozono	1771	1779
Kokaku	1780	1817
Ninko	1817	1846
Komei	1831	1867
Meiji[9]	1867	1912
Taisho[9]	1912	1926
Showa (Hirohito)[8]	1926	1989
Tenno Heika (current emperor, Akihito)[9, 10]	1989	n/a

1. Since at least the reign of Temmu, the title *tenno*, which translates to ''emperor,'' has been used to refer to the monarch of Japan. In earlier periods, such titles as *sumeramikoto*, which roughly translates to ''heavenly ruler,'' and *okimi*, which can be translated as ''great king,'' were used.
2. Regnal dates prior to the reign of Kimmei (539–571 CE) may be inaccurate.
3. Emperors prior to the reign of Ojin are mentioned in such ancient sources as the *Kojiki* (*Records of Ancient Matters*) and the *Nihon Shoki* (*Chronicles of Japan*) but are usually considered legendary. Thus, information about their reigns may be unreliable.
4. Kogyoku and Saimei were the same person.
5. Koken and Shotoku were the same person.
6. There is some overlap between the reigns of Antoku and Go-Toba, as both claimed the title of emperor for a time during the power struggle between the Taira and Minamoto clans.
7. Ashikaga (Northern Court) emperors during the Period of Northern and Southern Courts.
8. The Northern and Southern Courts were reunified during the reign of Ashikaga (Northern Court) emperor Go-Komatsu, who became the emperor of a unified court on October 21, 1392.
9. Since the reign of Showa, emperors have often been referred to by their personal name (*imina*) in Western sources, though this is uncommon in Japanese sources.
10. The current emperor, Akihito, is called Tenno Heika, which is usually translated as ''His Imperial Majesty, the Emperor,'' though his regnal period is known as Heisei, which is to be his posthumous imperial name.

Source: Gen Isataka, ed., *Kodansha Encyclopedia of Japan*, Vol. 2 (Tokyo: Kodansha International, 1983), 202–203.

PRODUCTION OF RICE AND LAND UNDER CULTIVATION, 1980–2005

Rice is Japan's most important crop, as it is not just a food but also has deep connections with early Japan. The following tables detail total Japanese rice production and cultivated land and rice production for each prefecture.

Table D. Production of Rice and Land Under Cultivation, 1980–2005

Year	Total Cultivated Land (hectares)	Utilization Rate of Cultivated Land (%)	Land under Rice Cultivation (hectares)	Production of Rice (metric tons)
1980	5,706,000	104.5	2,377,000	9,751,000
1985	5,656,000	105.1	2,342,000	11,662,000
1990	5,349,000	102.0	2,074,000	10,499,000
1995	4,920,000	97.7	2,118,000	10,748,000
2000	4,563,000	94.5	1,770,000	9,490,000
2003	4,450,000	94.0	1,665,000	7,792,000
2004	4,422,000	93.8	1,701,000	8,730,000
2005	4,384,000	93.4	1,706,000	9,074,000

Source: Statistics Department, Minister's Secretariat, Ministry of Agriculture, Forestry, and Fisheries (http://www.stat.go.jp/english/data/nenkan/1431-07.htm). Data are based on the Crop Survey.

PLANTED AREA AND PRODUCTION OF RICE BY PREFECTURE, 2005

Table E. Planted Area and Production of Rice by Prefecture, 2005

Prefecture	Total Cultivated Land (hectares)	Utilization Rate of Cultivated Land (%)	Land under Rice Cultivation (hectares)	Production of Rice (metric tons)
Hokkaido	1,164,000	99.6	119,100	683,000
Aomori	138,300	86.9	53,800	323,000
Iwate	134,800	86.1	60,600	326,000
Miyagi	121,700	88.2	79,500	424,000
Akita	133,300	87.6	94,600	544,000
Yamagata	112,800	90.3	71,700	430,000
Fukushima	131,900	86.1	82,800	449,000
Ibaraki	162,200	91.5	81,400	425,000
Tochigi	122,500	94.2	69,000	375,000
Gumma	73,100	93.1	19,500	96,000
Saitama	71,600	84.4	37,400	185,000
Chiba	126,300	94.7	63,100	339,000
Tokyo	8,010	96.0	230	900
Kanagawa	20,600	97.6	3,330	16,000
Niigata	154,400	87.2	121,000	652,000

(Continued)

Table E. Planted Area and Production of Rice by Prefecture, 2005 (*Continued*)

Prefecture	Total Cultivated Land (hectares)	Utilization Rate of Cultivated Land (%)	Land under Rice Cultivation (hectares)	Production of Rice (metric tons)
Toyama	54,300	90.3	41,100	221,000
Ishikawa	37,200	83.6	27,200	142,000
Fukui	40,800	98.6	28,300	148,000
Yamanashi	23,100	89.2	5,540	31,000
Nagano	101,300	89.2	36,700	237,000
Gifu	54,200	91.7	26,200	127,000
Shizuoka	68,700	91.5	18,500	96,000
Aichi	77,100	91.8	32,000	162,000
Mie	55,900	88.3	32,400	161,000
Shiga	53,400	97.8	35,300	189,000
Kyoto	27,200	82.4	16,400	85,000
Osaka	12,400	85.5	6,310	31,000
Hyogo	67,300	87.1	40,800	208,000
Nara	18,200	78.1	9,850	50,000
Wakayama	33,700	91.1	8,010	39,000
Tottori	30,100	84.6	14,400	73,000
Shimane	32,300	81.8	20,600	106,000
Okayama	57,600	81.1	35,000	182,000
Hiroshima	48,300	79.8	27,100	143,000
Yamaguchi	41,100	79.8	24,500	123,000
Tokushima	31,300	96.6	14,100	69,000
Kagawa	30,500	93.0	15,400	77,000
Ehime	52,600	92.4	16,100	79,000
Kochi	26,000	90.0	13,900	66,000
Fukuoka	100,600	111.9	41,600	201,000
Saga	74,400	132.9	29,500	145,000
Nagasaki	49,100	95.7	14,700	66,000
Kumamoto	116,700	96.9	42,700	204,000
Oita	57,400	95.0	26,200	120,000
Miyazaki	76,900	109.5	21,900	103,000
Kagoshima	123,200	98.2	25,900	121,000
Okinawa	35,400	90.1	1,060	3,000

Source: Statistics Department, Minister's Secretariat, Ministry of Agriculture, Forestry, and Fisheries (http://www.stat.go.jp/english/data/nenkan/1431-07.htm). Data are based on the Crop Survey.

SOYBEAN PRODUCTION AND LAND UNDER CULTIVATION, 1980–2005

Like rice, the food products made from soybeans are a major staple of Japanese cuisine. The following table details Japanese soybean production over a quarter-century.

Table F. Soybean Production and Land Under Cultivation, 1980–2005

Harvesting Year	Total Cultivated Land (hectares)	Soybeans		Soybeans, Green	
		Planted Area (hectares)	Production (metric tons)	Planted Area (hectares)	Production (metric tons)
1980	5,706,000	142,000	174,000	14,000	118,000
1985	5,656,000	134,000	228,000	14,000	116,000
1990	5,349,000	146,000	220,000	14,000	103,000
1995	4,920,000	69,000	119,000	13,000	79,000
2000	4,563,000	123,000	235,000	13,000	81,000
2003	4,450,000	152,000	232,000	13,000	77,000
2004	4,422,000	137,000	163,000	13,000	73,000
2005	4,384,000	134,000	225,000	13,000	77,000

Sources: Statistics Department, Minister's Secretariat, Ministry of Agriculture, Forestry, and Fisheries; Staple Food Department, General Food Policy Bureau (http://www.stat.go.jp/english/data/nenkan/1431-07.htm). Data are based on the Crop Survey.

FISHING CATCH AND AQUACULTURE, 1985–2004

Fish is a main staple of the Japanese diet, and the country's island location gives its fishing industry a wide selection of offshore waters to pursue this indispensable fare. The table on page 362 provides specific figures on Japan's fishing industry over nearly two decades.

TABLE G. Fishing Catch and Aquaculture, 1985–2004 (quantity of catches in 1,000 t)

Year	Total	Total Marine Fisheries and Aquaculture	Marine Fisheries	Pelagic	Offshore	Coastal	Marine Aquaculture	Total Inland Fisheries and Aquaculture	Inland Fisheries	Inland Aquaculture	Whaling (number of whales caught)
1985	12,171	11,965	10,877	2,111	6,498	2,268	1,088	206	110	96	3,087
1990	11,052	10,843	9,570	1,496	6,081	1,992	1,273	209	112	97	96
1995	7,489	7,322	6,007	917	3,260	1,831	1,315	167	92	75	174
2000	6,384	6,252	5,022	855	2,591	1,576	1,231	132	71	61	188
2002	5,880	5,767	4,434	686	2,258	1,489	1,333	113	61	51	157
2003	6,083	5,973	4,722	602	2,543	1,577	1,251	110	60	50	150
2004	5,776	5,670	4,455	535	2,406	1,514	1,215	106	60	46	111

Source: Statistics Department, Minister's Secretariat, Ministry of Agriculture, Forestry, and Fisheries (http://www.stat.go.jp/english/data/nenkan/1431-07.htm). Data are based on the Survey on Marine Production and the Survey on Inland Water Fishery and Aquaculture Production.

WHALING, 1980–2004

Japan remains one of the few countries in the world that continues to pursue whaling. Although Japan claims that most of its whaling expeditions are for research purposes, the figures in the table on page 364 illustrate the large volume of whales caught by Japanese whalers since 1980.

Table H. Whaling, 1980–2004

Year	Whaling				Whaling in the Antarctic Ocean[1]			Survey Whaling in the Northwest Pacific Ocean			
	Whaling Ships	Total Whales Caught	Humpback Whales Caught	Pilot Whales Caught	Whaling Ships	Number of Workers	Total Whales Caught	Whaling Ships	Number of Workers	Total Whales Caught	Minke Whales Caught
1980	8	413	31	1	7	431	3,279	–	–	–	–
1985	9	429	40	62	7	332	1,941	–	–	–	–
1990	9	96	54	18	3	135	330	–	–	–	–
1995	9	174	54	100	3	163	330	3	151	100	100
2000	9	188	62	106	3	174	439	3	169	88	40
2002	5	157	62	83	3	173	440	6	183	244	150
2003	5	150	62	69	3	176	440	7	184	260	150
2004	5	111	62	42	3	181	440	6	187	312	159

1. Data for 1980–1985 include commercial whaling; all other years are for survey whaling only.

Source: Statistics Department, Minister's Secretariat, Ministry of Agriculture, Forestry, and Fisheries (http://www.stat.go.jp/english/data/nenkan/1431-07.htm). Data are based on the Survey on Marine Production.

PRODUCTION OF SELECT BEVERAGES AND FOODS, 1985–2005

Such foods and beverages as miso, soy sauce, and sake will always be associated with Japan. The table on page 366 presents statistics on production of select food and beverage products over a 20-year period.

Table I. Production of Select Beverages and Foods, 1985–2005

Year	Refined Sake (kiloliters)	*Shochu* (kiloliters)	Beer (kiloliters)	Miso (metric tons)	Soy Sauce (kiloliters)	Wheat Flour (metric tons)	Soybean Oil (metric tons)
1985	928,000	668,000	4,852,000	573,000	1,186,000	4,243,000	711,000
1990	1,060,000	592,000	6,564,000	555,000	1,177,000	4,338,000	665,000
1995	980,000	675,000	6,797,000	541,000	1,122,000	4,633,000	680,000
2000	720,000	757,000	5,464,000	533,000	1,065,000	4,623,000	694,000
2003	601,000	923,000	3,959,000	510,000	981,000	4,662,000	760,000
2004	562,000	1,043,000	3,844,000	508,000	954,000	4,667,000	639,000
2005	533,000	1,042,000	3,650,000	497,000	939,000	4,624,000	575,000

Note: Figures for liquors are from the National Tax Administration Agency.

Sources: Canners Association of Japan; Director-General's Secretariat, National Tax Administration Agency; Japan Frozen Food Association (http://www.stat.go.jp/english/data/nenkan/1431-08.htm); Marketing Department, Food Agency; Statistics and Information Department, Economic Affairs Bureau, Ministry of Agriculture, Forestry, and Fisheries. Data are based on the Survey on Current Production of Processed Food from Rice and Wheat and the Survey on the Status of Processed Foods Production.

POPULATION AND POPULATION DENSITY, 1872–2006

For a country whose entire area is smaller than the state of California, Japan has a lot of people. The following table and graphs track the dramatic growth of Japan's population and population density from the late 19th century to the early 21st century.

TABLE J. Population and Population Density, 1872–2006

Year	Total Population (thousands)	Males (thousands)	Females (thousands)	Population Density (people per sq. km)
1872	34,806	17,666	17,140	91
1873	34,985	17,755	17,230	92
1874	35,154	17,835	17,319	92
1875	35,316	17,913	17,403	93
1876	35,555	18,030	17,525	93
1877	35,870	18,187	17,683	94
1878	36,166	18,327	17,839	95
1879	36,464	18,472	17,992	96
1880	36,649	18,559	18,090	96
1881	36,965	18,712	18,253	97
1882	37,259	18,854	18,405	98
1883	37,569	19,006	18,563	98
1884	37,962	19,199	18,763	99
1885	38,313	19,368	18,945	100
1886	38,541	19,480	19,061	101
1887	38,703	19,554	19,149	101
1888	39,029	19,716	19,313	102
1889	39,473	19,940	19,533	103
1890	39,902	20,153	19,749	105
1891	40,251	20,322	19,929	105
1892	40,508	20,443	20,065	106
1893	40,860	20,616	20,244	107
1894	41,142	20,755	20,387	108
1895	41,557	20,960	20,597	109
1896	41,992	21,164	20,828	110
1897	42,400	21,356	21,044	111
1898	42,886	21,590	21,296	112
1899	43,404	21,836	21,568	114
1900	43,847	22,051	21,796	115
1901	44,359	22,298	22,061	116
1902	44,964	22,606	22,358	118

(Continued)

Table J. Population and Population Density, 1872–2006 (*Continued*)

Year	Total Population (thousands)	Males (thousands)	Females (thousands)	Population Density (people per sq. km)
1903	45,546	22,901	22,645	119
1904	46,135	23,195	22,940	121
1905	46,620	23,421	23,199	122
1906	47,038	23,599	23,439	123
1907	47,416	23,786	23,630	124
1908	47,965	24,041	23,924	126
1909	48,554	24,326	24,228	127
1910	49,184	24,650	24,534	129
1911	49,852	24,993	24,859	131
1912	50,577	25,365	25,212	133
1913	51,305	25,737	25,568	134
1914	52,039	26,105	25,934	136
1915	52,752	26,465	26,287	138
1916	53,496	26,841	26,655	140
1917	54,134	27,158	26,976	142
1918	54,739	27,453	27,286	143
1919	55,033	27,602	27,431	144
1920	55,473	27,812	27,661	145
1920	55,963	28,044	27,919	147
1921	56,666	28,412	28,254	148
1922	57,390	28,800	28,590	150
1923	58,119	29,177	28,942	152
1924	58,876	29,569	29,307	154
1925	59,737	30,013	29,724	157
1926	60,741	30,521	30,220	159
1927	61,659	30,982	30,678	162
1928	62,595	31,449	31,146	164
1929	63,461	31,891	31,570	166
1930	64,450	32,390	32,060	169
1931	65,457	32,899	32,559	171
1932	66,434	33,355	33,079	174
1933	67,432	33,845	33,587	176
1934	68,309	34,294	34,015	179
1935	69,254	34,734	34,520	181
1936	70,114	35,103	35,011	183
1937	70,630	35,128	35,503	185
1938	71,013	35,125	35,888	186
1939	71,380	35,226	36,154	187

Table J. Population and Population Density, 1872–2006 (*Continued*)

Year	Total Population (thousands)	Males (thousands)	Females (thousands)	Population Density (people per sq. km)
1940	71,933	35,387	36,546	188
1941	72,218	(not available)	(not available)	189
1942	72,880	(not available)	(not available)	191
1943	73,903	(not available)	(not available)	193
1944	74,433	(not available)	(not available)	195
1945	72,147	(not available)	(not available)	195
1946	75,750	(not available)	(not available)	206
1947	78,101	38,129	39,972	212
1948	80,002	39,130	40,873	217
1949	81,773	40,063	41,710	222
1950	84,115	41,241	42,873	226
1951	84,541	41,489	43,052	230
1952	85,808	42,128	43,680	233
1953	86,981	42,721	44,260	236
1954	88,239	43,344	44,895	239
1955	90,077	44,243	45,834	242
1956	90,172	44,301	45,871	244
1957	90,928	44,671	46,258	246
1958	91,767	45,078	46,689	248
1959	92,641	45,504	47,137	251
1960	94,302	46,300	48,001	254
1961	94,287	46,300	47,987	255
1962	95,181	46,733	48,447	258
1963	96,156	47,208	48,947	260
1964	97,182	47,710	49,471	263
1965	99,209	48,692	50,517	267
1966	99,036	48,611	50,425	268
1967	100,196	49,180	51,016	271
1968	101,331	49,739	51,592	274
1969	102,536	50,334	52,202	277
1970	104,665	51,369	53,296	281
1971	106,100	52,076	54,024	284
1972	107,595	52,822	54,773	289
1973	109,104	53,606	55,498	293
1974	110,573	54,376	56,197	297
1975	111,940	55,091	56,849	301
1976	113,094	55,658	57,436	304
1977	114,165	56,184	57,981	306

(*Continued*)

Table J. Population and Population Density, 1872–2006 (*Continued*)

Year	Total Population (thousands)	Males (thousands)	Females (thousands)	Population Density (people per sq. km)
1978	115,190	56,682	58,508	309
1979	116,155	57,151	59,004	312
1980	117,060	57,594	59,467	314
1981	117,902	58,001	59,901	316
1982	118,728	58,400	60,329	319
1983	119,536	58,786	60,750	321
1984	120,305	59,150	61,155	323
1985	121,049	59,497	61,552	325
1986	121,660	59,788	61,871	326
1987	122,239	60,058	62,181	328
1988	122,745	60,302	62,443	329
1989	123,205	60,515	62,690	331
1990	123,611	60,697	62,914	332
1991	124,101	60,934	63,167	333
1992	124,567	61,155	63,413	334
1993	124,938	61,317	63,621	335
1994	125,265	61,446	63,819	336
1995	125,570	61,574	63,996	337
1996	125,859	61,698	64,161	338
1997	126,157	61,827	64,329	338
1998	126,472	61,952	64,520	339
1999	126,667	62,017	64,650	340
2000	126,926	62,111	64,815	340
2001	127,316	62,265	65,051	342
2002	127,486	62,295	65,190	342
2003	127,694	62,368	65,326	343
2004	127,787	62,380	65,407	343
2005	127,768	62,349	65,419	343
2006	127,770	62,330	65,440	343

Note: Data prior to 1920 are estimates of the Cabinet Bureau of Statistics as of January 1 of the year stated (as of the end of January in the lunar calendar for 1872). Data since 1920 are based on the Population Census and the Annual Report on Current Population Estimates as of October 1. Okinawa Prefecture is not included in figures from 1945 through 1970.

Source: Statistical Survey Department, Statistics Bureau, Ministry of Internal Affairs and Communications.

Figure J.1. Population of Japan, 1872–2006

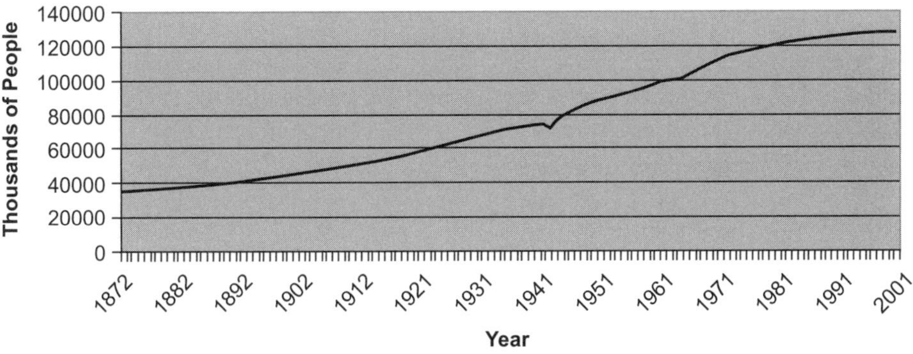

Figure J.2. Population Density of Japan, 1872–2006

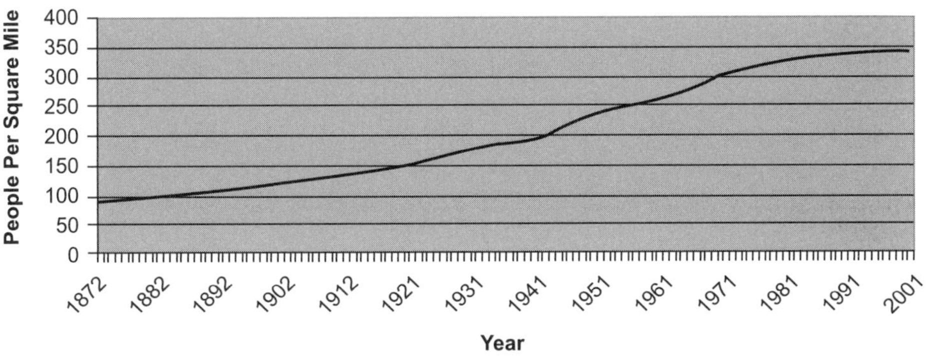

JAPANESE CITIES WITH MORE THAN 500,000 INHABITANTS, 2005

By the latter half of the 20th century Japan had become a predominantly urban nation and its cities are now some of the most crowded on Earth. The figures in the following table offer a snapshot of Japan's urban population by listing the populations of its 25 largest cities in 2005.

Table K. Japanese Cities With More Than 500,000 Inhabitants, 2005

City	Population
Tokyo	12,488,554
Yokohama	3,579,628
Osaka	2,628,811
Nagoya	2,215,062
Sapporo	1,880,863
Kobe	1,525,393
Kyoto	1,474,811
Fukuoka	1,401,279
Kawasaki	1,327,011
Saitama	1,176,314
Hiroshima	1,154,391
Sendai	1,025,098
Kitakyushu	993,525
Chiba	924,319
Sakai	830,966
Hamamatsu	804,032
Niigata	785,134
Shizuoka	700,886
Okayama	674,746
Kumamoto	669,603
Sagamihara	628,698
Kagoshima	604,367
Funabashi	569,835
Matsuyama	514,937
Higashiosaka	513,821

Note: The rate of population change is calculated on the basis of the population from the 2000 Census adjusted to the municipality boundary as of October 1, 2005.

Source: Statistical Survey Department, Statistics Bureau, Ministry of Internal Affairs and Communications. Data are based on the Population Census as of October 1.

POPULATION BY AGE GROUP, 1920–2006

During the period from the early 20th century to the early 21st century, the age demographics of the Japanese population slowly changed. In 1920, younger people made up a much more significant portion of the population than they do today. This aging of the Japanese population figures to be among the pressing challenges facing Japan in the 21st century.

Table L. Population by Age Group, 1920–2006

Age	1920	1930	1940	1950	1960	1970	1980	1990	2000
All ages	55,963,053	64,450,005	73,075,071	83,199,637	93,418,501	103,720,060	117,060,396	123,611,167	126,925,843
0–9	14,314,635	16,778,220	17,961,607	20,728,122	17,049,068	16,965,066	18,547,450	13,959,454	11,925,887
10–19	11,520,624	13,340,649	15,816,378	17,267,585	20,326,076	16,921,989	17,231,873	18,533,872	14,034,777
20–29	8,533,259	10,367,140	11,756,837	13,910,662	16,527,810	19,749,434	16,882,381	16,870,834	18,211,769
30–39	7,020,188	7,798,498	9,370,143	10,250,310	13,555,835	16,578,939	19,973,312	16,791,465	16,891,475
40–49	5,902,331	6,332,741	7,041,270	8,487,529	9,835,689	13,217,564	16,427,887	19,676,302	16,716,227
50–59	4,074,855	5,046,797	5,446,760	6,137,697	7,842,597	9,230,197	12,813,527	15,813,274	19,176,162
60–69	2,968,342	2,977,915	3,782,574	4,074,610	5,092,019	6,709,761	8,429,928	11,848,590	14,841,772
70–79	1,378,630	1,478,319	1,541,314	1,967,261	2,518,482	3,401,952	5,059,662	6,835,747	10,051,176
80–89	236,419	315,624	338,472	354,836	638,738	879,221	1,503,633	2,665,908	4,147,012
90–99	13,657	13,997	18,567	16,258	32,043	65,629	118,391	286,141	688,769
100 and over	113	105	187	97	144	308	989	3,223	12,256
Did not report	–	–	962	4,670	–	–	71,363	326,357	228,561

Source: Statistical Survey Department, Statistics Bureau, Ministry of Internal Affairs and Communications (http://www.stat.go.jp/english/data/nenkan/1431-02.htm). Data are based on the Population Census as of October 1. However, for 2006, data are based on the Annual Report on Current Population Estimates.

Japanese Population by Age Group, 1920

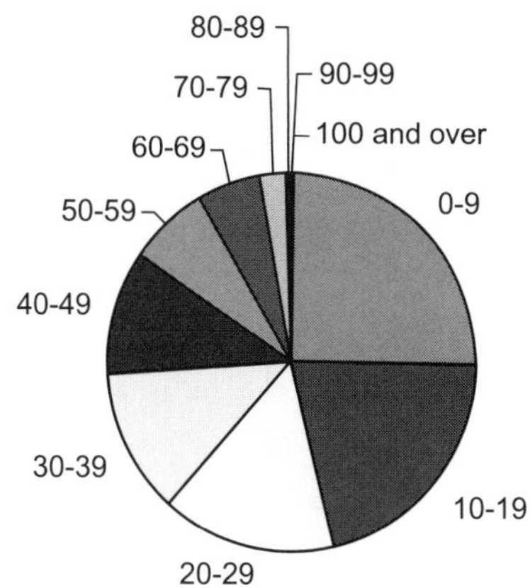

Japanese Population by Age Group, 2006

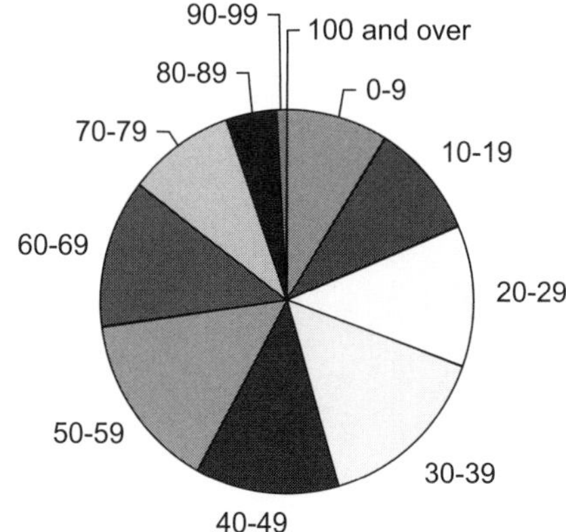

WORKFORCE BREAKDOWN BY INDUSTRY, 1975–2006

The evolution of Japan's industrial economy since the 1970s can be traced by using the table on page 376, which details the country's transformation from an agricultural nation to a world leader in manufacturing, information, and communications.

TABLE M. Workforce Breakdown by Industry, 1975–2006 (in tens of thousands of persons)

Year	Total	Agriculture and Forestry	Non-agricultural Industries	Fisheries	Mining	Construction	Manufacturing	Electricity, Gas, Heat Supply, and Water	Information and Communications	Transport	Wholesale and Retail Trade (including restaurants from 1975–2000)	Finance and Insurance	Real Estate	Eating and Drinking Places and Accommodations	Medical, Health Care, and Welfare	Education and Learning Support	Compound Services	Services (not elsewhere classified)	Government (not elsewhere classified)
1975	5,223	618	4,605	43	16	479	(not available)	32	(not available)	(not available)	1,127	(not available)	(not available)	(not available)	(not available)	(not available)	(not available)	(not available)	196
1980	5,536	532	5,004	45	11	548	(not available)	30	(not available)	(not available)	1,248	(not available)	(not available)	(not available)	(not available)	(not available)	(not available)	(not available)	199
1985	5,807	464	5,343	45	9	530	(not available)	33	(not available)	(not available)	1,318	(not available)	(not available)	(not available)	(not available)	(not available)	(not available)	(not available)	199
1990	6,249	411	5,839	40	6	588	(not available)	30	(not available)	(not available)	1,415	(not available)	(not available)	(not available)	(not available)	(not available)	(not available)	(not available)	195
1995	6,457	340	6,116	27	6	663	(not available)	42	(not available)	(not available)	1,449	(not available)	(not available)	(not available)	(not available)	(not available)	(not available)	(not available)	218
2000	6,446	297	6,150	29	5	653	(not available)	34	(not available)	(not available)	1,474	(not available)	(not available)	(not available)	(not available)	(not available)	(not available)	(not available)	214
2004	6,329	264	6,064	22	4	584	1,150	31	172	323	1,123	159	71	347	531	284	81	881	233
2005	6,356	259	6,097	23	3	568	1,142	35	176	317	1,122	157	75	343	553	286	76	916	229
2006	6,382	250	6,132	22	3	559	1,161	36	181	324	1,113	155	79	337	571	287	75	938	222

Source: Statistical Survey Department, Statistics Bureau, Ministry of Internal Affairs and Communications. Data are based on the Labour Force Survey.

AVERAGE MONTHLY HOURS WORKED, BY INDUSTRY, 1980–2006

Though still among world leaders in long workdays, Japan's workers have experienced a decrease in hours worked over the past two decades. The table on pages 378–379 specifies these changes by industry, while the second compares the average Japanese workweek to those of other highly developed countries.

TABLE N. Average Monthly Hours Worked, by Industry, 1980–2006 (in hours)

Year	1980	1985	1990	1995	2000	2002	2003	2004	2005	2006
Total	175.7	175.8	171.0	159.1	154.9	153.1	153.8	153.3	152.4	153.5
Mining	188.8	189.1	185.5	178.6	172.2	169.1	168.6	166.5	165.5	164.6
Construction	188.7	188.5	184.4	172.1	170.3	169.4	170.9	170.3	170.7	174.0
All Manufacturing	178.2	179.7	176.6	163.9	164.7	163.8	165.6	167.7	166.8	167.9
Food, Beverage, Tobacco, and Feed	(not available)	(not available)	(not available)	(not available)	157.9	156.8	158.3	161.7	160.2	159.8
Textiles	177.7	179.6	173.7	161.5	160.6	162.3	163.2	164.2	163.8	164.2
Pulp, Paper, and Paper Products	176.7	181.0	174.1	164.9	164.6	165.4	166.4	164.9	164.9	165.4
Printing and Associated Industries	(not available)	(not available)	(not available)	(not available)	175.4	177.7	177.2	178.4	174.9	175.2
Chemical and Associ-ated Products	164.8	167.5	163.9	156.1	156.6	157.3	157.3	156.9	157.0	159.0
Petroleum and Coal Products	171.9	170.0	167.5	160.6	158.1	158.0	157.7	160.2	160.9	164.2
Ceramic, Stone, and Clay Products	178.8	180.6	180.4	167.4	168.6	164.1	166.0	167.8	165.6	168.1
Iron and Steel	174.6	175.6	180.0	162.8	165.3	164.8	169.5	173.0	171.8	173.5
Nonferrous Metals and Products	177.2	181.1	180.7	167.2	168.4	165.9	168.4	166.5	165.5	167.2
Fabricated Metal Products	183.9	184.7	183.3	169.6	167.2	169.5	171.4	173.2	172.1	172.3
General Machinery	(not available)	(not available)	(not available)	(not available)	169.0	167.5	170.1	173.4	172.5	173.9
Electrical Machinery, Equipment, and Supplies	(not available)	(not available)	(not available)	(not available)	163.2	161.4	164.5	164.5	163.4	165.2

Information and Communication Electronic Equipment	(not available)	(not available)	(not available)	(not available)	162.5	158.8	162.4	163.8	163.1	164.6
Transportation Equipment	184.7	186.0	186.4	167.4	169.8	171.7	173.0	175.1	174.9	175.7
Precision Instruments and Machinery	173.1	175.7	171.8	160.9	165.0	161.6	163.6	164.2	163.3	165.6
Electricity, Gas, Heating, and Water	168.3	168.2	166.3	158.3	154.9	154.7	153.8	156.0	155.7	158.2
Information and Communications	(not available)	(not available)	(not available)	(not available)	162.9	162.4	164.4	162.3	161.6	162.5
Transport	(not available)	(not available)	(not available)	(not available)	174.3	174.1	176.1	177.3	176.8	176.6
Wholesale and Retail Trade	(not available)	(not available)	(not available)	(not available)	144.5	141.1	140.3	139.1	137.4	139.7
Financing and Insurance	(not available)	(not available)	(not available)	(not available)	149.8	148.6	148.2	150.1	150.8	153.4
Real Estate	(not available)	(not available)	(not available)	(not available)	153.6	153.3	153.6	152.1	152	153.4
Hotels and Restaurants	(not available)	(not available)	(not available)	(not available)	122.8	119.9	119.6	121.4	123.8	121.7
Medical, Health Care, and Welfare	(not available)	(not available)	(not available)	(not available)	148.3	148.3	148.2	149.7	148.4	148.6
Education and Educational Support	(not available)	(not available)	(not available)	(not available)	132.8	130.8	131.3	131.8	129.9	131.5
Compound Services	(not available)	(not available)	(not available)	(not available)	145.2	146	144.9	142.9	144.2	145.6
Other Services	(not available)	(not available)	(not available)	(not available)	149.4	146.8	147.5	146.9	146.1	147.2

Source: Statistics and Information Department, Minister's Secretariat, Ministry of Health, Labour, and Welfare. Data are based on the Monthly Labour Survey for establishments with 30 or more regular employees.

COMPARISON OF WORKING HOURS IN SOUTH KOREA, THE UNITED STATES, JAPAN, THE UNITED KINGDOM, AND GERMANY, 2005

Table O. Comparison of Working Hours in South Korea (ROK), The United States, Japan, The United Kingdom, and Germany, 2005

Country	Hours Per Week
South Korea (ROK)	46.9[1]
United States	43.6[2]
Japan	41.8
United Kingdom	39.6[3]
Germany	37.6

1. Figures are for manufacturing only.
2. Excludes hunting, forestry, and fishing.
3. Data are from 2004.

Sources: *Facts and Figures of Japan 2007* (Tokyo: Foreign Press Center, 2007); International Labor Organization, 2005.

WORKFORCE PARTICIPATION AMONG OLDER AGE GROUPS IN JAPAN, THE UNITED STATES, AND GERMANY, 2005

Members of older age groups make up a significant portion of the total Japanese populace. Unlike their counterparts in some other highly developed countries, however, many Japanese work well past the age of 65. The following table illustrates this by comparing workforce participation among older age groups in Japan, the United States, and Germany.

Table P. Workforce Participation Among Older Age Groups in Japan, The United States, and Germany, 2005 (in percent)

Country	Age 50–54	Age 55–59	Age 60–64	Age 65+
Japan	83.1	76.5	55.1	19.9
United States	79.8	71.4	51.6	15.1
Germany	84.6	73.2	31.6	3.3

Sources: *Facts and Figures of Japan 2007* (Japan: Foreign Press Center, 2007); Ministry of Internal Affairs and Communications of Japan, 2006.

AVERAGE MONTHLY WAGES BY SEX, 1990–2006

The historical disparity between male and female earning power in Japan is dramatically illustrated in this table, which shows in most fields that men's wages have consistently remained about twice those of women from the late 20th century to the present day.

Table Q. Average Monthly Wages by Sex, 1990–2006

Year	Overall Average	Male	Female
1990	826	1,100	551
1995	917	1,214	619
2000	909	1,212	605
2004	870	1,157	582
2005	874	1,162	585
2006	879	1,167	591

Note: In thousands of yen. Figures include bonuses and other special cash earnings.

Source: Statistics and Information Department, Minister's Secretariat, Ministry of Health, Labour, and Welfare. Data are based on the Monthly Labour Survey.

LABOR UNION MEMBERSHIP IN THE UNITED KINGDOM, SOUTH KOREA, GERMANY, JAPAN, AND THE UNITED STATES, 2005

Unions play an important role in the Japanese economy but are not as influential as those in some other highly developed countries. The following table compares the percentage of work performed by union members in Japan and four other major economic powers.

Table R. Labor Union Membership in the United Kingdom, South Korea, Germany, Japan, and The United States, 2005

Country	Unionized Work in %
United Kingdom	29.0
Germany	26.6
Japan	18.2
United States	12.5
South Korea	11.9

Sources: *Facts and Figures of Japan 2007* (Tokyo: Foreign Press Center, 2007); Japan Institute of Labor, 2007.

LIFE EXPECTANCY IN CHINA, JAPAN, AND THE UNITED STATES, 2005

Japanese people are some of the longest-lived in the world. The following table compares Japan's average life expectancies for men and women with those of the United States and China.

TABLE S. Life Expectancy in China, Japan, and The United States, 2005 (in years)

Country	Male	Female
Japan	78.5	85.5
United States	74.8	80.1
China	69.6	73.3

Sources: *Facts and Figures of Japan 2007* (Tokyo: Foreign Press Center, 2007); Ministry of Health, Labor, and Welfare of Japan, 2005; United Nations, *Demographic Yearbook, 2004* (New York: UN, 2007).

MOTOR VEHICLE PRODUCTION, 1995–2005

Japan has become well known around the world for the high quality and dependability of its cars, trucks, and other motor vehicles. Production figures detailing the country's motor vehicle industry are provided in the table below.

TABLE T. Motor Vehicle Production, 1995–2005

Item	1995	2000	2003	2004	2005
Motor vehicles (excl. motorcycles and combat vehicles)	10,196,000	10,145,000	10,286,000	10,512,000	10,800,000
Passenger cars	7,611,000	8,363,000	8,478,000	8,720,000	9,017,000
Buses	47,000	55,000	61,000	60,000	76,000
Trucks	2,538,000	1,727,000	1,747,000	1,731,000	1,707,000
Motorcycles and motor scooters	2,753,000	2,415,000	1,831,000	1,740,000	1,792,000
Powered industrial trucks and tractor trucks	180,976	141,069	130,188	148,171	167,563
Forklift trucks	121,688	111,385	109,454	123,453	141,432
Shovel trucks	20,282	13,890	12,262	15,334	17,366

Note: Data are from motor vehicle and motorcycle factories with 50 or more regular employees; for powered industrial trucks, data are from factories with 30 or more regular employees. Numbers for passenger cars, buses, and trucks include full-vehicle and chassis-only production.

Sources: Information and Research Department, Policy Bureau, Ministry of Land, Infrastructure, and Transport; Research and Statistics Department, Economic and Industrial Policy Bureau, Ministry of Economy, Trade, and Industry (METI). Data are based on the Current Production Survey of METI.

DESTINATION OF JAPANESE FOREIGN DIRECT INVESTMENT, 2004–2007

Japanese companies have long been among the leaders of the globalized world economy, and Japanese investment in foreign countries is substantial. The following table shows recent trends in foreign direct investment (FDI) in the three most important target countries.

TABLE U. Destination of Japanese Foreign Direct Investment (in US$ billion)

Country	2004	2005	2006	2007
United States	7.56	12.13	9.30	15.67
Netherlands	3.34	3.32	8.50	12.44
China	5.86	6.58	6.17	6.22

Source: Japan External Trade Organization, 2008 (http://www.jetro.go.jp/en/reports/statistics).

INTERNET USERS AND HOSTS PER 1,000 INHABITANTS BY COUNTRY, 2005

The Internet has transformed the Japanese economy and provided new communication, entertainment, and information-gathering options. Although many Japanese use the Internet, note that three countries with smaller populations than Japan have more Internet users.

TABLE V. Internet Users and Hosts Per 1,000 Inhabitants by Country, 2005

Country	Internet Users	Internet Hosts
Iceland	877.6	475.9
South Korea (ROK)	683.5	113.0
United States	630.0	664.5
Taiwan	580.1	139.0
Japan	502.0	128.7

Sources: *Facts and Figures of Japan 2007* (Tokyo: Foreign Press Center, 2007); International Telecommunication Union, 2007.

MOST POPULAR LEISURE ACTIVITIES, 2007

Japan is known for its vibrant consumer and leisure culture and the prevalence of popular media and technology. In addition to the wide variety of activities engaged in at home, many Japanese also vacation in other countries. The following tables present information about common Japanese leisure activities, tourism, and media consumption.

Table W. Most Popular Leisure Activities, 2007 (in millions of persons annually)

Activity	Participants
Karaoke	43.1
Video watching	42.4
Zoos, botanical gardens, museums, and aquariums	41.6
Computer use, computer games, and online communication	40.5
Cinema	40.1
Listening to music	38.0
Going to drinking establishments	34.4
Television-based video games	31.8
Gardening	30.5
Amusement parks	28.6

Source: Japan Productivity Center for Socio-Economic Development, *White Paper of Leisure 2008* (http://www.jpc-sed.or.jp/eng/research/2008_07.html).

MOST POPULAR ATHLETIC ACTIVITIES, 2005

Table X. Most Popular Athletic Activities, 2005 (in millions of persons)

Activity	Participants
Bowling	27.6
Calisthenics	23.0
Jogging, marathon	21.2
Swimming (at a pool)	16.4
Baseball	12.5

Sources: *Facts and Figures of Japan 2007* (Tokyo: Foreign Press Center, 2007); Japan Productivity Center for Socio-Economic Development, 2006.

AVERAGE AMOUNT OF TELEVISION VIEWING PER DAY, 1990 AND 2005

Table Y. Average Amount of Television Viewing Per Day, 1990 and 2005

	1990	**2005**
Weekday	3 hours 38 minutes	3 hours 56 minutes
Sunday	3 hours 55 minutes	4 hours 30 minutes

Sources: *Facts and Figures of Japan 2007* (Tokyo: Foreign Press Center, 2007); Japan's Ministry of Internal Affairs and Communications, 2007.

TOP FIVE TRAVEL DESTINATIONS FOR JAPANESE TOURISTS, 2005

Table Z. Top Five Travel Destinations for Japanese Tourists, 2005

Destination	**Visitors**
United States	3,883,906
China	3,389,976
South Korea (ROK)	2,439,809
Hong Kong	1,210,848
Taiwan	1,124,334

Sources: *Facts and Figures of Japan 2007* (Tokyo: Foreign Press Center, 2007); Japan National Tourist Organization, 2007.

MAJOR NEWSPAPERS IN JAPAN, 2006

Table ZZ. Major Newspapers in Japan, 2006 (circulation in 1,000 copies)

Newspaper	**Morning Edition**	**Evening Edition**
Yomiuri Shimbun	10,042	3,913
Asahi Shimbun	8,094	3,680
Mainichi Shimbun	3,975	1,563
Japan Times (English)	46	–
International Herald Tribune (English)	41	–

Sources: *Facts and Figures of Japan 2007* (Tokyo: Foreign Press Center, 2007); Japan Audit Bureau of Circulations, 2007.

MAJOR EARTHQUAKES IN 20TH-CENTURY JAPAN

Japan is a seismically active place, situated at the meeting point of continental and oceanic tectonic plates. As such, there were several disastrous earthquakes during the 20th century. With increased urbanization and population density, the potential for a quake to cause massive devastation has increased as well.

TABLE ZZZ. Major Earthquakes in 20th-Century Japan

Date	Earthquake Name	Magnitude	Fatalities
September 1, 1923	Great Kanto	7.9	142,807*
March 7, 1927	Kita Tango	7.3	2,925
March 3, 1933	Off Sanriku	8.1	3,008
December 21, 1946	Nankai	8.0	1,443
June 28, 1948	Fukui	7.1	3,769
January 17, 1995	Great Hanshin Awaji	7.3	6,437

* (Author's Note: This statistic is disputed as some sources report approximately 110,000 fatalities.)

Sources: *Facts and Figures of Japan 2007* (Tokyo: Foreign Press Center, 2007); Fire Defense Agency of Japan, 2007.

Holidays

JANUARY 1 (NATIONAL HOLIDAY)

*New Year (*shogatsu*)*

This is the most important holiday in Japan. Only January 1 is designated as a national holiday, but many businesses remain closed through January 3, and families gather to spend the days together. Work should be finished by the end of the year, while *bonenkai* parties, "year-forgetting parties," are held. Homes and entrance gates are decorated with ornaments made of pine, bamboo, and plum trees, and clothes and houses are cleaned. On New Year's Eve, *toshikoshi soba* ("buckwheat noodles"), symbolizing longevity, are served. January 1 is seen as a significant day. The day should be full of joy, everything should be clean, and there should be no work. Traditionally, people visit a shrine or temple during *shogatsu.* The most popular, such as Tokyo's Meiji Shrine, attract several million people during the three days. Various kinds of food and beverages are served during *shogatsu,* including *osechi ryori*, a sweetened rice wine. Sending New Year's cards, which are specially marked to be delivered on January 1, is a popular custom. Many people send several dozens of cards to friends, relatives, and coworkers.

SECOND MONDAY OF JANUARY (NATIONAL HOLIDAY)

Coming of Age (seijin no hi)

Twenty is the age at which Japanese are considered to be adults. Celebrations are held throughout Japan.

FEBRUARY 3

Beginning of spring (setsubun)

Setsubun is not a national holiday but is celebrated at shrines and temples throughout Japan, and festivals occur on February 3 or 4, the day before the beginning of spring according to the Japanese lunar calendar. Throughout history, this was a time to drive away evil spirits. Today, one ritual is to throw roasted beans around one's house and at temples and shrines. When throwing the beans, the custom is to shout, "*Oni wa soto*! *Fuku wa uchi*!" ("Devils out! Happiness in!"). Afterward, you should pick up and eat the number of beans that corresponds to your age. *Setsubun* celebrations vary throughout Japan.

FEBRUARY 11 (NATIONAL HOLIDAY)

National Foundation Day (kenkoku kinenbi)

Supposedly, on this day in 660 BCE the first Japanese emperor was crowned.

FEBRUARY 14

Valentine's Day

In Japan, women give chocolates to men on Valentine's Day. It is not a national holiday. St. Valentine's Day is celebrated on February 14, and White Day one month later on March 14. Supposedly, a Japanese confectionary company was responsible in 1958 for importing the holiday. In Japan, it is only women who give presents—mainly chocolate—to men. Men return the favors one month later on White Day. Both holidays are most popular among participants younger than 20. Valentine's Day is more popular among single people than married couples, and more popular among married people, with more than 50 percent celebrating both Valentine's and White Day. The most popular Valentine's present is chocolate.

MARCH 3

Dolls' Festival (hina matsuri)

Also called Girls' Festival. Families celebrate daughters in various ways.

MARCH 14

White Day

White Day, a Japanese creation, is the opposite of Valentine's Day: Men give cakes or chocolates to women. In the 1960s, a marshmallow manufacturing company supposedly started White Day. Various presents including candy and flowers are popular. According to *Japan Guide*, White Day is still less popular than Valentine's Day. It is not a national holiday.

AROUND MARCH 20 (NATIONAL HOLIDAY)

Spring Equinox Day (shunbun no hi)

Graves are visited during the week of the Equinox Day.

APRIL 29 (NATIONAL HOLIDAY)

Showa Day (Showa no hi)

The birthday of the Showa emperor, who died in 1989. Before 2007, April 29 was known as Greenery Day (now celebrated on May 4). Showa Day is part of Golden Week.

MAY 3 (NATIONAL HOLIDAY)

Constitution Day (kenpo kinenbi)

A national holiday commemorating the 1947 Constitution.

MAY 4 (NATIONAL HOLIDAY)

Greenery Day (midori no hi)

Now celebrated on May 4 and part of Golden Week. The day celebrates the environment; the Showa emperor loved plants and nature.

MAY 5 (NATIONAL HOLIDAY)

Children's Day (kodomo no hi)

Also called Boys' Festival (*tango no sekku*). Families pray for the health and future success of their sons by hanging up carp streamers and displaying samurai dolls. Both symbolize strength, power, and success in life.

JULY/AUGUST 7

Star Festival (tanabata)

Tanabata, also known as the Star Festival, takes place on the seventh day of the seventh month of the year by the old lunar calendar, when, according to a Chinese legend, the two stars Altair and Vega, which are usually separated from each other by the Milky Way, are able to meet. Because the seventh month of the year roughly coincides with August rather than July according to the formerly used lunar calendar, *tanabata* is still celebrated on August 7 in some parts of Japan, while it is celebrated on July 7 in other regions. One popular *tanabata* custom is to write wishes on a piece of paper and hang the paper on a specially erected bamboo tree. Colorful *tanabata* festivals are held throughout Japan in early July and August.

THIRD MONDAY OF JULY (NATIONAL HOLIDAY)

Ocean Day (umi no hi)

A recently introduced national holiday to celebrate the ocean.

JULY/AUGUST 13–15

Obon

Obon is a Buddhist festival to commemorate deceased ancestors. It is believed that annually during Obon, the ancestors' spirits return to this world to visit their relatives. Traditionally, lanterns are hung in front of houses to guide the ancestors' spirits, Obon dances (*bon odori*) performed, graves visited, and food offerings made at house altars and temples. At the end of Obon, floating lanterns are put into rivers, lakes, and seas in order to guide the spirits back into their world. Specific festival customs vary regionally. Obon is celebrated from the 13th to the 15th day of the seventh month of the year, which is July according to the solar calendar. However, since the seventh month of the year roughly coincides with August rather than July according to the old lunar calendar, Obon is still celebrated in mid-August in parts of Japan, while it is celebrated in mid-July in other regions. The Obon week in mid-August is one of Japan's three major holiday seasons. There is enormous travel in August and hotel rates increase.

THIRD MONDAY OF SEPTEMBER (NATIONAL HOLIDAY)

Respect for the Aged Day (keiro no hi)

Respect for the elderly and longevity are celebrated.

AROUND SEPTEMBER 23 (NATIONAL HOLIDAY)

Autumn Equinox Day (shubun no hi)

Graves are visited during the week of the Equinox Day.

SECOND MONDAY OF OCTOBER (NATIONAL HOLIDAY)

Health and Sports Day (taiiku no hi)

The 1964 Tokyo Olympics opening was on this day.

NOVEMBER 3 (NATIONAL HOLIDAY)

Culture Day (bunka no hi)

A day promoting culture, freedom, and peace. On culture day, schools and the government present individuals with awards for outstanding cultural accomplishments.

NOVEMBER 15

Seven-Five-Three (shichigosan)

A festival for children, *shichigosan* is not a national holiday. Girls aged three and seven and boys aged three and five are celebrated. On November 15 or the closest weekend, the young people visit a Shinto shrine dressed in kimono. Long candies in bags decorated with turtles and cranes are given to the children. The candy, the crane, and the turtle all symbolize longevity.

NOVEMBER 23 (NATIONAL HOLIDAY)

Labor Thanksgiving Day (kinro kansha no hi)

A national holiday for honoring labor.

DECEMBER 23 (NATIONAL HOLIDAY)

Emperor's Birthday (tenno no tanjobi)

The birthday of the current emperor is always a national holiday. The date changes with the accession of a new emperor.

DECEMBER 24–25

Christmas

Christmas is not a national holiday but in a *Japan-Guide* survey, 54 percent of Japanese thought Christmas was special. Europeans introduced Christmas in the 16th century. In recent decades it has become popular, despite the fact that less than 2 percent of Japanese are Christians. Increasingly more people decorate their homes, give presents to friends, and celebrate the event with a special meal. Retail stores and shopping malls display Christmas trees, Santa Clauses, and other seasonal decorations several weeks in advance. Some public places also feature seasonal illuminations. The traditional Japanese Christmas food is the Christmas cake, usually made of sponge cake, strawberries, and whipped cream.

DECEMBER 31

New Year's Eve (omisoka)

December 31 is not a national holiday but various festivities occur.

HOLIDAYS' REFERENCE

"Annual Events." *Japan-Guide.com.* http://www.japan-guide.com/e/e2062.html (accessed January 2008).

Organizations

BUSINESS AND ECONOMIC ORGANIZATIONS

Japan Economic Foundation
11th Floor, Jiji Press Building
5-15-8 Ginza Chuo-ku
Tokyo 104-0061 Japan
Telephone: (81-3) 5565-4821
Fax: (81-3) 5565-4828
E-mail: info@jef.or.jp
Internet: http://www.jef.or.jp

The Japan Economic Foundation (JEF) was established in July 1981 to deepen mutual understanding between Japan and other countries through activities aimed at promoting economic and technological exchanges. With this goal in mind, JEF engages in a broad range of activities; it provides information about Japan and arranges opportunities to exchange ideas among opinion leaders from many countries in such fields as industry, government administration, academia, and politics in order to break down the barriers to mutual understanding. It sponsors conferences on both sides of the Pacific for Americans, representatives of other foreign concerns, and Japanese.

Japan External Trade Organization
Ark Mori Building, 6F 12-32
Akasaka 1-chome, Minato-ku
Tokyo 107-6006 Japan

Established in 1958, the Japan External Trade Organization (JETRO) is a nonprofit, Japanese government–supported organization dedicated to promoting mutually beneficial trade and economic relationships between Japan and the rest of the world. Its focus is to help American and other nations' companies do business with Japan. Promotion of industrial cooperation, technology exchange, and direct investment in Japan are also areas of significant activity. In addition to directly assisting private companies, JETRO cooperates closely with national, state, and local economic development agencies as well as with industrial and trade organizations seeking to do business in Japan. JETRO also provides free subscriptions to e-mail newsletters, and information about how to access this service is available on their Web site.

JETRO Offices in the United States

Atlanta

245 Peachtree Center Ave.
Marquis One Tower, Suite 2208
Atlanta, GA 30303
Telephone: (404) 681-0600
Fax: (404) 681-0713
Internet: http://www.jetro.org/atlanta

Chicago

One E. Wacker Dr., Suite 600
Chicago, IL 60601
Telephone: (312) 832-6000
Fax: (312) 832-6066
Internet: http://www.jetro.org/chicago

Houston

1221 McKinney, One Houston Center, Suite 4141
Houston, TX 77010
Telephone: (713) 759-9595
Fax: (713) 759-9210
Internet: http://www.jetro.org/houston

Los Angeles

777 S. Figueroa St., Suite 2650
Los Angeles, CA 90017

Telephone: (213) 624-8855
Fax: (213) 629-8127
Internet: http://www.jetro.org/losangeles

New York

42nd Floor, McGraw-Hill Building
1221 Avenue of the Americas
New York, NY 10020-1079
Telephone: (212) 997-0400
Fax: (212) 944-0464
Internet: http://www.jetro.org/newyork

San Francisco

201 Third St., Suite 1010
San Francisco, CA 94103
Telephone: (415) 392-1333
Fax: (415) 788-6927
Internet: http://www.jetro.org/sanfrancisco

Nippon Keidanren–The Japan Business Federation
Keidanren-USA
Keizai Koho Center
1150 Connecticut Ave. NW, Suite 1050
Washington, DC 20036
Telephone: (202) 293-8430
Fax: (202) 293-8438
E-mail: Ms. Miho Tanaka at milhot@heidanren-usa.org
Internet: http://www.keidanren-usa.org

Keidanren-USA is the Washington, DC, office of Nippon Keidanren. Keidanren-USA's mission is to promote greater understanding in the United States of the importance of the bilateral trade and investment relationship to the U.S. and Japanese economies and to support policies that strengthen bilateral trade. Established in 1978, the Keizai Koho Center (KKC) is the information and outreach arm of Nippon Keidanren. KKC is an independent, nonprofit organization supported by individuals, industrial organizations, and foreign-affiliated firms. The center's mission is to promote dialogue and understanding of Japanese business and society by sponsoring informational programs and events and through study trips that bring foreign scholars, businesspeople, educators, and journalists to Japan to help them learn more about the nation and its economy. For further information about programs for educators and journalists, contact the Washington,

DC, office. The KKC also provides a number of free or low-cost English-language publications on a variety of economic, social, and political Japan-related topics.

CULTURE, EDUCATION, AND GOVERNMENT ORGANIZATIONS

AFS (AFS-USA)
Admissions Center
506 SW Sixth Ave., Second Floor
Portland, OR 97204
Telephone: (800) AFS–INFO
E-mail: afsinfo@afs.org
Internet: http://www.afs.org/afs_or/home

AFS (formerly the American Field Service) has provided international and intercultural learning experiences to individuals, families, schools, and communities through a global volunteer partnership for more than 50 years. AFS is a worldwide leader in international exchange programs and sponsors programs in 40 different countries. The Japan program is more than 50 years old. Although probably best known for high school exchange programs, AFS-USA also offers community service and university programs. U.S. students and families can also have opportunities to host foreign students through AFS. The Japan programs include year, semester, and summer experiences. Comprehensive information and online applications are available at the AFS Web site.

ASIANetwork
Teddy O. Amoloza, Executive Director
Illinois Wesleyan University
205 Beecher St.
Bloomington, IL 61701
Telephone: (309) 556-3405
Fax: (309) 556-3719
E-mail: tamoloza@iwu.edu
Internet: http://www.asianetwork.org

A consortium of more than 170 North American colleges, ASIANetwork strives to strengthen the role of Asian studies within the framework of liberal arts education to help prepare succeeding generations of undergraduates for a world in which Asian societies play prominent roles. The special focus of this organization is the liberal arts college, and a large number of member institutions sponsor Japan-related programs, including study abroad opportunities for students and faculty at member institutions. The organization hosts an annual conference with Japan-related sessions and publishes a newsletter.

Asian Studies Program: Kansai Gaidai University
Center for International Education
16-1 Nakamiyahigashino-cho, Hirakata-shi
Osaka 573-1001 Japan
Telephone: 072-805-2831, (81-72) 805-2831 (international)
Fax: (81-72) 805-2830, (81-72) 805-2830 (international)
E-mail: inquiry@kansaigaidai.ac.jp (general inquiry), aspadm@kansaigaidai.ac.jp (admissions)
Internet: http://www.kansaigaidai.ac.jp/asp/02_international_programs/05.html

Part of the universities' Center for International Education, the Asian Studies Program has a stellar reputation for both providing foreigners Japanese language programs and offering courses about Japan for international exchange students.

Asia Society
725 Park Ave.
New York, NY 10021
Telephone: (212) 288-6400
Fax: (212) 517-8315
Internet: http://www.asiasociety.org

The Asia Society is a national, nonprofit, nonpartisan educational organization that is dedicated to fostering understanding of Asia and communication between Americans and the peoples of Asia and the Pacific. The society sponsors art exhibitions, performances, films, lectures, seminars and conferences, publications and assistance to the media, and materials and programs for students and teachers to build awareness of the countries and peoples of Asia. A variety of Japan-related content is available at the Asia Society Web site including, as of the publication of this book, 144 classroom lessons on Japan.

Association for Asian Studies
1021 E. Huron St.
Ann Arbor, MI 48104
Telephone: (734) 665-2490
Fax: (734) 665-3801
Internet: http://www.asian-studies.org

The Association for Asian Studies (AAS)—the largest society of its kind, with approximately 7,000 members worldwide—is a scholarly, nonpolitical, nonprofit professional association open to all persons interested in Asia. It seeks through publications, meetings, and seminars to facilitate contact and an exchange of information among scholars to increase their understanding of East, South, and Southeast Asia. It counts among its members scholars, educators, businesspeople, diplomats, journalists, and interested laypersons. The AAS disseminates Japan content through its publications *Education About Asia*, the *Journal of Asian Studies*, and *Key Issues in Asian Studies*.

Association of Teachers of Japanese
240 Humanities Building, EALC Department, 279 UCB
University of Colorado: Boulder
Boulder, CO 80309-0279
Telephone: (303) 492-5487
Fax: (303) 492-5856
E-mail: atj@colorado.edu

The Association of Teachers of Japanese (ATJ) is an international, nonprofit, nonpolitical organization of scholars, teachers, and students of Japanese language, literature, and linguistics who work to promote the study of Japanese language and culture in precollegiate and higher education institutions. Founded in 1963, the ATJ has given scholars the opportunity to exchange academic and professional views, results of research, and news of the field. It holds an annual meeting in conjunction with the Association for Asian Studies and cooperates with its sister organization, the National Council of Secondary Teachers of Japanese, in presenting panels at the annual meeting of the American Council on the Teaching of Foreign Languages. It publishes the *Journal of the Association of Teachers of Japanese* twice each year and the *ATJ Newsletter* four times annually. As part of a multiorganizational effort to encourage more students to study in Japan during their college years, the ATJ has established a clearinghouse to collect and distribute information on study abroad programs in North America and international student programs at Japanese universities. The ATJ also provides information about positions in Japanese language and links to other useful Japan Web sites.

Center for Japanese Studies: Nanzan University
18 Yamazato-cho, Showa-ku
Nagoya 466-8673 Japan
Telephone: (81-52) 832-3123
Fax: (81-52) 832-5490
E-mail: cjs@ic.nanzan-u.ac.jp
Internet: http://www.nanzan-u.ac.jp/English/cjs/index.html

The Center for Japanese Studies (CJS) was established at Nanzan more than 30 years ago, and its comprehensive program now encompasses not only language-related studies but also courses in area studies as well as practical courses in traditional arts. In addition to the center's internationally famous language program, Nanzan University professors in the social sciences and the humanities also teach courses. The CJS is part of the Center for International Education that oversees the entire range of the university's international teaching, research, and exchange activities.

Embassy of Japan, Japan Information and Culture Center, Consulate General Offices
2520 Massachusetts Ave. NW
Washington, DC 20008
Telephone: (202) 238-6700
Fax: (202) 328-21287
Internet: http://www.us.emb-japan.go.jp/english/html

The Japan Information and Culture Center (JICC) is the cultural and public affairs section of the Embassy of Japan in Washington, DC. Its primary role is to promote better understanding of Japan and Japanese culture by providing a wide range of information, educational services, and programs to the American public. Areas served include Washington, DC, Maryland, and Virginia. Other Japanese consulates provide services in areas outside JICC's jurisdiction. The JICC and Consulates General offices offer excellent free publications on Japan in English as well as other educational materials and sponsor a number of programs including the Japan Exchange and Teaching Program where qualified American (and other English-speaking) university graduates can work in Japanese schools and local and prefectural government offices.

CONSULATES GENERAL

Guam

590 S. Marine Corp Dr., Suite 604
Tamuning, Guam 96911
Telephone: (671) 646-1290
Fax: (671) 649-2620
Internet: http://www.hagatna.us.emb-japan.go.jp

Anchorage

3601 C St., Suite 1300
Anchorage, AK 99503-5925
Telephone: (907) 562-8424
Fax: (907) 562-8434
Internet: http://www.anchorage.us.emb-japan.go.jp

Atlanta

One Alliance Center
3500 Lenox Rd., Suite 1600
1175 Peachtree St. NE
Atlanta, GA 30326
Telephone: (404) 240-4300
Fax: (404) 240-4311
Internet: http://www.atlanta.us.emb-japan.go.jp

Boston

Federal Reserve Plaza, 14th Floor
600 Atlantic Ave.
Boston, MA 02210-2285
Telephone: (617) 973-9772
Fax: (617) 542-1329
Internet: http://www.boston.us.emb-japan.go.jp

Chicago

Olympia Centre, Suite 1100
737 N. Michigan Ave.
Chicago, IL 60611-2656
Telephone: (312) 280-0400
Fax: (312) 280-9568
Internet: http://www.chicago.us.emb-japan.go.jp

Denver

1225 17th St., Suite 3000
Denver, CO 80202-5814
Telephone: (303) 534-1151
Fax: (303) 534-3393
Internet: http://www.denver.us.emb-japan.go.jp

Detroit

400 Renaissance Center, Suite 1600
Detroit, MI 48243
Telephone: (313) 567-0120
Fax: (313) 567-0274
E-mail: ryouji@globalbiz.net
Internet: http://www.detroit.us.emb-japan.go.jp

Honolulu

1742 Nuuanu Ave.
Honolulu, HI 96817-3294
Telephone: (808) 543-3111
Fax: (808) 543-3170
Internet: http://www.honolulu.us.emb-japan.go.jp

Houston

2 Houston Center
909 Fannin, Suite 3000

Houston, TX 77010
Telephone: (713) 652-2977
Fax: (713) 651-7822
Internet: http://www.houston.us.emb-japan.go.jp

Los Angeles

350 S. Grand Ave., Suite 1700
Los Angeles, CA 90071-3459
Telephone: (213) 617-6700
Fax: (213) 617-6727
Internet: http://www.la.us.emb-japan.go.jp

Miami

Brickell Bay View Centre, Suite 3200
80 SW Eighth St.
Miami, FL 33130-3047
Telephone: (305) 530-9090
Fax: (305) 530-0950
Internet: http://www.miami.us.emb-japan.go.jp

Nashville

1801 West End Ave., Suite 900
Nashville, TN 37203
Telephone: (615) 340-4300
Fax: (615) 340-4311
Internet: http://www.nashville.us.emb-japan.go.jp

New York

299 Park Ave., 18th Floor
New York, NY 10171-0025
Telephone: (212) 371-8222
Fax: (212) 319-6357
Internet: http://www.ny.us.emb-japan.go.jp

Portland

2700 Wells Fargo Center
1300 SW Fifth Ave.
Portland, OR 97201
Telephone: (503) 221-1811
Fax: (503) 224-8936
Internet: http://www.portland.us.emb-japan.go.jp

San Francisco

50 Fremont St., Suite 2300
San Francisco, CA 94105-2236
Telephone: (415) 777-3533
Fax: (415) 974-3660
Internet: http://www.sf.us.emb-japan.go.jp

Seattle

601 Union St., Suite 500
Seattle, WA 98101-4015
Telephone: (206) 682-9107
Fax: (206) 624-9097
Internet: http://www.seattle.us.emb-japan.go.jp

Ikebana International Headquarters
P.O. Box 2262, Ginza Branch
Japan Post Service 100-8698 Japan
Telephone: (81-3) 3293-8188
Fax: (81-3) 3294-2272
E-mail: office@ikebanahq.org
Internet: http://www.ikebanahq.org

Ikebana International is a nonprofit cultural organization dedicated to the promotion and appreciation of all styles of ikebana, the Japanese art of flower arrangement. The organization was founded in 1956 with the purpose of uniting the peoples of the world through their mutual love of nature and enjoyment of ikebana. Today its membership includes approximately 10,000 persons in more than 60 counties and 175 chapters.

Japan Center for International Exchange (JCIE/USA)
274 Madison Ave., Suite 1102
New York, NY 10016
Telephone: (212) 679-4130
Fax: (212) 679-8410
E-mail: info@jcie.org
Internet: http://www.jcie.or.jp

Founded in 1975, JCIE/USA is the North American counterpart of JCIE/Japan, one of the few independent and nonpartisan nongovernmental organizations in the field of international affairs in Japan. The JCIE serves as a bridge to Japan and the rest of the Asia Pacific region by conducting international political exchanges and fostering dialogue between policy makers and experts from the research community on both sides of the Pacific. The JCIE also works to enhance the role of civil society in domestic and international governance by promoting philanthropy in Japan and the Asia Pacific region and by helping construct an environment supportive of the nonprofit sector.

Japanese American Cultural and Community Center
244 S. San Pedro St., Suite 505
Los Angeles, CA 90012
Telephone: (213) 628-2725
Fax: (213) 617-8576
E-mail: info@jaccc.org
Internet: http://www.jaccc.org

The Japanese American Cultural and Community Center is the largest ethnic cultural center in the United States. It is a nonprofit organization established to preserve and encourage the appreciation of Japanese and Japanese American heritage and cultural arts.

Japan Foundation
Carnegie Hall Tower
152 W. 57th St., 17th Floor
New York, NY 10019
Telephone: (212) 489-0299
Fax: (212) 489-0409
E-mail: info@jfny.org
Internet: http://www.jfny.org

Established in 1972 by the Japanese Diet through special legislation, the Japan Foundation became an independent administrative institution in 2002. The Japan Foundation operates in several countries. It carries out a broad variety of cultural exchange programs, ranging from academic (including Japanese language instruction) to the arts, publications, audiovisual media, sports, and culture.

Japan Foundation Center for Global Partnership
152 W. 57th St., 17th Floor
New York, NY 10019
Telephone: (212) 489-1255
Fax: (212) 489-1344
Internet: http://www.cgp.org

The Center for Global Partnership (CGP) was established within the Japan Foundation in April 1991 with offices in both Tokyo and New York. The CGP seeks to provide collaboration between Japan and the United States in order to fulfill shared global responsibilities and contribute to the betterment of the world. The CGP also works to enhance dialogue and interchange between Japanese and U.S. citizens on a wide range of issues, thus improving bilateral relations. To carry out its mission, the CGP operates grant programs in three areas—intellectual exchange, grassroots exchange, and education—as well as self-initiated projects and fellowships. The CGP supports an array of institutions and individuals, including nonprofit organizations, universities, policy makers, scholars, and educators, and works for broad-based, multichannel approaches to effect positive change.

Japan Society
333 E. 47th St.
New York, NY 10017
Telephone: (212) 832-1155, (212) 715-1258 (box office)
Internet: http://www.japansociety.org

The Japan Society provides content on Japan for the United States and offers more than 100 events annually in the performing and visual arts, business and policy sector, and education fields as well as publications and online forums. Founded in 1907, the Japan Society is an internationally recognized nonprofit, nonpolitical organization that provides access to information on Japan, offers opportunities to experience Japanese culture, and fosters sustained and open dialogue on issues important to the United States, Japan, and East Asia.

Japan–United States Friendship Commission
1201 15th St. NW, Suite 330
Washington, DC 20005
Telephone: (202) 653-9800
Fax: (202) 653-9802
E-mail: jusfc@jusfc.gov
Internet: http://www.jusfc.gov

The Japan–United States Friendship Commission is an independent federal agency that provides support for training and information to help prepare Americans to better meet the challenges and opportunities in the U.S.-Japan relationship through grant programs for Japanese studies in the United States, public affairs and education, study of the United States in Japan, and the arts.

The Laurasian Institution
12345 Lake City Way NE, #151
Seattle, WA 98125
Telephone: (425) 398-1153
Fax: (425) 398-8245
E-mail: tli@laurasian.org
Internet: http://www.laurasian.org

The Laurasian Institution is a nongovernmental, nonprofit organization founded in 1990 that offers a variety of international and cross-cultural educational programs on Japan. Examples of Laurasian Institution programs include Japanese volunteers in American classrooms to assist American students with learning about Japan's culture, promotion of Japanese language in American schools, and study tours of Japan for American students and teachers. Currently, there are also programs that place Japanese language teachers in American schools and that extend Japanese cultural outreach programs to schools in the American southeast.

National Association of Japan-America Societies, Inc.
1150 Connecticut Ave. NW, Suite 1050
Washington, DC 20036
Telephone: (202) 429-5545
Fax: (202) 429-0027
E-mail: contact@us-japan.org
Internet: http://www.us-japan.org

The National Association of Japan-America Societies (NAJAS) is a private, nonprofit, nonpartisan organization that offers educational, cultural, and business programs about Japan and U.S.-Japan relations to the general public through its member Japan-America Societies. The NAJAS is the only national nonprofit network in the United States dedicated to public education about Japan. It consists of approximately 40 independent Japan-related organizations located in 32 cities around the country. Its membership cuts across usual group boundaries (business, political, academic, American, Japanese, etc.) and affords a variety of perspectives on U.S.-Japan relations. The NAJAS also cosponsors, along with the Keizai Koho Center, teacher study tours of Japan.

United States–Japan Foundation
145 E. 32nd St.
New York, NY 10016
Telephone: (212) 481-8753
Fax: (212) 481-8762
E-mail: info@us-jf.org
Internet: http://www.us-jf.org

The United States–Japan Foundation (USJF) is committed to promoting stronger ties between Americans and Japanese by supporting projects that foster mutual knowledge and education, deepen understanding, create effective channels of communication, and address common world concerns. The USJF, incorporated under U.S. law in 1980, was founded with a grant from the Japan Shipbuilding Industry Foundation (now known as the Nippon Foundation). The USJF's founder, the late Sasakawa Ryoichi, established the foundation to improve understanding between the United States and Japan. The USJF is the only private, independent American grant-making foundation dedicated to the mutual interests of the American and Japanese people. It also maintains a Tokyo office. The USJF funds grants for precollege education, communication and public opinion, and U.S.-Japan policy. It also presents the annual Elgin Heinz Outstanding Teacher Award to two teachers (humanities and Japanese languages) for exceptional service in promoting understanding of Japan.

TOURISM ORGANIZATIONS

Fodor's Travel Publications
Internet: http://www.fodors.com

Fodor's Web site provides a variety of information on travel in Japan and information on several Japanese cities. The company also publishes two separate travel guides for Japan and two different guides for Tokyo. In addition, the Web site has a link for air reservations. Information available on Fodor's Web site and in the guides includes recommended sights, activities, restaurants, hotels, shopping, nightlife, art exhibits, and travel tips.

Japan Association of Travel Agents
Zen-Nittu Kasumigaseki Building
3-3 Kasumigaseki 3-chome, Chiyoda-ku
Tokyo 100-0013 Japan
Telephone: (81-3) 3592-1271
Fax: (81-3) 3592-1268
Internet: http://www.jata-net.or.jp/English

The Japan Association of Travel Agents seeks to improve the quality of services provided to travelers to and from Japan. It contributes to the development of the travel and tourism industries by disseminating information, encouraging cooperation among members, and developing business and legal dealings that will benefit the membership and the industry at large.

Japan National Tourist Organization
2-10-1 Yurakucho, Chiyoda-ku
Tokyo 100-0006 Japan
Internet: http://www.jnto.go.jp

The Japan National Tourist Organization (JNTO) engages in a range of overseas tourism promotions encouraging individuals and companies to visit Japan on business, to hold conferences and meetings in Japan, or to simply deepen their understanding of Japanese history, culture, customs, and its people through travel. Established in 1964, the JNTO operates tourist information centers in Japan and in foreign countries, including the United States. The JNTO maintains an excellent Web site with a wide variety of information on Japan including travel, accommodations, history, culture, and top destinations.

Los Angeles

515 S. Figueroa St., Suite 1470
Los Angeles, CA 90071

Telephone: (213) 623-1952
Fax: (213) 623-6301
E-mail: info@jnto-lax.org

New York

One Rockefeller Plaza, Suite 1250
New York, NY 10020
Telephone: (212) 757-5640
Fax: (212) 307-6754
E-mail: visitjapan@jntonyc.org
Japan Travel Bureau
Internet: http://www.jtbusa.com

Established in 1964, the Japan Travel Bureau (JTB) provides information on travel to and around Japan, whether the visit is for business or for pleasure. The Web site for the U.S. branch is provided above. JTB-USA has branch offices in seven American cities and provides a variety of booking and reservation options for prospective visitors to Japan. This is the organization through which Japan Rail (JR) passes should be booked. JR passes are the most economical way to travel throughout Japan by rail, and passes are available that vary by length of duration. Special passes for specific regions of Japan are also available.

Lonely Planet Web Site and Guides
150 Linden St.
Oakland, CA 94607
Telephone: (510) 250-6420, (800) 275-8555 (toll-free)
Fax: (510) 893-8572
Internet: http://www.lonelyplanet.com

Lonely Planet's Web site provides a wide variety of interesting information and articles on travel in Japan. Lonely Planet's hard copy guide to Japan includes the best times to visit (as well as how to get there and how to get around), money and costs, events and attractions, activities (both popular and off the beaten track), and overviews of Japan's history, culture, and environment.

Annotated Bibliography of Recommended Works on Japan

These sources are organized in accordance with the subjects of the individual chapters. Every effort has been made to include accurate and readable sources that should assist those readers who want to know more about Japan. An attempt has also been made to provide readers with a diversity of viewpoints regarding controversial issues and interpretations. Although most of these works are intended for general readers, in some cases more scholarly works are included when few or no general sources exist. Given limited space, some of the selections for this section were difficult choices. Readers interested in a particular topic are also encouraged to examine the references at the end of relevant chapters.

GEOGRAPHY

"East Asia in Geographic Perspective: China, Japan, Korea, and Vietnam." *Asia for Educators*. Columbia University. 2008. http://afe.easia.columbia.edu/geography.

This component of the award-winning Columbia University Web site places Japanese geography within the context of the East Asian region. The component is an ideal multimedia learning tool for anyone who desires to better understand Japan. *Asia for Educators* also includes components on Japanese history, philosophy, literature, and society.

Facts and Figures of Japan 2007. Tokyo: Foreign Press Center, 2007. 224 pp.

This annual publication, available in paperback, is a superb compilation of statistics encompassing a wide variety of cultural, economic, political, and social topics. The publication is also available online at http://fpcj.jp/old/e/mres/publication/ff/index_07.html.

Karan, Pradyumna P. *Japan in the 21st Century: Environment, Economy, and Society*. Lexington: University Press of Kentucky, 2005. 401 pp.

This text, prepared for survey-level university courses, is the most current introduction to Japan's geography available in English. The book contains a wide array of photographs, maps, and other graphics.

Laing, Craig R. "Japanese Cultural Landscapes." *Japan Teaching Module*. University of Tennessee at Chattanooga. 2007. http://www.utc.edu/asia/teaching.

Photographs of varying Japanese urban, rural, and suburban landscapes will help interested users conceptualize important human geography concepts.

Tanaka, Hideaki, ed. *Japan 2007: An International Comparison*. Tokyo: Keizai Koho Center. 119 pp.

This small annual paperback booklet is a useful source of statistics on a variety of Japan-related topics including population, the economy, and natural resources.

Tym, Alice L. "Centripetal Forces in Japan." *Japan Teaching Module*. University of Tennessee at Chattanooga. 2007. http://www.utc.edu/asia/teaching.

In this Web site module, users through interactive activities learn of such forces as physical geography, rice, and Shinto that give most Japanese common cultural reference points.

HISTORY

Beasley, W. G. *The Japanese Experience: A Short History of Japan*. Berkeley: University of California Press, 2000. 317 pp.

This is a concise and well-done history of Japan from early times through the end of the 20th century. Cultural, economic, geographical, political, and social topics are addressed.

Ellington, Lucien, ed. *Education About Asia*. Ann Arbor: Association for Asian Studies.

This 72-page illustrated journal, published three times a year, contains articles on Japanese history as well as material on the humanities, social sciences, and contemporary topics in every issue. The journal is intended for educators and general readers. Sample materials and other information are available at: http://www.asian-studies.org/EAA/.

Ellington, Lucien. "Japan in World History." *Japan Teaching Module*. University of Tennessee at Chattanooga. 2007. http://www.utc.edu/asia/teaching.

In this interactive Web site component, users interested in Japanese history can learn about Japan's cultural, political, economic, and social history. The emphasis is on not only Japan as a country but its role in world history as well.

Holcombe, Charles. *The Genesis of East Asia, 221 B.C.–A.D. 907: Asian Interactions and Comparisons*. Honolulu: University of Hawai'i Press, 2001. 332 pp.

Japan is not just a self-contained entity but also part of a larger regional cultural milieu. This excellent book assists readers with understanding how the early Japanese were influenced by other East Asian cultures yet remained distinctive.

Huffman, James. *Modern Japan: A History in Documents*. New York: Oxford University Press, 2004. 224 pp.

In this innovative work, the author uses a variety of both print and graphic sources in assisting readers with understanding various aspects of Japanese history from 1600 until the present.

Jansen, Marius. *The Making of Modern Japan*. Cambridge, MA: Belknap Press, 2002. 936 pp.

This well-written book begins with the late 16th and early 17th centuries and offers a rich, broad, and interesting history of the archipelago.

Schirokauer, Conrad, et al. *A Brief History of Chinese and Japanese Civilizations*. Boston: Houghton Mifflin, 2005. 712 pp.

This best-selling university survey text provides readers with a solid historical foundation. The art included in the book is particularly well done.

GOVERNMENT AND POLITICS

Bowen, Roger W. *Japan's Dysfunctional Democracy: The Liberal Democratic Party and Structural Corruption*. Armonk, NY: M. E. Sharpe, 2003. 139 pp.

Although perhaps overly critical of Japan's democracy, the author does a good job of pointing out some problems with Japanese politics and government that are in need of reform.

Ennis, Peter, and Richard Katz, eds. *Oriental Economist Report*. New York: Japan Watchers, LLC.

This 16–20-page newsletter is clearly written and provides up-to-date information on a variety of Japan-related economic, political, and social topics. The editors do a particularly good job of relating political issues to economics.

Facts and Figures of Japan 2007. Tokyo: Foreign Press Center, 2007. 224 pp.

This annual publication, available in paperback, is a superb compilation of statistics encompassing a wide variety of cultural, economic, political, and social topics. The publication is also available online at http://fpcj.jp/old/e/mres/publication/ff/index_07.html.

Green, Michael J. "The US-Japan Alliance: A Brief Strategic History." *Education About Asia* 12, No. 3 (Winter 2007): 25–30.

This article by an academic who has advised both the Clinton and G. W. Bush White Houses on Japan policy is a succinct overview of U.S.-Japan political relations since World War II.

Inoguchi, Takashi. *Japanese Politics: An Introduction*. Melbourne, Australia: Trans Pacific Press, 2005. 235 pp.

This is an excellent overview of Japanese government and politics that draws on history and a variety of social science disciplines in explaining governmental structure, the political process, and public policy questions.

Japan Considered. http://www.japanconsidered.com.

This Web site, developed by University of South Carolina Professor Robert Angel, is a comprehensive introduction to Japanese politics, government, and policy issues for nonspecialists as well as a resource for scholars. The site includes archived and regular podcasts about Japan's contemporary political scene, audio and transcripts of interviews with leading experts on Japanese politics and government, and a host of excellent links ranging from the prime minister's office to political parties' official sites.

Miyamoto, Masao. *Straitjacket Society: An Insider's Irreverent View of Bureaucratic Japan*. Translated by Juliet Winters Carpenter. Tokyo: Kodansha International, 1994. 196 pp.

This now classic work by a psychiatrist who served in the national bureaucracy remains one of the best "insider" books ever written about Japan's bureaucracy.

Oros, Andrew L. "The Domestic and International Politics of Constitutional Change in Japan." *Education About Asia* 12, No. 3 (Winter 2007): 39–44.
This is an excellent introduction to one of Japan's most controversial and, as of yet, unresolved political issues that has both domestic and international ramifications.

ECONOMY

Allen, G. C. *A Short Economic History of Modern Japan: 1867–1937*. London: Routledge Press, 2003. 203 pp.
First published in 1946, this classic work provides readers with a solid foundation for understanding the roots of contemporary Japanese economic institutions.

Ennis, Peter, and Richard Katz, eds. *Oriental Economist Report*. New York: Japan Watchers, LLC.
This 16–20-page newsletter is clearly written and provides up-to-date information on a variety of Japan-related economic, political, and social topics. The editors do a particularly good job of relating political issues to economics.

Facts and Figures of Japan 2007. Tokyo: Foreign Press Center, 2007. 224 pp.
This annual publication, available in paperback, is a superb compilation of statistics encompassing a wide variety of cultural, economic, political, and social topics. The publication is also available online at http://fpcj.jp/old/e/mres/publication/ff/index_07.html.

Japan Productivity Center for Socio-economic Development (JPC-SED). http://www.jpc-sed.or.jp/eng/index.html.
This nonprofit organization that was founded in 1955 publishes a number of readable studies and reports focusing on Japanese productivity and management.

Karan, Pradyumna P. *Japan in the 21st Century: Environment, Economy, and Society*. Lexington: University Press of Kentucky, 2005. 401 pp.
Although used most as a geography text, this versatile work is also a valuable source of basic information on the national economy, resources, and regional economic problems and opportunities. The illustrations complement the lucid prose.

Katz, Richard. *Japan: The System That Soured*. Armonk, NY: M. E. Sharpe, 1998. 530 pp.
This is an accurate analysis of why many of the characteristics of Japan's economic system that fostered success before the 1990s contributed to Japan's lingering problems during that decade and afterward.

Lincoln, Edward J. "The Japanese Government and the Economy: Twenty-first Century Challenges." *Education About Asia* 12, No. 3 (Winter 2007): 31–38.
Written by an internationally famous economist who was special advisor to former Japan ambassador Walter Mondale, the article provides the general reader with an excellent overview of Japan's contemporary political economy.

Restall, Hugo, ed. *Far Eastern Economic Review*. Hong Kong: Review Publishing, Ltd.
This publication, founded in 1946, appears 10 times annually and regularly includes articles on Japan's economy, politics, and economic relations with Asia and the rest of the world.

Tanaka, Hideaki, ed. *Japan 2007: An International Comparison*. Tokyo: Keizai Koho Center, 2007. 119 pp.
Although this annual booklet is useful for a number of reasons, it is a good source of current economic statistics that allows comparisons and contrasts of Japan and a number of other countries.

Vogel, Steven. *Japan Remodeled: How Government and Industry Are Reforming Japanese Capitalism.* Ithaca, NY: Cornell University Press, 2006. 284 pp.
This is a lucid discussion of recent and ongoing economic liberalization efforts in Japan.

SOCIETY

Religion and Thought

DharmaNet International. http://www.dharmanet.org/index.htm.
This is an international online clearinghouse for Buddhist study with a variety of resources and succinct explanations of variants of Japanese Buddhism.

Facts and Figures of Japan 2007. Tokyo: Foreign Press Center, 2007. 224 pp.
This annual publication, available in paperback, is a superb compilation of statistics encompassing a wide variety of cultural, economic, political, and social topics. The publication is also available online at http://fpcj.jp/old/e/mres/publication/ff/index_07.html.

Kasulis, Thomas P. "Japanese Philosophy" in *Routledge Encyclopedia of Philosophy*, edited by E. Craig. London: Routledge, 1998. http://www.rep.routledge.com/article-related/G100SECT8.
This excellent online set of entries, written by an outstanding scholar of Japanese philosophy and religion, provides the layperson with an essential foundation for understanding developments in Japanese philosophy. The author does a good job of tracing religious and philosophical currents in Japan from prehistory to contemporary times.

———. *Shinto: The Way Home.* Honolulu: University of Hawai'i Press, 2004. 184 pp.
A good theoretical and factual overview of Shinto.

Minoru, Sonoda. *The World of Shinto: Reflections of a Shinto Priest.* Tokyo: International Society for Educational Information, 2002. 36 pp.
This short but informative booklet is a good overview of Japan's indigenous belief system and has an excellent section comparing Shinto to early Greek religious practices.

Reid, T. R. *Confucius Lives Next Door: What Living in the East Teaches Us about Living in the West.* New York: Vintage, 1999. 276 pp.
This popular book remains a good explanation for Westerners of the influence of Confucian teachings on daily life and Japanese society.

Suzuki, Daisetz T. *Zen and Japanese Culture.* Tokyo: Charles E. Tuttle Co., 1959. 478 pp.
A comprehensive treatment of the influence of Zen on a variety of aspects of Japanese culture including the arts.

Swanson, Paul, and Clark Chilson, eds. *Nanzan Guide to Japanese Religions.* Honolulu: University of Hawai'i Press, 2006. 466 pp.
This comprehensive work is one of the best broad overviews of traditional and contemporary Japanese religions available in English. There are chapters and sections on history, basic beliefs, and the sociology of Japanese religions.

Watt, Paul. "Buddhism in Japan." *Asia for Educators.* Columbia University. http://afe.easia.columbia.edu/japan/japanworkbook/religion/jbuddhis.html (accessed January 2008).
A short overview that is an excellent introduction to Japanese Buddhism and its influence on society.

Watt, Paul. "Shinto." *Asia for Educators.* Columbia University. http://afe.easia.columbia.edu/japan/japanworkbook/religion/shinto.htm (accessed January 2008).
A short reading that is an excellent introduction to Shinto.

Social Classes and Ethnicity

Douglass, Mike, and Glenda S. Roberts, eds. *Japan and Global Migration: Foreign Workers and the Advent of a Multicultural Society.* Honolulu: University of Hawai'i Press, 2000. 306 pp.
In this edited volume, a variety of issues regarding foreign workers are addressed including the history of foreign workers in Japan, the Japanese Brazilian return, and local settlement patterns of foreigners.

Dubruil, Chisato O. "Ainu-e: Instructional Resources for the Study of Japan's Other People." *Education About Asia* 9, No. 1 (Spring 2004): 9–17.
In this richly illustrated article, readers can learn of Ainu traditional culture through the art they created.

Facts and Figures of Japan 2007. Tokyo: Foreign Press Center, 2007. 224 pp.
This annual publication, available in paperback, is a superb compilation of statistics encompassing a wide variety of cultural, economic, political, and social topics. The publication is also available online at http://fpcj.jp/old/e/mres/publication/ff/index_07.html.

Kerr, Alex. *Dogs and Demons: Tales from the Dark Side of Japan.* New York: Hill and Wang, 2001. 432 pp.
There is an interesting chapter in this book that presents Japan from the perspective of Japanese who've chosen to leave.

Lesser, Jeffrey, ed. *Searching for Home Abroad: Japanese Brazilians and Transnationalism.* Durham, NC: Duke University Press, 2003. 219 pp.
In this edited volume, the experiences of Japan Brazilians, ethnically Japanese but culturally Latin Americans, are analyzed from a variety of perspectives.

Lie, John. *Multiethnic Japan.* Cambridge, MA: Harvard University Press, 2001. 248 pp.
This is probably the best general survey on ethnic groups in Japan and effectively refutes the notion that Japanese culture is homogeneous.

Moore, Joe, ed. *The Other Japan: Conflict, Compromise and Resistance since 1945.* Armonk, NY: M. E. Sharpe, 1997. 406 pp.
This anthology, now in its second edition, is an interesting treatment of class, race, and gender issues in post–World War II Japan.

Oyama, Shiro. *A Man with No Talents: Memoirs of a Tokyo Day Laborer.* Ithaca, NY: Cornell University Press, 2000. 139 pp.
These fascinating memoirs are written by a university graduate and former white-collar employee who left conventional work and lived on the streets and then in San'ya, a Tokyo slum that is the gathering and living place for day laborers.

Selden, Mark, et al., eds. *Japan Focus: An Asia-Pacific E-Journal.* http://japanfocus.org.
Articles and essays are published on a regular basis in this online journal on social class, cultural and ethnic minorities, and recent immigrants.

Sugimoto, Yoshio, ed. *An Introduction to Japanese Society.* Cambridge, UK: Cambridge University Press, 2003. 316 pp.

In this well-written survey, the author specifically addresses a wide range of issues including gender stratification, discrimination against minority groups, and diversity problems in education.

Women and Marriage

Arntzen, Sonja. "The Heart of History: *The Tale of Genji*." *Education About Asia* 10, No. 3 (Winter 2005): 25–30.

The author does a nice job in this article of connecting the lives of aristocratic Japanese women more than 1,000 years ago to still-existing general Japanese cultural proclivities.

Facts and Figures of Japan 2007. Tokyo: Foreign Press Center, 2007. 224 pp.

This annual publication, available in paperback, is a superb compilation of statistics encompassing a wide variety of cultural, economic, political, and social topics. The publication is also available online at http://fpcj.jp/old/e/mres/publication/ff/index_07.html.

Hooker, Richard. "Women and Women's Communities in Ancient Japan." *World Civilizations: An Internet Classroom and Anthology*. Pullman: Washington State University, 1996. http://www.wsu.edu/~dee/ANCJAPAN/WOMEN.HTM (accessed February 2008).

This online material is an interesting explanation, based on available evidence, of the position of women in Japan before the spread of Buddhism.

Imamura, Anne E. "The Japanese Family Faces Twenty-first Century Challenges." *Education About Asia* 8, No. 2 (Fall 2003): 30–33.

The author, a sociologist who prepares U.S. Foreign Service families who will be stationed in Japan, provides a comprehensive overview of historic, post–World War II, and contemporary Japanese family structures and problems.

———. "Marriage in Japan: Yesterday, Today, and Tomorrow." *Education About Asia* 13, No. 1 (Spring 2008): 25–29.

In this follow-up article, the author focuses on the evolution of marriage in Japan. The article is accompanied by a graphic with information about contemporary marriage customs.

Jansen, Marius B. *The Making of Modern Japan*. Cambridge, MA: Belknap Press of Harvard University Press, 2002. 936 pp.

In this survey, the author does a good job of describing women's issues in every era addressed in his book.

Katzenstein, Peter J., and Takashi Shiraishi, eds. *Beyond Japan: The Dynamics of East Asian Regionalism*. Ithaca, NY: Cornell University Press, 2006. 325 pp.

Chapter 3 in this edited volume offers an accurate overview of such single and married women's issues as employment and care for the elderly.

Education

DeCoker, Gary, ed. *National Standards and School Reform in Japan and the United States*. New York: Teachers College Press, 2002. 218 pp.

In this edited volume, a number of comparative issues are addressed including standards, textbooks, and curricula.

Duke, Benjamin C., ed. *Ten Great Educators of Modern Japan: A Japanese Perspective*. Tokyo: University of Tokyo Press, 1989. 237 pp.

This well-done edited volume of educational history uses biography as a medium for understanding the roots of Japan's contemporary educational system.

Eades, J. S., Roger Goodman, and Yumiko Hada, eds. *The "Big Bang" in Japanese Higher Education: The 2004 Reforms and the Dynamics of Change*. Melbourne, Australia: Trans Pacific Press, 2005. 337 pp.

The only full-length available book in English on the recent widespread higher educational reforms initiated in Japan.

Ellington, Lucien. "Japanese Education." *Japan Digest*. Palo Alto, CA: Stanford Program on Intercultural and Cross-Cultural Education, September 2005. http://spice.stanford.edu/docs/120.

This four-column, two-page digest is an overview of elementary, secondary, and tertiary education in Japan. It is now available online.

Facts and Figures of Japan 2007. Tokyo: Foreign Press Center, 2007. 224 pp.

This annual publication, available in paperback, is a superb compilation of statistics encompassing a wide variety of cultural, economic, political, and social topics. The publication is also available online at http://fpcj.jp/old/e/mres/publication/ff/index_07.html.

Fukuzawa, Rebecca Erwin, and Gerald K. Letendre. *Intense Years: How Japanese Adolescents Balance School, Family, and Friends*. New York: Routledge Falmer, 2000. 128 pp.

A succinct overview of the level of Japanese schooling that tends to be the most stressful. The lives of adolescents both in and out of school are examined.

Organization for Economic Co-operation and Development. "OECD Briefing Note for Japan." *Education at a Glance 2007*. http://www.oecd.org/dataoecd/22/2/39317152.pdf.

The test data included in this online report was national news in Japan. It in part resulted in modifications of the 2002 reforms discussed in the narrative of this book.

———. "OECD Briefing Note for the United States." *Education at a Glance 2007*. http://www.oecd.org/dataoecd/22/51/39317423.pdf.

Since often readers interested in Japanese education also desire to focus on comparisons with the United States, American data from the same study are provided here.

Postiglione, Gerard A., and Jason Tan. *Going to School in East Asia*. Westport, CT: Greenwood Press, 2007. 483 pp.

This recent survey includes a good chapter on Japanese education and allows readers to compare and contrast Japanese schools and universities with other educational systems in the region and beyond.

CULTURE

Language

Association for Japanese-Language Teaching. *Japanese for Busy People I*. Rev. ed. Tokyo: Kodansha International, Ltd., 1997. 232 pp.

This book, part of a series that includes audio supplements and workbooks, is an outstanding practical resource for readers who want to acquire a speaking knowledge of Japanese and must engage in self-study. There are books in the series that also provide instruction on written Japanese.

Hadamitzky, Wolfgang, and Mark Spahn. *Kanji and Kana: A Guide to the Japanese Writing System.* North Clarendon, VT: Tuttle Publishing, 1997. 436 pp.

This is a later edition of a classic guide to Chinese characters, or kanji, which constitute one of the three writing systems that are combined in printed Japanese language.

Imaeda, Kazuko. *Breeze into Japanese: Practical Language for Beginners.* Boston: Cheng & Tsui Co., 2004. 323 pp.

This is a book/CD self-study combination that is elemental but provides a good overview of spoken language basics.

Kaneda, Fujihiko. *Easy Hiragana: First Steps to Reading and Writing Basic Japanese.* Lincoln, IL: Passport Books, 1989. 153 pp.

This is an example of a number of similar workbooks that are for self-study of one of the two Japanese syllabaries.

Menton, Linda. "Borrowing Words: Using Loanwords to Teach about Japan." *Education About Asia* 6, No. 2 (Fall 2001): 28–30.

This article is recommended for those who are interested in the influence of foreign words in the Japanese language.

Wells, Tina. *Easy Katakana: First Steps to Reading and Writing Basic Japanese.* New York: McGraw-Hill, 1989. 160 pp.

This is an example of a number of workbooks that are for self-study of one of the two Japanese syllabaries.

Etiquette

"Etiquette." *Japan Guide.* 2008. http://www.japan-guide.com/e/e622.html.

This online resource provides detailed and reliable information about appropriate etiquette in a variety of situations.

"A Guide to Living in Japan." *ELT News.* 2008. http://www.eltnews.com/guides/living.

These online essays are written by assistant language teachers who are English-speaking young people in Japan through the courtesy of the national government. They contain good information on how Japanese etiquette is changing and what traditional elements remain.

Itasaka, Gen, ed. "Etiquette" in *Kodansha Encyclopedia of Japan*, 233–234. Vol. 2. New York: Kodansha International, 1983.

This entry is intended for readers who would like to better understand the psychological and sociological roots of Japanese etiquette.

Rowthorn, Chris, et al. *Lonely Planet: Japan.* 10th ed. Oakland, CA: Lonely Planet Publications, 2007. 868 pp.

This is one of several travel guides that include reliable information about etiquette for those visiting Japan.

Literature

Arntzen, Sonya. "The Heart of History: *The Tale of Genji.*" *Education About Asia* 10, No. 3 (Winter 2005): 25–30.

This is a superb contextual article on the most famous of all Japanese novels.

Asia for Educators. "Japanese Literature." 2008. http://afe.easia.columbia.edu.

This Web site contains a wide array of excerpts from Japanese literature ranging from early history to contemporary times.

The Japanese Literature Home Page. 2008. http://www.jlit.net.

This online site is a good place to learn about a large number of historical and contemporary Japanese authors.

Keene, Donald. *Anthology of Japanese Literature: From the Earliest Era to the Mid-Nineteenth Century*. New York: Grove Press, 1994. 448 pp.

One of several recommended works by the leading world authority on Japanese literature who publishes in English.

———. *Five Modern Japanese Novelists*. New York: Columbia University Press, 2003. 113 pp.

This is a brief but excellent sketch of influential modern novelists. The chapters on Tanizaki, Kawabata, and Mishima are particularly recommended.

———. *World within Walls: Japanese Literature of the Pre-modern Era, 1600–1867*. New York: Grove Press, 1979. 606 pp.

The focus here is on the genres of literature from the Tokugawa period that have come to be considered classic examples of Japanese prose.

Keene, Donald, ed. *Modern Japanese Literature: From 1868 to the Present Day*. New York: Grove Press, 1994. 440 pp.

The companion volume to the *Anthology of Japanese Literature*.

McCullough, Helen Craig, ed. *Classical Japanese Prose: An Anthology*. Palo Alto, CA: Stanford University Press, 1991. 178 pp.

This anthology has particularly good excerpts from the work of Heian period women authors.

Miller, Barbara, ed. *Masterworks of Asian Literature in Comparative Perspective: A Guide for Teaching*. Armonk, NY: M. E. Sharpe, 1994. 575 pp.

This anthology includes writers from Asia and situates Japanese literature within both Asian and international comparative frameworks.

Weston, Mark. *Giants of Japan: The Lives of Japan's Most Influential Men and Women*. New York: Kodansha America, 1999. 377 pp.

Several interesting biographies of authors are also included in this highly readable book.

Art

Freer Gallery of Art and Arthur M. Sackler Gallery. http://www.asia.si.edu/education/teacherResources/onlineGuidesJapanese.htm.

These Washington, D.C.–based galleries of Asian art have an excellent Web site that contains both examples of Japanese art and a curriculum guide for teachers.

Richie, Donald. (Arturo Silva, ed.). *The Donald Richie Reader: Fifty Years of Writing on Japan*. New York: Stone Bridge Press, 2001. 238 pp.

Donald Richie is one of the most outstanding film critics in Japan. There are several excellent essays about such filmmakers as Ozu and Kurosawa in this anthology.

———. *The Films of Akira Kurosawa*. 3rd ed. Berkeley: University of California Press, 1999. 280 pp.

This is a superb systematic introduction to Kurosawa's work.

Stanley-Baker, Joan. *Japanese Art*. Rev. exp. ed. London: Thames & Hudson, 2000. 224 pp.
This is a classic general introduction to the breadth of Japanese visual arts. Stanley-Baker's book is used by a wide variety of people and features excellent narrative and strong supporting illustrations.

Varley, H. Paul. *Japanese Culture*. 4th ed. Honolulu: University of Hawai'i Press, 2000. 400 pp.
Varley gives ample attention to Japanese visual and performing arts in a highly readable introduction to the history of Japanese arts, religion, and literature.

Music

Atkins, Taylor. "Edifying Tones: Using Music to Teach Asian History and Culture." *Education About Asia* 8, No. 3 (Spring 2003): 17–20.
The author of this article does an excellent job of explaining how history and culture influenced the development of traditional Japanese music.

Isataka, Gen, ed. *Kodansha Encyclopedia of Japan*. 9 vols. Tokyo: Kodansha International, 1983.
The Kodansha volumes have succinct and accurate descriptions of such traditional Japanese musical instruments as biwa, samisen, and shakuhachi.

The Kodansha encyclopedia is now available online at: http://www.ency-japan.com/public/default.asp?type=&value=

Koto World. http://www.kotoworld.com.
This is a well-done Web site devoted to a traditional Japanese instrument that is still enjoyed in Japan today.

Wade, Bonnie C. *Music in Japan: Experiencing Music, Expressing Culture*. New York: Oxford University Press, 2004. 184 pp.
This is the best book available on Japanese music in English for the general reader.

Food

"Dig In! Japanese Culture in the Kitchen." *Nipponia: A Quarterly Web Magazine* 36 (March 2006): 8–11. http://web-japan.org/nipponia/backnumber/index.html.
This issue, available at the above Web site, from a journal previously in print that is now online, has several superb articles on Japanese food. This is highly recommended as an introduction to Japan's traditional cuisine.

Japanese Cookbook for Kids. http://web-japan.org/kidsweb/cook/index.html.
This Web site provides basic information about Japanese cuisine (e.g., the word for "meal" in Japanese is *gohan*), explains many Japanese dietary and dining customs, and includes recipes. There is good information provided for both kids and adults.

Japanese Cuisines/Recipes. The Tokyo Food Page. http://www.bento.com/tokyofood.html.
This Web site includes a variety of information about Japanese food as well as Japanese and Tokyo-area restaurants. Free featured recipes are also included.

Moore, Richard. "The Japan Rice Paradox." *Education About Asia* 9, No. 3 (Winter 2004): 10–13.
Rice is more than a basic necessity and recreational pursuit and has political ramifications, as are depicted in this article.

Ohnuki-Tierney, Emiko. "Rice as Self: Japanese Identities through Time." *Education About Asia* 9, No. 3 (Winter 2004): 4–9.

In this article the social, historical, and cultural ramifications of rice are addressed.

Rowthorn, Chris, et al. *Lonely Planet: Japan.* 10th ed. Oakland, CA: Lonely Planet Publications, 2007. 868 pp.

This travel guide, as is the case with several others available in English, has an excellent overview of what types of Japanese and international cuisines are available and how to find them.

Tsuji, Shizuo, et al. *Japanese Cooking: A Simple Art.* New York: Kodansha International, 2007. 508 pp.

This classic of Japanese cooking was reissued in 2007 as a 25th anniversary edition. It includes a broad range of Japanese recipes and is recommended for the serious Japanese food lover.

Sports and Leisure

Cirulnick, Brian, ed. Anime.com. http://www.anime.com.

This is a comprehensive guide to both the latest anime and the classics.

Hayford, Charles. "Samurai Baseball vs. Baseball in Japan." *Japan Focus*, April 4, 2007. http://japanfocus.org/products/details/2398.

This is an excellent comparative essay on arguments by Japan watchers about the nature of Japanese baseball.

Itasaka, Gen, ed. "Karate" in *Kodansha Encyclopedia of Japan*, 158–159. Vol. 4. New York: Kodansha International, 1983.

Although considered a Japanese martial art, this fascinating entry depicts the international origins of this now "traditional" Japanese sport.

———. "Martial Arts" in *Kodansha Encyclopedia of Japan*, 118–120. Vol. 5. New York: Kodansha International, 1983.

This informative entry is a succinct description of the evolution of Japanese martial arts.

Japanese Baseball.com. http://www.japanesebaseball.com.

Professional soccer is now rivaling even professional baseball as a spectator sport, but despite the defections of some baseball stars to the U.S. major leagues, baseball has a huge following in Japan. This is the English-language Web site for Japanese professional baseball.

Japan Golf Tours. http://www.japan-golf-tours.com.

This organization, affiliated with the Japan National Tourist Organization, is a good source of information on Japan's most popular adult-participant sport for non-Japanese golf buffs.

J. League: The Official Site. http://www.j-league.or.jp/eng.

Japanese professional football (soccer) has a large and growing following, and curious Westerners can get a good overview of the sport from this Web site.

Mitsukuni, Yoshida. *Asobi: The Sensibilities at Play.* Tokyo: Cosmo Public Relations Corp., 1987. Available from the Asia Bookroom Web site: http://www.asiabookroom.com/AsiaBookRoom/index.cfm.

This is a classic if little-known work that is available at the site above and through other specialty book stores. *Asobi* can be translated as "play" but denotes something broader than the Western sense of the term. The book provides concrete examples and is visually striking as well.

Schilling, Mark. *The Encyclopedia of Japanese Pop Culture*. Boston: Shambala/Weatherhill, 1997. 344 pp.
Although a little dated, this book is considered to be the bible of Japanese popular culture and is still in print and in demand.

Schodt, Frederick. *Dreamland: Writings on Modern Manga*. Berkeley, CA: Stonebridge Press, 1996. 360 pp.
This remains an important guide to the wide world of Japanese comic books.

Contemporary Issues

DeWit, Andrew, et al., eds. *Asia-Pacific Journal: Japan Focus*. http://www.japanfocus.org.
This online journal, whose contributors include scholars and journalists, often contains essays on contemporary political and social issues.

Ennis, Peter, and Richard Katz, eds. *Oriental Economist Report*. New York: Japan Watchers, LLC.
This 16–20-page newsletter is clearly written and provides up-to-date information on a variety of Japan-related economic, political, and social topics. The editors do a particularly good job of relating political issues to economics.

Facts and Figures of Japan 2007. Tokyo: Foreign Press Center, 2007. 224 pp.
This annual publication, available in paperback, is a superb compilation of statistics encompassing a wide variety of cultural, economic, political, and social topics. The publication is also available online at http://fpcj.jp/old/e/mres/publication/ff/index_07.html.

Green, Michael J. "The US-Japan Alliance: A Brief Strategic History." *Education About Asia* 12, No. 3 (2007): 25–30.
This article by a former Japan advisor to two American presidents is an excellent overview of U.S.-Japan relations from 1945 until 2007.

Japan Considered. http://www.japanconsidered.com.
This Web site, developed by University of South Carolina professor Robert Angel, is a comprehensive introduction to Japanese politics, government, and policy issues for nonspecialists as well as a resource for scholars. The site includes archived and regular podcasts about Japan's contemporary political scene, audio and transcripts of interviews with leading experts on Japanese politics and government, and a host of excellent links ranging from the prime minister's office to political parties' official sites.

Lie, John. *Multiethnic Japan*. Cambridge, MA: Harvard University Press, 2001. 248 pp.
This book is a systematic overview of major minority and ethnic groups who live in Japan.

Tanaka, Hideaki, ed. *Japan 2007: An International Comparison*. Tokyo: Keizai Koho Center, 2007. 119 pp.
This small annual paperback booklet is a useful source of statistics on a variety of Japan-related topics.

Thematic Index

Contemporary issues

Economy

Geography

Government and politics

History

Language

Literature

Social class and ethnicity

Index

Throughout this index, *t* indicates a table.